International Society and its Critics

Edited by

ALEX J. BELLAMY

OXFORD

UNIVERSITY PRESS

This book has been printed digitally and produced in a standard specification
in order to ensure its continuing availability

OXFORD
UNIVERSITY PRESS

Great Clarendon Street, Oxford OX2 6DP

Oxford University Press is a department of the University of Oxford.
It furthers the University's objective of excellence in research, scholarship,
and education by publishing worldwide in

Oxford New York

Auckland   Cape Town   Dar es Salaam   Hong Kong   Karachi
Kuala Lumpur   Madrid   Melbourne   Mexico City   Nairobi
New Delhi   Shanghai   Taipei   Toronto
With offices in
Argentina   Austria   Brazil   Chile   Czech Republic   France   Greece
Guatemala   Hungary   Italy   Japan   South Korea   Poland   Portugal
Singapore   Switzerland   Thailand   Turkey   Ukraine   Vietnam

Oxford is a registered trade mark of Oxford University Press
in the UK and in certain other countries

Published in the United States
by Oxford University Press Inc., New York

ISBN 978-0-19-926520-6

Preface and Acknowledgements

This volume was first conceived almost immediately after I arrived to take up a position at the University of Queensland in January 2002. The project began with exchanges of emails about the continuing relevance and apparently insurmountable rise of the English School or international society approach to world politics. A number of people were quite bemused by the rise of English School thinking in international relations, inspite of the many objections that writers from all sides of the discipline had levelled against it. The problem, it seemed, was that there had been very little dialogue between proponents of the English School account and those of other approaches to the subject. Although there had been a number of exchanges between key English School thinkers and writers of a realist persuasion, there had been virtually no engagement with critical and postmodern theories, feminism, international political economy, environmentalism, and other approaches to international relations. The primary aim of this project was to address this issue in three steps: first, by re-evaluating the contribution of English School thinking to the study of world politics; second, by initiating dialogue between the English School and a variety of alternative approaches to the subject; and third, by interrogating what these conversations might contribute to our understanding of world politics in the post-September 11 era.

An undertaking such as this depends upon its contributors and I was very lucky to receive fifteen excellent chapters by outstanding authors. It was an immense and humbling pleasure to work with the contributors to this volume and my first set of thanks go to them, for contributing so much of their time and expertise to this project. As well as writing chapters, many contributors also read and reviewed other chapters, for which I am very grateful.

From its inception this volume received the support and guidance of Dominic Byatt at Oxford University Press. Dominic enthusiastically supported the idea from the very beginning and patiently worked through about ten drafts of the original proposal, offering sage advice and direction throughout. Once it got up and running, Dominic continued to provide advice and help. I would also like to thank Claire Croft at Oxford University Press for her patience and skill in navigating this project to completion.

As well as the chapter contributors, several other colleagues provided much help and assistance. To start with, I would like to single out Steve Smith who in his own way was instrumental in getting the project off the ground in the first place. My contributions to this volume were helped by Marianne Hanson, Paul Williams, and especially Sara Davies who provided me with excellent and insightful comments on earlier drafts of the introduction and conclusion. I am also grateful to Nick Wheeler, Richard Shapcott, and Matt McDonald for offering comments on some of the chapters and advice about the overall direction of the book. Finally, I would like to thank Joseph Grieco and

Robert Jackson, who were unable to contribute chapters but provided very helpful support and advice.

Last of all I would like to thank my darling wife, Sara. As well as giving me immeasurable love and support throughout the project, Sara read and commented on many of the chapters and offered excellent advice, especially on the many drafts of the introduction and conclusion that she read.

Alex J. Bellamy

Brisbane, April 2004

Contents

Notes on Contributors

Alex J. Bellamy is Lecturer in Peace and Conflict Studies at the University of Queensland, Australia.

Roland Bleiker is Reader in Political Theory and Peace and Conflict Studies at the University of Queensland, Australia.

Barry Buzan is Professor of International Relations at the London School of Economics, UK.

Richard Devetak is Lecturer in International Relations at Monash University, Australia.

Tim Dunne is Reader of International Relations at the University of Exeter, UK.

Richard Falk is Albert G. Millbank Professor of International Law and Practice Emeritus at Princeton University and Visiting Professor, Global Studies, University of California, Santa Barbara, 2002–5.

Richard Little is Professor of International Politics at the University of Bristol, UK.

Justin Morris is Senior Lecturer in International Relations at the University of Hull, UK.

Terry Nardin is Distinguished Professor of Political Science at the University of Wisconsin–Milwaukee, United States.

Jacinta O'Hagan is Fellow in International Relations at the Australian National University.

Matthew Paterson is Associate Professor of Political Science at the University of Ottawa, Canada.

Christian Reus-Smit is Professor of International Relations at the Australian National University.

Roger D. Spegele is Senior Lecturer in International Relations at Monash University, Australia.

Hidemi Suganami is Professor of International Politics at the University of Wales, Aberystwyth.

Jacqui True is Senior Lecturer in Political Studies at the University of Auckland, New Zealand.

Paul Williams is Lecturer in Security Studies at the University of Birmingham, UK.

Introduction: International Society and the English School

Alex J. Bellamy

Writing in 1992, Andrew Linklater raised the question of the 'next stage' in International Relations theory (Linklater 1992*a*). He argued that the ending of the cold war and the rise to prominence of globalization opened up new possibilities for the discipline. These developments created a need and an opportunity to move International Relations theory beyond the debate between realists and liberals that had, by and large, characterized the discipline. To be taken seriously, however, any such theoretical innovation would need to generate an empirical research agenda that met the needs of international relations in the post-cold war world. Since then, the discipline has been enriched by the multiplication and broadening of its theories. However, despite much talk about the withering away of the state and the emergence of new types of politics, some of the central features of the post-September 11 world have been the display of the overwhelming might of the world's most powerful state, the persistence of the use of violence for political ends and its continuing utility in both intra- and interstate settings, the return of particularism and religiously inspired fundamentalism to mainstream political discourse, and the seeming inability of internationally agreed norms and rules to constrain the world's most powerful actors.

While there is a 'new agenda' in international relations (Lawson 2002), it is not at all clear what it looks like. On the one hand, international society has never had so many systems of governance. There is an International Criminal Court, a global environmental protocol, and widespread agreement about how states should organize themselves and their societies internally and conduct themselves internationally. On the other hand, some states are apparently becoming more willing to use force against others and to break international law. In 2003 alone, a US-led war against Iraq and an Israeli air strike against Syria violated commonly accepted rules governing the use of international force, bringing the salience of these rules into question (see Bellamy 2003*c*).

I would like to thank Marianne Hanson, Paul Williams, and especially Sara Davies for their constructive comments on earlier drafts of this introduction.

How are we to make sense of these seemingly paradoxical trends? On close inspection, in the post-cold war era International Relations has witnessed the convergence of two trends rather than the emergence of new paradigms that purport to explain world politics in a scientifically rigorous manner. The first is a return of ideas and writers that were often undervalued during the cold war. Paramount among these was the re-emergence of interest in writers associated with the British Committee of International Relations and the English School. The second trend has been the production of the so-called constructivist synthesis (see Adler 1997 and Hopf 1998), which has established itself as one of the central paradigms of contemporary International Relations theory. As a result of these two trends, it has become increasingly apparent that English School and constructivist writers had much in common, in particular their belief that states form an international society shaped by ideas, values, identities, and norms that are—to a greater or lesser extent—common to all.

The constructivist interest in international society has elevated English School theorists to the forefront of a range of contemporary debates.[1] As Richard Falk points out in his contribution to this volume, the English School's conception of international society is able to capture the paradoxes of international life described earlier because it recognizes that the international realm contains particularist states who often pursue their own values and perceived interests but who are also able to create and share common values and interests and even learn from one another. Moreover, the rise of the English School and constructivism has seen the creation of a 'next stage' in International Relations theory characterized not by the domination of a particular paradigm—though some scholars complain about the 'emergence of an English School intellectual "imperialism"'[2]—but by a growing interest in particular issue areas, which can be understood as 'sociological', 'historical', and 'normative' turns. Each of these 'turns' requires a concept of international society, and writers associated with the English School are well placed to provide it.

There are broadly three ways of thinking about the contribution of the English School of International Relations and international society approach to the study of contemporary international relations. The first is to follow Barry Buzan in arguing that the English School is an 'underexploited resource' and that 'the time is ripe to develop and apply its historicist, and methodologically pluralist approach' to the subject (Buzan 2001: 472). Buzan argues that the English School has become recognized as a distinctive approach that has much to offer the discipline and needs to be given a more central role. At the other end of the spectrum, some writers call for the School's closure. The 'English School' label was first written down by Roy Jones in 1981 in an article calling for the 'School's' closure (1981). More recently, Ian Hall went one step further and argued that the School no longer existed because it had been too much distorted by contemporary proponents such as Tim Dunne and Nicholas Wheeler (Hall 2001). According to Hall, Dunne and Wheeler's commitment to solidarism and constructivism eschews some of the School's foundational ideas such as the centrality of states, the importance of power politics, and a deep scepticism about the possibility of different political communities reaching agreement on substantive political matters. A third perspective, somewhere between these two poles, has arisen as a result of the increased dialogue between English School ideas and other theoretical perspectives—most notably realism and constructivism. Both realists and constructivists alike have called for the further refinement of English School thinking to give it a more 'refined' theory capable of identifying the motors for change and lines of causation in world politics (Finnemore 2001; Copeland 2003; see also the contributions by Suganami, Reus-Smit, and Spegele, Chapters 1, 4, and 5, this volume).

The primary purpose of this book is to assess these three positions and question the utility of the English School and international society approach to world politics. Overall, this volume demonstrates that while our understanding of international society at present is flawed in several respects, thinking about international society and engaging with the English School marks an important contribution to the study of international relations and that, with further work, the importance of the English School is likely to increase as its theories become more sophisticated and supplemented with detailed empirical analysis. Most significantly, the School's approach combines a concept of international society that captures elements of conflict and cooperation in world politics and the tension between the pursuit of order and the promotion of justice with a form of methodological pluralism that promises to generate significant empirical insight on the subject. To return to the three ways of understanding the English School's contribution to the study of international relations, I argue in the conclusion that the School is *both* an underexploited resource *and* in need of further work, but that the case for closure is weak. This book aims to contribute to the development of English School thinking by opening up avenues for theoretical dialogue with other perspectives and suggesting new lines of theoretically informed empirical analysis.

INTERNATIONAL RELATIONS THEORY AFTER THE COLD WAR

The first important trend to become more apparent in post-cold war International Relations theory has been a re-emergence of old ideas and research agendas that were too easily overlooked or discounted in the past. The palpable failure of the neorealist and neoliberal theories of world politics to satisfactorily predict or explain the end of the cold war and the emergence of new types of politics and violence exposed their weaknesses and prompted many writers to revisit the work of earlier thinkers who had either been ignored or too narrowly interpreted. For instance, Karl Deutsch's work on pluralistic security communities (Deutsch et al. 1957), overlooked almost completely by his contemporaries, has been used with increasing regularity to explain the regionalization of security politics (see Adler and Barnett 1998; Acharya 2001; Bellamy 2004). In a similar vein, during the 1990s much deeper thought was given to international relations' own history and many of its core assumptions, such as the 'history' of the idealist–realist debate as recounted by E. H. Carr, have been called into question (Schmidt 1998; Wilson 1998).

So why should we still believe their predictions?

One of the most significant developments has been the elevation of the English School and the international society approach to the fore of the study of world politics. Originally pioneered by the British Committee in the 1960s and 1970s and developed by writers based largely at Oxford and the London School of Economics, by the end of the 1980s the English School had been effectively consigned to the history books of International Relations theory. For many, the School's professed methodological pluralism made many of its key writers difficult to discern from realists (an idea that persists today; see Fierke 2002: 133; Molloy 2003), and its commitment to interpretivism (Bull 1966a) meant that it could not rival the causal, ostensibly scientific, theories put forward by neorealism and neoliberalism.

In short, when Roy Jones called for the 'closure' of the School in 1981 there was very little dissent. There was no reply at all until 1988, when Sheila Grader (1988) insisted that the School could not be closed because it did not exist—a claim rapidly and convincingly disputed by Peter Wilson (1989). The School's key thinkers of that period, Hedley Bull, Martin Wight, Adam Watson, and R. J. Vincent (among others), were more concerned with unravelling contemporary political puzzles than explicitly identifying themselves within schools of thought. Bull spent the early 1980s grappling with questions of order and justice and the 'revolt against the West' (Bull 1984, in Alderson and Hurrell 2000); Martin Wight identified three traditions in international theory. Although Wight came to identify most closely with the 'rationalist' tradition (labelled 'Grotian' by Bull), he insisted that all three (realist, rationalist, revolutionist) were necessary components of the proper study of world politics. As Wight himself eloquently put it (1991: 260):

The three traditions are not like three railroad tracks running parallel into infinity. They are not philosophically constant and pure like three stately, tranquil and independent streams ... They are streams, with eddies and cross-currents, sometimes interlacing and never for long confined to their own river bed ... They both influence and cross-fertilise one another, and they change without, I think, losing their inner identity.

Adam Watson's work tended to focus on the historical evolution of the international system (1992)—a marginal issue until very recently—and the conduct of international diplomacy (1984a, b), while R. J. Vincent moved from detailed analyses of the principle of non-intervention (1974) to a landmark study of justice and human rights in international society (1986a, b). The important point to make here is that during this period none of the central writers made the defence of their collective position a central component of their research, though Bull and Vincent did in passing identify themselves as part of a common tradition of enquiry—labelled the 'British school' by Bull (Vincent 1983; Dunne 1998: 7).

The re-emergence of the English School after the end of the cold war changed all this significantly. When, in 2001, Ian Hall attempted to repeat Roy Jones' attack and deny the existence of the School, Barry Buzan and Richard Little replied swiftly and with devastating effect, demonstrating the theoretical and empirical flaws with Hall's argument (Buzan and Little 2001). To explain the fact that Hall's critique was so swiftly dealt with, while Jones' earlier critique was left unanswered, it is important to understand two interrelated developments. First, in the twenty years between 1981, when Jones' article was published, and Hall's essay in 2001, there was an exponential growth in the number of people who identified themselves either within the School's tradition of enquiry, allied to it but separate, or engaged in dialogue with it. Today, the number of scholars who fall into one of these three categories can be accurately counted in the 'hundreds' (Buzan and Little 2001: 944) whereby in earlier years only a handful of scholars identified themselves as part of a loose fitting common tradition. Contemporary scholars have access to an English School website and a variety of working groups housed within the British International Studies Association and the International Studies Association.

The second key change over past two decades is that the tradition's intellectual content has been elaborated on and more carefully demarcated from other approaches to the subject. This process of self-identification was greatly assisted by Tim Dunne's important study on the British Committee. Here, Dunne (1998: 5–11) identified three 'preliminary articles' of the English School which should be understood, he argued, as 'family resemblances'. They were

Self-identification with a particular tradition of enquiry. Although the key early thinkers such as Bull, Wight, and Vincent did not expend much energy justifying their common ideas (with the possible exception of Bull 1966*a*,*b*), since the mid-1990s writers have increasingly identified themselves in relation to a common tradition usually by referring to and utilizing the concept of international society.

An interpretive approach. Scholars within or related to this common tradition are deeply sceptical about scientism in international relations. Instead, they prefer to use a variety of methods drawn from historical, legal, and diplomatic studies. This has left the tradition exposed to the criticisms of constructivists like Finnemore and Wendt and realists like Copeland who insist that the English School needs to develop 'better' (more scientific, predictive) theories. However, the English School can make a strong theoretical case for rejecting scientism and Richard Little (2003) has convincingly argued that its broad historical canvas makes scientism and the quest for causal variables less useful.

International theory as normative theory. English School writers recognize that ethical enquiry lies at the heart of international theory. From E. H. Carr onwards, writers associated with this tradition of enquiry have acknowledged that the proper study of international relations not only involves questioning 'what is', but also 'what ought to be' (Reus-Smit 2001*a*).

By identifying the common features of the English School tradition, Dunne made an important contribution to the development of a self-conscious school of thought, able and willing to defend its key claims and characteristics.

Since the end of the cold war, the English School has developed from a loose collection of a handful of scholars, formally arraigned in the British Committee for a period, who pursued similar interests with a common mode of thought, into a significant, self-identifying intellectual movement that today challenges the idea that International Relations theory can be divided into 'realist', 'liberal', and 'critical'

camps. In so doing, however, the overlap between the English School and the most popular 'new' ideas in international relations—collectively labelled constructivism— has become more apparent (see Reus-Smit's contribution, Chapter 4, this volume). It is important to bear in mind that the re-emergence of the English School and its incorporation into international relations debates outside the United Kingdom and Australasia is due, in a significant way, to its relationship with constructivism.

Christian Reus-Smit has identified three common concerns shared by most constructivists (2001*b*: 216).[3] First, they argue that normative and ideational struc- tures are just as important as material structures. As Finnemore put it, 'states are embedded in dense networks of transnational and international social relations that shape their perceptions of the world and their role in that world. States are *socialized* to want certain things by the international society in which they and the people in them live' (Finnemore 1996*a*: 2). The second common concern is that ideational structures shape the identities and therefore interests of actors in world politics (see Wendt 1992: 398). The third common concern is the view that the relation- ship between agents and structures is mutually constitutive. It follows from these latter two observations that meaning is socially constructed (thus granting agency to actors) and that identities, interests, and behaviour are conditioned by ideational structures. Constructivism attempts to find a synthesis between approaches that focus on the actions of actors and the way that they create political institutions and ideo- logies and structural approaches, including neorealism and Marxism, which hold that political action is shaped by socio-economic and historical structures (see Wendt 1987; Dessler 1989; Cerny 2000). The idea of mutual constitution holds that although actors are constituted and constrained by ideational and material structures, 'those structures would not exist were it not for the knowledgeable practices of those actors' (Reus-Smit 2001*b*: 218). The social structures that constitute and constrain states in international society are themselves constructed and maintained by social interac- tion between states. Thus, constructivists hold that the structures which comprise international society can be altered by the conscious actions of agents.

The links between constructivism and English School thought have been well documented. Tim Dunne, for instance, noted in 1995 that the English School approach was a forerunner of contemporary constructivism (Dunne 1995*a*, *b*). Many leading constructivists have offered further support to this view: Alexander Wendt argued that his own theory was in the same 'quadrant' as Hedley Bull's (1999: 31–2); John Gerard Ruggie (1998: 11) admitted that constructivist thought—his included—was influenced by the English School; and Martha Finnemore (1996*a*: 17–18) identified English School thinking as one of three strands of thought that contributed to the development of her own constructivist ideas.

The English School/international society approach has therefore come to the fore of contemporary debates about the theory and practice of international relations, assisted by two of the most profound trends in post-cold war International Relations theory: the re-emergence of marginalised ideas and the development and spread of the constructivist synthesis. The first trend helped to create a wider circle of interest, particularly among North American constructivists, in the work of writers such as

Martin Wight, Hedley Bull, and R. J. Vincent. This produced a rapid expansion of the number of scholars who were self-consciously engaged with the ideas associated with the English School. At the same time, the School's distinctiveness became more apparent, particularly as the concept of international society came to the fore in other approaches to the subject, most notably constructivism, and as it began to shed light on some of the key issues in contemporary international relations—in particular, the relationship between human rights and state sovereignty, the role of norms in guiding change, and the dilemma of balancing the security of states with the security of individuals (see Bellamy and McDonald 2004).

The re-emergence of the English School and its developing relationship with constructivist approaches to international relations was associated with the rise of the disciplinary 'turns', discussed earlier, that have reshaped the discipline's subject matter. The first can be described as the 'sociological turn'. The sociological turn in international relations is, by and large, a product of the rise of constructivism. This perspective draws our attention to the idea that international relations are social relations given meaning by intersubjective actions. It suggests that actions are given meaning by human interpretation and thus international relations is guided by the rules, norms, and patterns of socialization produced by interaction. Above all, the sociological turn has helped to bring the idea of an international *society* to the fore.

The second 'turn' in contemporary international relations has been an 'historical turn'. In the past few decades many writers have questioned the supposedly 'timeless wisdom' of realism and begun to pose more complicated historical questions. In doing so, a number of key myths that were central to realist stories of world politics were exposed as historically inaccurate. For example, non-realist readings of Thucydides have revealed that the generals responsible for the Melian massacre and the famous 'might is right' argument that is so central to realist historiography were also responsible for the ill-fated Athenian invasion of Sicily just a few months later, which was the beginning of the end for the republic (Walzer 1977: 9–11). An alternative reading of Thucydides suggests that, in the long run, 'might' turned out not to be 'right' for Athens. Similarly, closer reading of the various 'Westphalian treaties' of 1648 revealed that a system of sovereign states did not suddenly appear overnight in Europe. Indeed, historical sociologists have correctly pointed out that our global system of states is less than fifty years old—it is the historical anomaly, not the norm (Hobden and Hobson 2002). Indeed, as late as 1917, much of Europe was ruled along imperial and neomedieval lines through the complex structures of the Habsburg and Ottoman Empires, rather than by sovereign states. Many writers have therefore recognized a pressing need to revisit the question of international history. For those interested in international society there are two major historical questions yet to be answered satisfactorily: how did today's international society emerge? And, why and how do the norms, interests, and rules that underpin international societies change and sometimes erode and dissolve?

The third key turn in contemporary international relations has been a 'normative turn'. This line of enquiry, as O'Hagan points out in her contribution to this volume, asks whether international society is a society worth living in and how we might bring

such a society about. According to Richard Shapcott, the normative turn prompted the asking of two questions about world politics. First, what are the ethical principles that underpin contemporary international society and what work do those principles do in guiding processes and outcomes? Second, how legitimate and morally satisfying are those ethical principles (Shapcott 2000: 148)? As noted earlier, English School writers have always emphasized the importance of normative questions, while their realist, neorealist, neoliberal, and behaviouralist contemporaries insisted on either the irrelevance or outright danger of thinking and acting morally in international relations. For instance, Hedley Bull's defence of 'order' was predicated on the idea that order is a morally appealing condition because it allows political communities to cooperate in pursuit of the elementary and secondary goals of social life (for a response see Bleiker's contribution, Chapter 10, this volume).

These three 'turns' have helped to propel English School approaches to international relations to the centre of the discipline's core contemporary debates. Indeed, it could be claimed that the School itself has played an important part in defining precisely what the discipline's core issue areas should be.[4] The question of whether understanding world politics through the concept of international society is an 'underexploited resource', a 'perspective in need of refinement', or an 'approach ripe for closure' is an important one. I return to this question in the conclusion. As a prelude to this, I will briefly identify two of the English School's key contributions to international relations: the concept of international society itself and the idea of methodological pluralism.

THE ENGLISH SCHOOL AND INTERNATIONAL RELATIONS

The central question to address when thinking about the English School's contribution to international relations is the relationship between the School and the concept of international society. Is the concept of international society the School's leitmotiv or one of only three ways of thinking about world politics? It is worth noting at the outset that the idea of international society did not originate with the English School. Many writers suggest that the idea was first mooted in the sixteenth and seventeenth centuries in relation to the commercial, cultural, and religious bonds that tied European states together (Keene 2002: 13; Clark 2003; and Dunne, Chapter 3, this volume). Nevertheless, today the idea of an international society is most often associated with Hedley Bull's famous definition:

A *society of states* (or international society) exists when a group of states, conscious of certain common interests and common values, form a society in the sense that they conceive themselves to be bound by a common set of rules in their relations with one another, and share in the working of common institutions. (Bull 1977: 13)

Since then, the English School and the concept of international society have often been taken as synonymous. However, both Bull and Wight identified three key traditions of thought and action that continually struggle to make their vision of what international society is like prevail over the others. Bull identified what he described as Hobbesian, Grotian, and Kantian traditions, while Wight referred to realist, rationalist, and revolutionist modes of thought and practice. Today, we still tend to think about these three modes of thinking but they are often labelled 'international system', 'international society', and 'world society' (see the contributions by Suganami and Little, Chapters 1 and 2, this volume). According to Chris Brown, the idea of the three traditions suggests that the English School's early thinkers did not conceive the concept of international society as the calling card of their tradition, but instead thought of it as only one of three elements that comprise world politics (Brown 2001: 425). As such, Brown argued, early English School theorizing was not much different from structural realism. Moreover, Brown argued, the School's preoccupation with international society as a *via media* between realism and idealism was only a product of 'second generation' writers such as Vincent.

Although Brown was correct to point out that 'international society' was not the sole concern of the English School's early writers, the concept has developed into one that can stand its ground in the discipline's conceptual marketplace and can also mark out a distinct line of enquiry. When reflecting on the contemporary era, the English School's early thinkers did recognize that states formed a society. Indeed, Martin Wight opened his discussion of the theory of international society with the observation that such a society was a 'political and social fact' (Wight 1991: 30). The key question, however, was what kind of society was it? It was in order to address this question that Wight and Bull introduced the 'three traditions'. Moreover, given the era in which they were writing (the cold war) it is not surprising that English School thinkers believed that the realist image of world politics had explanatory merit in many important respects (though not in others). Since the end of the cold war there has been growing evidence of a shift towards a different type of society in which factors such as the balance of power and strategies of deterrence play less of a role. Of course, there is evidence to suggest that had they not passed away so early in life, key writers such as Bull and Vincent would have recognized this shift. Indeed, Vincent remarked in private that he believed that the likelihood of allied intervention to restore the Kuwaiti government after the Iraqi invasion in 1990 signified the start of a new epoch in international society, where collective action would be given a higher priority vis-à-vis state sovereignty.[5] For the purposes of this volume, then, the concept of international society is taken to be the key concept that unifies the English School. The central dilemmas that have occupied much thought since the British Committee are 'what type of society is it?', 'what are the best ways of studying it?', and 'does it fulfil the elementary and secondary goals of social life?'

What Type of Society?

English School debates can be characterized as a dialogue between two different conceptions of international society that were first identified by Hedley Bull: pluralism and solidarism (Bull 1966*a*, *b*). Both conceptions agree that the states system is actually a society of states which includes commonly agreed values, rules, and institutions.

Bull argued that there was disagreement, however, about the normative content of this society, and on three important questions in particular: the place of war in international society, the sources of international law, and the status of individuals (Bull 1966*b*: 52).[6]

Pluralists insist that international society is founded on the acceptance of a plurality of states in an anarchical system, and that each state houses a political community that constructs its own idea of the good life and conceptions of justice. Because these ideas are created within communities, they are not compatible with each other and are liable to come into conflict. However, if anarchy were to translate into perpetual conflict, states would not be able to allow their communities to pursue their own ideas about the good life because they would be unable to provide the basic foundations of social life, which according to Bull are life, truth, and property. Thus, through the creation of a form of constitution based on the mutual recognition of the component units' right to exist, international society permits the diffusion of power to peoples via the plurality of states, allowing each nation and state to develop its own way of life. The normative content of such an international society is limited to a mutual interest in the continued existence of the units comprising the society. This is manifested in the reciprocal recognition of state sovereignty and the norm of non-intervention. For pluralists, states are unable to agree about substantive issues such as redistributive justice but do recognize that they are bound by the rules of sovereignty and non-intervention (Jackson 1990; Linklater 1990: 20; Dunne 1998: 100). State sovereignty and non-intervention are therefore powerful and important norms that combine state interests, moral principles, and formal laws. Pluralist international society, then, 'establishes a legal and moral framework which allows national communities to promote their diverse ends with the minimal of outside interference' (Linklater 1998: 59).

Pluralists argue that there is no agreement—nor any possibility of agreement—about substantive issues such as human rights or redistributive justice. They argue that substantive (or purposive) moral and political codes are constructed within specific cultural contexts and therefore cannot be universal. Moreover, proposals for universal ethics or common standards of humane governance are always culturally biased. Pluralists insist that the best that international society can hope to achieve is the creation of practical rules designed to manage interaction between the component units. Policy programmes based on misplaced ideas about universal ethics only serve to undermine international society's unwritten constitution, leading to higher levels of disorder in world politics.

In contrast, the solidarist conception of international society holds that diverse communities can and do reach agreement about substantive moral standards and that international society has moral agency to uphold those standards (Linklater 1998: 166–7). According to Hedley Bull, a solidarist international society is one in which the states that comprise it display a degree of solidarity in developing and enforcing international law (Bull 1966*b*: 52). The use of force in such a society will be considered legitimate only if it is an 'act of law enforcement' (p. 57). Such law enforcement includes the defence of a state against the crime of aggression (collective security) and the upholding of the society's moral purpose.

Solidarists find evidence for their argument in the sophisticated contemporary human rights regime that includes agreed and detailed standards of humane behaviour, accepted methods of governmental and non-governmental surveillance, and an increasing acknowledgement of universal criminal culpability. Just as this consensus has grown over time, so too has state practice developed towards a growing recognition of shared values and interests across a range of subject matters—particularly in the economic sector (see Buzan's contribution, Chapter 6, this volume).

Beyond the simple assertion that states comprise an international society, there are important differences about the type of international society we live in today and the type we *ought* to live in. Both pluralism and solidarism contain descriptive as well as prescriptive components. To date, both of these approaches have tended to assume that international society is a society of states and to focus on the types of diplomatic and legal intercourse and historical analyses that informed early English School approaches. The dialogue between pluralism and solidarism helps to highlight the important tension between conceptions of order and justice in international relations. However, as many contributors to this volume point out, this debate needs to become broader (in terms of recognizing that international society deals with a wider number of questions than has hitherto been acknowledged) and deeper (in terms of recognizing that international society, even narrowly conceived, is no longer a society of states—and probably never was) (for an important starting point see Foot, Gaddis, and Hurrell 2003).[7]

The Study of International Society

To answer the question of how we should study international society, English School writers prefer an interpretivist approach (discussed earlier) and methodological pluralism. As we saw earlier, both Wight and Bull argued that the proper understanding of international society required an approach informed by three traditions, each of which has its own methodological preferences. Wight believed that each of the three traditions cast light upon the subject matter and needed to be considered together. It is not the case, Wight argued, that one tradition should triumph over the others or that a single tradition could claim a monopoly of legitimate knowledge, as has tended to happen in international relations' 'inter-paradigm debate'. Other English School writers agreed that a variety of methodological tools, drawn from economics, law, history, and other humanities, were a necessary ingredient. Beyond this, though, the School's early thinkers did not spend much time on methodological issues or in defining what 'methodological pluralism' might mean.

The meaning of methodological pluralism was subsequently fleshed out by Andrew Linklater and Richard Little in particular. Linklater associated Wight's three traditions with three methodologies—positivism (for realism), hermeneutics (for rationalism), and critical theory (for revolutionism) (see Little 2000: 402). Each, of course, implies a different way of understanding and evaluating knowledge claims about international society. Moreover, Linklater also developed our understanding of the relationship between the three methodologies. While Wight had written vaguely about intellectual streams with 'eddies and cross-currents' (see earlier), Linklater suggested that the three traditions were dialectical with critical theory synthesizing the antitheses of the first two (Little 2000: 402). There are two main problems with these ideas. First, the idea that the three methodologies are dialectically related goes against the idea put forward by Bull, Wight, and their followers that none of the elements can be given priority and neither can a synthesis be reached. Second, it is important to remember that Bull expressly rejected positivism in its behaviouralist form—a rejection that has become one of the defining features of the English School approach to world politics (Bull 1969). Thus, Linklater therefore probably takes the task of codifying the English School's methodological pluralism too far. Nevertheless, it is useful to remember that the three traditions do imply different methodologies (positivism, hermeneutics, and critical) that should be used to develop a comprehensive study of world politics.

The English School approach to international relations can therefore be understood as having two central characteristics. First, there is a common view that there is an international society, though there is little agreement about where that society came from, what it looks like today, and where it might be (and ought to be) going in the future. In many ways, these three questions form the core of the English School's contemporary research agenda (see Dunne's contribution, Chapter 3, this volume). Second, English School writers and those sympathetic to the approach agree about the importance of methodological pluralism as the best way of studying international society. Because international society is composed of a large number of different material and ideational structures, agents, cultures, beliefs, and perspectives, we need to use a variety of methodologies to understand and explain the phenomena. Although Linklater may have taken the methodological implications of the three traditions further than its proponents envisaged, it is certainly useful to think of methodological pluralism as overlapping 'streams' of thought—sometimes competing, sometimes complementary—that help us to shed light on the key questions about international society.

INTERNATIONAL SOCIETY AND ITS CRITICS

Part I: The English School's Contribution to International Relations

In order to address the question of whether the English School approach to international relations is an 'underexploited resource', in need of closure, or in need of refinement, this book is organized into three parts. The opening part of the book sets the scene by precisely identifying the English School's contribution to the study of world politics and the role that the concept of international society plays in theory and practice. It begins with two chapters that assess the School's contribution to international theory and world history, respectively.

In the opening chapter, Hidemi Suganami argues that the English School is best understood as a cluster of scholars with interrelated stories to tell about the world.

Suganami interrogates the School's contribution to international theory by discussing three aspects of theorizing: 'explanatory', 'normative', and 'international'. Discussing the English School's contribution to 'explanatory' theory, Suganami echoes the realist and constructivist view, expressed above, that the English School does not have an explanatory theory comparable to those of other paradigms. The key problem, however, is not so much that the English School does not have a causal theory, the very search for which would cast doubt upon the presumption of methodological pluralism, but that to date the School has not amassed a large enough body of empirical work from which to draw conclusions about the causes and course of change in international society that can withstand the scrutiny of other paradigms.

The English School and the concept of international society have much more to say about 'normative' and 'international' theory, though once again Suganami remains unsatisfied with the ambiguity at the heart of discussions such as Bull's treatment of the order–justice divide and Wight's three traditions. By 'normative theory', Suganami means theories that can provide conclusions about what *should* be done. He finds such an argument in Bull's *Anarchical Society* and traces Bull's argument about the relationship between order and justice through seven steps, before identifying three core problems with Bull's normative case. First, Suganami argues that, despite its apparent systematicity, Bull's moral argument is disjointed. Second, Suganami criticizes Bull's treatment of order as a value. Whereas Bull initially described his work as a defence of the value of order, he went on to identify situations in which it may be overridden by the pursuit of justice. Finally, Suganami describes Bull's attempts to reconcile Western and non-Western conceptions of justice as 'vacuous'—an argument developed further by O'Hagan. In sum, Suganami finds that Bull's 'normative theory' should be understood as an instrumental theory rather than an ethical one. Vincent and Wheeler have since taken up the challenge of outlining a normative account of international society but, according to Suganami, the debate they have created (the pluralism–solidarism debate described earlier) is more an empirical one about the nature of contemporary international society than an ethical one, properly understood.

The English School fares a little better when Suganami turns to discuss 'international theory' and focuses on the work of Martin Wight and the 'three traditions' idea. He argues that although Wight's identification of the three traditions provided a useful pedagogical device, it was Hedley Bull that awarded the traditions their social scientific value by utilizing them in tandem in his study of international society. In sum, Suganami argues that the English School's 'explanatory' theory is 'woefully underdeveloped', its 'normative' theory is in need of further reflection, while its 'international' theory does offer a useful way of interpreting world politics.

Richard Little, on the other hand, argues that the School has made, and can continue to make, an important contribution to the study of world history. In particular, he suggests that the three traditions of world politics—international system, international society, and world society—provide a useful way of thinking about the many different types of international societies and systems that have permeated world history. The English School is perhaps uniquely placed to think about world history because the pluralistic approach can accommodate different standpoints over the *longue durée* and because, since its inception, the English School has emphasized the importance of locating contemporary international society within a proper historical context. In an era of uncertainty where questions about the legitimacy of international society and its members' actions abound (Clark 2003), questions about how international societies emerge, relate to each other, and decline are crucial.

Little begins his study by questioning whether distinguishing between international systems and international societies provides a useful method for understanding world history. Bull used the distinction to differentiate between relations characterized solely by the acknowledged existence of more than one unit (system) and those characterized by the existence of consciously common interests and values. According to Alan James, the distinction between system and society is a flawed one as once a state is conscious of another's existence, they will seek to establish some form of diplomatic contact and this alone leads to the establishment of a rudimentary society of states. Little shows that Barry Buzan disagrees and instead argues that states may be locked into a competitive international system without developing societal ties and that when they do, different types of society may be differentiated according to whether they are based on common cultures and values or contractual links designed to manage interaction. Although Little does not try to resolve the debate—seeing useful tools for the study of world history in the debate itself—he does propose three additional features to our understanding of world history that flow from it: the importance of empires in creating common interests and values; the possibility of international systems/societies incorporating different types of units; and the important distinction between 'open' systems capable of expansion and retraction and 'closed' systems where the environment allows no room for further expansion. For these reasons, Little argues that English School accounts of world history provide a more 'differentiated' and 'nuanced' perspective than neorealist approaches.

According to Little, the English School approach has helped to pioneer our understanding of world history by providing a framework that allows the comparison of different international systems/societies. In so doing, it permits us to identify what is distinctive and what is not distinctive about contemporary world politics. From this perspective, world history can be understood as the result of the constant interplay between forces of hierarchy and anarchy. Moreover, it becomes clear that international societies/systems tend to be predicated on historically contingent values and interests rather than the immutable global forces intimated by neorealists and neoliberals. Overall, Little demonstrates that while there may be problems with the theoretical substance of English School approaches to world politics, the value of such approaches are more discernible once we use them to unravel empirical puzzles.

In what ways can English School scholarship help to unravel contemporary empirical and theoretical puzzles? The final two chapters in Part One investigate the evolving English School research agenda and its contribution to contemporary international relations.

Developing these insights, Tim Dunne explores what may be described as the 'new agenda' in English School thinking about world politics. He begins by briefly tracing the long history of the concept of international society, noting how it has become synonymous with the English School despite the fact that other paradigms have also made use of the term. He moves on to reiterate one of the central claims of the first part of this volume: that the English School and the concept of international society have been propelled to the forefront of contemporary debates about world politics by important sociological and normative developments in mainstream international relations in North America. Dunne then identifies four core and as yet unsolved 'puzzles' that will frame the English School's 'new agenda' as it continues to develop. They are the relationship between agency and structure, the boundaries between international society and world society, the moral basis of international society, and the tension between forces of society and hierarchy in contemporary world politics.

On the agent–structure question, Dunne endorses Reus-Smit's claim (see below) that more work needs to be done on how agency is constituted by international society. It is important on the one hand, Dunne argues, to avoid taking states for granted by assuming that they are preformed entities that then interact in a society of states. Instead, we should acknowledge the fact that international society itself plays a crucial role in constituting and legitimating particular forms of political community. On the other hand, however, it is equally important to avoid societal structuralism and to resist the temptation to imply that states are simply constituted by international society. States and other forms of political community have a degree of agency and play an important role in constructing, sometimes deliberately, the societal structures that in turn constitutes and legitimates particular forms of agency. According to Dunne, therefore, the 'new agenda' needs to explore in more detail how key ideas and norms are spread throughout international society. This is a question explored further by Jacinta O'Hagan in her contribution to this volume, Chapter 12.

The second key puzzle, and—as already suggested—an issue that permeates this volume, is the relationship between international society, world society, and the international system. Here, Dunne identifies two competing trends within contemporary English School thought. On the one hand, 'classical' theorists (or 'hedgehogs' as Dunne labels them) attempt to blend the concepts of international society, world society, and international system into a single holistic account of world politics. On the other hand, 'Neo-English School' (or 'foxes') prefer analytical disaggregation in order to retain the analytical value of each of the terms. This distinction carries with it methodological as well as empirical implications. The former prefer 'historical-cum-normative' theorizing while the latter are more inclined towards structural theory. Both, Dunne argues, have important insights to offer and the debate between the two approaches promises to open up rich avenues for future research and debate.

The final two puzzles relate more to the practice of contemporary world politics than to its theory. The third puzzle, then, is the question of the moral basis of international society. Drawing upon recent work by Keene (2002) and Keal (2003), while recognizing its importance in terms of keeping ethical issues on the table, Dunne insists that the normative dimension needs to move beyond the pluralist–solidarist debate and the dilemmas of humanitarian intervention that were predominant during the 1990s. Keal and Keen provide new ways of thinking ethically about international society, showing that—for instance—there was a close link between the much heralded 'expansion' of international society and the destruction of indigenous peoples and the denial of indigenous self-determination. The challenge is to not only think ethically about the day-to-day praxis of world politics but also reflect on the ethical quality of the material and ideational structures that underpin international society. This is a task taken up to some extent in Chapters 7, 8, 9, and 12 by Williams, True, Paterson, and O'Hagan, respectively.

The fourth puzzle revolves around the question of how we respond to US power in the contemporary era and in particular how we think about the relationship between hierarchy and society. Dunne begins by perceptively pointing out that all international societies are hierarchical and that most actually incorporate elements of hierarchy into their constitutive rules, for instance through the written and unwritten responsibilities associated with the institution of great powers. What makes the contemporary era different from other eras, and in Dunne's view more dangerous, is that the United States is not prepared to grant other great powers the special rights that it claims for itself.

In Chapter 4, Christian Reus-Smit investigates the emerging dialogue between English School and constructivist approaches in order to explore how they help us understand the post-September 11 world. In particular, Reus-Smit argues that, taken together, both English School and constructivist scholarship can add much to our understanding of contemporary international society through their focus on the relationship between power and institutions, world society and international society, and order and justice. In doing so, he undertakes two central tasks. The first is to outline the potential scope for engagement between English School and constructivist writers. To date, he argues, the conversation between the two has been hindered by 'blinkered vision' and stereotyping. Thus, contemporary English School writers tend to locate constructivist thinking almost exclusively in terms of Alexander Wendt's work. Meanwhile, constructivists have taken on the concept of international society but have almost completely ignored the normative aspects of the work of writers such as Vincent, Mayall, Jackson, and Wheeler.

As a result of this stereotyping, potentially fertile avenues of discussion have been underexplored. Specifically, Reus-Smit identifies three 'big and important' questions that confront contemporary international relations. They are the relationship between power and institutions, international society and world society, and order and justice. Each of these issues, Reus-Smit argues, have been core elements of English School thinking to date, though addressing them fruitfully would not be possible without constructivist insights. Reus-Smit goes through each of these issues, detailing English School and constructivist responses. In each, he demonstrates flaws with both the English School and the constructivist account, revealing how the flaws may be overcome through less blinkered dialogue between the two.

Part One of the book, therefore, sets out the English School's contribution to international relations. It details the approach's main strengths and weaknesses in the fields of theory and history, its contemporary research agenda, and the potential for further collaboration between English School and constructivist approaches to the subject. In so doing, it provides an important starting point for the survey of critical conversations between the English School and other perspectives contained in Part Two.

Part II: Critical Engagements with International Society

Part Two of the book takes as its starting point the idea that international society is now at the forefront of debates about the theory and practice of international relations. If it is to remain there, it must engage more seriously with a variety of other perspectives and challenges. To date there have been few attempts to do this. Where such discussions have taken place they have almost always concerned the dialogue between realism, constructivism, and international society. The second part of this book broadens the debate by considering a much wider variety of engagements with international society and the English School, some of them more critical than others.

This section begins with a discussion of realist and English School approaches to writing international history by Roger Spegele. Spegele argues that the appreciation of history that underpinned early English School thinking was reminiscent of that which also framed 'traditional classical' realist approaches to the subject. Indeed, Spegele refutes Copeland's (2003) structuralist critique of the English School and argues that the School's early thinkers may provide a teleological account of agent-led historical change that could enable traditional realists to regain ground lost to the structuralists in the past few decades. Focusing on E. H. Carr's and Herbert Butterfield's conceptions of history, Spegele argues that their mix of English School and political realism offers an understanding of history that can challenge dominant neorealist and neoliberal accounts in two principal ways. First, it offers an account of history that focuses on the intentional actions of actors, and second it provides a convincing method for identifying the 'causes' of historical change by focusing on the 'reasons' for change.

Spegele begins by identifying the ascendancy of scientism in the study of world history in international relations and partially accounting for it in terms of a 'methodological quietism'. In other words, English School writers failed to develop the methodological claims made by Bull in his famous debate with Kaplan, leaving scientific empiricism with few competitors. One of the implications of this was traditional realism's loss of value and status within the discipline and the rise of neorealism. By drawing on the connections between traditional realism and the English School, Spegele attempts to unseat the pursuit of 'scientific' history. After detailed analyses of the historiographies proposed by Carr and Butterfield, Spegele puts forward the case for an alternative, teleological, approach to history based on the similar methods employed by English School writers and traditional realists. Spegele's contribution opens up important avenues for theorists of international society to develop pluralist methods for understanding change. This question is taken up again in the conclusion.

Chapter 6 deals with arguably the most pointed omission from English School thinking—international political economy (IPE). Barry Buzan begins his account by identifying and then accounting for this omission, arguing that it is both unnecessary and unjustified. Buzan points out that although Bull and Vincent referred to the importance of trade for international society, this interest played a small role in their thinking and was not followed up by subsequent writers, with the exception of James Mayall. He then turns to the vexing question of *why* English School writers paid so little attention to economic questions. Potential explanations include: their lack of knowledge of economics, the state-centrism of international society, the English School's focus on international society rather than world society, and the School's focus on the global level at the expense of the regional. In the proceeding section, Buzan evaluates the consequences of this neglect. Most significantly, he argues that the widespread agreement about the liberal rules of economic governance evident in contemporary world politics—and inclusion of this into our picture of international society—dramatically changes the salience of solidarism. If we acknowledge that the liberal international economic order is an example of solidarism, contemporary international society begins to look much more solidarist than it does if solidarism is defined exclusively in human rights terms, as it has tended to be do date.

Buzan then goes on to discuss the principal effect of including the economic dimension in our analysis of international society: the broadening of international society's ontology to include regions and institutions (see also Buzan and Wæver 2003; Buzan 2004). He turns first to the issue of institutions and identifies a long-running division in IPE between mercantilists and liberals. Over the past two centuries, liberalism has steadily become ascendant and the market became as important an institution as war. Indeed, Buzan argues that the institution of war proved problematic for the proper working of the market. As a result, economic actors were given increasing rights in international society whilst rights to wage war were increasingly curtailed, at least in part because of its negative impact on the market. The continuing growth of the market and the attendant ascendancy of the market may point the way to the transformation of international society. At the very least, it suggests a link between the English School and globalization that needs to be explored in more depth. The second important change that would be necessitated by the incorporation of the economic sector into our understanding of international society would be a greater prominence for regions. Viewed through economic lenses there is strong evidence to suggest that distinctive types of regional societies are developing in places such as Europe, Southeast Asia, and the Gulf. To date, English School approaches have failed to account for different types of regionalism and they need to consider the links between the subglobal and the global more fully if they are to provide a convincing picture of contemporary world politics.

A recurring theme in many of the subsequent chapters is that international society's state-centredness makes it an inappropriate vehicle for addressing many of the big questions of contemporary world politics. Following Buzan, we need to ask whether state-centrism is a necessary and justifiable element of international society or whether we could conceive such a society as comprising different types and levels of actors. Buzan's chapter therefore provides two vital insights that will be discussed further in the conclusion: the notion of many different types of solidarism and the idea that, contra Bull, international society need not be exclusively a society of states.

The idea that we need to think of international society as operating on different planes of social interaction rather than solely at the interstate level is developed further by Paul Williams. Whereas Buzan calls for the inclusion of the economic sector and regional actors, Williams draws upon Critical Security Studies (CSS) to suggest that the security of individuals should be incorporated into our understanding of international society. Williams begins by identifying CSS as a 'deeper' (in that it recognizes that 'security' is derived from societal assumptions about the nature of politics), 'broader' (in that it recognizes that security extends beyond the threat and use of military force), and more 'focused' (on emancipation) approach to understanding security.

Williams frames his discussion of CSS and the English School around four central questions. The first is, 'what is security?' Williams notes that CSS and English School writers share a belief that security is a process rather than an objective condition but that writers such as Bull did not move much beyond this recognition in their study of security. However, Williams argues that the 'three traditions' framework may present a useful way of interrogating the potential for a Kantian defence of world society in an era still characterized by Hobbesian and Grotian elements.[8] What CSS adds is the idea that human emancipation and the Kantian injunction that humans be treated as ends in themselves rather than as means needs to be the starting point for the study of security. Following on from this, Williams' second question asks, 'whose security' should be prioritized? For pluralist English School writers, the security of the state and the society of states ought to be privileged over the provision of security for individuals in cases where the two concerns collide. CSS, on the other hand, points out that this arrangement may serve to heighten the insecurity of individuals, as states exhaust precious resources that could be used to ease hunger or poverty on military preparations. Williams then goes to on to ask, what counts as a security issue? Here again, the English School contains latent potential for a more comprehensive account of security in its recognition of the importance of the intersubjective understandings of statesmen. If developed, this approach could provide useful insights into why some issues are treated as security issues while others are not, and whose interests are served by this prioritization. As with its answer to the other two questions, however, English School approaches offer a restricted response to this question and CSS challenges the English School's belief in the central value of international order by insisting that in the long run human emancipation may involve the removal of international order as the primary value. Finally, Williams asks 'what is to be done?' to promote an emancipatory politics of security in the contemporary era. He argues that locating the potential for change within states is likely to be a flawed enterprise, since the modes of politics that states represent tend to be particularist. He is therefore sceptical about the potential for emancipatory change within international society. Instead, Williams suggests that scholars should not seek to influence policy directly by engaging with policy-makers but should instead engage with, and give voice to, those who do not get a seat at the table of international society.

Broadening the scope of the study of international society to include individuals, a key tenet of the world society/Kantian/revolutionist tradition identified by Bull and Wight, should prompt us to ask questions about the relationship between gender and international society. In particular, as Jacqui True points out in her chapter, it becomes important to ask what types of gender roles are created and perpetuated by international society and, vice versa, how different ideas about gender shape and challenge the theory and practice of international society. True begins her analysis by demonstrating that ideas about gender play an important role in constituting the boundaries of international society. In particular, if we accept the proposition that state identities frame, and are framed by, international society then we must also accept that gender norms too play an important constitutive role because such norms help to frame national identities and interests. She points out, for instance, that gender relations are an integral part of the practice of diplomacy. The public/private divide results in women taking on the role of diplomatic wife, fulfilling a variety of functions in support of the male diplomat. As a result, if we understand diplomatic practice to be one of the main sources of the common interests and values that underpin international society, it is important to acknowledge that these practices are themselves informed by gendered identities.

Having identified the presence of gender in a variety of settings, True goes on to explain why—until now—it has been absent from the study of international society. In doing so, she concurs with Spegele that the English School and realism have much in common. In this case, it shares common ground with realism on a number of issues that feminists dispute. These include the apparent irrelevance of domestic politics, an acceptance of the public/private divide, and state-centrism. The effect of this neglect has been to blind English School theorists to the impact of cultural diversity and conflict on world politics. True argues that a dynamic concept of international society needs to reverse the prior tendency of English School writers to ignore the question of gender. She ends by sketching out what such a society would look like and insisting that reform to the currently predominant picture of international society is necessary if it is to remain relevant. Most significantly, True argues, a feminist international society would takes its link with 'world society' much more seriously and would rethink the public/private boundaries that currently inform the theory and practice of international society.

The subsequent chapter by Matthew Paterson adds a further level of complexity to both the question of the nature of global solidarism raised by Buzan and the ontological issues raised by both Buzan and Williams. In tackling issues connected to global environmental governance, Paterson echoes previous chapters by arguing that it is impossible to think about contemporary international society in a sophisticated way without thinking about its modes of production and the ideologies that underpin it. As least as important as the fact of international anarchy, if not more so, is the fact of global capitalism. Capitalism provides a set of fundamental ideational structures that organize both domestic and international societies and the spaces between them. It also shapes the material structures that frame international relations. However, the English School has to date said virtually nothing about the capitalist bases of global life.

Therefore, Paterson argues that if we take capitalism and the politics of globalization as our starting point rather than international society, we need to develop a more complex and multilayered understanding of world politics. That is, it is important to understand that layers of authority and political allegiance transcend and subvert international society, creating new forms of governance that have virtually nothing to do with states. Thus, he argues that if we are to understand political practices and change in the environmental sector, it is essential to consider new forms of governance and non-state sites of collective political agency—an argument that could be transposed into other sectors of social action.

In the final chapter of Part Two, Roland Bleiker addresses arguably the central stumbling block for those who would enlarge international society to incorporate elements of world society, alternative levels of analysis, and subject matters. Namely, the problem of order. Bleiker argues that a concern with order, in its methodological, theoretical, and empirical guises, is the principal feature of the English School's understanding of international society. While it may endorse methodological pluralism, Bleiker argues that the approach does not embrace it and has powerful canons that structure its work. One such canon, he argues, is the requirement that to count as valid knowledge about international society, a piece of work must begin by referring to the established fathers of the tradition—a trait perhaps evidenced by this introduction's reference to Andrew Linklater on the very first line. This preoccupation with order carries over into the empirical and theoretical work conducted by those associated with the School. Bleiker attempts to critique this by challenging the assumption, central to English School theorizing since Bull, that a degree of order is necessary for the achievement of social goods. Instead, Bleiker argues that an over-preoccupation with order (witness Nazi Germany, the Stalinist Soviet Union, and contemporary North Korea) can serve the cause of oppression.

Bleiker therefore insists that progressive change tends to come about through periods of disorder. It is, perhaps, international society's preoccupation with order that has produced the exclusion of so many of the concerns and actors discussed by Buzan, Williams, True, and Paterson. On the one hand, the desire for intellectual order has worked against perspectives that fall outside the English School's 'normal' subject matter. On the other, echoing Bull's concerns about solidarism, there is a sense in which the more we expect of international society (in terms of dealing with some of the practical problems discussed in these chapters), the more fragile it may become as the ideational and material differences that divide the society's actors become more apparent (Clark 2003).

Three sets of issues therefore emerge from this part of the book. First, although approaches to international society may eschew the very idea of causal theories, the question of causation needs to be explored more rigorously than has previously been the case. Second, for international society to act as an organizing concept for the way we study world politics, there needs to be a move away from Bull's idea that it is essentially a society of states towards incorporation of ideas about world society. Third, we need to rethink the pluralism–solidarism debate in two central ways. On the one hand, it is important to explicate the ideological, economic, and cultural structures that frame international society. Above all, we need to understand contemporary international society as an essentially capitalist society. On the other hand, we need to bear in mind that there are many forms of solidarism and modes of transmission, only some of which are morally appealing.

Part III: International Society after September 11

Part Three of the book turns to the question of what all this might mean for the study of international relations after September 11. The scene is set at the beginning of the section by Richard Falk, who argues that international society remains a useful starting point for studying today's globalized world because it is predicated on the dual assertions of international anarchy and a (potentially) global normative order. This duality provides a fertile breeding ground for different accounts of what the world should look like to come to the fore and compete with one another.

Falk goes on to identify five overlapping accounts of globalization that provide alternative and competing pictures of the future of global governance and international society. The first is 'corporate globalization', which refers to the growth of transnational business and the forging of common interests and values based on neoliberal economics. The second is 'civic globalization', which in many ways is a civil society response to the corporate variety. This form of globalization has manifested itself in a number of transnational anti-globalization movements but has now moved beyond straightforward opposition towards the articulation of new global political agendas. The third variety of globalization is 'imperial globalization' which is a US-led form of globalization that seeks not the creation of a genuinely multinational neoliberal global economy but rather the extension of American power and the satisfaction of US interests narrowly conceived. More so than the other variants, 'imperial globalization' is a matter of perception and hinges on how successful the United States is in persuading others of the legitimacy of its cause in the war against terror, the pursuit of global democratization, and other initiatives. The fourth type of globalization Falk labels 'apocalyptic'. This is the variant promoted by Osama Bin Laden and his followers and, as a classic case of pernicious revolutionism, aims to overthrow the society of states and replace it with an Islamic world state. The final type is 'regional globalization'. Around the world, a number of regions are developing their own subsystems as a way of moderating pressures created by the global flow of capital. The proliferation of regionalisms could encourage Huntington's inexorable 'clash of civilisations' or, alternatively, produce 'neo-medieval' (Bull 1977) forms of politics.

The key question for Falk, then, is which form of globalization will come to predominate? This is closely related to the following question: if international society is becoming more solidarist, which type of solidarism will come to prevail? Will it be a solidarism informed by American values and spread by its military power, or will it be a solidarism based on the recognition of difference and genuine intercultural dialogue? Falk argues that none of these forms of globalization is likely to predominate completely but that the relationship between them is likely to shape the nature of global governance for the foreseeable future.

Jacinta O'Hagan develops these questions further in Chapter 12. Here, O'Hagan poses two interrelated questions. First, whose cultural values are embedded within contemporary international society; and second, does international society provide a neutral space for cross-cultural coexistence and dialogue? In addressing the first question, O'Hagan suggests that international societies are predicated to some extent on shared cultural values, which were a product of the universalization of Western values. This process was not always as one-sided as some international histories have suggested. Although concepts like sovereignty and non-interference were new to some parts of the decolonizing world, they were well-established practices in other parts of the world (most notably Latin America and Southeast Asia). Moreover, as the evolution of the so-called 'ASEAN way' demonstrates, there has been some scope for non-Western regions to develop alternative types of international society. In the case of Southeast Asia since 1967, this was a pluralist international society based on a rigid non-interference principle. This leads into the second question. How can we ensure that contemporary international society creates a space for genuine cross-cultural dialogue that would permit a more consensual than coercive form of solidarism to emerge?

O'Hagan begins by identifying a number of cultural assumptions embedded within the theory and practice of international society. For pluralists, O'Hagan argues, international society provides an acultural space for the management of cultural difference. This is a flawed understanding and fails to acknowledge the extent to which the so-called acultural practices and ideas (such as the practice of diplomacy and the idea of sovereignty) are deeply imbued with Western cultural values. O'Hagan moves on to identify some of these Western cultural values that are embedded within international society before examining how contemporary international society might embark upon the necessary task of renegotiating the terms by which intercultural dialogue is managed. The answer, O'Hagan concludes, may lie in the creation of space for intercultural dialogic encounters. Before that, however, we need to understand and recognize the partisan interests and values that underpin international society today. Failure to do so will perpetuate perceptions of 'imperial globalization' in many parts of the world and ferment opposition to international society in the form of either 'civic' or—worryingly—'apocalyptic' globalization.

The final four chapters each deal with this question of the failure of contemporary international society to create consensual solidarism and address some of the dangers that this creates. In his chapter on the rise of terrorism, arguably one of the consequences of the failure to build consensual solidarism after the cold war, Richard Devetak points to two principal challenges to international society. First, terrorism challenges the state's monopoly of legitimate violence, which is also being eroded in a number of other ways, for instance through the emergence of private security companies and the 'warlordism' phenomenon in many of the world's contemporary conflicts (Bellamy and Williams 2004). Second, Devetak argues that the reaction that Al-Qaeda has drawn from the United States threatens to create as significant a problem for international society as terrorism itself, as the United States becomes a 'menace to international order' by setting itself up as an 'authoritative judge' of the 'global common good', to use Bull's terminology in the Hagey lectures (Bull 1984).

Devetak opens his discussion with a brief survey of the nature of terrorism and the position it has held in English School thought. With only one or two minor exceptions, English School writers tended not to incorporate terrorism into their study despite the proliferation of terrorist incidents in the 1970s. Indeed, Hedley Bull identified terrorism as simply one of several types of 'private international violence'. Devetak suggests two reasons for this apparent oversight: the School's state-centrism and its resistance to presentism. After a detailed discussion of the changing nature of terrorism in both its non-state and state varieties, Devetak moves on to address how terrorism poses a threat to contemporary international order. In particular, he focuses on terrorism as a breakdown of the state's monopoly on legitimate violence that is essential for the proper functioning of international society. However, Devetak concludes by arguing that US attempts to tackle terrorism by undermining the basic principles of international society may only help to exacerbate the problem by casting further doubt on the relevance and legitimacy of international order.

The problems caused by the US-led response to terrorism are addressed in more detail in the remaining chapters. Terry Nardin begins by offering a novel reformulation of 'justice' as 'coercively enforceable morality'. He argues that ideas about international justice and particularly about the rightness of the use of force in pursuit of the supposedly common interests of international society are intrinsically linked to common ideas about what is right or wrong. This suggests a need to rethink the order versus justice debate, as justice becomes the pursuit of those things that we agree are legitimate to pursue. Rather than seeing order and justice as polar opposites, Nardin argues that the very concept of international justice implies a basic level of agreement about the legitimacy of particular types of order. The key question that confronts us today, however, is how does international society manage competing ideas about justice, particularly when the sole global hegemon is convinced that its conception of coercively enforceable morality is universalizable despite a considerable amount of evidence to the contrary?

Nardin responds to this question by outlining a case for the recognition of a 'common morality' that should guide action in international society. Common morality, he argues, has three primary properties. First, unlike other ethical codes it is binding on all individuals. Second, it rests on the human capacity for reasoned argument rather than 'custom, contract, or legislation'. Finally, the precepts of common morality are obligatory restraints on choice, not mere recommendations. Nardin then moves on to discuss how common morality is applicable in international society. In sum, the creation of a common morality implies a shift to a solidarist international society that binds all its actors to a common moral code of action and shares moral responsibilities between them. The key tension within international society,

Nardin concludes, is not one between order and justice, but one between just and unjust coercive orders.

Finally, Justin Morris assesses what this might mean for the ability of norms to regulate recourse to force in contemporary international society. Morris asks whether the shift from a multipolar to unipolar society of states has led to normative change in international society, using the norm prohibiting the use of force as a case study. He argues that although material changes in international society do have an impact, the norms that underpin international society are not infinitely malleable and constrain even powerful actors like the United States. Thus, despite its overwhelming preponderance of power, the United States still feels obliged to justify its actions in terms of international law and still acts as if it is bound by such rules. If, as realists suggest, such justifications were merely idle rhetoric, why did the United States offer humanitarian justifications to support its case for war in Afghanistan, when most members of international society recognized that it had a right to act in self-defence? Morris suggests that the answer to this lies in the power of international society's peremptory norms to shape state behaviour.

Morris begins his chapter with a discussion of the relationship between power and norms, which reinforces the linkages between English School and constructivist approaches identified earlier by Reus-Smit. Morris dismisses realist and materialist arguments that norms play, at most, a peripheral role in international life by arguing that even powerful states prefer to act in accordance with international rules. In relation to the use of force, Morris argues, it is very difficult to find a case since 1945 where a state has not sought to justify its use of force with reference to the rules governing that discussion. After charting the evolution of norms pertaining to the use of force and the globalization of international society, Morris turns to the post-September 11 era. Although the United States continues to follow the rules to a large extent, Morris argues that its attempt to act as a 'normative innovator' by claiming an exceptional right to self-defence poses a grave danger to both the United Nations and the system of law that underpins the society of states.

The concluding chapter attempts to draw these ideas together and question the continuing relevance of the English School approach to international relations. It argues that although the School has made a significant contribution to the discipline, more work needs to be done if it is to maintain its relevance. In particular, the School needs to address the relationship between international society and world society in more detail, identify and explore the many structures that underpin international society, rethink the pluralism–solidarism debate, and shed more light on the drivers and dynamics of change in world politics.

Notes

1. That is not to imply that the English School was invisible during the 1980s. Writers such as R. J. Vincent, Andrew Hurrell, Marianne Hanson, and Iver Neumann among others continued to work on international society. However, the impact of their study

did not extend much beyond the United Kingdom and their ideas had very little impact on the main debates of the time. The most famous trenchant critiques of realism in this era made no reference to the English School. (See, for instance, Ashley 1984; Cox [1981]1986.)

2. Ken Booth used this phrase in an email to the author.

3. It is worth noting that many of these constructivist insights can also be arrived at through Marxist or dialectical approaches to history which acknowledge the interdependency between individual agents and the powerful socio-economic forces that constitute, enable, and constrain them. I am grateful to Paul Williams for bringing this to my attention.

4. I am grateful to Paul Williams for this point.

5. I owe this point to Marianne Hanson, who was a student of R. J. Vincent's.

6. It is interesting to note here that Bull implicitly recognized that international society and individuals were related to one another. This raises the question of whether international and world society are necessarily separate entities and whether the distinction between the two is a useful one. If we are to build a holistic account of contemporary international society it is necessary to either (*a*) think more carefully about the relationship between international society and world society; or (*b*) incorporate ideas about world society into our understandings of international society. These ideas are developed in the conclusion. Also see Buzan (2004).

7. This is arguably one of the most important debates. See n. 4, and the conclusion.

8. Bellamy and McDonald (2004) undertake precisely this task and argue that the emergence of human security and security communities suggests the development of 'weak' solidarist praxes of security that go some way towards privileging individual security while not undermining the security of international society.

PART ONE

The English School's Contribution to International Relations

1

The English School and International Theory

Hidemi Suganami

There has been an accelerating growth of interest, especially marked in the past few years, in the English School of international relations. Since its name entered the disciplinary history of international relations in the early 1980s (Jones 1981), there have, however, been some discrepancies in the ways that chief commentators on the School's life and work have characterized its identity and contribution to international theory.

The English School's main contribution has been seen by some to be in articulating the international society perspective on world politics, Manning being a founding figure, and the Department of International Relations at the London School of Economics (LSE) its initial institutional base (Jones 1981; Suganami 1983; Wilson 1989). According to some others, the English School has indeed to do with the international society perspective, but not with Manning (Brown 1997: 52; Dunne 1998), and in some commentators' view, the School has to do mainly or even exclusively with the British Committee on the Theory of International Politics led by Butterfield and Wight (Little 1995: 32, n. 1; Dunne 1998).[1] Some writers consider Carr to belong to the English School (Buzan 1993: 328; Jackson 1996: 213; Dunne 1998), while others do not (Suganami 1983; Wilson 1989; Brown 1997: 52). In the view of some commentators, even the international society perspective is not what distinguishes the English School (Little 2000: 395; Buzan 2001), while according to another there is no such thing as the English School in any case (Grader 1988: 42).

When, however, these differing contentions are subjected to critical textual and contextual scrutiny, and efforts are made to conciliate as well as adjudicate between them, the identity of the English School reveals itself—although, importantly, as a historically constituted and evolving cluster of scholars with a number of plaus-ible and interrelated stories to tell about them.[2] The English School, this approach reveals, is an evolving cluster of so far mainly UK-based contributors to international relations, initially active in the latter part of the twentieth century, who broadly agree in treating the international society perspective—or 'rationalism' in Wight's sense—as a particularly important way to interpret world politics, and whose views and intellectual dispositions show significant family resemblance due partly to exceptionally close personal or professional connections. These connections were initially formed at the LSE, but later extended to other academic institutions, and were also, to a large extent independently, cultivated within the exclusive British Committee on the Theory of International Politics.

A broad characterization of the English School given here suggests that Manning, Wight, Bull, James, Vincent, Watson, and perhaps also Butterfield have a strong case to be treated as the School's central figures in its early stages, though this is by no means to insist that there are no others, or that there will not be a slightly different, but perhaps equally plausible, conception of the English School. More recent contributors to the English School tradition include Hurrell, Dunne, Wheeler, and Jackson.

The purpose of this chapter is to outline and assess leading English School writers' contributions to *theory* in the study of world politics. To this end, I wish first to explain what in my view 'theory' is. Primarily, there are three kinds.

A first of the three may be called *explanatory* theory. This aims to help us understand better how it is that the realm of world politics works out the ways it appears to do. A second may be called a *normative* theory. This elucidates the steps through which some fundamental normative presuppositions lead to conclusions regarding what should be done in world politics. A third is *international* theory in Wight's specific sense of the term, 'a tradition of speculation about relations between states, a tradition imagined as the twin of speculation about the state to which the name "political theory" is appropriated' (Wight 1966a: 18).[3] In the following, I shall outline and assess leading English School writers' contributions to theory in these three senses in turn. As the discussion progresses, some other senses of the word 'theory' will be brought to attention to elucidate the activities of the English School.

EXPLANATORY THEORY

'Theory' in its most elementary sense may be said to help us see things better: it helps us understand better what we observe by alerting our minds to what we do not otherwise grasp. 'Theory', therefore, 'explains' in the most elementary sense of that word—'to make (more) plain', 'to make us understand (better)'. But not all that 'explains' is 'theoretical'. History, or historical explanation, typically explains how a segment of the world moved on from where it was at one time to where it came to be at another. But historical explanations, while not unconnected with what we normally mean by '(explanatory) theory', are not usually '*theoretical* explanations'.

To elucidate the last point, it is necessary to say a few words about the nature of historical explanation. How does historical explanation give us an improved understanding of how a segment of the world moved on from where it was at one time to where it came to be at another? In my view, it does so partly by confirming, explicitly or implicitly, what we already know, partly by challenging what we thought we knew, and partly by filling in the gaps in our knowledge which we wanted filled or did not know existed. And all this is done by supplying four kinds of information at a maximum. A first concerns how the relevant segment of the world was to start with. The other three correspond to what Clausewitz (1976: 89) called 'a remarkable trinity': (*a*) information concerning the occurrence of some historically significant chance coincidences; (*b*) information concerning a variety of relevant human interventions and non-interventions; and (*c*) information concerning some mechanistic forces in operation—all contributing towards elucidating the particular path the process of transition took.[4]

Now, I take it that what we normally mean by '(explanatory) theory' relates to (*c*) in this list: it consists in the elucidation of mechanistic causal processes in which causal forces operate without (and even against) human intentions and purposes. It follows that theoretical explanations, or explanations invoking (explanatory) theories, do occur in historical explanations, but historical explanations are not identical with, or reducible to, theoretical explanations.

Have English School writers made significant contributions to explaining world politics *theoretically*—by engaging in theoretical explanations, and offering explanatory theories? A short answer to that is 'no'. In my view, their contributions to explaining world politics *historically* are also somewhat limited, but it is beyond the concern of this chapter to substantiate this claim.[5] But when I suggest that English School writers have not made significant contributions to explaining world politics *theoretically*, I have in mind something very specific under the rubric of 'theoretical explanations'. What I mean here is that I do not think they have offered explanatory theories or identified mechanistic causal processes operative in the realm of world politics in any detail.

[margin handwriting: limited contribution to IR theory ?]

Of course, English School writers' central claim is that there are institutional bases to order that exists in the world of states (James 1973) and that, in Bull's version (1977: 74–5), the rules and institutions of modern international society have contributed, causally, to the maintenance of international order. But these are not very refined causal claims and not very different in quality from saying, for example, that traffic regulations exist, operate, and thereby contribute to road safety.

It may be helpful here to bring in a comparison with Wendt's *Social Theory of International Politics*. Making use of a tripartite distinction between the Hobbesian international political culture of enmity, the Lockean one of rivalry, and the Kantian one of friendship, Wendt offers a fairly detailed theoretical explanation as to how it is that, when states first form a states system, the system tends towards a Hobbesian culture (1999: 264, 322–3, 332), and how the system, once it reaches a Lockean state, may move from there towards a Kantian one.[6] In connection with the latter, Wendt refers to the 'three master variables' of interdependence, common fate, and homogeneity (1999: 343–57). His argument, advancing a set of causal hypotheses or what I am calling here 'explanatory theory', is briefly that, given the Lockean background, these factors can, both individually and in combination, contribute to bringing the system closer to the Kantian one. Such a transition, according to Wendt (1999: 360–3), is facilitated, among other things, by a process of social learning (or gradual internalization of the institutions of pluralistic security community through repeated compliance with the norms enjoining the peaceful settlement of international disputes) and democratic states' strong predisposition towards the peaceful settlement of international disputes with each other.

This is not a place to go into further details of Wendt's argument. Suffice it to say that there is nothing comparable to it in the English School literature, either with respect to Wendt's substantive argument about the process of collective identity formation or to his philosophical reflection on the nature of his own enquiry in the context of existing IR theories.[7] Finnemore is therefore quite right to remark: 'What, exactly, are they claiming theoretically? American IR tends to be interested in causation. I am not sure that the English School shares this interest' (2001: 510). Elaborating on this theme, Finnemore pertinently remarks:

need for more explanatory theory

How is it, exactly, that politics moves from an international system to an international society, or from an international society to a world society? Movement between what I have called these ideal-types [i.e. international system, international society, and world society] is not well theorized [or explained theoretically]: elaboration of mechanisms for change could galvanize English School scholars internally and open up new lines of research. (2001: 513)

Copeland is even more outspoken when he says: '[to answer this kind of question], the English School needs a theory; right now, it has none' (2003: 433). One exception to this general neglect, on the part of English School writers, of causal mechanisms in world politics may perhaps be said to be present in the writings of Watson. In his extensive comparative study of states-systems, he envisages a spectrum, beginning with a system of multiple independences at one end, going through hegemony and dominion, and ending with an empire at the other. He noted that in any given system there are tendencies—propelled by the desire for order—to move away from multiple independences in the direction of hegemony, dominion, and empire, but that this was countered by pressures—propelled by the desire for independence—towards greater autonomy that make empires and dominions loosen and break up (Watson 1990: 105–6).

To explain the tendency for states-systems to avoid the extremes and settle on some midpoint, he invites us to imagine the spectrum 'laid out in the form of an arc, with its midpoint at the bottom of the pendulum's swing, somewhere between hegemony and dominion' (1990: 105). He continues:

Was there in former systems, is there now, not merely oscillation to and fro, but a noticeable pendulum effect, in the sense of a gravitational pull on systems away from both the theoretical extremes and towards some central area of the spectrum, even though the momentum of change and other factors may carry the pendulum past that area? I am now (after twenty years of looking at the evidence) inclined to think that there is a pendulum effect, though the pattern varies from one system to another. (1990: 105)

So what, in Watson's view, explains the push towards each end of the spectrum and the gravitational pull towards the centre? In one version, Watson attributes the push towards empire to the desire for order and the push towards multiple independences to the desire for independence, adding that '[t]he desire for a balanced system, that is neither too tight nor too loose, causes the gravitational pull on the pendulum' (1990: 106). In a related version, the gravitational pull is said to be 'a metaphor for what in sociological terms are the constraints exercised by an impersonal net of interests and pressures that hold the system together: constraints which become greater as a system moves towards the extremes of independence or empire' (Watson 1992: 122). To these, he adds yet another version (1992: 131):

Three factors play major parts in determining what point in our spectrum is the most stable and generally acceptable for a given system at a given time. The first is the Sein, the balance of material advantage, both for the rulers and the ruled. The second is the Sollen, the point of greatest legitimacy, also for all concerned . . . Third there is the gravitational pull of the pendulum away from the high points of the curve, from direct empire towards autonomy and from anarchical independence towards hegemony. Thus the most stable point along the curve is not some invariable formula, but is the point of optimum mix of legitimacy and advantage, modified by the pull on our pendulum away from the extremes.

In this version, three factors are said to be among the causal determinants of the shape any given system would take: the balance of material advantage for both the rulers and the ruled; the understanding, on the part of all concerned, about the legitimate structure of the system along the spectrum; and (Watson adds) the gravitational pull. It is unclear what this third force is and whether this exists over and above the two other factors listed here—interests and legitimacy.

What we find in Watson then is perhaps a reasonably well-substantiated empirical observation that states-systems tend to settle on some midpoint between the two extremes of multiple independences and empire;[8] and this, we find, is accompanied by an attempt to account for the phenomenon theoretically, by pointing to causal mechanisms supposedly in operation. But Watson's account is at best an attempt to work out an explanation-sketch, pointing to a number of things scattered in the system that are thought to form a framework of constraints and pressures—the desire for order, the desire for independence, the desire for a balanced system, and the prevailing understanding about the legitimate structure of the system.

I cannot help but conclude that the English School's contributions to improving our explanatory theory of world politics are marginal in scope and significance. This is related to, though not necessitated by, the fact that leading English School writers' main interests lie in *Verstehen*, or explanation of what goes on in the world by penetrating the minds of the key actors and uncovering not only their motives but also the common premises and presuppositions that prevail among them about the nature of the game they are supposed to be playing. Here is one classic statement:

Let the student of International Relations think then of the international society as Malinowski did of his Trobrianders, and be content with nothing other than whatever may prove to be the nearest practicable approach to personal participation—in the role, as it were, of sovereign states—in the life of the international family. (Manning 1975: 204–5)

Manning also thought highly of Zimmern because he, according to Manning, was able to convey to his students what life was like as lived by the states of his day in their interrelations, just as Malinowski was able to teach his pupils about the life of the Trobriand

Islanders. Manning added: 'What fortune for those generations of grateful young men [*sic*] that it seems never to have occurred to him [Zimmern] to try to make his subject look like economic theory' (1975: 206). This is echoed by Bull: 'The student whose study of international politics consist solely of an introduction to the techniques of systems theory, game theory, simulation, or content analysis is simply to shut off from contact with the subject, and is unable to develop any feeling either for the play of international politics or for the moral dilemma to which it gives rise' (1969: 28).

There is nothing inappropriate in, and much to be gained by, stressing the importance of ideas in world politics. It is a pity, though, that in the case of the English School, its hostility to the rising tide of American behaviouralism went hand in hand with its failure, for the most part, to make significant causal enquiries into various puzzling features of world politics such as what causes, or what causal mechanisms contribute to, war, imperialism, exploitation, global inequalities, international cooperation, and the emergence of relatively stable pockets of peace and solidarity in the world.

Does this mean that there is no theory of any significance to speak of emanating from the English School about world politics? That, unfortunately, will have to be the verdict if by 'theory' we mean 'explanatory theory', and if by this we mean the elucidation of mechanistic causal processes, processes in which causal forces operate, or causation occurs, without and even against human intentions and purposes. English School writers are, of course, well known for their stress on the causal importance of the rules and institutions of international society for the maintenance of international order, but detailed analysis is not found in their writings about how the causal process works which links the rules and institutions, on the one hand, with order between states, on the other.

It may of course be that we do not wish to define '(explanatory) theory' so narrowly as is done here. In the most elementary sense, 'theory', as we saw, 'explains' or gives us a better understanding of what we observe and experience, and there is little doubt that the English School's *way of looking at, or reading, the world* has much to teach us about the workings of interstate relations. It does so mainly by alerting us to the institutional structure of contemporary international society within which the day-to-day interactions between sovereign states are carried out. If this is to be taken to count as a contribution to theory, however, it must clearly be understood that by 'theory' here we mean something quite broad such as 'a systematic representation of the world that gives us some coherent understanding of it (and thereby perhaps also a set of guidelines as to how to deal with it)'.[9] I shall return to this point when we come to discuss Wight's 'international theory'. But, for now, we should move to the subject of action-guidance.

NORMATIVE THEORY

By 'normative theory' I mean an argument that elucidates the steps through which some fundamental normative presuppositions lead to conclusions about what should be done. The best example of this, representing the English School, is Bull's key text, *The Anarchical Society*. His argument can be summarized in the following seven steps:

1. Security against violence, observance of agreements, and stability of property, private or public—or 'life, truth, and property'—are the three elementary, primary, and universal goals of social life (Bull 1977: 5). A society cannot be said to be orderly, or even to exist, if these goals are not met to some extent; and order is a pattern of activity that sustains such goals (Bull 1977: 4–5).
2. Order is not the only goal that is important; justice is also important. However, *The Anarchical Society* is dedicated to analysing how order is sustained in contemporary world politics through the workings of international society (Bull 1977: pp. xii–xiii).
3. As for international order, or order in international society, six elementary and primary goals are discernible, which have been pursued in modern international society especially by its leading members: (*a*) the preservation of the system or society of states itself against the challenges to create a universal empire or challenges by supra-, sub-, and trans-state actors to undermine the position of sovereign states as the principal actors in world politics; (*b*) the maintenance of the independence or external sovereignty of individual states; (*c*) peace in the sense of the absence of war among member states of international society as the normal condition of their relationship, to be breached only in special circumstances and according to principles that are generally accepted; (*d*) limitation of interstate violence; and (*e*) observance of international agreements; (*f*) the stability of what belongs to each state's sovereign jurisdiction (Bull 1977: 16–20).
4. These goals are sustained, and a degree of order is achieved, by a combination of rules and institutions that have evolved in modern international society. The former are of three types: (*a*) 'the fundamental or constitutional normative principle of world politics' in the modern era; (*b*) 'the rules of coexistence'; and (*c*) 'the rules concerned to regulate cooperation among states—whether on a universal or on a more limited scale' (Bull 1977: 67–70). The latter includes the sovereign states (Bull 1977: 71–3) and the five other institutions of modern international society: the balance of power, international law, diplomacy, war, and the concert of great powers (Bull 1977: chs. 5–9).
5. These institutions have worked reasonably well, and thereby sustained the elementary and primary goals of international society/order. This in turn has contributed to the maintenance of world order, defined as the pursuit of the three elementary goals of society transposed to the level of the community of humankind as a whole (see Bull 1977: esp. 20–2).
6. There are opinions often voiced to the effect that the contemporary institutional structure of the world organized as a society of sovereign states is not the most effective way to achieve the goals of peace and security, economic and social justice, or effective environmental management. But the current institutional arrangement works reasonably well; there is no good reason to think that it cannot work better, if appropriate conditions come to be met; and in any case there is no good reason

to believe that other institutional structures can work better than the existing one for the pursuit of such goals—for the factors preventing a more satisfactory achievement of these goals are deeper than the current institutional arrangement of the world (Bull 1977: ch. 12).

7. If, however, the existing framework is to contribute to the goals of economic and social justice and of efficient environmental management, in addition to the more basic goals of peace and security, the element of international society must be preserved and strengthened. For this purpose, collaboration among the great powers based on their sense of common interests is essential (Bull 1977: 315). The future of international society is likely also to depend on the growth of a more genuine cosmopolitan culture, incorporating non-Western elements to a much greater degree than at present (Bull 1977: 317).

This was quite an impressive argument at the time of its publication (1977), going far beyond anything that had been produced by the English School in response to the question of whether the current world political order, organized as a society of sovereign states, is more defensible than other historical and non-historical alternatives. It still represents the essence of the English School's defence of the states system. But there are a number of points at which more work is needed to sort out Bull's thinking. Three may be noted here.

First, notwithstanding its appearance of systematicity, Bull's argument is in fact quite disjointed. Compare steps 1, 3, and 6 in the above summary. Bull's discussion begins with (*a*) the purportedly universal values of 'life, truth, and property'; it then deals with (*b*) the goals said to be associated specifically with the modern Western international society, such as 'the preservation of the system or society of states itself'; and it ends with (*c*) 'peace and security, economic and social justice, and efficient management of the environment', or values presented as especially relevant to contemporary international society. Bull's inclusion of the second set of goals is justified by his argument summarized in steps 4 and 5: it is through the protection of these goals that modern international society has contributed to the goals of world order. Nonetheless, Bull's line is that international society is good for all these different sets of values, and that goes beyond what he sets out to argue at the beginning, which has to do with the basic goals of 'life, truth, and property'. This leads me to make my second observation.

There is an ambiguity in Bull's treatment of order as a value. On the one hand, he thinks of it as the most fundamental value without which society cannot even be said to exist, but on the other hand, he acknowledges that it is but one of a number of values that are important. His line seems to be that the goals of order may be sacrificed in pursuit of justice in a transitional period from one less just social system to another more just one, but that no system can achieve the degree of justice realisable within unless there is a degree of order there also (Bull 1977: ch. 4). Bull does not pursue this theme further, however, and insists that this book is a study of order in world politics, not a study of justice. But Bull seriously undermines this claim first by discussing the relationship between order and justice in the book—and thus the book is not *purely* about order—and second by advancing a defence of the current world political structure for the achievement of a number of goals, *including*, as we saw in step 6, economic and social *justice*.

Bull's view, as we saw in step 7, is that such higher goals could only be achieved within the framework of the society of sovereign states if the element of international society, and the cosmopolitan culture that underlies it, could both be strengthened. He writes:

The future of international society is likely to be determined, among other things, by the preservation and extension of a cosmopolitan culture, embracing both common ideas and common values, and rooted in societies in general as well as in their elites, that can provide the world international society of today with the kind of underpinning enjoyed by the geograph- ically small and culturally more homogenous international societies of the past . . . We have also to recognise that the nascent cosmopolitan culture of today, like the international society which it helps to sustain, is weighted in favour of the dominant cultures of the West. Like the world international society, the cosmopolitan culture on which it depends may need to absorb non-Western elements to a much greater degree if it is to be genuinely universal and provide a foundation for a universal international society. (1977: 317)

A third weakness is found here. What it means to integrate non-Western elements into the cosmopolitan culture that may develop is left unexplained, and who or what class of individuals, if any, has the power and responsibility to implement such a move is left unanswered. Bull's seemingly reasonable prescription here is, therefore, largely vacuous.

In discussing Bull's 'normative theory' of world politics, it is important to recall that he did not consider his argument as 'normative' in the ethical sense of that word. His own view (1977: introduction) of his argument was that it was an instrumentalist one: if order is what we think we ought to have in world politics, then his argument points to a plausible set of guidelines towards achieving it. This, admittedly, is not the same as suggesting that his prescriptions ought morally to be obeyed. He was reluctant to make such a suggestion because he was sceptical that what ought morally to be done could be given an objective answer (and he wished, as an academic, to remain within the realm of objectivity). He thought that what counts as a just social arrangement is essentially a matter of subjective, and ultimately arbitrary, opinion. He considered, however, that what counts as an orderly society was a question to which an objective answer could be given, and was presumably confident that his own, formulated in terms of the three values of 'life, truth, and property', was indeed such an answer.[10]

Bull's apparent dichotomy of social values into objective values coming under the rubric of 'order' and subjective ones subsumed under the rubric of 'justice', and his selection of 'life, truth, and property' as values of the first kind, strike me as ill-founded. Indeed, while Bull's work contains a 'normative theory', in the sense spe- cified above, the starting point of his argument is lacking in serious philosophical reflection.

Bull's response to this may be that philosophical theorizing was beyond his scholarly concern. As a non-philosopher, he was starting from some substantive position, showing its consequences, and qualifying the conclusion as merely an instrumentalist one. Those who are somewhat more philosophically inclined than Bull would not wish to let him off the hook so readily by accepting his simple jurisdictional pro-clamation; but, perhaps more to the point, it is unlikely that he could stay within the instrumentalist realm without straying outside of it from time to time, as witnessed in his discussion of what he called 'the revolt against the West'.

At first, he argued:

> The interest of the Western countries derives not chiefly from moral considerations or economic considerations ... but rather from considerations of international order. The Western peoples, who created the global international system of today, have a supreme interest in sustaining a viable international order that will endure into the next century. It is not credible that such an order can be sustained unless the states of the Third World, representing as they do the majority of states and the greater part of the world's population, believe themselves to have a stake in it. (Bull 2000: 243)

This, clearly, is an instrumentalist argument: Western governments should accom-modate the demands of the Third World governments if, as they would, they wish to enjoy orderly international relations. Nonetheless, Bull could not help add the following observations:

> For all the tawdry rhetoric with which it has been accompanied, the envy and self-pity that lies behind it, the false and shallow charges levelled against the historical role of the West, the vast gap between aspiration and achievement in the Third World, the bitter ironies of decay in the place of development, tyranny in the place of liberty, the cases of reversion to superstition and barbarism, these changes [or consequences of the revolt against the West] do represent at least in their broad direction a forward movement in human affairs and a step towards greater justice in international relations. (Bull 2000: 244)

A transition from an instrumentalist line of argument towards an ethical one is visible also in Vincent's writings. In *Nonintervention and International Order* (1974), Vincent took an instrumentalist line to the effect that the principle of non-intervention was a necessary means to securing the goals of order in the society of states. But in *Human Rights and International Relations* (1986*a*), his argument is more explicitly ethical. According to him

> Human rights now play a part in the decision about the legitimacy of a state (and of other actors and institutions) in international society, about whether what it is or what it does is sanctioned or authorized by law or right. It is not now enough for a state to be, and to be recognized as, sovereign. Nor is it enough for it to be a nation-state in accordance with the principle of self-determination. It must also act domestically in such a way as not to offend against the basic rights of individuals and groups within its territory. The question of what these basic rights are may not be resolved in international law ... but the argument here is that the right to life is basic if there are such things as basic rights. (1986*a*: 130)

Vincent's reasoning here is simply that no one can enjoy human rights unless she or he is alive, and therefore the right to life is the most basic of all human rights. But, he argues, 'the right to life is a nonsense unless it demands sustenance against deprivation as well as protection against violence' (1986*a*: 145). Of the various kinds of duty that correlate with this human right, Vincent argues that the duty to aid those incapable of providing for their own subsistence is the most elementary (1986a: 146).

Vincent's argument that in order for anyone to enjoy human rights, she or he must first be alive, while true, points only to the precondition of a particular person's ability to enjoy her or his human rights. I am not entirely persuaded that this (essentially instrumental reasoning at the level of the individuals) necessarily settles the political/moral question about which, among the total set of human rights, is the most primary, or which class of rights are more important than others. But this is to demand further reflection on what mode of reasoning is required in addressing the question; it is not necessary to doubt the rightness or otherwise of the conclusion reached.

Vincent's stress (1986a) on the primary importance of the right to life, and his view that, if this is a human right, there must be a correlative duty on the rest of humankind to protect such a right, have led some followers of the English School tradition to investigate whether, in case of acute humanitarian emergencies, exceptions should be made to the principle of non-intervention and non-use of force. Currently, opinions are divided between the 'solidarists', who argue that such exceptions could be permitted within certain constraints without thereby jeopardizing the minimalist goal of the orderly coexistence of sovereign states (Wheeler 2000), and the 'pluralists', who argue that such a system is likely to undermine international order and even that humanitarian intervention is a form of paternalism which is morally objectionable (Jackson 2000).

In this current round of debate, the disagreement between the two positions is to some extent an empirical one about how far, in the contemporary circumstances, it is possible to pursue higher goals such as the international protection of human rights without undermining the more basic goal of international order. But a difference can also be seen in the two parties' respective normative presuppositions.

Whereas Wheeler believes it to be the responsibility of the richer and more powerful states to take care of intolerable miseries experienced in other less successful states (2000: 306 *ff.*), Jackson holds that this is the responsibility of the states in which miseries are experienced. Whereas Wheeler thinks that, in order to help reconstruct such states, even the imposition of an international protectorate may become necessary (2000: 306), Jackson rejects such an idea as both impractical and *morally* objectionable because he sees it as paternalistic (2000: ch. 11). However, Jackson considers that the more successful members of international society can treat certain goals— such as the protection of human rights, respect for the rule of law, or the holding of democratic elections—as a condition for their international financial and technical aid to the failed states (2000: 312). It is, he maintains, also up to the members of international society to expel non-improvers from international organizations, and even banish them 'to the outer fringes of diplomacy and beyond' (2000: 312). Curiously, none of these policy alternatives are rejected as paternalistic. International society, Jackson also says, can get involved in the pacification, reconstruction, or development of any country, but only with the consent of its government (2000: 312), implying that where the country lacks an effective government it is not entitled to such assistance.

The difference between Wheeler and Jackson is, as we noted, partly empirical. It is also partly rooted in the difference between them regarding the location of moral responsibility. Here, their opinions differ because Wheeler assumes humankind, despite its division into sovereign political communities, to form a unified moral community, whereas Jackson sees sovereign political communities to be each responsible for their own citizens' welfare. Their normative difference may be expressed as a difference concerning what moral implications they each read into the concept of sovereignty. This issue is, of course, at the heart of (normative) international (political) theory.

INTERNATIONAL THEORY

Despite Jones's complaint many years ago (1981) that political theory is largely absent from English School writings, Wight's lectures on 'international (political) theory' are now quite well-known, thanks to their posthumous publication (Wight 1991). What Wight has done, however, is to exhibit a collection of specimens of Western international thought and classify them into three types, Realism, Rationalism, and Revolutionism. It may be said that 'international theory', in Wight's sense, is the name of his subject matter, and not the name of his mode of engagement with that subject matter, which is basically taxonomic. Nonetheless, Wight's contribution is of considerable significance in alerting us to the body of literature in which contending traditions of thinking about international relations can be discerned and studied with the help of his pioneering exposition and analysis (Wight 1991).[11]

What, we may ask, was this painstaking collection and meticulous classification for? There were, according to Wight, two conscious aims on his part. One was to challenge the prevailing 'two-schools' analysis of international thought, or the view that there are only 'idealism' on the one hand and 'realism' on the other. This view, Wight astutely remarked, may have served a useful purpose in the middle decades of the twentieth century, by enabling a realist critique of idealism, but, according to him, the inadequacy of the dichotomy was apparent in a wider historical perspective (1991: 267). The number of categories has had to be increased to do justice to the wide variety of thought. There were the basic three (realism, rationalism, and revolutionism), instead of the two (realism and idealism), and Wight added that contemporary 'realists' (in the dichotomy) are as much rationalists as realists (in his triple classification which took account of the 'classic realists') (1991: 267). Interestingly, he also suggested a fourth category, 'inverted revolutionists' (or pacifists), and acknowledged that 'soft revolutionists', from Kant to Nehru, may be detached from 'hard revolutionists like the Jacobins and Marxists' (1991: 267) to form yet another category. Clearly, the primary aim of Wight's collection and classification was to produce a more comprehensive and systematic analysis of the past and present thought than was available in his time.

That effort, in turn, was a means to an end, his second conscious aim. This is to show that 'there is very little, if anything, new in political theory, that the great moral debates of the past are in essence our debates' (1991: 268).[12] What Wight aimed to do was to present the known range of argument about matters international so that we could engage in great moral debates of our time with fuller knowledge of the range of ideas that constitute such debates. But the aim of such debates, for Wight, was in deliberation itself, not necessarily in solution. He remarked (1991: 268):

So I have not wanted to offer any definite conclusions, apart from these: to delimit the scope of international theory, to mark out its boundaries, stake its circle. The reflective person will perhaps feel free to move round the circle and enter into any position without settling anywhere. Of course, if one is preoccupied with the need to impart advice to those who conduct foreign policy, one will have to know where one stands. But it is desirable, and certainly not impossible, to combine the urgency of the committed citizen with the philosophical detachment of a student of international politics.

Wight's lectures on 'international theory' were therefore a pedagogical device, an aide to deepening our thinking about international politics, a means by which to bring up a politically reflective citizen with respect to matters international, and not a system of argument that would lead us to a single solution to our questions. As such, Wight's lectures themselves constitute a 'theory' in the sense of a framework of thought within which the activity of international thinking may take place. Moreover, his emphasis on detached philosophical deliberation, rather than search for a solution that enables an action, betrays his conviction that what is needed in the study of world politics is critical (communal) introspection into a range of answers many of us are prone to give out unreflectively. If this kind of activity comes under the rubric of 'theory', it does so in the sense in which a philosopher is a theorist, someone who specializes in scrutinizing the foundations of our practices (or ready-made answers).

But this is not to say that Wight's international theory (or his classification of the specimens he collected) was purely a means of philosophical pedagogy. Bull, it may be noted, gave a social scientific twist to Wight's pedagogical device when he turned them into a set of ideal-types, or three elements found in varying degrees of combination in the changing reality of world politics. Bull wrote (1977: 41):

The modern international system in fact reflects all three of the elements singled out, respect- ively, by the Hobbesian, the Kantian and the Grotian traditions: the element of war and struggle for power among states, the element of transnational solidarity and conflict, cutting across the divisions among states, and the element of co-operation and regulated intercourse among states. In different historical phases of the states system, in different geographical theatres of its operation, and in the policies of different states and statesmen, one of these three elements may predominate over the others.[13]

Finnemore is right, therefore, when she remarks that 'the English School's theoret- ical contribution is that it offers something like a set of Weberian ideal-types about international social structures' (2001: 512). But it is unclear in what sense their con- tribution in this respect can be said to be 'theoretical', for English School writers have not gone much beyond pointing to the irreducibility of the realm of world politics to a single logic of eternal conflict, of order, or of transcendence.[14] To the extent, however, that they, unlike realists, are not dogmatically committed to the inevitability of eternal conflict, and that they recognize the capacity for international society to progress towards a more rational world, while never losing sight of the possibility for world conditions to deteriorate, they can be said to subscribe to a 'theory'—in the sense of an 'interpretation'—of world history which embodies a cautious and mild form of progressivism.

CONCLUDING REMARKS

In the foregoing, I have examined a number of senses in which English School writers may or may not be said to have made contribution to 'theory' in the study of world politics. As far as 'explanatory theory' is concerned, where this term is understood to mean analysis of mechanistic causal processes, the English School's contributions are very modest indeed. They leave many important causal questions about world politics totally untouched, and the few causal claims they make are underdeveloped.

By comparison, their 'normative theory' is much better developed as can be seen chiefly in the works of Bull and Vincent. However, there are signs of weakness even there, and a number of them were noted above. More recently, the debate between the solidarists and the pluralists within the followers of the English School intellectual tradition has come to focus on normative issues quite explicitly. In my assessment, however, they are still at the stage of formulating and asserting their views against each other. They need to be more deeply reflective of the structure of their contentions and disagreements before they can make any further progress.

The English School has a theory of international politics in the sense that it offers a systematic representation of the realm of world politics that gives us a coherent understanding of it. Central to this representation is the international society perspective, or Wight's Rationalism. Wight and Bull did not argue, of course, that this perspective represented the world political realm satisfactorily in its entirety, but they attached a central importance to it nonetheless. Bull derived a set of ideal-types from Wight's three main categories of international thought—international system, international society, and world society—but he did not build an explanatory/causal theory of social transformation of the kind other theorists have attempted to do. Wight's analytical treatment of 'international theory/theories' may in turn be characterized as 'theoretical' in the sense that it provides a framework for thinking and debating about international relations. Moreover, the English School has a theory, or interpretation, of world history which is cautiously progressivist (see Richard Little's contribution, Chapter 2, this volume).

In my view, the most important contribution of the English School to 'theory' concerning world politics lies in the stress Wight's placed on philosophical deliberation. This is not to suggest that English School writers have already made a truly outstanding contribution in this area of activity. The examination in this chapter tends to show otherwise. Furthermore, English School writers seem unfamiliar with the idea that the point of 'detachment' is not thereby to enable privileged access to the world as it really is, but rather to reflect on the cause and effect of a particular claim to know what the world is really like.[15] Still, the English School's stress on reflective deliberation may be extended further to encompass that mode of critical enquiry.

Notes

1. The British Committee was founded in 1958 by the Rockefeller Foundation as a British counterpart of an American Committee (Butterfield and Wight 1966: preface). Chaired successively by Butterfield, Wight, Watson, and Bull, the Committee, comprising a number of academics and some officials, and holding weekend meetings three times a year, collectively produced *Diplomatic Investigations* (1966) and, in its last phase, Bull and Watson's *The Expansion of International Society* (1984). Separate publications by Wight (1977), Bull (1977), and Watson (1992) owe much to the work of the Committee, whose central importance as a site of the English School's evolution is now evident, thanks mainly to the work of Tim Dunne (1998).
2. For further details, see Andrew Linklater and Hidemi Suganami, *The English School of International Relations: A Contemporary Reassessment* (forthcoming), ch. 1.
3. In what sense Wight's engagement with 'international theory' is itself 'theoretical' will be discussed later.
4. I have made use of this line of thinking about the nature of historical explanation in a number of related publications. See Suganami (1996, 1997, 1999). 'Chance coincidences' include cases of confluence of causally independent conditions.
5. Copeland (2003: 432) rightly notes: 'For a school that prides itself on offering a "historical" approach to international relations, there are surprisingly few diplomatic-historical analyses that extensively utilise archival sources or documentary collections'.
6. Note that Wendt's tripartite scheme (1999) does not correspond exactly to the English School's. Wendt's Hobbesian culture does correspond to the English School's Hobbesian/Machiavellian Realism, but Wendt's Kantian international political culture does not correspond to the English School's Kantian/Revolutionism. Wendt's Lockean and Kantian cultures are close to the two versions of Grotian Rationalism—or 'realist' and 'idealist' versions in Wight's terminology (1991: 159–60) and 'pluralist' and 'solidarist' versions in Bull's (1966*a*, *b*).
7. See, for further details, Suganami (2001, 2002*a*, *b*).
8. Note, however, Finnemore's complaint (2001: 510):

   it is unclear why Adam Watson includes ancient China and Persia but not feudal Japan, Siam, or Abyssinia in his study of evolving international society. It may not matter that these were omitted; there may be good reasons for the sample of societies chosen. But without knowing what those reasons are, we cannot judge the effects of these omissions on the work's conclusion.

9. By this criterion, a map of the world is also a theory. Manning (1975: p. xxxv) aptly characterized his teaching of international relations as an exercise in 'global social Topography', and included oceanography among its close relatives (1975: 211). Needless to say, there are many ways in which the world—geographical or social—can be mapped. To suggest that any one map represents the social world 'as it is' is an effect of the power that the world so

represented has upon the person who so suggests; and such a person is contributing to the legitimation and reproduction of that particular representation of the social world.

10. 'Unlike order, justice is a term which can ultimately be given only some kind of private or subjective definition', wrote Bull (1977: 78).

11. As is well known, Wight's realism sees the world of states as in the eternal state of nature and therefore of war, whereas according to his revolutionism, the ultimate reality was the community of mankind, which exists potentially and is 'destined to sweep the system of states into limbo' (Bull 1991: p. xii). Rationalism is presented by Wight as a *via media* between these two extremes, and as holding that despite the anarchical structure of the world of states, a tolerable degree of order and some degree of justice are attainable in the anarchical society of states. See Wight (1991).

12. Note, however, Wight's view that history is not necessarily the best guide to politics (1997: 191–2). Compare Bull (1977: 255–6).

13. The Hobbesian, Grotian, and Kantian models are usually equated with 'the three constructs of international system, international society, and world society' (Finnemore 2001: 512). But in Bull's usage (1977: 10), the concept of 'international system' is somewhat ambiguous, and does not correspond exactly to the Hobbesian model—for, in his usage, 'international system' can be said to exist where the relationships between its members are not very intense whereas the Hobbesian model can be said to exist where the relationships are intense and hostile. This relates to the issue of the intensity of acculturation, not touched on by Bull (see Wendt 1999: 253 *ff.*).

14. This is taken by Little (2000) to suggest that what the English School stands for is not the rationalist international society perspective, but pluralism. This overstates the case. While Wight and Bull never argued that the rationalist perspective was sufficient on its own, they nevertheless attached very special significance to this perspective and were unsympathetic, in particular, to the revolutinist perspective.

15. See n. 10 above.

2

The English School and World History

Richard Little

As the reputed certainties of the cold war recede into the past, there is surprisingly little agreement to be found in the field of international relations about how to characterize the contemporary world. At one extreme, it is argued that we are operating under conditions of unipolarity in a *pax Americana*, while at the other extreme, it is insisted that we living in a global arena where long-standing civilizations are coming into violent confrontation. Sitting between these two extremes is the image of an international society that extends across the globe. From the perspective of this image, there is much more continuity and stability in international relations than either of the other images suggest. According to the dominant assessment of international society, we are operating in a global arena that can trace its origins back for several hundreds of years, to Europe in the seventeenth century and, according to some accounts, even earlier. From this perspective, Europe slowly but surely developed an international society made up of sovereign and equal states in the early modern period of European history, and these states then extended this society, until it embraced the entire globe (Bull and Watson 1984).

Although the dominant account is closely associated with the English School approach to international relations, a very different and much less Eurocentric assessment of the origins of international society can also be derived from this same school of thought (Wight 1977; Watson 1992). According to this alternative assessment, the existence of different kinds of international societies can be traced back for at least 5,000 years. The common interests, rules, institutions, and values that define these international societies have varied considerably, as have the political systems associated with these societies, which extend from anarchic structures, at one extreme, to hierarchical structures, at the other.

From this alternative, and much longer, time perspective, it becomes apparent that the European international society developed in the context of other much more established international societies, and, for several centuries, Europe must have coexisted and interacted with these other international societies. Indeed, it has been argued that it was only at the end of the nineteenth century that these international societies began to coalesce and form a single global international society (Onuma 2000). As interest in a constructivist approach to international relations has emerged in recent years, so the awareness of and a capacity to explore the variations between these different international societies is now being taken much further than the English School initially envisaged. It has been suggested, for example, that the European international society went through several transformations before it transmuted into a global international society (Barkin and Cronin 1994; Reus-Smit 1999).

There is, moreover, no consensus about whether this global international society is secure and firmly based or whether it will prove to be a transient phenomenon that will either evolve further or possibly even give way, once more, to coexisting international societies. Studying previous international societies on a comparative basis should help us to develop a more profound understanding of the distinctive characteristics of the international society that we now live in. At the same time, the current and growing interest in the idea of international society is helping to fuel the recognition that if the study of international relations is going to progress, then it must make space for world history. There is, as a consequence, the potential for a powerful synergy between the consolidation of a comparative framework for studying international societies and the developing interest in world history (Buzan and Little 1994, 2000; Hobden and Hobson 2002)

It is not the case, of course, that world history has been completely ignored in the mainstream study of international relations, although the prevailing tendency has been to draw on the past to provide evidence of continuity rather than change, and there is, in particular, an enduring belief in the 'timeless wisdom of realism'. This belief has always been a feature of classical realism, but it is now also manifest in attempts to draw on realist insights to establish a social scientific approach to the study of international relations. Neorealists have been especially prone to draw on the idea of an international system to reveal and account for what Waltz calls the unchanging 'texture' of international politics. What Waltz wants to do, therefore, is to find an explanation to account for the 'striking sameness in the quality of international life through the millennia' (Waltz 1979: 66).

Neorealism emerged in the final phase of the cold war, when it was still presupposed that the bipolar structure of the international system was going to be an abiding feature of international politics for the foreseeable future. At that time, attention was often drawn to the bipolarity that prevailed during the Peloponnesian War fought between Athens and Sparta at the end of the fifth century BC. Neorealists were confident that they had formulated a theory that could apply just as well to the relations among the Greek city-states as to the interactions among states in the cold war era (Waltz 1979; Gilpin 1981). So while they readily acknowledge that the component units in the international system have changed dramatically from the Greek city-states, through to the superpowers of the late twentieth century, neorealists insist that the patterns of state behaviour associated with the anarchic international system have remained essentially unchanged.

Like most other theorists, neorealists were surprised by the demise of the Soviet Union at the end of the twentieth century, but they were never under the illusion that great powers persist indefinitely. On the contrary, the rise and fall of great powers is acknowledged to be a perennial feature of the international system (Kennedy 1989). What neorealists claim that their theory can do, however, is explain the putative resilience of the anarchic structure of the international system.

At first sight, it might appear that the systemic and societal approaches to the analysis of international relations are fundamentally at odds with each other. The neorealist image of an international system, with its unchanging anarchic structure that constrains the behaviour of the component units, does not seem to be readily compatible with the alternative image of the changing and highly divergent structures of international societies. The English School, however, subscribes to a pluralistic methodology that has recognized the utility of both of these approaches (Little 2000). At the heart of their assessment lies the recognition that there is a need for a much richer and more complex theoretical framework for understanding international relations than currently exists. Although members of the English School have developed various aspects of the theoretical framework that can promote this pluralistic approach, a comprehensive assessment is still only in the early stages of development. Buzan and Little (2000), for example, have followed a similar pluralistic route and suggested that it is necessary to examine international relations from a range of perspectives that distinguish, or separate out, political, military, economic, societal, and environmental sectors from a single, complex reality.

This chapter adopts a world historical focus on the more familiar distinction drawn by the founding fathers of the English School between the political structures that define an international system and the social structures that define an international society. The aim is to demonstrate that a range of different international societies and systems have, across the course of world history, given way to a single worldwide international society/system. The chapter begins by examining the debate about the validity of distinguishing between international systems and societies. It then looks at the interaction between international systems and societies in the premodern world. The chapter goes on to outline the establishment of the European international system/society and its contact with other international systems/societies. It concludes by assessing the utility of adopting a world historical perspective and drawing a pluralistic distinction between international systems and societies.

THEORY AND THE INTERNATIONAL SOCIETY/SYSTEM DISTINCTION

According to Watson (1992: 4), one of the founding fathers of the English School, there is a 'seminal distinction' to be drawn between international systems and international societies when thinking about international relations. But it is not a distinction that has commanded much attention in mainstream International Relations theory. Moreover, it is a distinction that has generated debate even amongst theorists who are broadly sympathetic to the English School approach. Attention will be focused here on two conflicting lines of argument. The first, developed by James (1993), is that there is no meaningful distinction to be drawn between international systems and international societies. This position is contrasted with a second line of argument developed by Buzan (1993) that the distinction is important but that the first generation of English School theorists failed to make it with sufficient theoretical rigour. In a short coda to this section it will be suggested that Buzan does not push this argument far enough, because when measured against world history, it is impossible to avoid the conclusion that the concepts are more complex than he appreciated when he developed this argument.

The distinction between international systems and international societies has been made most clearly by Bull. He argues, in the first place, that it is possible to identify an international system whenever 'states are in regular contact with one another and where in addition there is interaction between them, sufficient to make the behaviour of each a necessary element in the calculation of the other' (Bull 1977: 10). By contrast, an international society exists when states are, on the one hand, 'conscious of certain common interests and common values' and, on the other, 'conceive of themselves to be bound by a common set of rules in their relations with one another, and share in the working of common institutions' (Bull 1977: 13). In developing this distinction, however, Bull, unwittingly generates a certain tension between the two concepts. The tension occurs because at some points in his analysis, Bull argues that international systems predate the emergence of international societies, whereas on other occasions he argues that it is important to recognize that international systems and international societies necessarily coexist.

Before exploring the debate sparked off by this distinction, however, it is worth noting that Bull's conception of the international system corresponds almost exactly with the one formulated by Waltz (1979). In other words, both theorists acknowledge the importance of anarchy for understanding international relations and they argue that in such a system every state takes into account what every other state is doing. In particular, all states have to accommodate the overall distribution of military power and the constant potential for war. But the two theorists then move off in rather different directions (Little 2003). Waltz argues that the anarchic structure of the international system encourages states to pursue policies that will ensure their survival; and an unintended consequence of these responses is the creation of a stable balance of power. As a consequence, anarchy represents a structure that ensures that the system constantly reproduces itself: hence, its resilience. By contrast, Bull argues that there is no automatic tendency for a balance of power to emerge within an anarchic arena. Such an outcome is seen to be purely fortuitous and that we can only imagine the balance of power to be 'a moment of deadlock in a struggle to death between two contending powers' (Bull 1977: 105). From Bull's perspective, stability and order are not a product of the anarchic international system, but the product of the common interests, institutions, rules, and values that characterize an international society.

Because of the tension generated by the way that Bull handles the distinction between system and society, it is unsurprising that the concepts have become a focal point for critiques of the framework developed by the English School (Little 1998). In an endeavour to resolve the tension, critics have approached the distinction from two very different perspectives. In the first instance, James (1993) insists that the distinction reflects a false dichotomy and, as a consequence, he argues that none of the criteria used by Bull to distinguish international systems and international societies can be sustained. In the first place, Bull is seen to assume that although there is regularized contact in both systems and societies, only in the case of international societies is this contact rule-governed. James asserts, however, that it is impossible to sustain regular contact in the absence of established rules and, more importantly, he shows that Bull acknowledges the force of this argument at various points in his analysis.

A second criterion is the existence of diplomatic machinery, which is considered to be an essential component of any international society but is not a feature of an international system. James argues, however, that diplomatic machinery is essential to ensure regular communication between states and he then goes on to show that Bull also acknowledges that communication is essential for sustaining an international system, thereby dissolving the distinction between system and society.

Finally, James attacks the argument that common interests and values underpin international societies but not systems. In the first place, he denies that common values have ever underpinned international relations. Indeed, he argues that common values are unnecessary for any kind of society because all societies are characterized by diverse and competing values. From this perspective, there is no reason, therefore, to associate international society with the idea of common values; indeed, according to James it would be perverse to do so. On the other hand, he considers it equally perverse to suggest that the regular patterns of interaction that are seen to define the existence of an international system could come into existence in the absence of common interests.

James concludes that it is necessary to dispense with the distinction between international systems and international societies, and simply to accept that states interact in an international society. By contrast, Buzan seeks to show that the distinction is useful but has been under-theorized. As a consequence, some of the important benefits to be gained from the historical insights generated by the English School are partially undermined by its theoretical deficiencies. Buzan attempts to build bridges between the systemic perspective developed by the neorealists and the societal perspective that he associates with the English School. However, he agrees with James that the attempt by Bull to demarcate an analytical boundary between a system and a society fails. Buzan acknowledges that systems, like societies, display evidence of rules, common interests, and institutions. What distinguishes a society from a system, he argues, is a sense of common identity. An international system develops into an international society, therefore, when this sense of common identity is made manifest. Buzan argues that this point is reached when states engage in mutual recognition of sovereign equality. Wight (1977: 23) and Reus-Smit (1999: 6) adopt a similar position. By laying down such a clearly defined boundary, Buzan is able, in principle, to identify the historical points when international societies have emerged or collapsed.

But Buzan aims to do more than this. He wants to establish a theoretical framework that can account for the emergence and expansion of international societies.

The English School, he argues, is firmly wedded to the assumption that international societies have only developed in the context of a common culture. It follows that an international society presupposes the prior existence of what the English School call a world society made up of individuals, or at any rate members of an elite, who all adhere to the same culture and share a common identity, as did the ancient Greeks or the early modern Europeans. Buzan accepts, therefore, that the English School provides a useful starting point for understanding international society. But the problem with its formulation is that it cannot account for how the contemporary multicultural international society emerged. Buzan's solution is to draw on the well-established sociological distinction between *gemeinschaft* and *gesellschaft* societies. *Gemeinschaft* societies are built upon 'bonds of common sentiment, experience, and identity'. It is this conception of society that the English School employs. Buzan (1993: 333) then contrasts the 'sentimental and traditional' ties between individuals that underpin an international society built on common culture with the 'contractual and constructed' links that hold together the states which form an international society of the *gesellschaft* type. Although a *gemeinschaft* society is seen to be more developed than a *gesellschaft* society, both are seen to emerge at that point when states engage in mutual recognition of each other's sovereign equality.

Having established this distinction, Buzan draws on the functional logic associated with neorealism to show how states locked into a competitive international system and lacking any common culture can nevertheless be pushed into establishing rules to mediate their interaction until eventually they will trade mutual recognition, transmuting the international system into an international society. Buzan starts from the assumption that in an anarchic system, states will constantly monitor what is happening within their competitors and emulate any developments that advantage their competitors—a process identified by Waltz in terms of 'internal' and 'external' balancing. As a consequence, states become progressively more similar in structure and interaction between states becomes increasingly regularized. Buzan argues that as this process evolves, rules that help to promote the regularized interaction will become progressively more elaborate until a sense of common identity will be generated and states will exchange mutual recognition and the benchmark that distinguishes a system from a society is crossed.

There is a powerful logic to the argument developed by Buzan, but by developing the argument in evolutionary terms, with international systems transforming into international societies, he eliminates the space that Bull was wanting to open up in order to establish a more complex framework for examining international relations. Bull presupposes that international systems and international societies can coexist within a complex reality. Moreover, Bull (1977: 22) insists that it is important not to reify either of these elements. And Bull (1977: 55) then argues that 'it is always erroneous to interpret events as if international society were the sole or the dominant element'. In the same vein, Watson (1987: 153) concludes that the distinction between international systems and international societies is useful 'not because it causes the complex reality of international relations to be simplified into this category or that but because it allows that reality to be illuminated by considering it from a particular point of view'. In other words, international systems and international societies are seen to be different aspects of a common but complex reality.

There are four additional features to this complex reality flowing from the English School approach that tend to get overlooked in the mainstream study of international relations. The first relates to the importance attached to empires. Watson, for example, is quite certain that empires represent the dominant political entity in the ancient world. But the crucial point is that empires are not viewed as a type of state, but as a kind of international system/society, and Watson (1992: 125) makes reference to 'imperially organized societies of states'. He employs Larsen's (1979: 91) definition of an empire as 'a system of political control' that may have 'either a city-state or a territorial state at its center'. It follows, according to Watson, that imperial authorities do not administer the entire region that they dominate or influence. Watson (1992: 38) argues that 'the inner core' of administrative control 'is surrounded by a ring of domination with a degree of local autonomy, and then a ring of hegemony where the imperial power controls external relations and extracts a financial contribution to the imperial structure'. Watson goes on to suggest that historical atlases which 'paint empires of the ancient world one uniform colour are misleading'. In the first place, the empires lacked any clearly delimited boundaries; instead, moving away from the imperial centre, influence became increasingly attenuated. In the second place, the activity and authority of empires 'were radial rather than territorial and spread along lines of penetration' (1992: 38). This formulation takes us a long way from the position adopted by neorealists who are only concerned with anarchical systems. The English School, by contrast, argue that for much of world history, international systems/societies need to be located on a continuum that extends from pure anarchies, where the component units are completely autonomous, through to pure empires where the component units operate within a clearly defined hierarchy (Watson 1992).

A second feature extends the first, with the English School acknowledging that an international system/society can embrace units that are structured in radically different ways, with city-states, for example, interacting with empires. This feature has been discussed at length in subsequent literature (Buzan, Jones, and Little 1993; Buzan and Little 1996) and Buzan and Little (2000) have stressed that very different units come to the fore, depending upon the sector of international relations that is being focused on. Their position, therefore, in the context of the political sector, is radically different from the one adopted by the neorealists, whose theory leads to the conclusion that, over time, structural differences will be eliminated and the states interacting within the international system can be characterized as 'like units' (Waltz 1979).

A third feature, which pulls the English School and neorealism even further apart, is the assumption made by the English School that international systems/societies need to be treated as open systems, because, in the past, their boundaries had 'indeterminate limits' which could expand or contract. By contrast, a 'closed' society/system has no external environment because the society/system has 'reached its maximum extension' (Wight 1977: 75). Only when we come to the contemporary worldwide international system/society is it possible to find evidence of a closed system and it can, as a consequence, be considered in a very significant way to be unique. Shortly after the Second World War, a number of world historians, Toynbee (1954) and Dehio (1962), for example, were acutely conscious that a new type of system was coming into existence. Both forecast that this system would develop unique qualities. In the short term, their prognoses proved incorrect, because the cold war intervened, but with the cold war now ended, interest in their assessments of system transformation may be resurrected.

The open nature of previous international systems and societies gives rise to a fourth distinctive feature of the English School approach and this is that the boundaries of international systems and societies do not necessarily have to coincide and so it is possible, for example, to envisage two international societies existing within a single international system. Again, this feature has the effect of distancing the English School from the neorealists. When combined, it follows that these distinctive features of the English School open the way to a much more differentiated and nuanced account of world history than can be provided by the neorealists.

INTERNATIONAL SYSTEMS AND SOCIETIES IN THE ANCIENT WORLD

Until recently, little interest has been displayed in the origins of international relations. Neorealists (Waltz 1979) simply presuppose that states develop in isolation, but that as their capacity to interact increases, so they eventually come to a point where they can threaten each other. At this juncture, an international system emerges. Using anthropological and archaeological evidence, Buzan and Little (2000) come to a very different assessment. They demonstrate that state-based international systems and societies formed in the context of much more extensive pre-international systems, established, in the first instance, by hunter-gatherer bands. Moreover, because of these very extended pre-international systems, international systems/societies that formed in very different locations rapidly came into contact with each other and quickly established trading systems, with the result that interaction in the economic sector extended far beyond the interaction that took place in the societal and political/military sectors.

Buzan and Little (2000) also show that international systems and societies can emerge from two very different pathways, with one pathway leading to the establishment of anarchic systems of city-states and the other leading to the formation of more hierarchically structured empires. Although unable to account for this difference, neorealist theory does, however, predict that the anarchic structures will prove to be resilient. In fact, the historical evidence suggests that anarchy is a much more fragile structure than the neorealists predict, invariably giving way to the hierarchy of an imperial system. The origin of empires such as Babylon and Assyria, for example, can be traced back to the Sumerian city-states that were grouped at the head of the Persian Gulf. So although there is a pathway that gives rise to city-states, with the passage of time, these city-states, in turn, give way to empires.

The initial city-states and imperial systems, however, were both associated with a *gemeinschaft* form of society that reflected the existence of a common culture. Because of this common culture, the major international actors adhered to the same normative principles, and on the basis of these principles, actors could establish 'collective judgements' that bestowed legitimacy on international actions (Wight 1977: 153). For example, the Sumerian city-states and the Babylonian Empire are seen by Watson to have accepted a common set of religious beliefs that generated a legitimate sense of authority within these settings. These beliefs then tend to counter an unadulterated *realpolitik* conception of international relations. As Watson observes, within a common culture, people are 'inclined to favour what they believe ought to be, even when it is not in their material interest'. This assessment leads to the conclusion that because 'law and theory and the sense of what is proper and fitting are culturally conditioned and associated with tradition and precedent', they are 'comparatively solid and resistant to change; and so is the legitimacy which they confer' (Wight 1977: 152; Watson 1992: 130).

There is, however, good reason for wanting to qualify this conclusion or at least treat it with some caution. It suggests that when a *gemeinschaft* form of society underpins an anarchic society then there should be clear evidence of restraint exercised by the units in the system. Reus-Smit (1997, 1999), for example, provides ample evidence that the Greek city-states represented a *gemeinschaft* type of society. But it is also possible to find examples that reveal how rapidly societal restraint can disappear and be replaced by conditions that correspond to a Hobbesian state of nature. Although it is not possible to spell out the details here, this line of argument corresponds to a very persuasive reading of Thucydides by Price (2001: 5) who argues that the Peloponnesian War needs to be seen as 'a destructive internal conflict'. In such a war, Price (2001: 190) argues, communication breaks down and people 'who in the past had shared language, religious beliefs and practices, moral systems, and social and political institutions, not only stop sharing all those elements of mutual identity but also lose the ability to understand each other—even when they want to—once those bases for mutuality disappear'. The breakdown of communication was also matched by extraordinary acts of brutality and the persistent violation of long-established religious and ethical norms (Price 2001: 273 and 328). This phenomenon represents a significant anomaly that neither the English School nor the constructivists have addressed. By the same token, it is a phenomenon that neorealists fail to identify, much less explain.

Putting this anomaly to one side, however, founding members of the English School did manage to lay the foundations for Buzan's *gemeinschaft/gesellschaft* distinction. As we have noted, the initial international societies were all underpinned by a common culture and an extant world society. The inhabitants of the different city-states in Sumeria, for example, shared a common set of religious beliefs and these helped to provide legitimacy for international actions. There was, for example, a belief that each city belonged to a particular god. Among the various gods there was an overlord who acted as the supreme arbiter. By the same token, the king of the city associated with the heavenly overlord acted as a king of kings and performed a similar function among the cities. Later, inhabitants of the Semetic kingdoms, who lived upstream on the Tigris and the Euphrates, overpowered the Sumerian cities but they adapted to the prevailing common culture, absorbing their religious beliefs, so both the Babylonian and Assyrian empires legitimated their imperial authority by virtue of possessing a god that acted as an overlord in heaven. The existence of such a legitimating principle helps to confirm that these empires embraced a *gemeinschaft* society.

Watson acknowledges, however, that not all empires operated on the basis of such a principle, thereby creating space for the idea of a *gesellschaft* society. The Persian Empire, for example, was not only far more extensive than the previous empires, but it was also founded by monotheistic tribes whose religious beliefs negated the indigenous, legitimizing, pantheistic principle. The Persians, as a consequence, had to rely on persuasion and consent rather than legitimacy, so that their survival was 'based on providing a balance of advantage to those willing to work with or at least acquiesce in Persian authority' (Watson 1992: 46). It can be suggested that international societies of this kind were working on the basis of *gesellschaft* principles.

The Persian Empire coexisted with the Greek city-states and, as a consequence, the relationship between these two entities provides a useful case to draw upon in order to illustrate the distinctive features that the English School associate with international systems and societies. The Greeks are almost invariably depicted as operating within an anarchic international system made up of about 1,200 Greek city-states (*poleis)* that emerged some time after the eighth century BC. The vast majority of these city-states were very small, little more than fortified villages. There was then a set of middle rank city-states, such as Megara, Aegina, and Sicyon, although most attention is paid to those city-states that were seen to be at the top of the power ranking— Thebes, Athens, Corinth, Argos, and Sparta—and states such as Syracuse on the islands in the Aegean Sea (Starr 1986: 46; Cohen 2000: 13). The English School are clear that the Greek city-states formed a nascent international society, identified by the existence of panhellenic institutions, a primitive diplomatic system, and 'rules of war and peace, of mediation, and of communication' (Watson 1992: 50; Reus-Smit 1997, 1999). The Greek city-states are also seen to have formed a distinct cultural unit reflected in 'common language, common theatre, architecture and religious observances' (Watson 1992: 50). As a consequence, the Greeks established a well-defined boundary, separating them from outsiders who were identified as barbarians. Initially, this was a neutral term, but over time it developed pejorative connotations (Wight 1977: 85). It follows that the Greek international society was underpinned by a well-developed world society.

By contrast, the Persians are seen to have operated within a hierarchically structured imperial international system and a *gesellschaft* form of multicultural international society. Because of its rapid expansion, the Persian Empire embraced a variety of divergent and ancient cultures. It is unsurprising to find that in centres where there was a pervasive culture, as in Egypt and Babylon, there was also constant disaffection with the Empire. This disaffection, however, had more ominous implications after 545 BC when the Persian Emperor, Cyrus, turned his attentions to Asia Minor, and subduing the Ionian Greeks who had established cities in Ionia on the east of the Aegean.

Although the Spartans sent a delegation threatening to punish Cyrus if he harmed the Ionian Greeks, in fact, the Persians discovered quite quickly that they were so riven by internal factions that they were unable to unite to resist the Persians and it also proved possible to encourage this factionalism by means of financial incentives (Balcar 1995: 63). By functional means, therefore, the Greeks in Asia Minor were brought inside the Persian international system/society. But in terms of world society, they remained within the ambit of mainland Greece and acted as a potential Trojan horse.

The relationship between the Persian imperial system/society of states and the Greek international system/society of city-states is therefore of particular interest from an English School perspective. Wight (1977: 73) acknowledges that from a systemic (political/military) perspective, the Greek city-states were dominated 'to an unparalleled extent' by the neighbouring 'world empire'. But at the same time, he draws attention to the fact that the boundary describing the Greek 'world society' was an open one, with the result that communities of non-Greeks could be 'hellenised' and brought within the Greek 'world society'. The Greeks became increasingly aware of the potential for cultural transformation as barbarians absorbed hellenic cultural norms and that the hellenic culture was 'inherently expansive', and, as a consequence, 'by force of circumstances or by desire barbarians might be *converted into* Hellenes' (Wight 1977: 86). This process of hellenization took place to the north in Macedonia as well as on the western edge of the Persian Empire. Inevitably, the steady hellenization of the empire accentuated the difficulties arising from competing cultures and complicated the task of maintaining the cohesion of the empire.

Accepting the *gemeinschaft* thesis, it is to be expected that as the world society boundary extends, so the boundary of the international society will be extended. The clearest example of this feature is provided by Macedonia. Alexander (498–454 BC), despite unwilling collaboration with the Persians against the Greeks, pursued a systematic policy of hellenization. He eventually persuaded the Greeks to allow Macedonia to participate in the Olympic games, suggesting that the boundary identifying the Greek international society could be extended provided that the necessary cultural transformation had taken place.

If the boundary of international society can move, then it raises questions about the location of the political and military boundary associated with the international system. This boundary is established primarily on the basis of threat perception. As a consequence, the systemic boundary will be extended very quickly if a peripheral state suddenly becomes more powerful. From the inception of the Persian Empire, it posed a threat to the Greek city-states. According to Wight, however, this threat was only partially reciprocated. He insists that 'the greater part of the Empire lay beyond the system', presumably because the Greek city-states lacked the capacity to mount an attack on the further reaches of the empire (Wight 1977: 90). There is no doubt that the Persians saw the process of hellenization as a threat and their first response was to mount an attack on the Greek city-states. When this strategy failed, the Persians turned to a subtler one. It was recognized that the Greek threat could be managed provided that no city-state dominated all the others. The Persians were able to maintain their own security by adopting a policy of keeping the Greek city-states divided. Watson argues that the Greeks were prepared to accept this arrangement 'not because they trusted the Persians more than they trusted each other, but because they knew that the Persians were not strong enough to dominate the system' (1992: 65).

There are problems with this conclusion because the Persians did come close to overpowering the Greek city-states (Balcar 1995), but in any event, the point can still be made that there is the potential for complex interaction between international systems and international societies and that the boundaries of these divergent sectors may not coincide. It is possible, for example, for two international societies to coexist within a single international system. Of course, James (1993) denies that such a distinction can be meaningful, but the Greek/Persian case supports its utility, although Wight (1977: 34) pondered whether there was enough community between the Greeks and Persians to suggest that an international society was at least 'approximated'. Buzan (1993) resolves this dilemma by distinguishing between *gemeinschaft* and *gesellschaft* international societies and arguing that both can be present, thereby identifying uneven development within a single international society. But this resolution still fails to take on board the utility of sectoral divisions and distinguishing between societal and political/military perspectives. Overall, the Greek/Persian case supports a decision to distinguish international systems, international societies, and world societies.

This section has largely drawn on the history of Persia and Greece to illustrate the emergence and consolidation of international systems and societies. But it is crucial to keep in mind how developments of this kind were taking place all around the world (Watson 1992; Buzan and Little 2000). It is clear from this discussion, however, that it is not possible to suggest that there is an evolutionary trend operating within international relations that is taking us from anarchy to hierarchy or that there is a developmental process that moves us from an international system through to an international society or from a *gesellschaft* to a *gemeinschaft* international society. Anarchy and hierarchy have coexisted from the origins of international relations and so too have international systems and international societies, as well as *gemeinschaft* and *gesellschaft* international societies. But we need much more comparative research to get close to a comprehensive understanding of the world history of international relations.

ORIGINS OF THE EUROPEAN INTERNATIONAL SOCIETY AND SYSTEM

At this juncture, theorists in the field of international relations are still struggling to find theoretical concepts and frameworks that can make sense of the complex international environment that preceded the emergence of modern Europe. Sovereignty during this period was parcelled out in a complicated and multilayered fashion. As a consequence, it is generally agreed that it is inappropriate to define medieval Europe in terms of either an imperial hierarchy or an international anarchy, but there is simply no consensus on any alternative characterization. Waltz (1986) insists that too much can be made of the complexities of the medieval world and that his model of an international system can effectively cut through these complexities. But most theorists have sided with Ruggie (1983) who argues that the problem with Waltz's position is that it then makes it impossible to describe, let alone explain, the most important change of the last millennium: 'the shift from the medieval to the modern international system'. With the growing influence of constructivism, Waltz's emphasis on the virtues of theoretical parsimony appears to be increasingly out of tune with current theoretical concerns. There is a growing desire for much more fine-grained constructivist analysis in preference to broad neorealist brush strokes.

Members of the English School, without doubt, recognize the complexity of medieval Europe but they have not yet managed to find a way of successfully analysing this complexity. Part of the problem, as Wight (1977: 132) frankly acknowledged, is that 'our political vocabulary is inadequate for writing in the same sentence about the states-system and its medieval precursor'. It is also the case that medieval Europe covers a very long period of time and embraces some very significant changes. Teschke (1998: 349), for example, distinguishes three major phases: feudal empires (650–950), feudal anarchy (950–1150), and a feudal state-system (1150–1450). But it is not possible in this brief section to survey such attempts to capture the complexities of medieval Europe. Instead, attention will be focused on the concepts of international system and international society. What becomes apparent is that while it is possible to describe medieval Europe in terms of an international society, to employ the concept of an international system is more problematic.

The central difficulty with trying to conceptualize medieval Europe as an international system is that it fails to fit anywhere along the political spectrum established by Watson (1992) that extends from anarchical international systems at one extreme to imperial international systems, at the other. Medieval Europe was constituted politically by a patchwork of overlapping and sometimes competing authorities. The Roman Church and the Holy Roman Empire, for example, both claimed authority over the same constituency of Christian believers. But in practice, neither possessed sovereign authority. During the era of what Teschke (1998) calls feudal anarchy, an even more decentralized mode of political organization operated based on personal ties of obligation. So it was not only the Roman Church and Empire that claimed to exercise authority in Europe; there were also, among a host of political actors, kings, barons, city burghers, trade guilds, and bishops. The resulting political structure is sometimes labelled as heteronomy, but theorists in international relations increasingly acknowledge that their existing concepts simply cannot begin to capture the complexity of medieval political organization.

Even if it is accepted that with the demise of the Roman Empire, 'successor states' emerged—and Reynolds (1997: 132) goes further to suggest that 'a good deal of Western Europe was governed throughout the Middle Ages by polities that can reasonably be called states'—it is still erroneous to assume that medieval Europe can be characterized in terms of the international anarchic system formulated by both Waltz and Bull. Their notion of strategic decision-makers taking the anticipated reactions of all other actors into account whenever they make a move is not a plausible scenario. For example, it is now generally accepted that the kind of strategic thinking that we associate with the modern state system was alien to the medieval world. As Honig (2001: 113) points out in a discussion of medieval warfare, it simply fails to meet 'the benchmark of good strategy'. Nineteenth century strategists attributed this absence of strategy to political immaturity. But Honig insists that the failure to engage in decisive battles was mainly a consequence of a very different mindset. There was an unquestioning belief in an omnipotent and omniscient God and, therefore, battles where blood would be spilled—a sinful activity in the absence of a just cause—were 'not a simple test of strength, but a test of divine favour and justice' (Honig 2001: 121). War, as a consequence, rarely took the form of pitched battles, because of these divine ramifications; when they did take place, they were highly ritualized occasions. Yet, warfare was a perennial feature of the medieval world, but instead of pitched battles, warfare took the form of ceaseless acts of plundering in order to acquire commodities that could then be given to the supporters of a war leader in order to retain their loyalty. From this perspective, therefore, war was not a mechanism associated with a balance of power and the reproduction of an anarchic international system. It needs to be conceived of as a source of social order.

By contrast, it can be suggested that Christianity helped to form the basis for a common culture and it provides evidence for the existence of a world society and a *gemeinschaft* form of international society. So however the complex political system is characterized, common interests, institutions, rules, and values prevailed throughout the medieval period. All these elements can be illustrated by reference to the crusades. This was a European-wide institution and the crusaders had a clear strategic goal of defending Christendom or *respublica christiana* against its enemies. The traditional image of the crusades being directed against the Muslims in the area east of the Mediterranean is much too circumspect. It is now widely accepted that crusades were fought in many theatres including the Iberian Peninsula, the Baltic region, Eastern Europe, North Africa, and the interior of Western Europe. So in addition to the Muslims, enemies of Christendom included Mongols, pagan Balts, Orthodox Greeks and Russians, heretics, as well as internal opponents of the papacy. Riley-Smith (2001: 128) insists, furthermore, that the crusades lasted for a very long time, from the eleventh to the sixteenth centuries. It has also been noted that crusades were often criticized because men and money were being diverted to the wrong theatre-of-war. Riley-Smith (2001: 132) concludes, therefore, that 'the competition between different theatres shows that the notion of a single Christendom responding to threats from whatever quarter was alive'. By the same token, the crusades also demonstrate that there were common European interests and that medieval Europe formed an independent international society. But this open society operated within a wider environment that embraced other international systems/societies.

The emergence of increasingly autonomous political units brought the medieval era to an end. But considerable attention is now being paid to the fact that, initially, modern states were not the only significant units to emerge. In northern Europe, the city league known as the Hanse became the dominant unit in this region, while in southern Europe, the Italian city-states flourished. Empires also survived into the modern era, although they increasingly came to resemble modern states, and in central Europe the Holy Roman Empire retained many medieval features of political organization until it was replaced by the new German state in the nineteenth century. But in the long haul, as Spruyt (1994*a,b*) explains, national states proved to be the most effective economic units in the European international economic system. Tilly (1990) argues, by contrast, that modern states emerged as the dominant unit in the global arena primarily because they proved to be more successful than any of their competitors when it came to waging war. In practice, of course, military and economic strength are closely related (Kennedy 1989).

Elements of the medieval European international society survived this political transformation, but an unintended consequence of the emergence of these powerful modern states was the crystallization of an anarchic European international system as characterized by Bull (1977) and Waltz (1979). The modern European states were highly competitive and very security conscious and they did closely monitor each other's activities. Although these elements were present in previous international systems, modern European states proved to be very much more efficient and dynamic than the more long-established types of political units. As a consequence, they eventually began to pose a threat not only to each other, but also to political actors in international societies in other parts of the globe.

THE EMERGENCE OF A GLOBAL INTERNATIONAL SOCIETY/SYSTEM

Escaping from long-established Eurocentric accounts of the European international society/system as well as Europe's relations with the rest of the world is not easy because much of the research that would allow us to develop what Onuma (2000) calls an 'intercivilisational perspective' is only just beginning to be produced. In recent decades, however, there has been a 'growing appreciation of non-European societies and civilizations' (Goffman 2002: p. xiii). As a consequence, Goffman observes that we are now gaining access to the views of members of these different civilizations instead of relying on the views of often hostile outside observers. It is only in very recent years, for example, that Europeans have gained an insight into how the court of the Chinese Emperor responded to the first official contact made by the British in 1793. Peyrefitte (1993) has provided an account of this meeting based on Chinese documents that had never previously been available to Western scholars. Prior to the nineteenth century, then, diplomatic relations between Europe and China had been very limited. By contrast, relations with the Ottoman Empire were very much richer, more complex, and long-standing. But, as Goffman (2002: 4–5) argues, understanding this relationship has suffered from 'Eurocentric mythologising' and an 'almost irresistible temptation to view the globe "downward" from Paris and London' so that 'the Ottoman empire joins the ranks of the "others"—exotic, inexplicable, unchanging and acted upon by the powers of ruling authorities in Europe'.

It would be surprising if the founding fathers of the English School managed to avoid criticisms of this kind. Writing in the 1950s and 1960s, they were, undoubtedly, men of their time. Critics have noted, for example, that there is a pervasive tendency to equate European international society with the idea of international society itself (Onuma 2000). In other words, there is a failure to adopt an intercivilizational perspective and acknowledge that for 400 years, the European international society operated in the context of a much more extensive environment, containing other international societies. Reference to the 'expansion of international society' (Bull and Watson 1984), therefore, not only ignores these other international societies, but also fails to note that it was a specifically European society that was expanding during the course of the nineteenth century. Keene (2002) also observes that Bull and others fail to note that throughout this period there were, effectively, two very different types of international order in place. Within Europe there was an international society where states recognized each other's sovereignty and tolerated their differences. By contrast, outside of Europe, there was a very different pattern of order in the extra-European empires and colonies, which did not tolerate difference, and 'which was dedicated to the goal of promoting a particular idea of civilization, transforming "uncivilized" cultures and social, economic and political systems along the way' (Keene 2002: p. xi). From Onuma's (2000) perspective, however, this formulation also fails to acknowledge the existence of a third type of international order that linked Europe to more long-standing international societies.

Other critics are much more hostile to English School omissions and commissions, noting, for example, how the English School fails to note that the ruthless pursuit of empire and colonization is without doubt one of the most central common institutions that defined the European international society. Even the use of expressions like 'the expansion of international society' is seen to be a rhetorical device that serves to sanitise an exceptionally brutal process. A genealogical assessment is seen to reveal that the English School focus on international society is essentially a nationalistic one, reflecting an 'intellectual response to decolonization and its attendant post-imperial anxieties' (Callahan, forthcoming).

There is, without doubt, an element of truth to these various criticisms. But they also oversimplify the way that the first generation of English School theorists endeavoured to characterize the complex process whereby a global international society has evolved. In the first place, in the context of European expansion, it was recognized that it is necessary to identify two quite separate spheres. Wight suggests, for example, that the Peace of Cateau Cambresis, 1559, specifically acknowledged that Europe formed one sphere with the creation of colonies operating within an outer sphere. The treaty is depicted as establishing 'amity lines' which separated Europe from areas where colonization was taking place. The amity lines established a zone of peace in Europe and a zone of war elsewhere, and Wight observes that this division 'became almost a rule of law, giving freedom to plunder and attack and settle without upsetting the peace of Europe' (1977: 125). Although Wight argues that this rule of law persisted for some time, by the eighteenth and nineteenth centuries, states were very concerned about the colonial possessions of their neighbours and they figured prominently in international agreements. The Berlin Conference of 1884–5, for example, 'legitimated' the partitioning of Africa among the European states (Bull 1984a: 109–11).

Bull and Watson also fully acknowledged that Europe operated initially in a global arena of 'regional international systems' that reflected the existence of long-established civilizations. From their perspective, Europe slowly but surely expanded until it had absorbed these other systems. But Bull and Watson were under no illusion that the resulting global international society can be considered European. As they saw it, from the end of the Second World War, there has been 'a massive revision of international rules and conventions carried out by African, Asian, and Latin American states' (Bull and Watson 1984: 1–2). Wight, however, adopted a more radical stance, drawing attention, in particular, to the views of Alexandrowicz (1967) who argued that the expanding European powers 'were compelled by the facts of the case to treat with non-European powers in regular diplomatic relations, whose principles were derived as much from non-European practice as from European' (Wight 1977: 118). Wight infers from this proposition that Alexandrowicz is hinting that the Europeans and non-Europeans mutually established a global states-system during the process of coming into contact with each other. This assessment has the virtue of questioning the prevailing Eurocentric perspective, but Wight does not consider that it provides a correct characterization of the process. It is clear that it is an area where more research is required.

A third complication supplied by the English School perspective relates to the relationship that they identify between international systems and societies. Wight (1977: 121) notes that in the second half of the fifteenth century the Ottomans began to pose a threat to Christendom 'of a kind and a scale that had never been known before'. At that juncture, therefore, it can be argued that the Europeans and the Ottomans became bound together at a systemic level. Wight notes that once this happened, the Ottomans were quickly caught up in European political alignments, and began to play a significant role in European balance of power politics. The role might be compared to the one played by the Persian Empire in the Greek states-system.

Once it is accepted that Europe and the Ottoman Empire were linked at the systemic level, questions inevitably arise about relations at the societal level. Wight looks at the implications of this development very carefully. According to James (1993), as discussed earlier, once systemic interactions are taking place, there are inevitable societal consequences. Wight fully recognizes the force of this argument. Once the Ottoman Empire was engaged in European political alignments and playing a role in European political struggles, it was inevitable that they had to participate in Europe's diplomatic community and develop common interests with European states. Nevertheless, Wight still wishes to maintain that the Ottoman Empire was not part of the European international society. Despite the systemic links, the European states-system and the Ottoman imperial system remained deeply divided at the world society level of analysis.

Wight's solution to the problem posed by James is to accept that there were societal links between the Europeans and the Ottoman Turks, but then to distinguish them from European societal links. Watson endorses this line of argument, observing that although relations between the European international society and the Ottoman empire were clearly rule-governed and reflected a societal dimension, the Turks and the Europeans formed an international society of a looser kind (1992: 217). Watson observes how the Ottoman Empire was systematically excluded from what Voltaire referred to as the *grande republique*. The Turks were not Christian and they did not adhere to European international law. They were not present at the settlements of Westphalia, Utrecht, or Vienna. Wight notes that there was never any regular exchange of diplomatic representatives which provided the 'test of full membership of the European diplomatic community' (1977: 122). The relations that European states established among themselves were not, therefore, comparable to the relations established with the Ottoman Empire.

The English School stress, however, that the establishment of the boundary line did not simply come about at the instigation of the Europeans. The Ottoman Turks had no desire to locate permanent diplomatic representatives in Europe. By the same token, they had no wish to build their relations with the Europeans on the foundations of European international law. Instead, they preferred to operate on an Islamic basis. So whereas the Europeans established their relations with each other by means of international law, relations with the Ottoman Empire were maintained on the basis of Islamic capitulations. These capitulations represented the mechanism used by Muslims to formulate rules to govern relations with citizens of infidel states. The Europeans agreed to these capitulations in order to facilitate the investment of European capital outside of Europe and to ensure the protection of Europeans within the Ottoman Empire. As the Europeans moved further afield, they extended the idea of capitulations to regulate their relations with other areas of the world.

It is clear that the assessments by Wight and Watson map very closely on to the distinction drawn by Buzan between *gemeinshaft* and *gesellschaft* international societies. The overall analysis in this section suggests, moreover, that the emergence of the global international system/society was the product of a much more complex process than can be captured by the familiar account of the expansion of the European international system/society. Much more research needs to be conducted, however, before an adequate picture of this process can be presented.

CONCLUSION

The English School is now widely associated with the idea that we can characterize international relations in terms of an international society constituted by norms that are considered to be very durable and highly institutionalized (Krasner 1999). The aim of this chapter has been to demonstrate that this assessment underestimates the ambition of the founding fathers of the English School. In the first place, they acknowledged that it is necessary to take account of political as well as societal international structures. At the same time, they also acknowledged the need to probe below the level of political structures and take account of common culture, although we have only touched on this dimension in this chapter. In other words, the English School has always recognized the need for a pluralistic approach to the study of international relations. Although it has been argued, subsequently, that the founding fathers failed to push this argument hard enough, and their neglect of the economic sector is considered to be a particular flaw, the focus on both political and social structures can certainly be seen to be a step in the right direction.

In the second place, the English School helped to pioneer the attempts to locate the study of international relations in a world historical setting. But in contrast to realists who drew on the past to emphasize the importance of continuity in international relations, members of the English School were interested in world history because it can help us differentiate international systems/societies and, in doing so, provide the basis for a comparative framework that can help to reveal what is distinctive about contemporary international relations. Working from a world historical perspective, for example, it became obvious to analysts such as Watson (1992) that an exclusive emphasis on anarchy is inappropriate for a comprehensive understanding of international relations. A comparative framework, therefore, helped to highlight the importance of hierarchical political structures in international relations. By the same token, the English School has helped to open up questions about boundary problems, open and closed systems, and sectoral differentiation. But these issues tended to be raised in a somewhat ad hoc fashion because the founding fathers of the English School did not come close to establishing a comparative framework that could be considered systematic or comprehensive.

Of course, it is possible that such a framework is a chimera and that we need to adopt a rather more modest approach to theory building. Certainly the most successful attempts to date to employ world history on a systematic basis have been more limited in scope. Reus-Smit (1999), for example, starts with an ambitious reconceptualization of the normative foundations of international societies, but then focuses more concretely on the question of why international societies have been characterized by different fundamental institutions. He illustrates his argument by focusing on the international societies that emerged in ancient Greece, Renaissance Italy, absolutist Europe, and the modern international society that emerged in the middle of the nineteenth century. Reus-Smit's approach reveals very effectively how important disjunctures have occurred in world history. The Renaissance city-states are not seen to have provided the prototype of the modern state system. On the contrary, Reus-Smit argues that they were characterized by fundamental institutions that are completely alien to the modern world.

Such an approach, of course, raises the question of what happens when these fundamentally different international societies come into contact. This was a question which undoubtedly preoccupied the founding fathers of the English School. As discussed, they provide some insights into this question, but not in a systematic or comprehensive fashion. The overall conclusion has to be that while the English School have raised a large number of interesting questions about the world history of international societies, there is a long way to go before satisfactory answers are likely to be given.

3

The New Agenda

Tim Dunne

During NATO's bombing of the Federal Republic of Yugoslavia, Prime Minister Tony Blair flew to the United States to try and persuade President Clinton to commit—or at least, not to rule out—the use of ground forces. One of the high points of his visit was to give the keynote speech to the Economic Club of Chicago. Given that context, the theme of the speech was to be the relationship between sovereignty and human rights. It was decided by the Cabinet Office to invite a leading international relations academic to write the first draft. The centrepiece of the speech was the enunciation of 'new rules' that would constitute criteria for just intervention in the affairs of a sovereign state. The Prime Minister read it properly for the first time on the journey to the United States. As he pondered over the draft, he kept repeating the word 'international community'. He then 'yelped with delight' when he hit upon the formulation "'the doctrine of the international community!'" (Kampfner 2003: 52). It was as if it had been discovered for the first time.

This vignette illustrates three important points about the idea that states form a community or society in their relations with one another. First, its invocation signifies the presence of a social totality dominated by collective actors called states. In this sense, international society is a general and inclusive term that gives an observer 'a frame of reference' (Onuf 1994: 9). Second, like all key concepts in the social sciences, it is slippery, contested, and underdetermined. It is slippery in so far as other terms are invoked to signify approximately the same social totality—practitioners as we have seen prefer international community (with some exceptions).[1] It is contested in so far as the boundaries of the concept are unclear—how did *it* evolve, and when does *it* become something else? And it is underdetermined in that the complexity of politics on a global scale is such that the meanings we give to concepts are always contingent, fallible, and in some sense inadequate. It stands to reason that none of the above are good reasons for abandoning the search for a coherent account of international society, in the way that a leading sociologist urged his discipline to give up on the idea of 'society' (Mann 1986: 2).

I would like to thank Alex Bellamy for his enthusiasm and patience. In addition, two of my colleagues at Exeter, David Armstrong and Theo Farrell, provided helpful comments on an earlier draft.

Like all concepts, international society has a history. Sadly for the British Prime Minister, it was not created on a jet plane over the Atlantic. The social totality that his 'new' doctrine refers to stretches back at least four centuries. From the early sixteenth century, the idea of a great 'society of societies' has been invoked by various natural law and natural rights thinkers. The belief that states form a society is based on two connected claims about common interests and shared values. At the most basic level, states take into account the impact their decisions have on other members of their society. Failure to do this could jeopardize the survival of the system as a whole, on which their independence is predicated. At a deeper level, international society can signify the presence of intricate patterns of social interaction, evident in the balance of power and in their general fidelity to the rules of the game. This does not mean that states will always act in accordance with agreed rules and conventions, only that this is the regular pattern and not the exception.

To claim a certain discursive resemblance in the manner in which interstate relations have been conceived over the centuries is not the same as saying that the structure of international society is unchanging. In the history of international society, the discontinuities are as interesting as continuities. This simple point, as Foucault reminds us, becomes a complicated one when we reflect on the fact that anything with a history does not have an 'essence', to presume it does is to look for 'that which was already there' (Foucault 1987: 223). Questions such as 'when did international society begin?' and 'what are its essential features?' do not lend themselves to straightforward answers. What came before is part of what evolved after. The precise moment when a social structure changes is often unclear—sometimes imperceptible until a radical rupture interposes itself as in the case of a revolution.

While it is possible to trace a genealogy of the idea back at least to the sixteenth century, the academic focus on 'international society' proliferated at the beginning of the twentieth century. It was a term that was widely used by international lawyers (Reeves 1921) and political scientists who recognized the dual nature of state sovereignty (signifying authority on the inside and rights/duties on the outside) and the fact that states were increasingly party to international legal contracts (or treaties). Early idealists from the inter-war period also used the term in their effort to displace power politics as the dominant framework for informing what states do and how they should behave. Realists have also been known to use the term. Morgenthau associated it with the realm of diplomacy and statecraft performed by or on behalf of the nineteenth century monarchs (1948: 237–41). Even Waltz, famous for his theory of a mechanical international system (1979), was unable to avoid it (1986: 326).

It is clear from the above that the term international society has been used by a variety of theoretical orientations as a general signifier of the institutional context within which interstate interactions take place. This generic usage needs to be bracketed from a particular meaning given to the term by the leading figures in post-1945 British international relations. To them, international society signalled a rejection both of a hard-headed realism and a big-hearted idealism. For writers such as C. A. W. Manning, Martin Wight, Hedley Bull, Adam Watson, and R. J. Vincent, there was 'more to international relations than the realist suggests but less than the cosmopolitan desires' (Linklater 1996*b*: 95). The work produced by these writers became known as the English School, a history that has received considerable attention in recent times (Dunne 1998; Suganami 2003*b*). While the writings associated with the first wave of the English School continue to be published (Wight 1991; Watson 1992; Alderson and Hurrell 2000), there is an emerging English School literature that is more inclined to engage with new currents of thinking in the American heartland of international relations (see Reus-Smit's contribution, Chapter 4, this volume).[2] This endeavour is one that all new currents of thinking on the English School are agreed upon.

If the 'frame' for macro-sociological research in international relations is 'how the world hangs together', then the picture that begins with an English School account of international society needs less justification today than it did at any time in the last two decades. Such a change of fortune can be discerned from comparisons with earlier historiographical debates in international relations. In reflections on the 'state of the discipline' in the 1980s, the English School was nowhere to be seen (Banks 1984; Smith 1986), neither did it figure in early representations of the debate between neorealism and its critics—what many have termed the 'third debate' (Keohane 1988; Lapid 1989). By the mid to late 1990s, interest in the English School was on the increase. Many influential textbooks began to include it as an alternative approach to the subject, placing it alongside realism, liberalism, and various critical approaches (Der Derian 1995; Brown 1997; Roberson 1998; Jackson and Sorensen 1999). Added to these, weighty monographs and doctoral dissertations proliferated, all taking the English School as their point of departure (*inter alia* Armstrong 1993; Welsh 1995; Neumann 1996; Korman 1996).

This sense of a resurgent English School paradigm was heightened by theoretical developments in the North American mainstream. As the new debate was constructed around the rationalist/constructivist fissure, the English School found itself represented as a form of constructivism. The leading rationalist, Stephen Krasner, referred to it as 'the best known sociological perspective' in international relations (in Buzan 2004: 46). Similarly, those who self-identified with constructivism openly acknowledged the insights of classical English School theory (Finnemore 1996*a*; Wendt 1999; see the Introduction and Chapter 4 by Reus-Smit, in this volume). The extent to which both 'old' and 'new' institutionalism can learn from one another has been extensively debated in the field (Dunne 1995*a,b*; Wæver 1998; Reus-Smit 2002*a*).

Such momentum prompted an attempt to pull together the diverse strands in English School theorizing into a coherent research programme, led by Barry Buzan and Richard Little. Buzan's agenda-setting paper 'The English School: an under-exploited resource in IR' was published in the *Review of International Studies* in 2001 as the lead article in a forum on the English School (Buzan 2001; Finnemore 2001; Guzzini 2001; Hurrell 2001; Neumann 2001). This agenda has also been debated in other journals, most recently in a Special Issue of *International Relations* in which the editor's foreword speaks of how the School has 'flourished' in recent years (Cox 2003: 251–2).

While the English School has produced a significant body of work on international society, there is much that can be learned from other approaches to the institutional context of international relations. Just as one can study norms without being a constructivist, or the material basis of the international system without being a neo-realist, it is possible to theorize international society without being a member of the English School. By decoupling English School theory from international society we are able to open up the macro-institutional context to a range of theoretical perspectives. The 'driver' of this agenda should not be to vindicate one paradigm over another, but to understand the social totality we call international society. This endeavour requires engaging with classical and new English School writings but it also demands a dialogue with a wider literature in international relations and beyond. These various connections will be evident below, where I show the various unresolved puzzles at the heart of the English School's theorization of international society, and begin to suggest the outline of a new agenda to address these puzzles.

AGENCY AND STRUCTURE

[handwritten margin note: def of society of states]

The first theoretical conundrum concerns the question of membership. Bull's classical definition in *The Anarchical Society* argues that a society of states is constituted 'when a group of states, conscious of certain common interests and common values, form a society in the sense that they conceive themselves to be bound by a common set of rules in their relations with one another, and share in the working of common institutions' (Bull 1977: 13). At first glance, such a definition is open to the charge of *state-centrism* leading to the conclusion that the English School is little more than a polite form of realism (Rosenberg 1994). Even though Bull acknowledged the fact that states defined as 'independent political communities' predated the emergence of modern sovereign states (1977: 9), what the English School account of international society lacks is an adequate theorization of *how* states are capable of social relations.

Robust answers to this question are required in order to protect the theory from objections rooted in reductionist accounts of the social world. Individualists, from J. S. Mill onwards, deny any coherence to the idea that collective entities can be meaningful. 'Men in a state of society are still men . . . Men are not, when brought together, converged into another kind of substance with different properties' (Archer 1995: 3). If this claim is persuasive at the level of domestic society, then it is arguably more damaging to an ontology whose constituent parts are *themselves* collectives. For philosophically informed theorists (Rengger 2000: 77–8), there is a problem in positing which agents are authorized to act in the name of international society (a problem that has no parallel in domestic societies in which governments claim legitimate authority).

This touches upon the issue that international society should be thought of in ontological terms (as a social structure) and agential terms (a capacity for action). The former refers to powers, tendencies, emergent properties, and rules, that take the form of enablements and constraints on action. The latter captures the residual truth that nothing happens in international society without something being done by those who act in the name of governments (and what predecessors in these roles have done).[3] Agency captures the way in which representatives of 'international society' have clarified and codified rules about diplomatic immunity, the laws of war, principles of coexistence following a breakdown in order, and so on.

No major event happens in world politics without a politician or activist calling for the 'international community' to 'do something'. New problems generate calls for international action across a vast range of issue areas from security, to trade, to global communications networks. This implies that international society has certain competences, ranging from agreements in the form of international treaties and concerted diplomatic pressure on one end of the spectrum to imposing its will through the collective use of force on the other. That said, international society is not reducible to the question of agency; in other words, it can be said to exist even if this is not manifested in observable instances of collective action. In this respect, international society is a social fact, one that is external to each state but also internal to all.

More work needs to be done on the question of agency. It is important not to regard states as preformed units as Bull implies. In the history of international society, membership has been ascribed to dynastic monarchies, imperial states, states that meet 'a standard of civilisation'. It has been denied to 'backward' peoples, secessionist groups, and latterly to authoritarian states who are suspected of acquiring weapons of mass destruction. But what exactly is the relationship between regime type and the character of international society? We need a theoretical account of international society that highlights the relationship between variable domestic structures and the creation and reproduction of frameworks of shared norms and purposes. The converging research agenda with constructivism is providing an important opening here, and much can be learned from the debate between constructiv*isms* on interstate–society relations (cf. Reus-Smit 2002 and in this volume; Wendt 1999).

The danger with taking states for granted is that we have implicitly answered one of the central questions of international politics, namely, where does authority lie and how is it exercised. The danger of ignoring states, especially the great powers, is also very real. After all, international society would be unthinkable if there were no agreed rules. In a decentralized system, it is great powers that set the rules and enforce them. This begs the question how rules and institutions come to be 'shared', and the various mechanisms and instruments by which new members (and recalcitrant ones) are socialized into the prevailing norms of international society. Historically, force, calculation, and persuasion have all played a part (Wendt 1999). Arguably, the English School is well placed to understand the relationship between power, interest, and norms, avoiding the twin pitfalls of denying the legal–normative domain any independent validity (as realists do), or underestimating the extent to which power creates a normative framework convenient to itself (as cosmopolitans are prone to). That said, there is work to be done in showing how socialization takes place, and the relative balance of coercion and persuasion in particular instances. Historically informed work on revolution and counter-revolution (Armstrong 1993), and 'the standard of civilisation' (Gong 1984; Foot 2000; Zhang 2001), offer rich possibilities for a synthetic account of large-scale historical and normative change.

SYSTEM, SOCIETY, WORLD SOCIETY: BOUNDARIES IN QUESTION

The theoretical puzzle about membership slides into the question of 'boundaries': in other words, what lies *outside* this vexatious entity we call international society? Bull was absolutely clear that international society was only 'one element' in the reality of world politics. It coexisted uneasily with systemic forces such as war and conquest, and transnational economic and social forces. The classical English School literature is ambiguous as to whether it is seeking to provide an account of the relationship *between* the three elements, or whether in its aim was the vindication of the societal dimension. Within the new English School literature, this ambivalence has become an issue that divides, in Isaiah Berlin's terms, 'hedgehogs' who are more inclined to holistic accounts of the social world (Jackson 1990*b*: 112, Hurrell 1998; Almeida 2003) from 'foxes' who are more inclined to analytical disaggregation (Buzan and Little 2000; Little 2000; Buzan 2004).[4] In the former camp are those who believe it is increasingly problematic to distinguish between system, society, and world society. Bull's initial configuration of a system, suggesting mere contact between states in the absence of shared rules, lacks plausibility given the high degree of interdependence today. 'All relations between human beings—including people who speak and act in the name of states—necessarily rest on mutual intelligibility and communication'. Such an observation leads Robert Jackson to argue that we should abandon the system/society distinction (1990*b*: 112; see also James 1993).

What Jackson means here is that international society is an essentially normative business, in contrast to the 'the abstract logic of the system of states' (Bull in Alderson and Hurrell 2000: 25) that characterizes Waltzian neorealism. We know international society exists, according to Jackson, because it is present in the 'normative vocabulary' of practitioners (Jackson 2000: 5). The society of states is a human construct which is produced and reproduced by the activities of statespeople and other representatives of institutions. While Jackson provides a strong 'insider' account of international society, at times he comes close to embracing what philosophers would call an 'anti-realist' position. In Jackson's words, '[i]t is not something "out there" that is independent of human beings' (Jackson 2000: 33). Such an anti-realist ontology has a long history in the English School, going back to Manning (1962) and re-emerging in Osiander (1994: 9).

Bull's view is closer to a realist ontology. Agreed, international society exists in the minds of men and women, but crucially, his position is that *it is not reducible to them*. Social facts—norms, expectations, habits—*do* exist 'out there' in that they will endure even if individuals resist or dispute them. As Durkheim argued in his *Rules of Sociological Method*, social facts exist prior to the individual and function independently of the individual (Giddens 1971: 87–98). On this account, there is an international social reality which is composed of structures that are unobservable yet constrain and compel actors. The theoretical task is to show how properties of international society, such as legal rules, enable certain actions, such as the legitimacy of colonial possessions overseas, in one historical era and proscribe them in another. This requires a causal account of how 'really existing' social structures operate.

Although Jackson and Bull implicitly work with different ontologies, they share the view that international society is a permanent feature of world politics. As Bull wrote in his *magnum opus*, 'the element of a society has always been present, and remains present, in the modern international system' (1977: 41). Such a position is mature in the sense that it recognizes that the 'darker' forces in world politics are also *social*. War and interstate violence are only intelligible in the context of competition among sovereign states for rewards which are valued intersubjectively be they priced in territory, status, security, or wealth. Moreover, this competition takes place within an established framework of rules and practices. An understanding of war without an understanding of this wider context would be like trying to explain the meaning of a five-pound note without providing an account of the social system of production and exchange.

[handwritten margin note: War is also 'social' & Must be placed in its wider context]

The difficulty with the 'hedgehog' account is that international society becomes an undifferentiated category. Too much is folded in to this account. International society is repeated in the hope that each iteration will make it come true, as Blair hoped with use of the term 'international community' on his way to Chicago. Blind faith is no substitute for an account of how an institutional order emerged, is reproduced, and has potentiality (or not) for transformation. The kind of sociological functionalism that often underpins a holistic account of international society is partly responsible. Functionalism blurs differentiation and causation, goals become causes, and description merges imperceptibly with normative adequacy. At a minimum, an adequate theorization of international society needs to be able to disentangle emergent properties from their consequences.

Barry Buzan has for some time been an eloquent exponent for analytically disaggregating international society from other domains. While his early work focused on the system/society boundary (1993), his new book (2004) examines at great length the world society dimension of English School theorizing. His motivation for this shift is to reposition the School in a manner that enables it to deal with the increasing density of interstate/society relations under conditions of globalization (see Buzan's contribution, Chapter 6, this volume). It is important to dwell on Buzan's argument both because of its intrinsic merit as a statement of grand theory, and because he articulates a position that is open to objections from those wanting to resist disaggregating the *via media*.

Buzan sets out his stall with a great sense of purpose. As he tells the reader at a number of junctures, the 'three pillars' of the English School 'triad' must be preserved because of their explanatory potential. The problem lies in the fact that the connections between the pillars are have not been properly worked through. It is worth pausing on an intriguing claim he makes about the meaning of international society. He argues that within the English School there are three answers to the question 'what is international society?' It either exists 'as a set of ideas in the minds of statesmen' (Manning being an exponent), or 'as a set of ideas to be found in the minds of political theorists' (which he likens to a Wightean approach), *or* 'as a set of externally imposed concepts that define the material and social structures of the international system' (2004: 48). It is this understanding of system/society/world society as 'analytical concepts' that Buzan adopts.

Taking the system/society boundary first, we see that a marked shift in his thinking has occurred. Buzan argued previously, in his co-authored book with Richard Little, that we need to draw a distinction between shared ideas (belonging to the societal sector), and the kind of mechanistic material power that Waltz and fellow neorealists regard as an attribute of the system (Buzan and Little 2000: 103–5). The influence of Wendtian constructivism has led Buzan to revise his position. As Wendt argues in *Social Theory of International Politics*, materialist theories of society can explain cooperation, just as shared ideas and norms explain war (2000: 253).

The central thrust of Buzan's argument is not about the system/society boundary so much as the international/world society boundary. He rightly points out that traditional English School thinking in this area is 'both incoherent and under-developed' (2004: 143). In terms of 'actors', world society has often been treated as a 'residual category' in which we place all kinds of entities that do not fit into the system or societal sectors. This problem is compounded by the fact that too much writing on world society has been framed around normative theoretical concerns about the rights of states versus the rights of individuals replaying an old debate between positive and naturalist conceptions of international law (Bull 1966*b*). In the context of today's human rights culture, the effect of this move is the 'merging' of the two pillars, to the detriment of analytical progress (Buzan 2004: 107). By way of example, the sectors where shared values and institutions are most in evidence is political economy (particularly in a regional context). The tendency to frame the question of the degree of convergence of values in terms of pluralism and solidarism has further impaired our vision of the boundary between international and world society.

Buzan's reconstructive surgery of the English School rests on the following moves. Abandoning the category of the system on constructivist grounds, Buzan focuses on the interstate/world society boundary. Each side of this divide is subject to extensive rethinking. Interstate society is opened up to a spectrum of variations, from 'thin' to 'thick'.[5] In addition, it is a layered phenomenon where the global institutional order is accompanied by subglobal structures, each of which can be mapped according to the degree of social solidarity on the thin–thick spectrum. The global and regional macro-social structures are held together by an admixture of coercion, calculation, and belief. Using these analytical categories, it is possible to see how the international social structure has changed historically, something that Buzan hints at in his conclusion. The classical English School treatment of world society is reworked by way of a distinction between the transnational domain and the interhuman domain (the society of peoples). This is how Buzan sets out the relationship between these three domains:

The three units are now separated by the hard boundaries resulting from defining them in terms of different types of constitutive unit. They are *not* a spectrum as the three traditions of the classical English school model were generally taken to be (Mayall 2000: 13). Consequently, interest shifts from what defines these borders (now clear) to how the three domains as so constituted interact with each other... The key English school idea that the three traditions are understood to be simultaneously in play is preserved, but now on the grounds that social formations involving the three types of unit are always expected to be present in international systems to some degree. At a minimum, each domain in the triad constitutes part of the operating environment for the other two. At a maximum, conditions in one domain may determine what options are possible in others. (2004: 277)

One reply to this agenda from the 'hedgehog' corner might be to press Buzan further on the relationship between the domains. The values and institutions of international society are intimately connected to the transnational and interhuman domains. At the beginning of the 2000s, it is hard to think of transborder interactions that are independent of international society: even email interaction between 'world citizens' is enabled by international rules (technology transfer, trade) and regulated (to some degree) by public international law. The point at which Buzan's reconstruction overlays with the classical English School agenda is over the vital question about how the domains relate to one another. What connects and infuses them are the underlying meta-values and moral purposes (Reus-Smit 1999). The question then becomes whether the best way to access these principles is through a structural theory or by way of a historical-cum-normative enquiry. The key conceptual challenge for those wanting to resist the logic of desegregation is to provide a clearer account of *how* states and non-state actors are creating the normative framework of international society. Buzan is right to argue that we can gain much in this regard from constructivist work, although the over-reliance on Wendt's statist interpretation of constructivism might hinder rather than further this goal.

There is no doubt that Buzan's *From International to World Society?* has set out a new point of departure for the English school. Greater analytical clarity has been the result and new avenues have been untapped, including the question of the relationship between global international society and regional international societies. Does this mean that the body of English School theory should follow Buzan and Little down the analytical avenue? Is his 'structural' agenda compatible with the historical/normative one evident in the writings of classical English School scholars (as Buzan claims)? This issue will be taken up in the conclusion. In the meantime, for those who do not want to run with the foxes, there are plenty of puzzles that have been thrown up by dynamics in world politics. The remainder of the chapter considers two challenges to international society, one from above and one from below.

EVALUATING THE MORAL BASIS OF INTERNATIONAL SOCIETY

For much of the 1990s the normative debate within the English School fractured along a pluralist/solidarist divide. As Wheeler argued at the beginning of that decade, the vexed question of humanitarian intervention threw the divide into sharp relief (Wheeler 1992: 463–4). When should we respect the pluralist norm of non-intervention, and under what conditions should states suspend the norm in accordance with the solidarist injunction that states be 'burdened with the guardianship of human rights everywhere' (Bull 1966: 63)? Leading members of the English School engaged in a heated debate on this question, with Jackson (2000) making the case for upholding pluralist norms and Wheeler (2000) setting out a constructivist case for intervention. It is worth noting that this academic debate connected in important ways to the evolving policy-making agenda evidenced by Blair's Chicago speech and the report by the International Commission on Intervention and State Sovereignty (2001).

Buzan is right to argue that one of the negative consequences with the debate between pluralism and solidarism is that it hived off other important normative issues. More critically inclined scholars have also added their reservations to the way the problematic has been constructed (Reus-Smit 2002a; Bellamy 2003: 326–9). If the English School is serious in its claim to incorporate constructivist insights, then the identity of international society will generate institutional norms that constrain and enable state practice: in this respect, the language of agency deployed by the English School is too voluntarist. States might not have a choice between acting in pluralist or solidarist ways; rather, the question becomes one of how such norms are transmitted and internalized.

Such critiques offer lessons to those working on the politics of humanitarianism. Not the least of these is the over-reliance on the questions of force and the dangers of remaining within an ethnocentric just war framework. What we must not lose sight of, however, is the fact that the pluralist–solidarist debate brought ethical considerations to the fore and in doing so, further underlined the different enterprises that realism and the English School are embarked upon. More significantly, both sets of protagonists were addressing the same central question: is the purpose of international society to maintain interstate order (even if it is unjust) or is the goal to provide for the conditions of justice everywhere (the only stable order).

As many have remarked, Bull's answer to this question was ambivalent (Linklater 1996a,b; Wheeler and Dunne 1996). Those inclined to a more solidarist understanding of the moral connectedness of international society to the global community of humankind point to passages in his writings where world order becomes the litmus test for the moral adequacy of international society (Dunne 1998: 145–6). If we accept this formulation, there is a moral audit to be done.

One example of just such an undertaking is Paul Keal's new book *European Conquest and the Rights of Indigenous Peoples* (2003). He declares international society to be 'morally backward'. Over five centuries, its language, institutions, and rules have enabled the destruction and dispossession of indigenous culture and territory. An English School account of the relationship between European and the non-European world is capable of reinventing itself but never fully escaping the exclusionary terms of its construction.

Writers such as Keal and Keene (2002) present a different reading of history to that which is found in the classical literature on the development of international society (Bull and Watson 1984; Mayall 1990). Keal reminds us that expansion and dispossession were two sides of the same coin: 'the expansion of Europe resulted in a progressive erosion and denial of the rights of indigenous peoples' (2003: 35). In classical political thought, erosion and denial came about through a double movement: to escape the state of nature, rights had to be transferred to a sovereign who would protect the natural right of individuals to security and property. Outside of Europe, the absence of 'evidence' of individual property rights led Locke and others to argue that indigenous inhabitants had no legitimate title to their land.

Where Keene and Keal are in agreement is in the intimate relationship between international society and domination. Failure adequately to represent this connection in previous English School writings leads us wrongly to conclude that international society is now 'universal'. Drawing on insights from critical theory, Keal shows us that the expansion story is incomplete for the reason that an estimated 250–300 million indigenous peoples have not been accorded self-determination. Until this is achieved, the legitimacy of international society is in question. Such a line of thought leads to a further question about whether the politics of autonomy and recognition of indigenous peoples needs to be pursued in opposition to a statist concept of world order. But as Keene shows, international society has invented many diverse forms of divided sovereignty in its history—we should not therefore presume its inability to accept (and protect) a non-territorial account of self-determination that is acceptable to indigenous peoples.

SOCIETY AND HIERARCHY

Keal's book shares with the classical international society literature the view that the main challenge to international society is the decolonization process. Bull thought the primary challenge to international society was the 'revolt' against the West by newly decolonized states and peoples, but in the wake of September 11 and the 'war on terror', we have to pose the question of whether the main threat today would appear to be a revolt against the institutions of international society by the United States and its allies. In the same way that the liberal moment of the post-cold war period engendered a debate about justice, will September 11 put the spotlight back on order?

To begin to answer this question we first need to reflect on why a concentration of power in the hands of a single actor (be it a sole superpower or empire) is a threat to international society. The answer to this question takes us straight to the origins and purpose of international society. From the earliest consciousness of the idea of common rules and institutions agreed to by sovereign states, the primary justification has been anti-hegemonic in character. International society exists to protect diverse political communities from being overrun by more powerful neighbours.

In the absence of a world government, it is up to the great powers and other institutions to ensure that the rights of sovereign states are protected. The fact that Bull referred to the great powers as one of the institutions of international society suggests that he was very aware of the ambiguous relationship between law and power: law needs to act as a constraint upon those states looking to act in ways that are contrary to the greater good, while at the same time law requires enforcement, a burden that falls disproportionately on the shoulders of the great powers. The members of international society generally accept that order has to be managed. This explains why it is that in a system of legal equality, certain privileges are nevertheless accorded to great powers. In the UN system, the Security Council is responsible for international peace and security, and that council is dominated by the permanent members. More broadly, all the major peace settlements since Westphalia have been dominated by the great powers (Clark 1989).

Hierarchy is not something that is new in international politics—in fact, sovereign equality is a thin veneer masking the vast inequalities of power that exist in the international system (Krasner 1999). So what makes *this* challenge to international society different from the threat posed by other hegemonic powers? In the case of classical European international society, the members agreed to accept the legitimate nature of the hierarchical order *and* extended the same privileges reciprocally. What is potentially different today is that international society does *not* appear to accept the special privileges that the United States now demands.

In a recent article, I presented two clusters of reasons for this tension (Dunne 2003). First, if we look at the dynamics of international society at the beginning of the twenty-first century, we find many abnormalities. In a system characterized as anarchic, order requires a stable distribution of power and a commitment on the part of the great powers to manage the system. An anarchical society therefore requires some inequality but not to such an extent that, in Vattel's words, one state is able to 'lay down the law to others' (Hurrell 1995: 240). The actions of the United States in the build-up to the war against Iraq suggests that the United States is both willing and capable of laying down the law to those it sees as rogue states, even when it has conspicuously failed to persuade the majority of Security Council representatives (see Justin Morris' contribution, Chapter 15, this volume).

It is plausible to argue that cooperation among great powers is not a necessary condition for international order. The cold war is an example where there was little evidence of concerted action but a fragile international society was able to persist because of a general balance of power that dictated mutual respect for strategic parity and a broad agreement on the respective spheres of influence. A key characteristic of the post-September 11 order is the absence of effective countervailing institutions against the primacy of American power, exacerbated by the fact that maintaining such an imbalance has become a goal of US grand strategy.[6]

The combination of the growth in US military power and its post-September 11 doctrine of pre-emption together signal the emergence of a hierarchical pattern of power and authority. This does not mean that the United States will oppose the rules and institutions of international society in all respects, but it will retain an option to disregard the rights of other members. Like a suzerain power, it will seek to conduct international relations bilaterally while overseeing the multilateralism of others. The right of states to remain neutral should no longer be taken for granted, and with it, the debate between pluralists and solidarists is being recast.

The existence of hierarchy does not mean the end of international society. In part this is because the hyperpower will continue to engage with other sovereign states in accordance with the settled norms, particularly in relation to low politics issues. The motivation to cooperate on trade stems from the extraordinary high levels of economic and financial integration on which American prosperity depends. But over questions about vital national interests, concerned with the use of force and the management of world order, we see that hierarchy represents a threat to international society and a source of ongoing tension. We should also leave open the possibility that disagreement over large-scale questions about international order might exert a reverse spillover effect, such that the consensus in low political issue areas comes under strain and possibly unravels.

CONCLUSION

The resurgence of English School theorizing had added considerably to the body of knowledge generated by earlier exponents. In light of developments in social theory, we know more about the integrative forces in international society, in particular, how norms emerge and become accepted or contested. New histories of international society have explored the relationship between global social formations and patterns of domination. And further thinking on ethics continues to draw our attention to the question of moral adequacy and normative change.

It is clear from the preceding discussion that theoretical innovation has been a dual track process. There is evidence of an ongoing conversation within the English School, where ideas first mooted in British Committee discussions are resurrected and innovatively applied to a different context: the debate about pluralism and solidarism is a case in point (Wheeler 2000). Alongside, we find a parallel track in which new theories have been imported from other fields in order to refine knowledge about complex processes such as socialization or the formation of institutions.

Buzan's *From International to World Society?* is an example of theoretical innovation. He strips the classical English School tradition of its philosophical idealism—out goes the dialogue between realism, rationalism, and revolutionism. In its place he puts a reconfigured structural theory that seeks to identify connections between global and regional dynamics. His theory downgrades the importance of states and brings in the dense web of economic interactions among states, corporations, and individuals. While Bull often remarked about the need to take political economy seriously, Buzan has actually done so in his reconfiguration of English School theory.

There will be some, as Buzan acknowledges, who will question whether in fact his account bears any resemblance to the English School. Such a conclusion would, in my view, be misplaced. Rather, what we see in the work of Little and Buzan is the articulation of a neo-English School theory that is multilayered and explicit about its methodology and ontology. Little's view in particular is that their agenda is in fact more faithful to Wight and Bull because it brings back the other two elements of system and world society and reconnects them to plural methodologies. Such an interpretation is also, in my view, misplaced. Wight and Bull's persistent reminder that international society was only 'one element' in world politics disguised a normative commitment to a rule-governed order based on the institutions that had evolved in European international society. It is this normative agenda that became a point of departure for Vincent, Jackson, Wheeler, and others.

To regard this debate as a contest over rightful succession is unhelpful. Instead, it would be more useful to clearly delineate the defining elements of these two contending interpretations and to regard them both as legitimate. Just as the latest debate within realism has been cast in terms of followers of Waltz (structural- or neorealists) and those who want to bring agency back in (neoclassical realists), one could posit a similar bifurcation within contemporary English School thinking. Neo-English School writers such as Buzan, Little, and Wæver not only draw on the writings of Bull and Watson (in particular), they have also been profoundly influenced by Waltz. This engagement has brought to the fore the parallels between Waltz's analysis of the balance of power and what Bull and Watson conceive of as systemic forces. They also share with Waltz an analytical approach to ontology, where domains (geography) are specified and sectors (political, social, *and* economic) are traced. The task for the researcher is to identify the patterns that define a historic international order, and to be able to make comparisons with other international societies both in time and through time.

Neoclassical English School writers are less interested in transhistorical comparison. Their focus has been the history of ideas which constituted European international society and the process of global isomorphism. This explains why Hurrell (1996), Keene (2002), Suganami (2003*a*, *b*), Welsh (1995), and others privilege a hermeneutic method recovering the meaning of a global order structured by shared rules and institutions. In contrast to the position set out by Buzan (2004: 48–52), international society is generated by the relay between thinkers and practitioners, past and present.[7] Once meanings have been recovered, the task becomes political and normative: why should we value this arrangement? Should it be measured against a transcendental moral standard, or an immanent standard? If it is failing, what is to be done?

There is much that can be gained by a dialogue between the analytical and normative wings of the English School. In this respect Buzan is right to argue they are different but not incompatible. Outside of this dual track process of intellectual regeneration, it is important to note that changes in the world—spectacular events such as September 11—also trigger new readings of old ideas. Given the dark period of world politics that we have entered, we are likely to see realist sentiments creep back in to the English School. While the humanitarian agenda focused our attention on the international society/world society border, there may now be a good case for bringing the system back in. To the extent that the United States has contracted out of certain shared rules, it could be said to be in the system but not in the society, rather like the Americas in the sixteenth century. The United States is trying to manage international order on realist principles, in which it is above the laws it creates and enforces, as against the accepted norms of the society of states in which all sovereigns are bound by the rules. How will international society cope with the challenge of hierarchy? Within the English School, two sets of answers suggest themselves. The foxes will no doubt point to the fact that there is a tendency in all states-systems towards hegemony, while hedgehogs will claim that international society is more resilient than their cunning companions fear.

Notes

1. A recent exception can be seen from the following quotation from the French President: 'In an open world, no one can isolate themselves, no one can act alone in the name of all, and no one can accept *the anarchy of a society without rules*' (Chirac 2003).
2. The characterization of a wave of neo-English School writing is useful in so far as it connects recent writings to the post-Waltzian debates that have dominated international relations in the last twenty-five years.
3. This is a reformulation of Bhaskar's argument in *The Possibility of Naturalism* (1979: 148).
4. The metaphor is taken from a fragment in the writings of the Greek poet Archilochus. The essence of the distinction is that 'The fox knows many things, but the hedgehog knows one big thing' (Berlin 1953).
5. Buzan refers to these models as: Asocial, Power Political, Coexistence, Cooperative, Convergence, Confederative.
6. New thinking on the cold war suggests that maintaining this imbalance has always been part of US grand strategy. If this is the case, then 9/11 represents a moment in which the pursuit of global dominance becomes more entrenched. I am grateful to Theo Farrell for this point.
7. Without seeking to stretch the parallel too far, it is worth noting that this emphasis on practice—how the external order is perceived and acted upon—is a defining marker of neoclassical realism.

4

The Constructivist Challenge after September 11

Christian Reus-Smit

Traditionally, thinking about 'society' has not been the forte of international relations scholars. The social world was thought to reside within the boundaries of sovereign states; the world beyond those boundaries was considered a realm of power, strategic interplay, and constant, often violent, competition. To speak of society beyond the state was to engage in quaint yet dangerous idealism, to imagine naively that the higher forms of human life that the security of the state facilitates could take root in a realm so lacking in central authority. For the self-styled 'realists' who colonized the mainstream of the field, notions of 'international' or 'world' society were oxymorons par excellence.

This does not mean, of course, that international relations has been devoid of social theorizing altogether. In particular, members of the 'English School' have long emphasized the social bases of order among sovereign states. As Hedley Bull famously argued, states (like individuals) share certain elementary goals of social life, such as physical security, the protection of property rights, and the need for promises to be kept. To achieve these goals, states formulate rules of coexistence and create and maintain international institutions, the most important of which are diplomacy, international law, the balance of power, management by the great powers, and war itself. Instead of international society being an oxymoron, as realists have long held, Bull and others have argued persuasively that relations among states constitute an 'anarchical society, an institutionally sustained order without central authority' (Bull 1977).

By the early 1990s this tradition of thought appeared in decline. Some of its most influential thinkers had died, critics had called for its closure as an intellectual project, and it had little more to say about the momentous changes that attended the end of the cold war than the other mainstream paradigms. Most importantly, it was displaced by a new 'constructivist' perspective on the social bases of international relations. Informed by a mixture of French and German social theory on the one hand,

The arguments advanced in the first two sections of this chapter draw extensively on Reus-Smit (2002a).

and American sociological institutionalism on the other, constructivists stressed the constitutive power of normative and ideational structures, the way in which actors' identities shape their interests, and the mutual constitution of agents and structures (Price and Reus-Smit 1998). They deployed these ideas to explain a broad range of empirical phenomena in international relations, tackling everything from arms control and the demise of apartheid to the end of the cold war and the roots of multilateralism.

The advent of constructivism provoked the reformulation of several established perspectives on international relations. A new variety of 'neoclassical' realism emerged to tap the rich ideas of Thucydides, Carr, and Morgenthau (Wohlforth 1994/95); liberalism was refashioned as a 'nonideological and nonutopian' social scientific theory (Moravscik 1997); and, most importantly for our purposes, the English School was rejuvenated as a major 'non-American' research programme (Dunne 1998; Buzan 1999; Little 2000). In a curious mixture of acclamation and critique, a new generation of English School scholars simultaneously staked out a position close to constructivism (at the 'social vanguard' of the field), highlighted the well-acknowledged debt constructivists owe Martin Wight, Bull, and others, and condemned the subterranean positivism they believe robs constructivism of much of its potential.

This chapter undertakes two tasks. It revisits an argument I have made elsewhere that although constructivism and the English School share much in common, and there is considerable scope for productive engagement, scholars on both sides are currently mired in an unproductive dialogue of stereotypes. Constructivists draw little more from the English School than the well-rehearsed proposition that states can form international societies not just systems, and English School scholars focus too heavily on the statist, positivistic form of constructivism associated with the writings of Alexander Wendt. It is far more fruitful, I shall argue, to see both perspectives as bounded realms of debate, each characterized by significant internal debates over ontology, methods, and ethics. Only by highlighting these debates can we see the rich potential for cross-fertilization. In particular, it enables us to move beyond some of the serious limitations in both perspectives' approaches to the politics of international society. The chapter's second task is to suggest how an enriched dialogue between constructivism and the English School could be productively deployed to grapple with some of the central research questions of the post-September 11 world: namely, the relationship between power and institutions, international society and world society, and order and justice.

BLINKERED VISION

It is all too common in the study of international relations for scholars to reify rival theoretical perspectives. This is partly driven by a belief that know-ledge is advanced by gladiatorial contests between paradigms, by the testing of competing sets of parsimonious assumptions against the facts of the empirical world

(Legro and Moravscik 1999). But it is also driven by the imperatives of identity construction that so permeate our scholarly universe. Too often, scholars mould their intellectual identities by constructing theoretical 'others', highlighting the merits of their own positions by defining what they are not. This invariably involves processes of reification, as aspects of rival paradigms are emphasized or suppressed to magnify points of difference. Liberals, constructivists, and postmodernists all criticize realists for doing this, and realists criticize all of these for the same thing. In a field where interparadigm wars are the norm, and in which identity construction is consequently so important, reification of alternative perspectives will be the order of the day.

Unfortunately, this tendency is already apparent in the dialogue between constructivists and members of the English School. It is important to stress here that this dialogue has been largely amicable, a dialogue among fellow travellers, so to speak. There is broad agreement that the two are engaged in a similar, if not common, project—to understand the social bases of international relations. When plotting international relations theories against individual/holist and material/idealist axes, Wendt places constructivism and the English School in the same holist/idealist quadrant, subsuming all theories in this field under the general rubric of 'Constructivism' (1999: 31–2; also Finnemore 1996a; and Reus-Smit 1999: 5). Tim Dunne, a key figure in the new wave of English School scholarship, argues that there is 'an affinity between the international society tradition and the work of constructivists like Alexander Wendt. Both assume the centrality of states, and both interrogate the meaning of international system/society according to the intersubjective practices through which it is constituted' (1995a: 384; and 1998: 187–90).

Despite this sense of common purpose, however, scholars in both camps have read the literature of the other to find what is comfortable and convenient, consciously or unconsciously ignoring other significant strands of thought. When discussing the English School, constructivists focus almost exclusively on its core ontological propositions; in particular, the idea that states can form international societies, not just systems. From the perspective of the English School, Jepperson, Wendt, and Katzenstein write, 'the international system is a "society" in which states, as a condition of their participation in the system, adhere to shared norms and rules in a variety of issue areas' (1996: 45; also Finnemore 1996a: 18; and Reus-Smit 1999: p. xi). What constructivists have missed altogether is the English School's strong tradition of normative inquiry into the relationship between order and justice in international relations. From the writings of Bull (1977, 1984) and R. J. Vincent (1974, 1986a) to recent works by Robert Jackson (2000), James Mayall (2000), and Nicholas Wheeler (2000), scholars of the English School have consistently explored the potential for moral action in a world of sovereign states, fuelling an ongoing debate between pluralists and solidarists. Martha Finnemore notes that much of Bull's work 'stems from his philosophical examination of the moral implications of order' (1996a: 18), but this is a notable exception to the rule and Finnemore fails to explore it further.

English School theorists are no less guilty of selective representation. Reading their writings one could easily be excused for thinking that Wendt's articles and major book constitute the bulk and essence of constructivist scholarship.

In seeking to cast the English School as constructivist, Dunne draws exclusively upon Wendt's understanding of what this might mean. Even though Wendt's state-centrism, systemic theorizing, and scientific realism are hotly contested by most other constructivists, Dunne treats Wendt's writings as indicative of 'the key elements of constructivism' (1998: 187; 2001: 70). Similarly, when characterizing and dismissing constructivism, Jackson refers solely to Wendt's writings, arguing that he 'captures the mood of constructivism in the study of international relations' (2000: 53–5). Wheeler makes considerable use of Friedrich Kratochwil's work on norms and communicative action, but still identifies Wendt's *Social Theory of International Politics* as the 'key text on constructivism' (2000: 4). Nothing here suggests that Wendt's work has been insignificant in the development of constructivism, far from it. The problem is that English School theorists tend to conflate Wendt's writings with constructivism more generally, and to treat other constructivists as a chorus amplifying Wendt's central themes. This encourages the mistaken view that constructivism is state-centric, systemic, structuralist, positivist, and focused on continuity rather than change. Some extraordinary conclusions have resulted from this tendency. Jackson reaches the erroneous conclusion that constructivists 'see themselves as involved in building a scientific discipline of international relations in a positivist sense' and 'do not see themselves as accepting the more modest goals of a humanistic science of international relations' (2000: 54). This would almost certainly surprise leading constructivists such as Kratochwil and John Ruggie (1986; Ruggie 1993*a*, *b*; Kratochwil 2000), not to mention many others (Price and Reus-Smit 1998).

BOUNDED REALMS OF DEBATE

Because constructivists and English School theorists view each other through intellectual blinkers, the potential for cross-fertilization is unnecessarily reduced, undermining the capacity of both schools to generate comprehensive understandings of the social bases of international relations. To move beyond this we need to broaden our understandings of both perspectives, to see them as bounded realms of rich debate. As we shall see, the proposition that constructivism and the English School are fields of debate, not monolithic conceptual or theoretical edifices, is easy to sustain. The notion that they are 'bounded', however, requires more explanation. If a literature is wracked by debate, in what sense can it constitute a bounded school of thought? Here, I would return to processes of identity construction. With regard to both constructivism and the English School, the debates that animate them have a strong identity-constitutive dimension. That is, they are ultimately debates about what ought to define 'constructivism' or the 'English School'. As they divide, therefore, they also constitute.

Over the past decade, three axes of debate have emerged within constructivism, broadly defined. The first is between constructivists inspired by sociological institutionalism, Habermasian communicative action theory, and Foucauldian writings on knowledge and power. The roots of much American constructivism lie in sociological institutionalism, an approach originally identified with the work of John Meyer and 'the Stanford School' of sociology. Meyer's central proposition is that 'world culture' constitutes social agents, affecting how they define their identities and interests. In Finnemore's words, 'the social structure is ontologically primary. It is the starting point for analysis. Its rules and values create all actors we might consider relevant in international politics, including states, firms, organizations, and even individuals' (1996*b*: 333). If this variant of constructivism emphasizes 'logics of appropriateness'—the constitutive power of norms over identities and interests—a second, 'Habermasian' variant stresses 'logics of argument', or the role of communicative action in mediating between agents and intersubjective values (Kratochwil 1989; Onuf 1989; Reus-Smit 1999; Risse 2000). Norms do not constitute identities and interests in any straightforward or uncomplicated way; in many situations, actors encounter multiple norms of behaviour, open to varied interpretations, some of which contradict one another. Contrary to Krasner's claim that in such situations actors simply revert to self-interested, power-maximizing behaviour (1999: 6), Habermasians argue that actors engage in argument, in which 'they try to figure out in a collective communicative process (*a*) whether their assumptions about the world and about cause-and-effect relationships in the world are correct (the realm of theoretical discourses); or (*b*) whether norms of appropriate behaviour can be justified, and which norms apply under given circumstances (the realm of practical discourses) (Risse 2000: 7). In contrast to these forms of constructivism, Foucauldians focus on the relationship between power and knowledge. In Richard Price's words, 'the production of discourses is a form of power, as it constructs categories that themselves make a cluster of practices and understandings seem illegitimate or even inconceivable. This disciplinary power defines what is normal and natural and what is unthinkable and reprehensible' (1997: 9). Exponents of this strand of constructivism employ a distinctive 'genealogical' method, one that 'is strategically aimed at that which looks unproblematic and is held to be timeless; its task is to explain how these present traits, in all their vigour and truth, were formed out of the past' (Bartelson 1995: 73).

This first, largely ontological debate is paralleled by a second line of difference between constructivists, that concerning levels of analysis. Wendt is virtually alone in advocating pure systemic theorizing, drawing a sharp distinction between the international and domestic realms, and explicitly bracketing the latter as theoretically irrelevant (1994, 1999). This contrasts sharply with the focus of unit-level constructivists, who concentrate on the relationship between domestic social and legal norms and the identities, interests, and actions of states (Katzenstein 1996*a*, 1999). Contrasting Germany's and Japan's responses to domestic terrorism, Peter Katzenstein writes that the former's 'strengthening of state power through changes in legal norms betrays a deep-seated fear that terrorism challenges the core of the state', while the latter's 'close interaction of social and legal norms reveals a state living symbiotically within its society and not easily shaken to its foundation' (1996*a*: 153–4). A third group of 'holistic' constructivists have challenged this dichotomy between the international and the domestic, seeking instead to bring them together into a unified analytical perspective that treats the internal and the external as two faces of a single social and political order (Ruggie 1993; Hall 1999; Reus-Smit 1999; Rae 2002).

The final axis of debate within constructivism concerns methodology. Early constructivists insisted that studying the role of ideas, norms, and culture in international relations demanded an interpretive methodology. Actors attach meaning to their actions, these meanings are shaped by an existing field of intersubjective meanings embedded in language and other symbols, and the effect of such meanings on human action cannot be understood by treating them as measurable variables that cause behaviour in a quantifiable manner (Kratochwil and Ruggie 1986; Kratochwil 1989; Neufeld 1993; Price 1994). An interpretive methodology requires scholars to grasp 'the relationship between "intersubjective meanings" which derive from self-interpretation and self-definition, and the social practices in which they are embedded and which they constitute' (Neufeld 1993: 49). This insistence that an analytical emphasis on ideas, norms, and culture requires a distinctive methodology has been challenged recently by 'methodological conventionalists' who claim that their explanations 'do not depend upon any specialized separate "interpretive methodology"' (Jepperson, Wendt, and Katzenstein 1996: 67). The differences between interpretive and positivist constructivists is most apparent in the contrast between those who employ quantitative methods (Johnston 1995; Cederman 1997) and those who adopt a genealogical approach (Bartelson 1995; Price 1997).

Significant axes of debate also characterize the English School. The first is between pluralists and solidarists. Bull laid the foundations for this debate when he argued that there is a fundamental distinction between those who see international society as bound together in solidarity by common values and purposes and those who hold that states have a plurality of different purposes and that international society rests solely on the observance of common rules of coexistence (1966). This distinction provides the basic framework for debate within the English School about the scope for, and desirability of, moral action in international relations (Nardin 1983; Vincent 1986a; Dunne 1998; Jackson 2000; Mayall 2000; Wheeler 2000). Nicholas Wheeler's impressive book on humanitarian intervention, *Saving Strangers*, is not only built around the distinction between solidarism and pluralism; he searches for evidence of a new solidarism in international relations of the last decade, and when he finds only partial movement in this direction, he marshals a strong normative argument for greater solidarist consciousness and action (2000). This contrasts with Jackson's recent work, *The Global Covenant*, which identifies two enduring forms of pluralism in contemporary world politics. International society is, first and foremost, 'an association of multiple political authorities based on the values of equal sovereignty, territorial integrity, and non-intervention of member states'. It is also an arrangement 'in which the domestic affairs of states are their own affair, which means that statespeople and citizens are free to compose their own domestic values and orchestrate them in their own way' (2000: 178–9).

A second point of difference concerns the relationship between the English School and international society theory. For many outsiders—including most constructivists—the proposition that sovereign states can form international societies is the School's leitmotiv (a position endorsed in the introduction). Yet, this has become an important point of contention among contemporary English School theorists. There are those, like Dunne, who identify the School with the idea of international society. Having called his history of the English School *Inventing International Society*, he argues that in the early meetings of the British Committee on International Theory a consensus emerged 'around the idea that sovereign states constituted a society' (1998: 183). There is, however, an ambiguity in the writings of Wight, Bull, and others that opens space for an alternative interpretation of the School's commitments. Bull argued that the 'modern international system in fact reflects ... the element of war and struggle for power among states, the element of transnational solidarity and conflict, cutting across the divisions among states, and the element of co-operation and regulated intercourse among states' (1977: 39). This has encouraged some to see the English School as more eclectic than is commonly assumed. Richard Little argues that in the writings of Wight and Bull '[n]one of the elements are given ontological priority. It is assumed that they are operating within a single complex reality ... Although attention may be focused on only one of these elements, it must never be forgotten that this element is lodged in the context of the other two' (Buzan 1999: 5; Little 2000: 402).

The final divide within the English School is methodological. In seeking to rejuvenate the School, critically inclined scholars have pointed to Bull's oft-cited defence of a 'classical approach' to suggest that the School fits within a broad family of reflective or interpretive approaches. Dunne identifies an interpretive approach as one of 'preliminary articles of the English School' (1998: 7), and Roger Epp claims that its 'hermeneutic orientation ... is at its best the source of distinctive attentiveness to language, an openness to the world, and a critical cultural and disciplinary reflexivity' (1998: 63). This attempt to cast the English School as post-positivist has been rejected, however, by those who see it as methodologically eclectic. Building on his argument that Wight, Bull, and others saw realist, Grotian, and Kantian dimensions of international relations coexisting, Little claims that this ontological pluralism led to methodological pluralism: 'International societies and international systems ... rest on very different ontological assumptions and, as a consequence, they need to be examined by means of very different methodologies' (2000: 408). The English School should thus been seen as employing an array of methodological tools, from positivist to interpretive. 'A comprehensive assessment of the English School', Little concludes, 'makes it clear that they rely on interpretivist, positivist and critical assumptions' (2000: 398).

BIG AND IMPORTANT QUESTIONS

Opening up constructivism and the English School in the above manner suggests numerous points of productive dialogue. Rather than enumerate these in the abstract, however, I want to concentrate on the very considerable research challenges exposed by the events of 11 September 2001, and the opportunities these provide for bridge building between constructivism and the English School. At one level these events seem to empower traditional realist thinking about international relations. Questions of power and hegemony are back on the agenda, states are busy reasserting their authority, international institutions appear in turmoil, and the spectre of widespread violence seems to be eroding the chances of peace or order through law and trade. On deeper reflection, however, some of the really big and important research questions are ones where constructivism and the English School have significant home-field advantages. Three of these stand out as particularly important: the relationships between power and institutions, international and world society, and order and justice. As we shall see, these questions are familiar to the English School in particular, but they are unlikely to be addressed fruitfully without insights drawn from constructivism.

Power and Institutions

The prevailing understanding of power in international relations is possessive and materialist. It is seen as something atomistic actors possess, and it is a possession defined principally in terms of material resources. To paraphrase Thucydides, states that possess lots of guns and money 'do what they will'; those lacking such resources 'accept what they must'. In this conception, power has little to do with institutions, understood as norms, rules, and decision-making procedures that shape actors identities, interests, and strategies. Institutions neither constitute power, nor do they exert any constraint on power. Institutions may exist, but only so long as they serve the interests of the powerful.

Contemporary world politics suggests, however, that the relationship between power and institutions is considerably more complex than this understanding suggests. If power were determined solely by the material resources states possess, or by the balance of such resources across the international system, it would be far easier for the administration of George W. Bush to achieve its global objectives than presently seems to be the case. An administration not shy of flexing its material muscle is experiencing significant diplomatic frustration, and at least part of this has to do with relationship between US power and international institutions. This is most palpable in the diplomatic standoff the administration has encountered in the United Nations Security Council, where institutional rules and procedures have served as obstacles to the free play of American grand strategy, if not the physical exercise of war. Beneath this, however, lies a more complex relationship between American power and international institutions. Stable, effective political power is never the product of material resources alone; it is also the product of legitimacy, of the perception, on the part of other social actors, that the exercise of power is rightful. Because international institutions enshrine social understandings of legitimate statehood and rightful state action, they play a critical role in structuring perceptions of legitimacy, and hence power. American power is thus not only constrained by international institutions; it also constitutes it.

Most commentators on contemporary international relations are blind to these complexities, and appear content to catalogue the multiple indices of America's material preponderance. This brief discussion, however, suggests two pressing research questions: how is American power constituted, as well as constrained, by international institutions? And what are the implications for American interests and world order when the United States, in a new phase of material preponderance, sets about eroding, rather than augmenting, the institutional architecture of international society? Hegemonic stability theory suggests that aspiring hegemons tend to construct institutions to embed their interests and ensure their medium- to long-term power, as were the cases of Britain in the nineteenth century and the United States after the Second World War. What happens, however, when a predominant state seeks to renew its hegemony by undermining a spectrum of institutions that continue to serve the interests of other major and minor powers?

Of constructivism and the English School, it is the former that offers the richest resources for tackling the first of these questions, that relating to the constitution of American power by international institutions. This is not to suggest that the English School has little say about such questions; Wight's writings on legitimacy and Bull's arguments about the special rights of great powers are relevant here. Constructivists have, however, pushed the theoretical envelope in three useful directions. The first concerns their insights into the relationship between the social identities of states and international institutions. American commentators constantly remind us that the United States enjoys considerable 'soft' power, the capacity to achieve its objectives by winning the hearts and minds of others. But if soft power means anything, it means that the social identity of the United States is closely 'identified' with prevailing norms of legitimate statehood within the international system. Constructivists, such as Wendt, have much to say about how state identities are constituted by prevailing institutional frames, and vice versa. Second, as the Security Council debate about war with Iraq amply demonstrates, the relationship between state identities, legitimacy, and institutional norms is constituted through communication, or 'logics of argument'. Again, constructivists—particularly those of a Habermasian bent—have much to say about this. Finally, there is already a strong literature within constructivism that brings the above insights to bear on the question of American power. Ruggie's work on the relationship between the liberal identity of the American state, the domestic institutional strategies of the New Deal, America's sponsorship of post-1945 multilateral institutions, and the subsequent embedding of liberalism in the fabric of international society (1993*b*) is directly relevant, as are Bruce Cronin's writings on American hegemony and multilateralism (2001).

When it comes to the second of our questions—that concerning the implications of the Bush administration's undermining of international institutions—the advantage goes to the English School. We find in Bull's writings, especially, an expansive understanding of the relationship between great powers, international institutions, and international order. Here Bull's 1980 article, titled 'the Great Irresponsibles', is particularly instructive. As we know, Bull was centrally concerned with the factors that sustain international order, of which he gave special emphasis to the fundamental institutions of international society. Among these he included 'management by the Great Powers'. He strongly believed that these powers 'contribute to international order in two ways: by managing their relations with one another; and by exploiting their preponderance in such a way as to impart a degree of central direction to the affairs of international society as a whole' (1977: 207). In 'The Great Irresponsibles' Bull rebuked the United States and the Soviet Union for failing to fulfil these roles, placing international order at risk. 'What we have been witnessing sine the mid-1970s', he wrote, 'is the abandonment by the superpowers of their postures as responsible managers' (1980: 446). Not only was this bad for international society—encouraging the 'disintegration of international order'—it was also bad for the authority of the powers concerned. Bull saw the relationship between the great powers and international society as a two-way street; they had special duties to sustain international order, but they also gained special rights, such as the right 'to play a part in determining issues that affect the peace and security of the international system as a whole' (Bull 1977: 202). If the United States and the Soviet Union abrogated their responsibilities to sustain international order, Bull concluded, they would undermine their claims to special rights, effectively undercutting their social power (1980: 446). The relevance of this line of reasoning to thinking about the implications of the Bush administration's undermining of international institutions is not difficult to see.

International Society and World Society

Since 11 September 2001, one thing has become clear—international society is not a self-contained realm autonomous from the forces of world society. The rise of transnational anti-systemic violence has exposed in stark relief the deep interpenetration of the society of states by non-state actors and processes, with profound implications for the juridical and empirical sovereignty of 'rogue' states, for state–society relations across the world, for the nature and viability of international public law, and for state and human security. Comprehending the nature and implications of this interconnection is central to the contemporary study of international relations, a fact emphasized by Bull's perhaps prescient suggestion that 'a sign of the decline of the states system and its transformation into a secular reincarnation of the medieval order is the resort to violence on an international scale by groups other than the state, and the assertion by them of a right to commit such violence' (1977: 268).

Unfortunately, the English School's capacity to respond to this challenge is handicapped by the pluralist insistence on developing a theory of international society as a relatively discrete social realm, with relative autonomy from the actors, structures, and processes of the surrounding world society. Their goal is develop a political and ethical theory 'of international relations understood as a "society" with its own distinctive standards of conduct' (Jackson 1995: 111). Because of this, pluralists go to some length to deny that world society is encroaching on the society of states. In Jackson's words, '[w]orld society is . . . a client of the society of states rather than the reverse' (1995: 111). This claim rests on the concomitant idea that non-state actors do not fundamentally alter the basic principles and dynamics of the society of sovereign states. Here, the question is almost always posed in terms of whether non-state actors are displacing the primacy of sovereign states, with pluralists supposedly winning the broader argument by claiming that this is not the case (Jackson 2000: 107). As I have argued elsewhere, posing the question is this way is deeply misleading. The issue is not whether actors in world society are displacing the society of sovereign states; it is whether they are affecting its basic principles and dynamics. It was hard to deny this before September 11; it is now virtually impossible.

While pluralists within the English School have been challenged by solidarists over questions of moral progress in international relations, solidarists have devoted little attention to the empirical relation between international and world society. For this we must turn to the holistic strand of constructivism. Writers such as Margaret Keck and Kathryn Sikkink have systematically explored the way in which 'transnational advocacy networks' of domestic and international NGOs and international organizations have contributed to the development of international norms and to the domestic reform of authoritarian states (1998). Arguing that sovereignty is an inherently variable principle, the meaning of which changes from one historical context to another, they have documented how non-state actors have worked to shape the domestic and international normative contexts in which states constitute their identities, define their interests, and conduct their relations. Given this, Keck and Sikkink argue that we need to move beyond the simple imagery of a society of states. They find 'that enough evidence of change in the relationships among actors, institutions, norms, and ideas exists to make the world political system rather than an international society of states the appropriate level of analysis' (1998: 212).

At first glance one might question the relevance of these ideas for contemporary concerns. Scholars like Keck and Sikkink are talking about world society's forces for moral progress, not its less palatable anti-systemic movements. It is important, though, to recognize the lessons that can be learnt from this scholarship, as well as the conceptual and analytical challenges that the rise of anti-systemic violence pose. Constructivists have focused on the way in which non-state actors use forms of moral suasion and symbolic politics to define the terms of political discourse affecting state interests and actions. At one level, groups such as Al-Qaeda are engaged in similar politics, but with the lethal difference of conscripting violence to the task. The novelty and magnitude of the violence they unleash often blinds us to the fact that they are ultimately seeking to transform ideas and values, both those of the 'West' and those of politically disaffected and economically alienated Muslims. Constructivists have taken two steps in the right direction by considering the way in which world society forces constitute the political fabric of international society, and by highlighting the politics of values that attends this process of constitution. Their task now is to confront three questions: what is the relationship between the exercise of violence and the erosion and propagation of social and political values, both by states and non-state actors? How has this constituted international society historically? And what are the implications of this nexus between violence and normative changes for international and global order?

Order and Justice

The overwhelming tendency of Western governments since the attacks of September 11 has been to deny any connection between the advent of such violence and questions of global justice. The United States and its closest allies have steadfastly defended the retributive justice of the 'war against terrorism', as well as their right to self-defence. And the Bush administration, in particular, has celebrated, with proselytizing zeal, the justice of America's global leadership. But the idea that the acts of groups such as Al-Qaeda could in any way be connected to issues of global justice or injustice is rejected out of hand. On one level this is entirely understandable. To sanctify such violence in the name of justice would be perverse. However, to deny any connection between the rise of anti-systemic violence and questions of global justice is simple-minded and self-defeating. Do we truly believe that there is no connection—complex and puzzling as it may be—between one billion people living below the World Bank's lowest poverty line, widespread cultural alienation in the face of globalization, and the proliferation of failed and unresponsive political institutions? If our answer is no then it would be hard for us to deny the need to address, with renewed vigour, the question of the relationship between order and justice in world politics.

Of all of the major schools of international thought, it is the English School that has the strongest tradition of inquiry into this relationship. Other traditions of international ethics exist, but members of the English School have ruminated in greater breadth and depth about the opportunities and constraints a society of states presents for moral action and progress. As noted earlier, the School is divided between pluralists and solidarists, the debate between which has becoming increasingly ritualized, predictable, and confining. On the one hand, there are those like Nardin, Jackson, and Mayall who hold that the pluralist nature of international society—the fact that it is a 'practical' not a 'purposive' association—seriously delimits the scope for moral change. Within such a world, only a circumscribed 'situational ethics' is possible. 'This is not the ethics of the ideal choice or the best choice or even the least costly choice ... Rather, it is the ethics of the best choice in the circumstances, or perhaps the least damaging choice if in the circumstances prevailing at the time all choices are deplorable and destructive to some degree—which is common in war' (Jackson 2000: 147). Solidarists, on the other hand, see the opportunities and constraints of international society differently. Normatively, they hold that individuals, not states, are the appropriate moral referent; empirically, they question the boundaries between international and world society, and they see evidence in contemporary international politics and law of the cosmopolitanization of international society (Linklater 1998; Wheeler 2000). In this world, more demanding ethical standards are possible than the situational ethics of the pluralists, and a more expansive politics of ethics is desirable.

For these intellectual resources to speak to contemporary issues of global order and justice they would need to confront five principal research questions. What constitutes international or world order at this historical juncture? How should we define international and human justice, and what are their political, economic, and cultural dimensions? How are these conceptions of order and justice related? When is the exercise of hegemonic, or quasi-hegemonic, power ethically justifiable? And, finally, how are answers to these questions to be negotiated within the present global political order?

Although the English School is to be credited for opening up questions of order and justice, it is not clear that it, alone, has the intellectual resources to deal with these issues. On the question of order, established ideas of peaceful coexistence among sovereign states may be insufficient in a world characterized by the globalization of security, economics, and culture, and by the proliferation of state and non-state agents. With regard to questions of justice, it may no longer be possible to privilege politically the pursuit of international justice over world justice, as Bull so tentatively proposed (1977: ch. 4). What if the ability to sustain the rights of states depends on confronting deep, systemic problems of human injustice? On the question of how order and justice are related, it is fruitful to consider Bull's argument about 'the revolt against the West', but also to recognize its limits in the present context. In the last of his writings, Bull worried that unless issues of justice were addressed Third World states would reject the rules and norms of international society, threatening international order. How do we think about this when developing states are no longer at the vanguard of the revolt, when it is clandestine, transnational, anti-systemic groups such as Al-Qaeda that are fanning resistance? With regard to the question of hegemony, the English School's notion that great powers have obligations to uphold the institutions of international society may take us part of the way we need to go. But does the United States have to fulfil wider ethical obligations before we can deem the exercise of American power ethically defensible? How do our answers to previous questions affect our judgements here? Finally, on the issue of how answers to these questions ought to be negotiated, it is not clear that the statist processes stressed by pluralists are sufficient to the task, and as we observed in the previous section, solidarists have an underdeveloped appreciation of the political processes linking international and world society.

What might constructivism offer here? As others have noted (Price and Reus-Smit 1998; Shapcott 2000), constructivists have shied away from explicit norm- ative theorizing, even if their normative commitments often lie just below the surface. There are, however, a number of constructivist insights that might prove valuable. First, when considering the nature of order beyond the state, the social ontology of holistic constructivism is potentially illuminating. There are other holistic sociologies of the world system, such as Wallerstein's world systems theory, and the world polity theory of the Stanford School. But holistic constructivism is more attuned to state identities, international institutions, and diverse forms of political agency. Second, when thinking about the nature of justice, holistic constructivism offers insights into the way in which international justice, pertaining to the rights and obligations of states, is conditioned by the justice politics of a wider world society. It also suggests ways of thinking about the importance of identity and culture in framing claims to justice within, between, and beyond states. Finally, constructivist work on communic- ative action is potentially useful when confronting the issue of how problems of order and justice ought to be negotiated. Nothing in constructivism tells us how this should be done, but the lessons it provides into how state and non-state actors negotiate new norms of international conduct are useful in defining the realm of the possible (Reus-Smit 2000). For instance, communicative or dialogical ethicists have upheld the principle that norms cannot be considered ethical unless they are endorsed by all of those affected. We learn from constructivists, however, that this is seldom how progressive norms are constructed—they generally originate when small groups of small to medium states, encouraged by domestic and international NGOs, push issues onto the international agenda, and through pain of embarrassment garner support from the majority of states (Keck and Sikkink 1998; Price 1998).

CONCLUSION

In titling this chapter 'The Constructivist Challenge After September 11', I sought to exploit the double-meaning of the term 'challenge'. On the one hand, I wanted to draw attention to the way in which the advent of constructivism prompted a renaissance in the scholarship of the English School. But I also wished to highlight how aspects of English School Scholarship challenge constructivism; particularly, the way in which it encourages constructivists to move beyond the politics of ethics to reflect on the ethics of politics. These are not merely intellectual niceties, or academic parlour games. They come to the fore when we consider the most pressing research questions facing our field, questions that should equally animate national and international policy-makers. My list is by no means exhaustive, but it would be difficult to deny the importance today of re-examining the relationship between power and institutions, international and world society, and order and justice. To grapple with these questions effectively, however, requires constructivists and members of the English School to transcend their dialogue of stereotypes, to recognize the 'other' as a complex yet bounded realm of debate, rich in intellectual resources of comprehending the social bases of international life.

PART TWO

Critical Engagements with
International Society

5

Traditional Political Realism and the Writing of History

Roger D. Spegele

Why should anyone care about what Realists have to say about the English School? Well, perhaps they should not when it takes the form of 'using' the English School as a foil to mount yet another argument based upon the decisive superiority of 'scientific empiricism'.[1] On the other hand, perhaps they should if what realists have to say will assist the English School (or anyone else) to get out from underneath dominant scientific empiricist orthodoxies in international relations by presenting an attractive and viable alternative methodology. To see why this would be of special interest to the English School and a particular version of realism identified here, hopefully not misleadingly, as 'traditional political realism' is the stage-setting goal of this introduction.[2]

Beginning with the first prop of the stage-setting, the crucial objective is fundamentally practical, namely, to get the members and followers of the 'older' version of the English School, understood as primarily grouped 'around a Wight-Bull-Vincent axis' (Epp 1998: 48), to recognize that the School, notwithstanding its recent revival, is caught between the rock of reinvention and the hard place of calls for its closure (see the Introduction to this volume). The resulting reverberations between these two interpretive moments, at the very least, raises substantial doubts about the School's epistemic viability which hinders renewal of the School's original self-conception, bound up, as it is, with classical realism (Little 2003: 445–51), and promotes a gross distortion of the School's main ideas. This consequence has not been helped by the School's reluctance to respond to either of these strategies which, one way or another, could only damage its reputation and stifle its resuscitation.[3] Nor is this the first time the English School has practised what might be called 'methodological quietism', the effective treatment, whether intended or not, of philosophical debates about method as unproductive and unnecessary: genuinely *useless*. For, during the so-called Bull–Kaplan debate in the mid-1960s one member of the English School, Hedley Bull, constructed a rigorous and systematic critical argument on the epistemological assumptions and presuppositions of the scientific approach on behalf of 'the classical approach', which the overwhelming majority of the members of the

English School practice regularly in their research (Bull 1969: 20–38). The response of Morton Kaplan, idiosyncratic and fragmented, resulted in a disciplinary judgement of 'nondebate' in whose aftermath representatives of the scientific school, in particular, produced telling and effective arguments against the classical approach and one of its major beneficiaries, the English School. At this point it would have been natural to expect the English School to respond by distinguishing its 'methodological offerings' from those favoured by an increasingly dominant scientific empiricism, but it did not do so: it practised 'methodological quietism'. In retrospect its silence was a mistake. It encouraged the idea that scientific empiricism was the 'correct' conception of science and rationality, without effective competitors, that the English School was indeed ready for 'closure', and that all other approaches reliant on the classical approach, such as traditional political realism, needed to be either discarded or replaced by a scientific empiricist version of their core ideas. Eventually, the English School became hostage to the reverberating pulls of reinvention and the shrill insistence on closure in favour of some version of scientific empiricism.[4]

One implication of the debate that followed the Bull–Kaplan performance was the growing belief that among the various contenders for the mantle of realism only neorealism could, and should, survive the self-evidently correct standards of scientific empiricism. Other contenders began to lose ground in the complex social processes that make for success in intradisciplinary struggles. Traditional political realism suffered a great loss of prestige and favour and became widely regarded as anachronistic and structurally incapable, given its commitment to the classical approach, of adapting to the valuable improvements in the philosophy of science that could make realism what it needed to be: a more reliable instrument for the accumulation of knowledge better able to explain past events in terms of causal generalizations, and, where possible, more adept at providing accurate predictions of future events and processes in the international system (Spegele 1987: 189–210; 1996: 14–19 and 88–92). But although neorealism dominated the field for several years, its victory over all contenders turned out to be Pyrrhic since it could not be sustained in the face of the aggressive criticism from within the very scientific empiricism it aspired to make its own (Legro and Moravcsik 1999: 5–55).

A good place to begin in the indispensable task of saving traditional political realism from a scientistic death sentence is with renewing our understanding of the thinker many scholars, including some neorealists like Robert Gilpin, regard as the founding father of realism in international relations: Thucydides (Gilpin 1984: 287–304). Contrary to what neorealists may say, there are good grounds for holding that Thucydides should not be regarded as a 'scientific historian' whose goal is to discover the causes of war and the laws of human nature. This would eventually lead to lining up Thucydides as an early and particularly prescient predecessor of scientific empiricism, struggling to find causal generalizations about war and political leadership. Such an interpretation would constitute a mistaken interpretation of Thucydides's purposes, the means he used to achieve them, and his contribution to the study of international relations. A better interpretation portrays the Greek historian as taking seriously the questions for which the dramatis personae themselves seek answers, notably the reasons, not the causes, which explain the actions of their adversaries and friends. From this perspective the central questions that drive Thucydides's *History of the Pelopennesian War* are, for instance: what reasons do political and military leaders give for going to war and conducting the war the way they did? Are these reasons justified in terms of commonly accepted standards of the limits of political action and its 'built-in' standards of moderation and prudence? Who, in the final analysis, is to blame for the self-destructive war and its brutalizing consequences? Although such questions motivate the political actors in the *History*, they would be of no interest to scientific historians searching for causes and natural laws. At the same time it would be to deny that Thucydides was a traditional realist, for he acutely recognized the persistence of power politics, that in the counsels of men it had to be given due weight, that tragedies are inextricable from the human condition, and that agonizing moral and political dilemmas inevitably arise from these dominant features of the world in which we live. With this as content, what would be the point, Thucydides might well have asked, of scientific history?

But there is more to be extracted from Thucydides's search for reasons and the kind or explanations they endorse, for Thucydides's explanations are clear examples of teleological, rather than causal, explanations of the sort endorsed by scientific empiricism. According to scientific empiricism, teleological explanations are either reducible to causal explanations or are not scientifically genuine explanations at all. Scientific empiricism here reflects the wider community of philosophers of science who have generally regarded 'teleological explanations' as rationally disreputable. But, I argue in this chapter, the time has come to overturn this orthodoxy and to carve out a robust alternative to scientific empiricism's causalism. And, perhaps more to the point for those who favour either the older English School or traditional political realism, this is a project which should generate great *joint interest*, notwithstanding the differences at the core of these two conceptions. As argued above, both the older English School and traditional political realism are being reinvented, reinterpreted, or reintegrated into paradigms, approaches, theories, or discourses in which their original identities are being gradually effaced. In joining together to defend teleological forms of explanation, these two worthy conceptions of international relations will be better able to resist such strategies; they will be better placed certainly to introduce greater epistemological content into their complaints by offering an attractive and plausible alternative to the causal explanations that scientific empiricism requires (see n. 1). For reasons explained below, the appreciation of history by the English School and traditional political realism can be turned to good purpose by showing just how many historical explanations are teleological in character and, in terms of the new respect accorded to teleology, provide perfectly acceptable explanations of agent action. Understood in this way, it would seem that the English School and traditional political realism should investigate the possibilities of overturning the causal dogma of scientific empiricism, an unnecessary obstacle standing in the way of giving teleological explanations a central place in the core philosophical ideas of these rich and often overlapping perspectives on international relations.

This chapter aims to build on the English School's claim that history, properly conceived, is admirably suited to understanding and explaining international relations
and to show how this may assist traditional political realism. In advancing to this goal,
I shall critically examine the 'approaches' to teleological explanation in history of two
distinguished members of the English School: E. H. Carr and Herbert Butterfield.
Although there are other members of the English School who had some original ideas
about the study of history and how it should be at the centre of the study of international relations—Martin Wight and Adam Watson come to mind—the choice of
these two historians is not arbitrary. There are at least three good reasons for it. First,
although their views of history are in some respects diametrically opposed, both Carr
and Butterfield resonate with traditional realist views. Second, a cursory examination
of their lives reveals very different experiences and reactions to the world (Coll 1985;
Haslam 1999: *passim*; Hall 2002: 719–36). Butterfield's world was very much bound
up with the groves of academe while Carr, though he occupied the first chair of international relations at Aberwystwyth, also held a variety of government positions and
wrote a great deal of journalism. Thus, we get the benefit of thinkers of history who,
though contemporaries, viewed the world from different locations. And, third, both
had different understandings of history, a significant advantage when undertaking
comparisons. While Carr underlined, justified, and applauded the *progressive* changes
that took place in history over time, Butterfield focused on the extent to which history itself resisted the dangerous and counterproductive 'ideological' conceptions of
it, of the sort Carr espoused. Butterfield saw himself as replacing this view of history with a philosophically and politically driven urge to tell stories that have their
own integrity, coherence, and meaning and resist ideological history. Yet, although
neither explicitly made a case for it, I will argue that both implicitly accepted different renditions of a teleological view of history. Once their commitments are drawn
out from their texts, I will advance a case for treating human actions as directed to
the agent's—individual and collective—goals and purposes, an idea that scientific
empiricism would be obliged to reject but which may unite the English School and
traditional political realism. There is, then, a good deal at stake here.

TELEOLOGY AND CARR'S CONCEPTION OF HISTORY

This section seeks to show that Carr understood historiography in capacious terms
to include teleological explanations as indispensable to what history is in its essence.
'History properly so-called', he wrote, 'can be written only by those who find and
accept a sense of direction in history itself' (Carr 1987: 132). If Carr is correct about
this—and his argument does not, I think, suffice to establish it—the result would
be considerable since it would open a path for thinking of Carr as a potential critic
of the dominant scientific empiricist epistemology in recent international relations
(Spegele 1996: ch. 2). For, if it can be validly claimed that at least certain teleological explanations in international relations are not reducible to causal analysis, then
anti-scientific empiricists, including in particular traditional political realists and

English School theorists, would be better placed to develop and sustain an alternative perspective. And although it is beyond the scope of this chapter to argue for a *particular* alternative, nonetheless, when we open the possibility that teleological explanations are consistent with accepted scientific norms of rationality, we begin to shake long-held orthodoxies with some possibly unpredictable consequences.

This way of understanding Carr's contribution to international relations has received scant, if any, attention. Part of the reason for this failure to engage with Carr's views on the teleological possibilities in history may lie in the general tendency to compartmentalize knowledge, reinforced by the belief that Carr's most important contribution to International Relations lies in his incisive, and historically significant, analyses of utopianism and realism in international relations. This understandable, if skewed, focus has effectively marginalized Carr's reflections on the nature, character, and role that history, understood teleologically, might play in a reconstructed version of political or 'historical' realism in carving out a distinctively different conception of knowledge and methodology (Goldfischer 2002: 715). The 'return' to Carr here should not be seen, then, as 'historical' in character; on the contrary, against the backdrop of the continuing theoretical strife in the discipline to say what international relations really is, or should be, the goal of this revisit is to advance a case for the partial resurrection of a teleological conception of history in terms of which we can distinguish reason-based explanations of human conduct and actions from the monolithic causalism that conceives individuals as the passive site of causal processes beyond their control.

To get Carr's conception of teleology in history into the most perspicuous frame, the place to begin is with what Kant wrote about history. Although scant in volume, what Kant did write was remarkable, not least because of its self-conscious effort to overcome the pervasive scepticism—just as much a problem in Kant's age as in our own—concerning the capacity of history to provide genuine knowledge of the past (Kant 1991: 41–53 and 176–234). Paradoxically, Kant achieved this goal by conceding limits on theoretical knowledge itself, which might well be construed as accepting the core idea in the sceptic's armoury. For example, in his essays on history Kant argues that theoretical reason can never determine whether mankind is progressing or not. This is a decisively important conclusion since one of Carr's most important contributions to historiography is that history is constitutive of progress and knowable by reason. Carr wrote: 'Certainly, without the hypothesis of progress, there is no history' (Carr 1960: 118). But although Kant and Carr may appear somewhat at odds with one another here, they are not. Kant is simply making the valid epistemological point that insofar as 'theoretical' reason cannot determine whether there has been progress, human beings need to rely on 'practical reason'. That is, the form of reason which provides knowledge and understanding of morality, religion, aesthetics, and history. Moreover, even with so little in hand we can already press an important analogy between Kant's view of morality and Carr's view of history. Morality, as Kant understands it, makes sense only if certain background conditions are met, that is, conditions showing at least a modicum of freedom of conscience, speech, and action (Kant 1991: 54–60). Unless such conditions hold, a despairing *pointlessness* threatens action directed by the moral law, and a rational agent cannot act while thinking her action pointless. Freedom is, for Kant, a necessary requirement of action. The belief in freedom is needed because otherwise we would lack the assurance that we can do what the moral law requires of us. Carr holds that something quite similar is true for history and especially for political activity in history (Carr 1960: 118). Carr's formula is paradigmatically Kantian: 'No history, no freedom: and conversely, no freedom, no history' (Carr 1960: 118). This is not to say that Carr develops an account of teleology which matches Kant's account of teleology at all. Carr's commentary should be considered suggestive only, such that any school of thought—the English School, certain revisionist forms of political realism, and so on—would be stimulated to excavate the central insights of Kant's theory of history in order to develop a genuinely compelling substantive account of teleology in history.

Although Carr is silent in *What is History?* and *The New Society* about the influence of Kant, he is explicit in citing Hegel as a predecessor. In reflecting on the predicament of the historian, Carr presents a self-consciously Hegelian view in claiming that man, except perhaps in earliest infancy and in extreme old age, is not totally involved in his environment and unconditionally dependent on it. On the other hand, he is never totally independent of it and its unconditional master. The relation of historian to conditions or, more broadly, to facts is dialectical. The historian without facts is rootless and futile; the facts without their historian are dead and meaningless. On the basis of this simple idea we already have, Carr thinks, one answer to his engaging book's title *What is History?* The answer is that history begins as a process of interaction between the present and the past and ends in their reconciliation (Carr 1987: 122). Carr, however, goes even further in this overtly Hegelian direction and in so doing suggests how a teleological view might be understood. He writes: 'Only the future can provide the key to the interpretation of the past; and it is only in this sense that we can speak of an ultimate objectivity in history' (Carr 1987: 123). Here, Carr identifies 'the future' as the condition that enables the historian to pick out those actions and events from the past which provide a continuous sequence to the identified future and, thereby, to provide whatever meaning there is to be teased out from the notion of historical objectivity. To be sure, although this claim about the future does not result in a fully fledged teleological view in terms of which the *end* causally *directs* the past to achieve successive steps to the prescribed goal, it nonetheless intimates the kind of 'immanent subjectivity' on which Hegel's teleological understanding of history relies (McCarney 2000: 129).

Other features of Carr's view of history serve to strengthen the idea of attributing to him a robust conception of teleology. One of the most promising of these lies in Carr's tenacious commitment to progressivism. Although the classical Greeks and Romans, we are told, had a cyclical view of history, Jews and Christians 'introduced an entirely new element by postulating a goal towards which the historical process is moving—the teleological view of history. History thus acquired a meaning and purpose' (Carr 1987: 110). Following in the Judaeo-Christian wake, Enlightenment thinkers retained the 'Jewish-Christian teleological view, but secularised the goal; they were thus enabled to restore the rational character of the historical process itself. History became progress towards the goal of the perfection of man's estate on earth' (Carr 1987: 110–11). Since teleology is here bound up with the intertwining of history and progress, Carr licenses us to use these terms more or less interchangeably.

Having got this far, it is useful for this and the next section to make a distinction between externalist and internalist teleology. The former refers to identifying goal-directed or purposive events, processes, and forces that are outside and independent of human agency itself; such events and processes are necessary to attaining the future goal. The form of an externalist teleological explanation would be: 'X [an event or process] took place because its having done so was necessary for progress in domain Y'. By contrast, internalist teleology, described and analysed more fully in the next section, offers an account of teleology based upon human action, volition, and intention which, though related to externalist teleology, is perhaps best regarded as bearing a 'family resemblance' to it. The form of internalist teleological explanation would be: 'X (a human agent) did Y in order to Z'.

Apart from appealing to Hegel and Marx (Carr 1987: 135–7), there are three other ways in which Carr's commitment to externalist teleology may be marked. First, like Kant, Carr specifically avoids claiming that a commitment to progress can be validated in some a priori or speculative way (Carr 1987: 112–13); it needs, on his view, to be treated as an empirical hypothesis that may or may not be sustained. Following such a path will help to circumvent the widespread idea that all appeals to teleology are scientifically dubious and must, as such, be avoided. Moreover, an understanding of progress-conceived teleology requiring empirical testing is consistent with Carr's evident belief that teleology is compatible with causalism, in other words the belief that '[t]he study of history is the study of causes' (Carr 1987: 87). This puts Carr in a space, critically examined below, endorsed by many philosophers, to wit, that whatever teleology may turn out to be, it cannot be opposed to causes (Davidson 1980; Mele 1997: 1–26).[5] More significantly for our purposes here it illustrates one sense in which Carr accepts externalist teleology as driven by forces outside and independent of human action.

Second, in the course of examining 'the [m]uddle about progress and evolution' (Carr 1987: 113), we learn of Carr's commitment to Hegel's distinction between nature and history (or culture); specifically, Hegel distinguished 'history, which was progressive, from nature which was not' (Carr 1987: 113). This distinction not only helps Carr resist naturalistic conceptions of history that reduce it to categories outside the realm of culture and action, but also to define history as 'progress through the transmission of acquired skills from one generation to another' (Carr 1987: 114). This feature of Carr's views cannot be overestimated. For, in accepting it, Carr holds that he avoids two egregious but common errors: the 'mistake' of conceiving progress as having a finite beginning or end and the equally gratuitous error of thinking of progress as a continuous unbroken advance (Carr 1987: 114–17). In holding to his definition of progress, Carr echoes Hegel's persistently expressed belief in the progressive development of human potential; but, while Hegel evidently held that such development would end in the coming of Absolute Spirit, Carr, quite reasonably, saw progress as in principle unlimited, insisting that 'progress is subject to no limits that we can or need envisage' (Carr 1987: 119). Carr justifies this strong view of progress elsewhere by arguing that without the idea of unlimited progress, the very idea of society's 'survival' is put in doubt. Survival, on this view, rests upon one generation making substantial sacrifices for the sake of future generations in the name of a better world (Carr 1960: 118). And so it may be. To his credit, Carr also recognized, *pace* Kant, that this way of looking at progress was a secular version of a religious idea, of justifying progress 'in the name of divine purpose' (Carr 1960: 118). This way of looking at progress, too, resonates with Carr's adherence to an externalist conception of teleology.

Third, in turning to Carr's discussion of *absolute truth* we get a clearer picture of what his externalist teleological view consists of. Carr's view is a version of the ortho-dox time-honoured idea that history in the material sense constitutes a single process of goal-directed change in which successive steps or stages of history are regarded not only as indispensable to 'higher' stages but also in which the end-stage 'directs' the entire process. As Carr appreciates, this view has been thoroughly discredited and he makes no attempt to resurrect it. However, what he replaces it with is something that appears to be, in some sense, a permutation of this older idea.

Carr holds that the historian needs a criterion to distinguish significant from acci-dental facts and events (Carr 1987: 120–1), but informs us that such a standard cannot be 'absolute' in the static sense of something that is the same yesterday, today, and forever for, such an 'absolute is incompatible with the nature of history' (Carr 1987: 121). And although the absolute is not in the past nor in the present (Carr 1987: 121), the criteria historians use are 'absolute with respect to the interpretation of the past' (Carr 1987: 121). But what does this mean? We need to apply this statement to the relation between means and ends upon which teleological interpretation depends. When the historian knows in the present that certain agents, institutions, and organ-izations have achieved some goal or purpose, his or her job is to cast around in history for an explanation of how that goal was achieved. It is vitally important to recognize that the historian is able to choose the activities of historical agents only to the extent that they satisfy a certain prospective description by which the actions are logically tied to the realization of the goal that the historian knows has been realized. So the relationship between choice and action is different from the situation in which the goal is located in the future and there are a variety of possible means for achiev-ing it, some of which will turn out to be unsuccessful. In the case of the past, the historian *knows* the goal has been achieved and he or she is now required to find not the possible ways it could be achieved but to 'order and interpret the events of the past' (Carr 1987: 121). The interpretation of the past, shaped, as it must be, by continued forward movement towards a future condition, cannot logically invoke a static criterion of interpretation in the present and cannot, therefore, be absolute (Carr 1987: 121).

So, although Carr 'drops' the orthodox teleological idea of a fixed 'end-stage' directing the past and present as part and parcel of Hegel's 'mystical . . . world spirit' (Carr 1987: 122), he nonetheless retains the two related ideas of past and present directed by the future, and the historian, as orderer and organizer, as the agent responsible for history as a 'progressive and dynamic' process (Carr 1987: 122). Thus, while the time-honoured understanding of teleology posits a Superintending Agent to control history's wayward events and guarantee meaning and progress in the face of the chaos of competing forces, Carr suggests a non-metaphysical agent—the progressive historian whose task it is to interpret, order, and 'control', as far as possible, both past and future via a constantly modifying and evolving end understood teleologically (Carr 1987: 122). On this understanding, history can retain a reasonably firm grip on the future's directedness of the past and present but without plunging into a metaphysical and scientifically discredited conception of teleological explanation.

To sum up this section: although there are, as we have seen, several teleological notions in play in Carr's insightful reflections on history, it must be admitted that, notwithstanding the potential fertility of his views on teleology when inextricably bound up with progress, he provided not much more than an intimation of what would be required for a more compelling analysis. On the other hand, this complaint might well be considered unfair given his wide-ranging contributions to our understanding of international relations and Soviet history. More to the point, perhaps, is that he did not evidently perceive the possibility of a tension between cause and teleology, between an account of history that explains actions in terms of prior non-psychological events and an account that explains actions by appeal to reasons. More specifically, Carr did not see that his discussion of causation in chapter 4 of *What is History?* would create difficulties for his assumption of teleological progress in chapter 5. In chapter 4 he says that the historian is like the ordinary man in believing that human actions have causes which are in principle ascertainable. 'History, like everyday life, would be impossible if this assumption were not made' (Carr 1987: 95). But this is inconsistent with what he says about what people do when they engage in certain human actions, such as, for instance, extending human rights or reforming a penal code, namely, that they are 'consciously seeking to do just these things' (Carr 1987: 117). This way of putting the matter implies that since human actions are 'consciously' chosen, they might well be explained by a reason-giving account in which appeal to causes would be out of place. On this construal of what is at issue, it would be legitimate to give a reason-giving, noncausal explanation; and there seems no good reason in principle why such an account could not have an epistemically valid role to play in historical or everyday explanations.

In the last analysis, in developing his ideas of history Carr may have been too much in thrall to the causal account of history to give sufficient philosophical space to a more fully developed conception of teleology (Carr 1987: ch. 4). Such an account would doubtless have had to make considerable conceptual space for a revised conception of *meaning*, an essential element in any external understanding of teleology (Lowith 1949: 1–19). Had he done so, he might have been able not only to reject empiricist interpretations of knowledge (Carr 1991: 73), but also, more imaginatively and daringly, assisted the English School to carve out an alternative teleological conception of history in the interest of challenging the shibboleths of positivist reductions of history to scientific causalism. This is a missed opportunity from which the English School and traditional political realism, among other schools, still suffer.

BUTTERFIELD: INTERNALIST TELEOLOGY AND NARRATIVE HISTORY

At first blush it would be hard to find a historian more diametrically opposed to Carr than Butterfield. While Carr scorned facts and their seekers, Butterfield held that facts constituted the very basis of an historian's craft, and that collectors of them should be honoured for their scholarship. While Carr held that political and philosophical detachment were impossible and in any case unnecessary, Butterfield argued that it was attainable, at least, somewhat paradoxically, for the believing Christian. Although Carr argued strenuously for the view that all of us are embedded in history, thus making history an unavoidable necessity, Butterfield believed that history itself was contingent, that men can have basic views of life which deny the very significance of history. In these respects (and many more) Butterfield's views differed from Carr's; yet there is an important sense in which they are in agreement, namely, they both believed that history has to be understood, at least in part, in teleological terms, even if those terms differ.

Butterfield, like Carr, failed to develop an explicit conception of history as teleological; however, close analysis of his views on historiography shows that he not only *possessed* the basic idea of teleological history, but also accepted it as one way in which history could be conceived to be rational, and therefore, in a certain sense, 'scientific', without having to accept a natural–scientific model of what knowledge consisted of and how to understand its accumulation (Butterfield 1960: 41–57; 1979: 33 and 151–71). Butterfield, I claim, was implicitly committed to what I have called above internalist teleology.

By deploying the term of art internalist teleology, I mean to convey three things: first, that the provenance of action derives from an agent's internal processes; second, that action is paradigmatically individual; and third, that we explain human action in ordinary life and history by creating narratives of human activity, individual and collective. To be an agent is not to be a passive responder to happenings; it means thinking about goals to be pursued and directing one's behaviour toward an identifiable goal or set of goals. The bringing together of internal processes and of directed behaviour to specified goals is what makes an activity internally teleological. The way we capture such activities is typically through writing historical narratives. To be sure, what Butterfield called 'technical history' was an alternative methodology whose advantages (and drawbacks) he marked (Butterfield 1950: ch. 1; 1979: 26–31); but whatever its virtues and defects, this kind of history should not be confused with the *genre* which assumes the self-directed behaviour of individual agents upon which history relies (Butterfield 1950: 12–25; 1979: 17–26). All these features of internalist teleology are discernible in Butterfield's historiography.

In 'The Role of the Individual in History' he explicitly refers to the source of 'historical events'. Butterfield wrote: 'The genesis of historical events lies in human beings. The real birth of ideas takes place in human brains . . . It is men who make history' (Butterfield 1979: 18). This shows a clear and obvious commitment to the idea that the source of 'historical events' lies *within* the individual brain, by which I take Butterfield to be referring to cognitive processes that, having taken place and having been deliberated upon, permit human agents to make things happen. The idea stands in marked contrast to externalist teleology, as discerned in Carr, which depends on events and processes outside and independent of human agency as such.

For Butterfield, internalist teleology has a second function, that of rendering individual actions historically intelligible. In giving a teleological account of an agent's behaviour, the historian answers a certain type of 'why' question, a question whose answer requires identifying and rendering intelligible the purpose or goal of self-directed actions. Such actions are paradigmatically individual and irreducible to causal generalization. Although Butterfield conceded that collective forces and institutions shape historical events, he never resiled from the idea that individual human personalities take—and will continue to take—centre-stage in historical writing; it is a constant theme that runs throughout the corpus of his work. In this respect Butterfield self-consciously contrasted his own approach to that employed in Whig, Marxist, and Positivist history (Butterfield 1951: 66–100; 1968: 64–89; 1979: 27–36). Quite early on in his historical writing Butterfield stressed the extent to which history turns on what individual human beings do as a consequence of the indisputable fact that people have wills and purposes that matter to them and to us. For Butterfield, in contrast to Carr, it is the single individual as agent who is the principal source of historical action.[6]

As to the third function of internal teleology concerning how we *explain* human action Butterfield lays considerable stress on the skills and inventiveness of historians in creating narratives that capture the contingency of teleological behaviour in human agents. Thus he writes that 'there is something in history to which we can do justice only by reproducing the course of events as a story, the kind of story in which we do not know what is going to happen next' (Butterfield 1979: 19). For Butterfield, this last condition has an important 'philosophical' implication, namely, that only when actions are understood as if they were 'present' can we be in a position to say whether individuals 'make history or merely go where history takes them' (Butterfield 1979: 25). In other words, only if we see past events as possible present actions which we too could have performed does it make sense to think of them as actions for which agents could be responsible rather than as happenings that occur to passive entities and for which the concept of responsibility is out of place. So whether we can think of them as present actions in the intended sense may turn on passing the 'test' of being meaningful, if not necessarily desired, by present norms. If the test is passed, the event provides the raw material for reconstruction as narrative history.

Understood in terms of these three features, internalist teleology offers a robust defence of narrative history. Butterfield stresses the way in which the stories we tell ourselves and others have the practical function of organizing our 'ready-made' prestructured experiences. Our lives are originally organized to bring out the unity of a life-story, no matter how much riven it is by conflict, and the 'human touches' that abound in it (Butterfield 1951: 11–15; 1979: 25–6). In this respect historical narrative is endowed with ontological significance; it is constitutive of our very being; it is our way of existing, of constituting ourselves as the beings we are. Moreover, it is not merely as individuals that we exist in this way, though, as emphasized above, individualizing processes are of primary significance. To be sure, communities, large and small, can be said to have the same narrative form of self-institution as individuals. A community whose members refer to themselves as 'we', or in some comparable way exists in a reflexive form which draws together a remembered past and projected future, and these jointly serve to make sense of the present that is being lived through.

Such an 'ontological' interpretation of narrative has the decided advantage of removing formal obstacles to the truthfulness or fidelity of narratives. It puts paid to the claim that narratives are necessarily incapable of 'representing' the events they depict because the form of the narrative itself will always be at variance with 'reality'. We must still allow, of course, for the possibility that stories may sometimes be untrue to events, that historians may distort them or that the motives for studying the past may turn out to be instrumental rather than intrinsic. Thus, for example, Butterfield distinguishes between storytelling that is motivated by 'a genuine interest in the past' and 'mere storytelling for its own sake' (Butterfield 1981: 158). Genuine *historical* narrative ushers in a certain characterization of historical narrating as an activity in its own right, with a social function in its own community, namely, as extending and refining the human drama that constitutes the community (Butterfield 1981: 158). In this sense communities, like history itself, are always filled with contingency and surprises. For instance, with the Hebrews, '[t]here emerges a people not only supremely conscious of the past but possibly more obsessed with history than any other nation that has ever existed' (Butterfield 1981: 80–1). The communal story of this nation is constantly being revised in a way that results in the rise of agonistic factions. But if the Jewish nation's stories differ from one another and their visions are ultimately irreconcilable, the community itself may become fragmented and, paradoxically, this may occur in a manner similar to the way the Israelites became fragmented into Christians and Jews. Here, once more, the struggle within a community can be justifiably likened to those between individuals in the picture Butterfield provides in *Napoleon* (1939) and *George III and the Historians* (1957). On the basis of such distinctions and examples there should be no obstacle to construing narrative as a principle that could express either a collective or individual ontology, thus meeting Carr's complaint about the excessive individualism in the common sense view of history (Carr 1987: 35–55).

Having extended Butterfield's conception of historiography to tease out an ontology of historical being, we need to consider whether these narrative assumptions invoke epistemic dimensions of history that could provide reliable knowledge of the past. For Butterfield, traditional narrative histories claim to tell us what really happened and though sometimes this claim may be wrong, there seems no good reason to accept the sceptical thesis that they are never true. In his first book, *The Historical*

Novel (1971: 13–21), Butterfield, made a distinction between events that are narrated in works of fiction and those narrated in history: fictional events never happened, even though if portrayed with imagination and sensitivity they may be said to be true-to-life. For they tell us how certain events might have enriched readers' lives if they had really occurred. Some stories, it is true, may be incredible and some others deliberately fanciful, but nothing in principle prevents such narratives from succeeding in their aim. The structure of fictional narratives is simple enough: it consists of meaningful fictional events, in which fictional characters engage in human actions in order to achieve certain purposes or goals.

For Butterfield, historical understanding is in general to be accounted for with the same teleological structure. Consider Butterfield's description of Napoleon's Continental System:

> The Continental System, the attempt to seal Europe against English commerce . . . implied a further intensification of his tyranny . . . in the regions over which he possessed influence . . . it entailed the expansion of empire . . . the purpose which the whole Napoleonic order was meant to subserve. In the course of time Napoleon occupied Rome, drove his brother Louis from the throne of Holland and annexed the country, and incorporated Hamburg and Oldenburg in his empire, and undertook the expedition to Moscow . . . in other words, the Continental System is in fact the Grand Empire. (Butterfield 1939: 89–90)

The meaning of these changes lay in metamorphosis of the Continental System into Napoleon's Grand Empire; the human actions involved Napoleon's increasing tyrannical behaviour as manifested in 'the expansion of empire', Napoleon's 'occupation of Rome', the removal of 'his brother Louis from the throne of Holland' and its annexation, and so on; the goal or purpose of these actions, as Butterfield also makes clear in the sequel (Butterfield 1939: 90), was to 'seal Europe against English commerce' (Butterfield 1939: 89–90). All of this, Butterfield implies, was driven by Napoleon's 'reasons' and, presumably, captured by the historian's 'reason-explanations'. Here one might ask rhetorically: what does 'cause' have to do with it? On the widely held view of knowledge, alluded to above, according to which explanation involves correctly answering 'why' questions, it seems difficult to fault Butterfield's narrative history.

Now, against this common-sense view of historical knowledge there are, one must concede, many philosophers of history who declare it naive and scientifically invalid. Real events, goes the argument, simply do not hang together in a narrative way, and if historians treat them as if they did, they are, whether consciously or unconsciously, imposing a form that is untrue-to-life. So it is not simply for lack of evidence or of verisimilitude, but in virtue of its very form, that any narrative account will present us with an impaired picture of the events it relates. Even apart from this complaint, some well-known philosophers of history have questioned narrative's scientific credentials. For example, Maurice Mandelbaum has argued that historical narratives 'ensure explanatory incompleteness', and necessarily constitute a 'gross distortion of the subject-matter' (Mandelbaum, quoted in Norman 2001: 182).

Although this is clearly not the place to examine this issue in depth, two comments are in order. First, the main source for many of these antinarrative views is positivism, a philosophy that has been increasingly discredited as an underpinning for the social sciences and subjects like international relations and history. Second, and more importantly perhaps, there does not seem to be any conceptual basis for denying that the statements made in historical narratives may be true, once one has the 'correct' understanding of truth in place. By this latter phrase I am referring to the many misguided efforts to hold that any realist understanding of truth *must* be some version of the 'correspondence theory of truth', a conception of truth thoroughly bound up with a metaphysical theory that neither the English School nor traditional political realism ever adopted or would ever be inclined to accept. In its place the traditional political realist would want to offer a non-metaphysical conception of truth to the effect that a proposition is true when the world is what that proposition says it is.[7] This conception of truth, with its anti-metaphysical and anti-absolutistic character, should assuage the worry of such realist philosophers of history as A. P. Norman whose defence of historical realism stops at the water's edge of truth.[8] But, if this conception of truth is justifiable, there seems no good reason to avoid making truth-claims in narrative history. A teleologically based form of historical narrative is defendable not only ontologically but epistemically as, in principle, truth-bearing as well.

Although it is beyond the scope of this chapter to defend any particular theory of human agency, it is nevertheless the case that a certain version of such a theory underpins narrative history: human agency rests upon a voluntaristic not a deterministic conception of agency. The behaviour of agents is voluntary—exercises of the will—and manifested in actions of which the historian lacks foreknowledge (Butterfield 1979: 19). The relation to teleology here is perspicuous: voluntary control consists generally in an agent's capacity to direct his or her will to ends or goals he or she selects by nominated means. To be sure, the structure of human action, so understood, may be exceedingly complex. Things do not always work out as planned and so on. Still, on the narrative view, it is false to claim that ordinary action is a 'chaos' of unrelated terms in the way, say, certain postmodernists have postulated. What makes historical events into identifiable patterns of action is that in the typical case *reasons* are advanced (or implied) to accompany the voluntary actions of human beings. Once again, teleology is in play, not, to be sure, that form of it which posits an a priori goal or end-state towards which history as a whole is said to be inexorably moving, but, rather, in the modality of it which gives central place to concrete, individual human actions and choice (Butterfield 1968: 65–73). Deterministic accounts of history flounder on the recognition of a 'myriad of alternative courses' that people 'decide at every moment of their lives' (Butterfield 1979: 26).

CONCLUSION

The main purpose of this chapter has been to resurrect, via the English School's understanding of history as discernible in E. H. Carr and Herbert Butterfield, a teleological conception of history as one possible route to distinguishing a still dominant scientific empiricism in international relations from what the English

School and traditional political realism ought to pursue. We have held that both Carr and Butterfield advanced views about history which would help in the construction of a distinctly different conception of history's relation to the study of international relations. Carr's work provides indispensable groundwork for regarding international relations as inextricably bound up with history. He had original views on history which we may summarize here. History is anti-empiricist (Carr 1987: 69); dialectical (Carr 1987: 30); social (Carr 1987: 52); and progressivist (Carr 1987: 117–19). For Butterfield, history is partially subjective (Butterfield 1955: 23); individualistic (Butterfield 1979: 17–36); particularistic and concrete (Butterfield 1968: 65–6); conflictual (Butterfield 1968: 41); Augustinian or pessimistic (Butterfield 1950: 28–9); continuous (Butterfield 1966: 182); and narrativistic (Butterfield 1979: 18). What emerges from the tensions between these alternative views is that in my view Butterfield's narrative account of history is superior to Carr's anachronistic non-narrative account.[9] Butterfield's account is superior for two reasons: first, it locates historical activity in the intentional action of human agents and, second, it tries to discover what Von Wright calls an 'efficacious reason', the actual or, as we might put it, real reason for the action, a time-honoured realist objective since Thucydides (Von Wright 1971: ch. 3; 1997: 1–20). A conception of teleology—internal teleology as it has been labelled in this chapter—is a highly defensible alternative to the fully blown 'causal' conception of human action that scientific empiricism endorses.

For instance, Butterfield accounted for Napoleon's behaviour as goal- or purpose-directed. He wrote of the great French leader:

His masterly moves, his heroic feats, his infectious spirit, his stirring bulletins [in Italy against the Austrians] had given the soldiers supreme confidence in their leader. So he was able to change the original purpose of the campaign, and to turn the Italian war into an end in itself instead of a mere diversion against the Austrian left wing. (1939: 28)

The aspiration that motivates a teleological interpretation rather than a causal one here is simply that citation of the agent's reasons may well explain why the agent performed his action by naming the goals and purposes of the action for the agent. There is no reason to suppose that such reasons have any explanatory value if treated as efficient cause(s) of Napoleon's behaviour. To say this is not, of course, to deny the commonplace claim that reasons are causes in some sense (Wilson 1997: 65). It is to recognize, rather, that such an admission will be of little assistance to the causalist since it amounts to a trivial platitude that any sensible appeal to reasons will take in stride. What the causalist needs is not a gesture to an analysis that goes missing but, rather, a compelling analysis identifying the causes for which the agent acted. According to some philosophers, such an analysis has not been forthcoming (Sehon 1994: 63–72; Wilson 1997: 74; Hutto 1999: 381–401).

From within the presuppositions of scientific empiricism, appeal to causality would do nothing to eliminate or discredit any of the rationalizations historians in the Butterfield mould would provide. What is required in cases where rationalizing plays the dominant role is, rather, a sensitivity to the specific detail of the subjective stance of others. When a historian provides rationalizing explanations, he or she is effectively making an action intelligible by adopting the agent's perspective on it. From that perspective the goals and purposes of others are detected as desirable and appropriate to the situation. Here we discern at work Butterfield's *desideratum* that narrative historians should see actions as present as a precondition to discussing whether agents were making history or being made by it (Butterfield 1979: 25). These features, however, are not objective in the sense of being describable from a notional 'view from nowhere' (Nagel 1986). The narrative historian's task is to use historical imagination in taking up the standpoint of an agent deciding how to act without 'knowing the outcome'. Needless to say, this standpoint is not that of a detached observer of the sort required by scientific empiricism. On the contrary, it is a standpoint which gives agents a privileged and authoritative position. As Johnston writes

The individual is treated not as a site of causal processes but as an agent, and *qua* agent he is attributed a privileged role, for by citing a consideration he authoritatively locates his action in the wider network of aims and intention which gave it its sense. (Johnston 1989: 45)

Appreciating the rationality of actions in history requires an appreciation of their normative character. To understand why an agent finds a certain path desirable is to appreciate what is involved in finding something desirable and thereby to appreciate the appropriateness of pursuing it; or vice versa. History cannot be decoupled from the normative engagements which come to light by taking up the perspective of the historical agent. In making a case for why the English School and traditional political realism have a joint and not insignificant basis to resuscitate a teleological conception of history, we need to recognize the indispensability of the normative, even though, following Thucydides, we construe the normative as ineluctably bound up with power. The scientific empiricist has disparaged, to the point of ridicule, teleology in all its varied forms (Fodor 1990: part one); such arguments, however, have been challenged and a philosophical pathway cleared for teleology's redemption from the sentence of causal reduction (Wilson, G. M. 1989: 258). If there remains, even among the best of philosophers sympathetic to realism, a tendency to associate teleology in history with its worst excesses (Williams 2002: 253), one can put this down to the still continuing echoes of moribund theory. Realist thinkers above all will certainly be alert to the 'gap' between making rational, truth-bearing arguments and putting those arguments to work in *practical* political contexts. Nevertheless, it might still be considered a reasonable achievement to have shown that it is not impossible to move towards reducing that gap by keeping 'teleology in history and international relations' on the expanding agendas of both the English School and traditional political realism.

Notes

1. See, for example, Copeland (2003: 427–41). Copeland argues that American realism (i.e. neorealism) is a more useful starting point than the English School for 'building strong explanatory and predictive IR theory' (p. 427). Copeland continues that it is often 'difficult to figure out what the English School is trying to explain, what its causal logic is, or how one

would go about measuring its core independent (causal) variable, "international society"' (p. 427). Moreover, the English School is less a 'theory that provides falsifiable hypotheses to be tested (or that have been tested) than a vague approach to thinking and conceptualising world politics' (p. 427). Interestingly enough, Copeland tries to persuade us that any objection to his essay on the grounds that it 'amounts to artificial forcing of thought in a "positivist" mold is "mistaken"' (p. 428). Is this an example of the rigorous testing Copeland insists upon or its very opposite: dogmatism?

Terminological confusion abounds in this arena. My term of art 'scientific empiricism' seems better than Bull's 'scientific approach' because, first of all, as Jones notes, several members of the English School said they were scientific (Jones 1981: 7); second, and relatedly, scientific empiricism attempts to bridge the gap between the natural and social sciences and thus retains the older positivist insistence on the unity of the sciences which serves to retain continuity over time; and third, scientific empiricism is committed to causalism which holds that desires and beliefs of agents are causes or causal conditions of agent action. By scientific empiricism, I mean the view, shaped by Quine and his followers, that all knowledge is ultimately obtained from experience and that the best method for acquiring reliable knowledge is to be found in the natural sciences and, in particular, in devising theories which help to establish laws and discover causal generalizations that are rigorously tested before they are *tentatively* accepted. The goal of scientific empiricism is to explain and predict phenomena of interest to scientists and researchers.

2. Although I have identified the version of Realism at issue in this essay as 'traditional political realism', I am using the term to refer to a large group of realists who have the following identifying marks: (*a*) a commitment to reject the 'methodological' orthodoxies of neorealism; (*b*) a sympathetic and appreciative attitude to the political philosophy of international relations; and (*c*) a view of history that makes it the centrepiece of international relations scholarship and research. Such a view also includes my own version of realism which I have called 'evaluative political realism' (Spegele 1996), but I am not pushing that barrow in this chapter. For the purposes of this chapter I am, for what it is worth, a follower of traditional (or classical) realism, an idea accurately described and sympathetically interpreted by Richard Little (2003: 443–60).

3. The evident reluctance to respond has been noted by Hall (2001: 932).

4. Copeland argues for an interpretation of the English School which would make it, without its members' permission, into a version of scientific empiricism with 'new and improved arguments' (2003: 439–41).

5. For a contrary view which the writer of this chapter accepts, see Wilson (1997: 65–82) and Sehon (1994: 63–72).

6. In an early work, *The Peace Tactics of Napoleon 1806–1808*, Butterfield wrote

The story has been told with special reference to the personalities engaged in the work of diplomacy, so that it might become apparent how much in Napoleonic times the course of events could be deflected by the characters and the idiosyncracies of ambassadors and ministers who were far removed from the events of the time. It is intended that the result should be at least a sample picture of the Napoleonic era, and should illustrate the strange tangle, the hidden undercurrents and the clash of personalities, that lay behind a Napoleonic war. (Butterfield 1929: p. vii)

Here (and in countless other cases that we need not labour) Butterfield shows commitment to the view that human actions are the primary events with which the historian deals.

7. The philosopher who has worked this out in some detail is Alston (1996: *passim*). IR theorists interested in how realism can avoid the correspondence theory of truth should refer to this well-argued book.
8. Norman (2001: 192–4) also asserts that realism can legitimately claim truth for its accounts, but does not say, in general, what truth consists of.
9. Bernard Williams provides good reasons for rejecting a certain kind of 'teleological history' that comes uncomfortably close to Carr's view (Williams 2002: 253).

6

International Political Economy and Globalization

Barry Buzan

The English School has failed to engage with international political economy (IPE). This failure has had serious and negative consequences for how the understanding of international society has developed. Another consequence of this failure is that the English School has so far not exploited its considerable potential to act as the theoretical framework through which globalization can be analysed. Nothing stands in the way of bringing IPE into the international society tradition, and much is to be gained by doing so. In the first section, I place the economic sector within English School thinking, look at what has been said about it, and examine why it has been neglected. In the second section, I explore the consequences of that neglect for the debate about pluralism and solidarism. In the third section, I examine regions and institutions as ways of bringing IPE and the English School together, and in the final section, I argue that this combination holds the key to a more effective study of globalization.

THE ENGLISH SCHOOL AND THE ECONOMIC SECTOR

To argue that the English School has neglected the economic sector is not to say either that it has never mentioned it, or that English School writers have explicitly rejected the international economy as an element of international society, or that the logic of international society somehow necessarily excludes IPE. The oddity is that one can find many favourable references in the English School classics to the need to bring the economic sector into the study of international society. What one cannot find is much follow up to these references. There seems to be no reason in principle why the economic sector should not feature in discussion of international and world society, and this rather glaring omission is often pointed out (Miller 1990: 70–4; Richardson 1990: 148 and 184; Hurrell 2002*a*: p. xvii). At various points along the way, English School writers have acknowledged the economic sector. Wight (1991: 7–8) talked

This chapter draws some of its argument, and in places some of its text, from Buzan (2004).

of the Rationalist position in terms of diplomacy and commerce. Bull (in Wight 1977: 16) noted trade as one of the four institutions in Wight's understanding of a states-system, and he also mentions it (1977: 70) in his discussion of rules about cooperation in society. Although Bull (1991: pp. xix–xx) was critical of Wight's disinterest in economics, he nevertheless failed to develop this aspect in his own discussions of international society, though his later work on justice (Bull 1984*a*, *b*, *c*) can be read as raising the question of international political economy. This is all the more surprising given that he made a feature of the economic sector in his critique of those who wanted to take a Hobbesian interpretation of international anarchy. Bull (1966*c*: 42) argued that 'trade, symbolic as it is of the existence of overlapping through [*sic*] different interests, is the activity most characteristic of international relationships as a whole'. Vincent, although critical of Bull for ignoring the economy as a key component of international order (Vincent 1988: 196 and 204) also failed to develop the topic, though he did put it on the agenda in a major way. His book on human rights (Vincent 1986*a*) developed a case for making the right to subsistence the floor of a global human rights programme. He was fully aware that this implied 'a radical reshaping of the international economic order' and that such a project 'might require a radical shift in patterns of political power in order that resources can reach the submerged 40% in developing countries'. That he understood the political side of the international economy was clear from his statement that: 'in regard to the failure to provide subsistence rights, it is not this or that government whose legitimacy is in question, but the whole international system in which we are all implicated' (Vincent 1986*a*: 127 and 145).

As Gonzalez-Pelaez (2003) pointed out, though, this opening into IPE was not followed up either by Vincent or by his followers, who have focused instead on the more directly violent abuses of citizens by their states such as torture and genocide. The one exception to this rule was James Mayall (1982, 1984, 1989) who began to think about economic liberalism in international society terms, and at one point (Mayall 1982) even argued for the existence of a sense of community in the economic sphere despite differences between North and South. However, he seemed to lose faith in his earlier interpretation (Mayall 1984). His more recent work (1990, 2000) focused largely on nationalism, and saw economic nationalism returning on the back of national security concerns in such a way as to undermine economic solidarism. This sidelining of the economic sector in representations of international society is surprising given both the enormous development of norms, rules, and institutions (including ones with powers of collective enforcement) in this sector, and the growth of IPE as a major branch of the study of international relations. What explains this absence?

There certainly does not seem to be any intrinsic reason why IPE should be excluded from the study of international society. Indeed, the basic construction of English School theory and IPE suggests the opposite. The founding fathers of the English School were trying to position themselves between liberalism and realism in the debates about international relations. The English School's founding thinkers had also to position themselves in relation to the great clash between universalist liberal and communist ideologies. The English School's task of finding a *via media* between liberalism and realism pointed almost unavoidably to engagement with the IPE agenda.

Perhaps even more important is the holistic and methodologically pluralist frame that defines English School theory (Little 1998, 2000). The English School posits three elements as composing the 'whole' of international relations: international system (basically a materialist, Realist, Hobbesian, power-politics view), international society (a rationalist, historical, legal, Grotian, and constructivist view), and world society (never very clearly defined, but containing cosmopolitanism, revolutionism, non-state actors, and other Kantian elements). These can be understood as either structural elements, or as ways of understanding and debating the practice of international relations. Either way, in the English School's perspective all three of these elements are in continuous coexistence and interplay. The question is, how strong they are in relation to each other (Bull 1991: pp. xvii–xviii; Dunne 1995*b*: 134–7). Although each element is conceptually and methodologically distinct, they blur into each other at the boundaries. This framework is both compatible with, and congenial to, IPE, which also requires a holistic and methodologically pluralist approach. In principle, there are no epistemological or ontological barriers between English School theory and IPE, and there is much practical ground for interoperability between them. By introducing international society as a third element, not only as a *via media* between realism and liberalism/cosmopolitanism but also as the keystone to an interdependent set of concepts, English School theory transcends the binary opposition between them that for long plagued debates about both IR theory generally, and IPE in particular. By assuming not only that all three elements always operate simultaneously, but also that each carries its own distinctive ontological and epistemological package, English School theory also transcends the assumption often made in the so-called interparadigm debate, that realist, liberal, and Marxist approaches to IR theory are incommensurable (McKinlay and Little 1986).

If there is no intrinsic barrier to the linkage of English School theory and IPE, a strong case for compatibility and mutual benefit, and no principled position against it among the School's founding fathers, why were these linkages not explored? Perhaps the most obvious explanation is that writers such as Manning, Wight, Bull, and Vincent were largely ignorant about, and not very interested in, the study of economics. Such a perspective was reinforced both by theory (which put an emphasis on states as actors, and on power politics) and by the practice of the cold war (with its extreme emphasis on military matters). It was also reinforced by the growing methodological gap between the study of politics and the study of economics in academic life. Most of the founding fathers of the English School rooted their expertise in political theory, international law, and international politics and were not well equipped to deal with economic questions. Their study focused on a Westphalian model of international society, effectively a pluralist, high politics approach that largely excluded economics except as one of the underpinnings of state power. That said, state-centrism by itself cannot explain the neglect of economics because the state focus is also apparent in much IPE.

Another way of thinking about this neglect of economics is in terms of the three pillars, or traditions, of English School theory: international system, international society, and world society. Bull (in Wight 1991: p. xi) nicely characterizes Wight's position on these three traditions as follows: realism is about 'the blood and iron and immorality men', rationalism is about 'the law and order and keep your word men', and revolutionism is about 'the subversion and liberation and missionary men'. The primary concern of the classical English School tradition was to construct the international society pillar as a *via media* between the extremes of the other two. The international system pillar was well taken care of by realists, and the world society pillar became a kind of intellectual dustbin into which to put whatever did not fit elsewhere. Wight, Bull, and many others in the rationalist tradition felt themselves to be distant from revolutionism. This explains why they did not devote much thought to the world society dimension of English School theory (Suganami 2002a: 5). To the extent that they did so, it was largely in the context of a concern with human rights and the cosmopolitan dimension of international morality. The general rule was that the things to be found in the world society pillar, whether outright revolutionism or cosmopolitanism, or even the emergence of human rights law, could threaten the stability of the society of states which was the crucial provider of such little order (and in some eyes therefore also justice) as humankind possessed or was likely to possess in the forseeable future. In Wight's view of revolutionism (1987 [1960]: 223–6) the economy is one of the dangers. His focus was on those who want to change the world, have an idea of how it should be, and (usually) have some mechanism in mind (he mentions commerce, enlightenment, revolution, war) that will bring their visions to reality.

A third possible reason for the English School's neglect of the economy is the way in which it has focused most of its thinking about international society at the global level, in the process ignoring or even opposing subglobal/regional societal developments. This move derives partly from its historical account of how European international society expanded to global scale, and partly from a political theory concern with 'universal values' such as human rights, which easily get transferred to a global scale. The fear of subglobal/regional developments made good sense during the cold war, when it was exactly such rival, subglobal international societies that were endangering the world. Many English School writers assumed that regional developments would necessarily compromise the global level and generate conflict. By blinding themselves to the subglobal in this way, they made it much more difficult to see the actual developments in the economics of international society that were taking place at that level.

While all of these reasons explain the English School's neglect of the economic sector, none of them justifies the continuance of that neglect. If simple disinterest and lack of knowledge among the founding fathers is the main reason, then there is no excuse for the perpetuation of this tradition, and an urgent need to reject it. So long as day-to-day world politics was dominated by the international system and international society pillars, with world society only a residual element in the background, the English School could perhaps get away with treating world society as a Cinderella. But if, as many people now think, both the subglobal/regional level and the world society element are rising in significance, this neglect becomes untenable.

THE CONSEQUENCES OF NEGLECT FOR
THE ENGLISH SCHOOL

The neglect of IPE has been a lost opportunity for the English School. Potential synergies have remained dormant, the audience for English School thinking is smaller than it might be, and the understanding of what international society is about has remained narrowly cast. If that was all, it would be bad enough, but the costs have in fact been considerably larger and deeper. Neglecting IPE has contributed to a profound distortion in the English School's theoretical development, particularly the way in which its core debate between pluralism and solidarism has unfolded (see the Introduction and Suganami's contribution, Chapter 1, this volume). The problem is that leaving out the economic sector has seriously weakened the solidarist position, and in so doing has reinforced the more pessimistic, pluralist interpretation of international society. This in turn has consequences for both how the history of international society is (mis)understood, and how the English School is able (or not) to position itself in the wider debates about International Relations theory.

Pluralism fits most comfortably with economic nationalist and/or mercantilist understandings of, and attitudes towards, the economic sector, and solidarism reflects more liberal views. In practice, however, neither side of the debate has addressed economic issues. Both have kept their focus largely on the military–political sector and high politics concerns about sovereignty, great power management, and human rights. Pluralists have failed to address how the emergence of a liberal international economic order impacts on their model. Solidarists have failed to consider whether the collective commitment to joint gain that is the foundation of a liberal international economic order counts as the sort of shared norm that differentiates pluralism's restriction to rules of coexistence from their own belief that international societies are both empirically and theoretically capable of developing shared norms that are wider and deeper than mere coexistence. The English School has remained silent on these questions, leaving them to be taken up by neoliberal institutionalism and regime theory.

This neglect carries significant costs. Neoliberal institutionalists and regime theorists are mainly interested in 'particular human-constructed arrangements, formally or informally organised' seen as 'specific institutions . . . that can be identified as related complexes of rules and norms, identifiable in space and time' (Keohane 1988: 383–5). Keohane puts particular emphasis on rules, arguing that specific institutions exist where there is a 'persistent set of rules' that must 'constrain activity, shape expectation, and prescribe roles'. This confines his meaning of institution either to formal organizations with 'capacity for purposive action' or international regimes comprising 'complexes of rules and organizations', a distinction also made by

Kratochwil and Ruggie (1986). This comes close to making the meaning of institution synonymous with intergovernmental organizations and legal frameworks. The English School, by contrast, is primarily concerned with 'historically constructed normative structures' (Alderson and Hurrell 2000: 27); the shared cultural elements that precede rational cooperation, or what Keohane (1988: 385) calls enduring 'fundamental practices' which shape and constrain the formation, evolution, and demise of the more specific institutions. Onuf (2002) labels this distinction as 'evolved' versus 'designed' institutions. From here on in, I will label as *secondary institutions* those that are the main focus of regime theory, and as *primary institutions* those that are the main focus of the English School. Among other things, this distinction means that the English School has placed a lot of emphasis on the way in which the institutions of international society and its members are mutually constitutive. To pick up Manning's (1962) metaphor of the game of states, the English School institutions define what the pieces are and how the game is played. Regime theory tends to take both actors and their preferences as given, and to define the game as cooperation under anarchy. This difference is complemented and reinforced by one of method, with regime theory largely wedded to rationalist method (Kratochwil and Ruggie 1986), and the English School resting on history, normative political theory, and international legal theory. The cost of leaving the economic sector to neoliberal institutionalists and regime theorists is that the whole question of how the economic sector plays into the English School's deeper sense of primary institutions—enduring fundamental practices which shape and constrain the formation, evolution, and demise of secondary institutions—remains unaddressed. Among the consequences of this silence is that consideration of the economic sector either gets confined to the relatively superficial level of secondary institutions or else gets subordinated, as in hegemonic stability theory, to the pluralist's primary institutions of sovereignty and great power management.

It was Bull (1966*b*) who set out the pluralist–solidarist framework, and so his conception of society is a good place to begin. Bull's (1977: 53–7) conception of society comes out of a kind of sociological functionalism in which all human societies must be founded on understandings about security against violence, observance of agreements, and rules about property rights. He sees rules as the key to sharpening up mere common interests into a clear sense of appropriate behaviour (1977: 67–71). The making of rules ranges from the customary to the positive, but whatever type they are, they fall into three levels.

(1) Constitutional normative principles provide the foundation, setting out the basic ordering principle (e.g. society of states, universal empire, state of nature, cosmopolitan community, etc.). In Bull's view what is essential for order is that one of these principles dominates: because the principles are usually zero-sum, contestation equals disorder. Contestation at this level is what defines Wight's revolutionists. For an international society, the key principle is sovereignty. This level is similar to Waltz's (1979) first tier of structure (organizing principle of the system), though Bull's range of possibilities is wider than Waltz's.

(2) Rules of coexistence are those which set out the minimum behavioural conditions for society, and therefore hinge on the basic elements of society: limits to violence, establishment of property rights, and sanctity of agreements. Here we find Bull's 'institutions' of classical European international society: diplomacy, international law, the balance of power, war, and the role of great powers.

(3) Rules to regulate cooperation in politics, strategy, society, and economy (1977: 70). About these Bull says: 'Rules of this kind prescribe behaviour that is appropriate not to the elementary or primary goals of international life, but rather to those more advanced or secondary goals that are a feature of an international society in which a consensus has been reached about a wider range of objectives than mere coexistence' (1977: 70). Here, one would find everything from the UN system, through arms control treaties, to the regimes and institutions for managing trade, finance, environment, and a host of technical issues from postage to allocation of orbital slots and broadcast frequencies.

Note that Bull's first and second levels of rules (constitutional principles and rules of coexistence) define the the de facto pluralist position on international society. Solidarism finds its scope mainly in the third tier of 'more advanced' but 'secondary' rules about cooperation. It is worth keeping this third tier in mind when considering Bull's position in the pluralist–solidarist debate. As presented here, it seems to offer an open-ended scope for the development of solidarism. Yet, in his defence of pluralism, and his fear of solidarism, Bull seems to forget about this third tier. Since this is where the big growth has been in contemporary international society, especially in the economic sector, the placing of this as a kind of shallow third tier comes into question, and the odd juxtaposition of the classifications 'more advanced' but 'secondary' begins to look contradictory. Develop enough down these 'secondary' lines, and the 'more advanced' elements begin to bring the constitutive principles themselves into question. The development of the European Union illustrates this potential, and shows that the two are not necessarily contradictory in the disordering way that Bull seemed to think inevitable.

Why did Bull's underlying concern with order, and his pessimism about its prospects, drive him to box himself into a relatively closed pluralist position when the underlying logic of his concepts does not seem to require doing so? This question is important, because the answer to it frames what solidarism is understood to be, and whether its relationship to pluralism is one of necessary opposition and mutual exclusivity, or one of degrees of difference along a single spectrum of societal development. If liberal international economic orders belong to solidarism, and if solidarism is mutually exclusive to pluralism, then the placement of IPE within the English School becomes extremely problematic.

One explanation for Bull's position, and for the view that pluralism and solidarism are mutually exclusive, is the strong linkage of solidarism to cosmopolitanism that marks much English School thinking. This linkage arises out of political theory concerns (about the relationship between states and peoples), and underpins the almost exclusive concern of solidarists within the English School with the issue of human rights. Sticking with the cosmopolitan view of solidarism confines one to a perilously narrow liberal view in which the issue of human rights dominates what solidarism is understood to be, and casts it into tension with the key pluralist institution of sovereignty. It also leaves one unable to describe as solidarist, international societies that make no concession to individuals as subjects of international law, but which nevertheless display a rich and deep array of shared norms, rules, and institutions, some of which may give individuals extensive rights as objects of international law. On the face of it, the inability to label such international societies as solidarist makes a nonsense of much of what the pluralist–solidarist debate is about in terms of whether international society is limited to mere rules of coexistence or embraces a wider set of norms.

If Bull's rules of cooperation do not provide the key to differentiating pluralism from solidarism, what does? Obviously one cannot go on stretching the meaning of coexistence forever. Just as obviously, solidarism almost certainly builds on the foundations laid down by pluralism, or at least must do so in its early and middle stages, whatever it might evolve into in its more advanced forms. If pluralism is defined by norms of coexistence, then there are two principles on which a departure into solidarism might be constructed. Both could be added to coexistence, yet both also move away from key defining qualities of pluralism.

First, states might abandon the pursuit of difference and exclusivity as their main *raison d'être*, and cultivate becoming more alike as a conscious goal. One might expect that there would be a correlation, on the one hand, between solidarism and a substantial degree of homogeneity among the domestic constitutions of the members, and on the other between diversity in the domestic constitutions of members and pluralism.

Second, states might acknowledge common values among them that go beyond survival and coexistence, and which they agree to pursue by coordinating their policies, undertaking collective action, creating appropriate norms, rules, and organizations, and revising the institutions of interstate society.

The first of these principles reflects a Kantian logic of convergence. The second is suggested by Mayall's (2000: 21) idea of 'an enterprise association . . . that exists to pursue substantive goals of its own'. Mayall clearly thinks that 'pursuing substantive goals of its own' transcends an understanding of pluralism as based on coexistence, and I imagine most pluralists would agree. He links this idea to cosmopolitanism, but that link is not necessary to the idea, and in what follows I will take it as being only one among several possibilities underpinning solidarism. In practice, convergence and pursuit of a joint project will often overlap, sometimes substantially, but this overlap is not a necessary one for all possible scenarios. Mayall's more open understanding of solidarism makes it much easier to see pluralism and solidarism as ends of a spectrum, and therefore opens the way to incorporating the IPE agenda into international society without seeming to call its pluralist foundations into question.

If homogenization is a route to solidarist international societies, then IR theory offers grounds for optimism. Several powerful trends in IR theory note the existence of homogenizing forces, and this would seem to work in favour of the normative approach to international society—at least so long as liberal states are in the ascendant in the international system as the model around which homogenization occurs. Halliday (1992) focuses on the issue of homogenization of domestic structures among states as one of the keys to international (and by implication world) society. He implicitly picks up on themes from Wight, and carries the same blurring of categories: pluralist/realist, transnational/non-state links, and homogenization among states in their internal character and structure. Halliday notes the normative case for homogenization (Burke and democratic peace), the Marxian idea of capitalism as the great homogenizing force, and the Kantian/Fukuyama idea of science and technology and democracy as homogenizing forces. Halliday ignores entirely Waltz's (1979) argument about the operation of socialization and competition as homogenizing forces, an idea I adapted to thinking about international society (Buzan 1993). Interestingly, the Stanford school (Meyer et al. 1997: 144–8) also ignore the powerful homogenizing argument in Waltz. Unlike Halliday, they acknowledge Waltz, but they dismiss him as a 'microrealist' even though they also take the striking isomorphism of the 'like units' of the international system as their key phenomenon for explanation. If homogeneity is overdetermined in the international system, then the implications of this for solidarism need to be more closely investigated. And since economic liberalism is a key aspect of the homogenization game, here too is another strong reason for bringing English School theory and IPE into closer contact.

To sum up, the widespread acceptance of liberal rules for the world economy cannot reasonably be characterized as coexistence. It represents a clear move into the solidarist logic of collective pursuit of shared values (economic growth and development). Placing it there both reinforces the case for seeing pluralism and solidarism as positions on a spectrum rather than as opposites, and expands the breadth of solidarism. It expands it theoretically, by breaking the dependence of solidarism on cosmopolitanism, and opening the way to thinking about solidarism in terms of domestic convergence and/or the pursuit of jointly held values beyond coexistence. It expands it empirically by requiring the inclusion of IPE into English School thinking. Making that inclusion should change the balance of power between pluralists and solidarists within the English School. If the development of a liberal international economic order counts as solidarism, then international society even on a global level looks much more solidarist than if solidarism is only about human rights. Not only that, but if homogenization is an overdetermined quality of state systems, then solidarists have a powerful structural ally. If global markets and all their attendant rules and institutions are part of contemporary international society, then some very hard questions can be put to the pluralists about their contention that international society is confined to coexistence and has little or no developmental potential. And last, but not least, a blow can be struck against the pessimistic renderings of the history of international society that the pluralists have provided. Add in the economic sector, and things look a lot different.

BRINGING IPE INTO INTERNATIONAL SOCIETY:
REGIONS AND INSTITUTIONS

If there are no conceptual obstacles to bringing IPE into the study of international society and many benefits to be gained, the question becomes how best to proceed towards that end. In terms of English School theory, two moves seem necessary. The first, and the most basic to the theory, was already hinted at in the discussion of pluralism and solidarism: the economic sector has to be brought into the English School's conceptualization of the norms, rules, and institutions that constitute international society. In particular, the primary institutions arising within the economic sector need to be identified, and integrated with the English School's discussion of the other primary institutions of international society (sovereignty, international law, diplomacy, balance of power, great power management, nationalism, and war). As I have argued elsewhere (Buzan 2004; also Holsti 2002) this move needs to be part of a general sharpening of the English School's focus on primary institutions. Among other things, bringing the economic sector into this discussion will require a retelling of the English School's account of how international society rose in Europe and spread to global scale. Once this is done, the second move, almost equally important in its consequences, is to open the whole discussion of international society to the subglobal/regional level. The existing English School opus has largely focused on the global level, which is where international society is most likely to be thinnest and pluralist. At the subglobal level the possibilities for solidarism are greater, as demonstrated by the European Union. The tendency in English School thinking has been either to ignore the regional level, or to see it as necessarily threatening to the global level (because different centres would clash for control of the global level, as during the cold war). This is certainly one possibility, but there are others. A subglobal international society could become a vanguard leading the way for the rest. The English School's own story of the expansion of international society can be read in this way. Alternatively, a variety of subglobal international societies might coexist in a type of second-order pluralism, tolerant of or indifferent to each other and sharing a thinner, global-level international society. The economic sector plays significantly into this question of levels, and needs to be incorporated there.

Institutions

The most obvious exemplar of solidarism in the pursuit of joint gains lies in liberal understandings of how to organize the economic sector. In order to realize joint gains, a liberal international economy has to be organized around a host of rules about trade, property rights, legal process, investment, banking, corporate law, and suchlike. According to liberal theory, unless states can cooperate to liberalize trade and finance, they will remain stuck with lower levels of growth and innovation, higher costs, and lower efficiencies than would otherwise be the case. In order to realize these gains, states have to both open their borders and coordinate their behaviours in selected but systematic ways. In other words they have to agree, up to a point, to homogenize their domestic structures. Over the past half-century this has in fact been done to a quite remarkable degree. Although initially subglobal, this development of solidarism is now nearly global in extent. The pursuit of joint gains in the economic sector is in part based on shared belief in the tenets of economic liberalism, but its mainstay is calculations of advantage, and some weaker players are simply coerced into going along. It even includes some significant enforcement measures, thus meeting the hard test of willingness to support the collective enforcement of international law that was one of Bull's (1966*b*: 52) benchmarks for solidarism.

To the extent that the founding fathers of the English School thought at all about the economic sector, the aspect that drew most of their attention was trade. Trade, like war and diplomacy, is a very old practice in human affairs, arguably perhaps *the* oldest candidate for the status of a primary institution defining the relations between the highest level of organized human grouping at any given time (Buzan and Little 2000). Trade (or in some places tribute) was the primary economic institution for much of human history until fairly recent times, often carrying with it secondary institutions such as the particular rights accorded to enclaves of foreign traders in most of the city-states and empires of the ancient and classical world. The picture got more complicated with the rise of Europe and its rapid takeover of the rest of the world. A nascent banking system with increasingly sophisticated means of international financial exchange emerged in late medieval Europe. This was not an unprecedented development, but it did become the one that spread worldwide, in the process adding an ever larger and more complicated world of finance to trade as a core part of economic practice.

Another key development was the emergence in Europe from the eighteenth century of a doctrinal struggle over how best to understand the political economy of interstate relations. On the one side was mercantilism, which was close to the traditional practices of the ancient and classical world. Under mercantilism, states saw themselves in a zero-sum competition with others and sought to maximize their wealth, power, and autonomy, not least by seeking favourable trade balances and the accumulation of specie. Crudely put, mercantilism meant that self-reliance was preferred to trade because the national interest was defined in terms of an ability to wage war. On the other side was liberalism, which held that trade was a good in and of itself, lowering prices, increasing technological innovation, prosperity, and social dynamism, and reducing the incentives for war. Mercantilism enhanced the power of the state, while liberalism elevated the power of the market and a variety of non-state actors. The two represented not only different approaches to solving economic problems, but also markedly different ways of understanding how best to pursue national and international security. They also have radical implications for the standing and interpretation of other primary institutions. Mercantilism is broadly in harmony with sovereignty/non-intervention, balance of power, nationalism, and war. Liberalism has complex effects. It requires sovereignty/non-intervention to be reinterpreted to allow more porous borders. It sits badly with war as a regular practice of great power relations, and therefore creates pressure to narrow the scope of war as an institution of international society. It is also in some tension with nationalism, and the sort of distinctive political projects that rest on nationalist ideas (Mayall 1990). It weakens balance of power as a primary institution, since within a liberal international economic order hegemony might well be acceptable in a way that it would not be under mercantilism. Liberalism in practice greatly increases and extends the content of international law, and from the empirical record also encourages and supports multilateralism as a derivative institution of diplomacy.

From the middle of the nineteenth century there was a battle between these two principles as to which would be the dominant derivative of trade. This battle not only affected the whole character of the IPE, but also radically altered the balance and meaning of the primary institutions of international society. For more than a century this struggle was a, and arguably *the*, central issue of international relations. During the nineteenth century, under pressure from the burgeoning wealth and opportunity generated by the industrial revolution, liberalism made steady gains. Late in the century came the first development of secondary institutions in response to growing trade and communication and the rapid shrinking of the world by technologies of transportation and communication. Although liberalism made gains, late industrializing powers reformulated mercantilism into economic nationalism as a strategy for industrial development. The communist revolution in Russia placed a significant great power strongly in the mercantilist camp and mercantilism had a brief but significant surge during the 1930s with the widespread collapse of the international trading and financial regimes. This development culminated in the Second World War during which the fascist version of mercantilism was defeated. The struggle between mercantilism and liberalism continued on in the guise of the cold war, with the Soviet bloc organized on mercantilist principles, the West increasingly organizing itself and parts of the Third World along liberal lines, with other parts of the Third World playing between the two and exploring their own versions of development via economic nationalism. As far as the great powers were concerned, this struggle largely came to end with the collapse of the Soviet Union, leaving the liberal powers led by the United States as the final victors. Whatever else might be said about it, liberalism had certainly demonstrated that it was a more effective generator of national power over the long haul than any version of mercantilism.

As a result of this long process, the market has emerged clearly as one of the major primary institutions of contemporary international society. The market means more than just trade, or even trade and finance together. It is a principle of organization and legitimation that affects both how states define and constitute themselves, what kind of other actors they give standing to, and how they interpret sovereignty and territoriality. In looking at the institutional structure of contemporary international society there is room for thinking that in many ways the market, its close associate multilateralism, and the host of secondary institutions associated with them, had taken over from war, balance of power, and their derivatives as the institutions that now shaped how sovereignty and territoriality were to be understood. The market does not necessarily eliminate balance of power as an institution, but it does make its operation much more complicated and contradictory than it would be under mercantilist rules, not least by undermining many of the reasons for supporting the principle of anti-hegemonism that underpins the balance of power as a social institution.

War as an institution also becomes more problematic in the presence of the market as a primary institution. This problematization is not derived from technical issues such as the advent of weapons of mass destruction, which might well bring war into question even within interstate societies not having the market as a primary institution. War simply becomes increasingly incompatible with the operation of the market. How is one to link this perspective to the more materialist one made famous by Tilly's phrase that 'war makes the state and the state makes war', which implicitly underpins much realist theorizing about international relations? From this perspective, war is constitutive of states not in the form of a constitutive rule, but as a mechanical, Darwinian structure which favours the survival of more state-like units, and drives into extinction or subordination less state-like ones. If war itself gets driven towards extinction, what then becomes of the state? Although the logics driving this type of structural thinking are different from those underpinning primary institutions in the English School sense, the two do cross paths when one comes to consider the impact of the market. Like war, the market can be seen both as a mechanical structure and as an institution of international society. In both perspectives there are some areas of overlap and complementarity between the two, but also an underlying contradiction that becomes more powerful as the market approaches global scale. War might, up to a point, support the market when the game is to grab control of subglobal shares. But when the market becomes global, war becomes a costly disruption to trade, production, and financial markets. As institutions, war and the market become increasingly incompatible in solidarist international societies. As mechanical structures, they seem also to fall into a zero-sum game for what makes the state and what the state makes. It could well be argued that in contemporary interstate societies it is the market that makes the state and the state that makes markets. To the extent that this is true the shift in balance between these two constitutes not just a shift in the institutions of interstate society, but also a transformation in the Darwinian structures that shape the principal units in the international system (Buzan and Little 2000: 362–7).

In addition to having major impacts on the other institutions of international society, the market also changes the composition of the actors who are in one way or another members of or at least participants in international society. Under liberal rules, both individuals and non-state actors have legal rights against the state even if those rights are granted by the state. In principle, liberalism as a doctrine and the market as a practice favour a minimal state and the maximum liberty for individuals consistent with maintaining social order. In practice this means the empowerment of civil society and the right of people to establish organizations for a wide range of purposes. Translated to the international sphere, this means that state borders have to be permeable to trade, travel, ideas, capital, and a wide range of international non-governmental organizations (INGOs), including multinational firms, interest groups, and lobbies. A liberal international society is likely to open up a substantial transnational space in which transnational actors (TNAs) of various kinds have legal rights and considerable autonomy to act across state borders. This feature creates a strong pressure on states to harmonize their domestic arrangements on a wide range of issues from property rights and border controls to accounting practices and product standards. This pressure, in turn, underlies a tendency towards convergence, and thus a Kantian model of international society.

In a liberal international society, TNAs can (and have) become very powerful actors. Huge global corporations command wealth, resources, and knowledge that surpass that of many of the poorer, weaker states in the system, and pressure even the more powerful states to compete for their investment. Transnational interest groups and lobbies can harass states directly over issues such as human rights and pollution, and a host of quieter TNAs can slowly leach away the authority and character of the state by providing alternative points of reference for its citizens. Because liberalism ties its political legitimacy and fortune to sustained economic growth, the rise of the transnational domain as a crucial element in the global economy itself becomes a crucial element in the wealth, power, and legitimacy of the core capitalist political economies. In parallel with these developments, liberal interstate societies need to promote (and/or allow) the development of a corresponding transnational civil society sufficient to carry the political burden created by moves into wider identities and more global markets. And while liberal solidarist interstate societies will need to encourage transnational *civil* society, the states comprising them will need to adapt themselves by creating IGOs (Inter-Governmental Organizations) to deal both with the complex coordination necessary to manage the market and keep it stable, and with the forces of transnational *uncivil* society to which the processes of integration also give space. In other words, liberal solidarism will be unable to develop far unless the interstate domain can carry with it degrees and types of interhuman and transnational society appropriate to the degree and type of norms, rules, institutions, and identities that they want to share among their members. A liberal interstate society will require parallel developments of cosmopolitanism in the interhuman domain, and of economic and civil society actors in the transnational domain. Without such developments the pursuit of the interstate project will be impossible beyond a rather basic level. In a liberal perspective, more interstate solidarism requires more cosmopolitanism in the interhuman domain and more TNAs, and cooperation among TNAs to support it. Conversely, the desired cosmopolitan developments in the interhuman and transnational domains cannot take place without the provision of law, order, and security from the interstate domain. Liberal solidarism develops as a close nexus among the three domains.

All of this is, of course, the stuff that drives the idea of globalization. At a minimum, the transnational sector becomes a driving force in favour of reinterpreting primary institutions such as sovereignty and non-intervention, and promoting new ones such as the market and human rights. At a maximum, as thought by some globalization enthusiasts, the transnational domain becomes the location of the vanguard driving the social structure of humankind towards some form of world society. It is this approach through primary institutions that provides the link between the English School and the problem of how to study globalization.

Regions

If the argument just made about bringing the economic sector into international society is accepted, then the question arises as to how the idea of primary institutions deriving from that sector shapes the distinction between the global and the regional level. In my view, the neglect of the economic sector and the subglobal/regional level in English School thinking is partly reciprocal. The subglobal level has been less visible because the economic sector was ignored, and the economic sector was ignored in part because of the disinclination to focus on subglobal developments in international society. If the English School had paid more attention to the economic sector, it could not have ignored developments such as the EU, NAFTA, and Mercosur, and if it had paid attention to these regional developments as distinctive instances of international society, it could not have ignored the economic component of international society. Thus bringing the economic sector into international society thinking should raise the profile of the subglobal level, and vice versa.

The general model I am proposing is that in any large, diverse international system in which distance and geography matter, and differences of culture and level of development are substantial, one is likely to find developments of international social structure at both the global and the subglobal/regional level. Given the simple logics of numbers and distance, it is reasonable to expect that as a rule, the development of international social structure will be thicker on the smaller scale (because numbers are smaller, cultural differences fewer, and distance and geography less of a barrier) and thinner on the global one. In this model it is an open question as to what the relationship is between the global and subglobal levels. In principle they could be quite harmonious, with the global level defining a second-order pluralism among the various subglobal international societies. On the other hand, they could be conflictual, with rivalry between subglobal societies dominating the global level. In the case of harmony, the global level could be quite thickly developed. In the case of conflict it will necessarily be thinner. This perspective also opens up the issue of what forces drive the development of the global level, and here one important option is the presence of a subglobal vanguard that leads the development of the global level. That, in turn, raises questions about the binding forces that hold the global level international society together, whether coercion, calculation, belief, or more probably some mixture of these.

IPE already has a well-developed perspective on this layered understanding of international society. In IPE it is broadly accepted that regional economic groupings are both alternatives to a global economic order and ways of operating more effectively within such a global order (Buzan, Wæver, and de Wilde 1998: 112–15). Subglobal social structures thus serve simultaneously as fallback positions in case of structural failure at the global level, and as bastions within which to build stronger players within the global game. Within the framework of the liberal international economic order, subglobal structures play a delicate game both with each other (competitors in some senses, co-dependent in others) and with the global level (too much subglobalism will destroy the global level to the potential disadvantage of all). From an IPE perspective, the European Union, east Asia, and North America all stand out as subglobal interstate societies that are more thickly developed within themselves than is the global level. If one looks through economic lenses, there is thus strong empirical evidence that the distinctive development of interstate societies is flourishing at the subglobal level. What is more, this evidence suggests a balanced assessment of how subglobal interstate developments interact with global international society. There is no simple 'either/or' choice about global and subglobal developments. In the contemporary international system, the thinner global interstate society is shared by all, and the subglobal developments build on top of that. A second-order pluralism is possible when subglobal interstate societies seek rules of coexistence with each other at the global level. Once economic institutions are factored in, there are clearly no grounds for any automatic assumption that subglobal developments must fall into rivalry with each other and so weaken global social developments. This *can* happen, as the cold war showed all too clearly, especially when rival ideologies are in play. Fear of conflict across levels can certainly be found in that body of (mostly liberal) concerns that regional economic blocs will undermine the liberal international economic order at the global level, creating some kind of replay of the 1930s. But against this is the argument that regional economic groupings are mainly responses to the global economic order, and that their existence may well serve to stabilize that order against the periodic instabilities that affect the trading and financial arrangements of all liberal economic orders. Short of that, such blocs offer options to strengthen the position of participating states within the global economy, so creating synergies rather than contradictions between the two levels. The ending of the cold war thus appears as an interesting and important transition in the development of international society. It marks the end of a period of harsh confrontation over economic institutions, and the spread of the market from being a strong but subglobal institution of Western international society, to being an effectively global institution, albeit one held in place as much by Western power as by belief in it in all parts of the international system. The market is still held in place coercively in some parts of the system, and by calculation in others, but it too has a substantial worldwide constituency of believers, more numerous and more influential in some places than in others. What starts out as imperial imposition can become internalized and accepted by those on whom it was imposed, though there is nothing inevitable about this, and imposition can just as easily breed rejection (as demonstrated by the demise of the Soviet Union). Where the values imposed by coercion bring improvement to the lives of peoples, whether in terms of wealth, or power, or social cohesion, they have a chance of enduring beyond the coercion that originally carried them.

There are reasons other than concern about the economic sector in English School thinking for paying more attention to the subglobal/regional level than has so far been the case in the study of international society. The point to be made here is that in relation to contemporary international society, there are particularly strong synergies between the subglobal level and the economic sector.

CONCLUSIONS: THE ENGLISH SCHOOL AND GLOBALIZATION

Having established that there are no good reasons for leaving the economic sector out of the consideration of international society, and having also shown both the high costs of doing so and how IPE and English School thinking can be brought together, the way is now clear to discuss the English School and globalization. The case I want to make is that English School theory should be of interest to all of those in international relations who acknowledge that 'globalization' represents an important way of labelling a set of substantial changes in the international system, but who despair about the analytical vacuousness of 'the "G" word'. English School theory, and particularly its solidarist side, is a good solution to the problems of how to think both analytically and normatively about globalization. It has not so far been much used in this way, in part because it has not taken either the economic sector—still the main element in globalization—or world society—still a Cinderella—properly on board. Once these failings are remedied, the English School's triad of concepts exactly captures the simultaneous existence of state and non-state systems operating alongside and through each other, without finding this conceptually problematic. It keeps the old, while bringing in the new, and is thus well suited to looking at the transition from Westphalian to post-Westphalian international politics, whether this be at the level of globalization or in regional developments such as those in the European Union. Through the study of primary institutions, English School theory can handle the idea of a shift from balance of power and war to market and multilateralism as the dominant institutions of international society, and it provides an ideal framework for examining questions of intervention, whether on human rights or other grounds.

Managing this expansion from interstate to world politics is important to international relations as a discipline. International relations' core strengths are in the state system, and it needs to combine these with other elements of international system, and to avoid ensnaring itself in the trap of unnecessary choices between state and non-state alternatives. In my view, English School theory shows how this can be done better than any available alternative. If this approach is thought to privilege the state, it is not out of line with much mainstream thinking on globalization. There is nothing unusual in privileging the state in this way, and it does not make one a realist to do so. The state remains special because of its central role in the processes of law, organized violence, taxation, political legitimacy, territoriality, and in some ways social identity. This view is, of course, central to all forms of political realism. But there are many other routes, including the English School, to the same conclusion. Marxians, historical sociologists, and IPE have all 'brought the state back in'; the Stanford school (Meyer et al. 1997) reach the same conclusion from a more legal and normative perspective. So too do Brown (1995*a*: 105–6) discussing world community from the perspective of political theory, and Rosenau (1990) with his distinction between 'sovereignty-bound' and 'sovereignty-free' actors.

Ironically, it is the relatively neglected concept of world society that provides the key to linking English School theory to the debate about globalization (Weller 2000: 47). Scholte (2000: 8–9 and 59–61) argues that globalization is defined by a deterritorialization of social life, which has created new actors and networks alongside the existing territorial ones: 'territoriality and supraterritoriality coexist in complex interrelation' (8). The more sensible globalization writers all agree that there is no simple zero-sum game between globalization and the state system. Both Woods (2000) and Held et al. (1999) agree with Scholte's idea that the state system and the non-state system(s) coexist side by side, and argue that states, especially stronger states, have played a major role in bringing globalization into being and steering its development. Some even think that 'the word "globalisation" is really a contemporary euphemism for American economic dominance' (Kapstein 1999: 468; see also Woods 2000: 9). Either way, English School theory is ideally tailored to address this problem because of the way in which it takes on board both the territorial and non-territorial elements. International society covers the system of states as the main political framework for humankind, and the principal provider of law and order. World society covers the cosmopolitan and transnational domains both as allies and confederates of international society (Risse 2002), and as opponents to it (Vincent 1978: 28; Anheier, Glasius, and Kaldor 2001: 15), and the normative side of English School theory is able to handle the fact that globalization has both a positive side and a dark one, and that there are strong differences of view on what belongs in which category. The English School's ability to think about the state and non-state domains within a single theoretical frame is what makes it attractive as an approach to globalization.

Many other users of the term 'world society' use it as a near synonym for globalization (Burton 1972; Luard 1990; WSRG 1995; Meyer et al. 1997; see discussion in Buzan 2004: ch. 3). Some approaches to IPE also take this holistic line: Cox (1986, 1994), Strange (1988), and Underhill (2000) all talk about the close interlinkage of states and markets, and try to unfold a conceptualization that expresses the simultaneous interplay of political, economic, and social forces. These approaches try to understand world society, or the IPE, as the whole package of state and non-state all bundled together as a single nexus. There are some in the English School who also take this view (Vincent 1978: 37; 1992: 253–61), wanting 'world' to be used as a holistic umbrella term to include everything in the international system, state, non-state, and individual. Rengger (1992: 366–9) also argues for incorporating the narrow idea of international society into a cosmopolitan frame. On analytical grounds, I oppose any attempt to lump too much together under a single heading. The rather sorry condition of the globalization debate stands as a warning against creating intellectual dustbins. I have no problem with holism, but the 'whole' should be composed of analytically distinct parts whose operation and interaction becomes the subject of study. Wholes that subsume everything within them have the same attractions and the same drawbacks as the idea of god—they explain everything and nothing.

My inclinations lean towards the strategy of Rosenau (1990) and Bull (1977), which is to find the point of interest in the balance between the state and the non-state worlds. In some future that I will certainly not live to see, the state may well become obsolete, and humankind may well find itself organized in some deterritorialized neomedieval form. In the meantime we seem to be in the presence of a shift away from a Westphalian mode of international relations, in which the key tension is among rival states. For now, and for some decades to come, the interesting question is about how the state and the non-state worlds interact with each other. What makes this question interesting is more than just shifts in the distribution of power, or immediate relevance to real world events. On top of these is the deep and excruciating tension between the state and non-state worlds. In some ways they are profoundly antagonistic, both in concept and in practice. In other ways they are heavily interdependent, again both in concept and in practice. This tension, it seems to me, is the big political question of our time, and in order to get at it analytically, it is vital to keep the two worlds conceptually distinct. English School theory, if properly revised, is exceptionally well suited to this task. It keeps a view of the whole without losing sight of the parts. Through English School lenses one can see the state, transnational, and cosmopolitan domains all in play with each other, and not just in the political sector, but also in the economic and social ones. This, it seems to me, is how we need to approach the study of globalization.

7

Critical Security Studies

Paul Williams

In 1994, Fred Halliday chastized the English School for its preoccupation with 'kings and queens, congresses and battles, treaties and laws' (1994: 26). As if in response, recent work within the English School tradition has addressed Halliday's concerns (Buzan and Little 2000). More recently, several prominent 'insiders' have urged their schoolmates to draw more heavily upon critical theory in order to develop the English School's wide-ranging but loosely defined research agenda (see Linklater 1990, 1998; Wheeler 1996; Little 2000; Buzan 2001). Substantial efforts have already been made to integrate the English School's concept of international society with realist and constructivist approaches to international relations (for instance Buzan 1993; Reus-Smit 1999, 2002). In comparison, critical approaches have been left relatively unexplored. But according to Richard Little (2000: 414), a debate has recently emerged within the English School that 'has taken on a critical theory dimension' and which 'reflects a profound concern about the potential for human emancipation'. So far, however, this debate has remained predominantly state-centric in its terms of reference, and preoccupied with the concept of intervention and discerning the most appropriate occasions when military force should be deployed under the banner of humanitarianism (for instance Wheeler 1992, 1996, 2000; Jackson 1993; Roberts 1993; Dunne 2001). And despite calls from some insiders (such as Wheeler 1996: 132), the English School has been virtually silent about the economic, gender, racial, and ecological dimensions that must form an integral part of any project of human emancipation.

Addressing these issues undoubtedly represents an important part of 'filling the gaping gaps' in the English School's 'original research programme' (Little 2000: 398). This chapter, however, concentrates upon the English School's understanding of security, which, as Hedley Bull noted, is one of the 'elementary or primary goals' of social life—without security against violence there can be no society (1977: 4). I submit that in order to help develop its apparently 'profound concern for human emancipation' and its concept of world society, the English School could usefully engage in a dialogue with the literature emerging under the umbrella label of

I would like to thank Alex Bellamy, Barry Buzan, and Richard Devetak for their constructive comments on earlier drafts of this chapter.

Critical Security Studies (CSS). After providing a brief description of CSS, this chapter compares its approach with the English School's answers to four funda-mental questions about security, taking the work of Hedley Bull as its primary point of reference.[1] I suggest that although Bull's work shares several concerns with the emerging CSS agenda and provides some useful avenues and pertinent insights for exploring questions of security in world politics, neither he nor subsequent genera-tions of the English School have devoted much energy to developing them further. Obviously, Bull dedicated much of his own time to analysing the military dimensions of security in international politics but his work contains fewer insights into the non-military and non-state dimensions of security. This may be because, as Bull (1977: 146) noted on more than one occasion, the pursuit of genuine security for human beings is necessarily subversive of the very foundations of international society.

WHAT IS CRITICAL SECURITY STUDIES?

There appear to be two rather different ways in which CSS is understood (Wyn Jones 1999: p. ix). First, CSS has been used as a typological device referring to all approaches critical of the prevailing realist-inspired orthodoxy within security studies. Altern-atively, some understand CSS as a distinct project in its own right that is based on a commitment to promoting emancipatory theories and practices of security. These two different meanings are reminiscent of Chris Brown's (1994) distinction between 'critical theories' (lower case) in the more generic sense of the entire list of anti-foundational approaches, and 'Critical Theory' (capitalized) in its Frankfurt School sense. This chapter adopts this capitalized, Frankfurt School-inspired understanding of what the 'Critical' of CSS is and should be about.

The immediate origins of the CSS label lie in two recent developments: the end of the cold war; and major debates within the social sciences in general and international relations in particular, as to their nature, method, and purpose. As one analysis noted, 'given the symbiotic relationship between Security Studies and the cold war, it is not surprising that the end of the latter has led to a crisis in the former' (Bilgin, Booth, and Wyn Jones 1998: 141). In contrast to realist-inspired perspectives, CSS aims to develop an approach to the theory and practice of security that is dedicated to the promotion of emancipatory politics. This has led proponents of CSS to analyse forms of domination and insecurity that have either been ignored or marginalized by realist-inspired security studies. This has involved a reconceptualization of security that is (*a*) *Focused*: the theory and practice of security should promote emancipatory politics; (*b*) *Deeper*: security is understood as a derivative concept inasmuch as different understandings of world politics will deliver different conceptions of what security means and who are its ultimate referents; and (*c*) *Broader*: the threat and use of military force is neither the only (or necessarily most important) threat to security, nor the only means of providing security (see Wyn Jones 1999).

At a deliberately general and abstract level, Ken Booth (2004*b*) has defined CSS as:

Both a theoretical commitment and a political orientation. As a theoretical commitment it embraces a set of ideas engaging in a critical and permanent exploration of the ontology, epistemology and praxis of security, community and emancipation in world politics. As a political orientation it is informed by the aim of enhancing security through emancipatory politics and networks of community at all levels, including the potential community of communities—common humanity.

This entails a commitment to both perpetual criticism of the dominant understandings and practices of security—a commitment Bull apparently shared (Dunne 1998: 140)—and a reconstructive element to re-vision what security and security policies might look like in different parts of the world. CSS thus seeks to prioritize emancipatory politics and the building of community by embracing Critical Theory and the normative dimensions of radical traditions in international relations proposed by world society thinking, feminist theorizing, peace research, social idealism, and Third World security specialists (see Booth 2004*a*, *b*).

To date, the CSS agenda has centred on four tasks: to provide critiques of traditional theory, to explore the meanings and implications of critical theories, to investigate security issues from critical perspectives, and to re-vision security in specific places (Booth 1997: 108). Arguably, the CSS project will stand or fall on how effectively it can fulfil the last of these tasks and provide viable alternative visions and security policies in different parts of the world. This is already underway but there is little room for optimism, especially within the confines of an agenda currently dominated by the US-led 'war on terrorism' (see Tickner 1992, 1995; van Aardt 1993; Booth and Vale 1995, 1997; Vale 1996, 2003; Swatuk and Vale 1999; Stamnes and Wyn Jones 2000; Booth 2004*a*, *b*; Stamnes 2004). The need to undertake empirical investigation of real historical contexts is something CSS shares with the English School but the former aims to do so without bringing the ethnocentric baggage that the latter has been accused of carrying (Little 2000: 414–5; Dunne 2001: 242).

CSS can be most closely identified with Wight's revolutionist tradition and more recent solidarist approaches to international and world society in English School theorizing, especially R. J. Vincent's (1986*a*) focus on the need to fulfil the 'basic rights' of all individuals to security and subsistence. Indeed, Kantian ideas underpin many of the central assumptions of CSS (see Booth and Wheeler 1992; Williams and Booth 1996) and its proponents are committed to a notion of common humanity as opposed to ideas of cultural or communitarian essentialism (Booth 1999). Despite recent claims that the English School is best characterized as epitomizing intellectual pluralism rather than a commitment to the rationalist tradition per se (Little 2000), the sympathies of its key architects such as Martin Wight and Hedley Bull clearly lay with the rationalist and to a lesser extent realist traditions, and there is general agreement that the main thrust of the School's work has been rationalist (Buzan 2001: 476). By comparison, the revolutionist tradition has received short shrift. Moreover, when revolutionism and the related concept of world society have been explored, a large degree of incoherence has been evident in the approaches of various English School theorists, including R. J. Vincent (see Buzan

2001: 477). And given the significant differences between Wight's ideas on revolutionism and recent work from the English School's solidarist wing, it is doubtful whether the latter should be characterized as the heirs apparent of Wight's conception of revolutionism.[2] Nevertheless, if the English School is indeed committed to promoting ideological pluralism, it is the Kantian/revolutionist tradition, the related concept of world society, and solidarist approaches to international society that stand in most serious need of conceptual and historical treatment. Engaging in a constructive dialogue with the emerging CSS literature would constitute a step in this direction. Encouragingly, there are signs that such a dialogue is underway (see Dunne and Wheeler 2004).

The rest of this chapter illustrates the CSS approach and how it relates to some of the central assumptions of the English School. It does so with specific reference to four fundamental questions about security, namely: what is security? Whose security are we talking about? What counts as a security issue? And, who or what can provide security?

WHAT IS SECURITY?

Both the English School and CSS see the concept of security as being of fundamental importance to the study of world politics. Both approaches also share Emma Rothschild's (1995) view that security is a process as much as a condition and throughout history this process has focused on determining the most appropriate relationship between individuals and political communities. 'Unless men enjoy some measure of security against the threat of injury or death at the hands of others,' Bull observed, 'they are not able to devote energy or attention enough to other objects to be able to accomplish them' (1977: 5). Yet despite the fact that Bull's work left open some potentially promising avenues for exploring the theory and practice of security, with few exceptions (Makinda 1997), English School theorists have not felt the need to elaborate upon the way in which they understand this central concept, presumably because during the cold war at least, they felt the ground had been well trodden by the political realists such as Arnold Wolfers (1962) and later Barry Buzan (1983).

In definitional terms, Bull does not shed much light upon his own conception of security. In international politics at least, he defines security as meaning 'no more than safety: either objective safety, safety which actually exists, or subjective safety, that which is felt or experienced' (1977: 18). However, since Bull appears to use the two words (security and safety) interchangeably this does not clarify his conception but instead merely shifts the debate onto an alternative semantic plane. More revealing is the next sentence: 'What states seek to make secure or safe is not merely peace, but their independence and the continued existence of the society of states itself which that independence requires'. Throughout the rest of *The Anarchical Society*, Bull makes clear his preference for a Grotian conception of security that is concerned primarily with promoting order within the society of states.

But this is not all Bull has to offer to students of security. As Samuel Makinda (1997) has argued, Bull's potential contribution to more critical approaches to security has been overlooked. Specifically, Bull's framework of analysis and some of his later work on justice implicitly provides for a wide-ranging agenda for security studies encompassing individuals, human rights, culture, the economy, and the environment. This might seem an odd claim given that the major figure in the CSS project has been one of the fiercest critics of the society of states (Booth 1995). Nevertheless, although the majority of Bull's work addressed the military dimensions of international security, notably disarmament, arms control, and nuclear proliferation, he also emphasized the need for international society to address poverty, injustice, and the unfair distribution of power and economic resources between the North and South (Bull 2000), sentiments that resonate with much contemporary work within CSS. Bull also confirmed the derivative nature of security through his argument that the policies of nuclear deterrence were merely one particular set of means for addressing the fundamental political issue of how the great powers should relate to one another within an international society (Makinda 1997: 10). In this sense, Makinda (1997: 2) argued that 'Bull indirectly helped establish a foundation for critical security theory'.

So although for the majority of his career Bull's sympathies undoubtedly lay with a Grotian defence of international society, his framework for analysis (based on Wight's realist, rationalist, and revolutionist traditions) provides avenues for other analysts to explore and develop the Kantian defence of security understood in terms of promoting emancipation, individual justice, and world society. At this philosophical level, CSS shares many concerns with the revolutionist tradition and those English School theorists more inclined to defend the solidarist conception of international society (Vincent 1986a; Wheeler 2000).

As noted above, CSS sees security and emancipation as being intimately related. The most concerted effort to think through the relationship between the two concepts within CSS has come from Ken Booth. Initially, Booth (1991) saw security and emancipation as 'two sides of the same coin' but now prefers to think in terms of security being the means, and emancipation as an end, in much the same way as Gandhi saw the relationship between *ahimsa* (non-violence) and 'Truth'. 'In a similar spirit', Booth (2004b) argues, 'to practise security (reducing the threats that impose life-determining conditions of insecurity on individuals and groups) is to promote emancipation (freedom from oppression, and so some opportunity to explore being human), and to realize emancipation (becoming fully human) is to practise security (opening up space in which people can feel safe from threats, and so act accordingly)'.

Booth (1999: 41–5) has defined emancipation in both negative and positive terms. In negative terms, emancipation cannot be defined in some timeless fashion, as a unitary, end-point to human history but instead 'recognises that every emancipation creates a new margin, just as every technological fix only creates new problems'. Emancipation is thus not a state of being but a condition of becoming. Nor can emancipation be defined at some else's expense, except, that is, those who benefit materially from oppression. However, drawing on Aristotle, Booth suggests that arguably even the beneficiaries of oppression are being freed spiritually. Finally, emancipation must not be seen as synonymous with Westernization. While some advances to emancipation have emerged from the West, it must not be viewed as holding a monopoly on wisdom. In positive terms, Booth identifies three roles for the concept of emancipation. First, because all claims to knowledge rest on something, emancipation should provide a philosophical *anchorage* that will serve as a point of reference to evaluate the current practices of world politics, and help identify better possibilities latent within the current order.[3] Emancipation should also be seen as a strategic process. Booth's preference is to identify and take reformist steps 'calculated to make a better world somewhat more probable for future generations' instead of attempting to construct grandiose blueprints of a utopian future. In practice, some positions are more emancipatory than others (although this may not always be clear at the time) and even those writers who deny the existence of progress theoretically usually behave as though it exists. Finally, emancipatory politics should be seen as a tactical goal that requires specific policies and 'clever and committed human agency'. Emancipation for Booth is thus both easy and difficult: it 'is easy because we know what it is not; it is difficult because we do not know with the same confidence what it looks like in terms of specific struggles'.

In practice, emancipation will become manifest in different ways across time and space. At its heart, however, remains the Kantian notion that *I* cannot be fully emancipated until *everybody* is emancipated (Williams and Booth 1996: 79). Thus, by defining security in terms of emancipation rather than the themes of power or order associated with realism and rationalism, CSS offers one avenue for developing the English School's neglected revolutionist tradition.

WHOSE SECURITY?

The meanings given to 'security' emerge from intellectually prior accounts of who or what is to be secured. Without a referent object there can be no threats and no discussion of security because the concept is meaningless without something to secure. As noted above, Bull's 'implicit defence of the states system' (1977: 307) does not necessarily mean that he saw states as the ultimate referent object of security. And despite the English School's preoccupation with states, the common analogy depicting states as 'eggs' within the 'egg-box' of international society is more accurately understood as seeing states as the 'egg-shells' protecting 'their' citizens (the yolk and egg-white). After all, egg-shells are worth very little in their own right if they protect a rotten interior. What this strained analogy is meant to suggest is that even according to their own terms of reference, English School theorists agree with proponents of CSS that states are simply a means to achieving the end of security for human beings. This was a position that was implicit in *The Anarchical Society*. As Wheeler (1996: 126) observed, 'Although he does not spell it out, the logic of Bull's position is that the rules and norms of the society of states are only to be valued if they provide for the security of individuals who stand at the centre of Bull's ethical code' (see also Dunne 1998: 146). CSS simply spells out this logic and seeks openly to defend the position that human beings are the ultimate referent of security (see Booth 1991; Smith 1991; Tickner 1995; McSweeney 1999). But human beings are not the isolated, society-less, *homo economicus* of neoliberal theory. Rather, proponents of CSS recognize that although 'security is an objective of individuals', it 'can only be achieved in a collective political process' (Rothschild 1995: 70).

So while acknowledging the importance of collective identities and community, CSS maintains that human beings are the ultimate referents of security because it is only with reference to real people that the concept of security has any meaning. The point has been well made by Bill McSweeney who has argued that the ultimate referent of security can *only* be human beings. 'It would be absurd,' McSweeney (1999: 33) claims:

> to postulate a subject of security other than people, even for the scientists of [the] 'golden age' [of security studies]. It is from the human need to protect human values that the term 'security' derives its meaning . . . and that a security policy derives its legitimacy and power to mobilize resources. The primacy of the state in the political science tradition has permitted a gap to develop between the meaning of the term 'security' as applied to individuals and its meaning for the state. In effect, the means have become the end; the object has become the subject of security when the state is made its ultimate referent.

In short, 'security must make sense at the basic level of the individual human being for it to make sense at the international level' (McSweeney 1999: 16).

The important praxeological question then becomes: which human beings should students of security focus upon? The English School, including its most solidarist members, has traditionally focused upon the perceptions and histories of diplomats and statesmen to provide them with the raw material to understand how world politics works. But from a CSS perspective, adopting this top-down view of the history and structures of world politics does not provide a sound basis on which to understand the realities and dynamics of insecurity that persist throughout the globe. This requires placing the experiences of those rendered insecure by the present world order at the centre of the agenda (Tickner 1995; Wyn Jones 1995). To borrow from Edward Said (1994: 84), CSS therefore 'ought to remain an organic part of an ongoing experience in society: of the poor, the disadvantaged, the voiceless, the unrepresented, the powerless'. In this vein, its proponents should publicly raise embarrassing questions, confront orthodoxy and dogma (rather than produce them), avoid being easily co-opted by governments or corporations, and help represent all those people and issues that are routinely forgotten or swept under the rug (Said 1994: 9).

Obviously, at a conceptual level the need to focus upon those individuals and groups who are currently rendered insecure by the prevailing structures and practices of world politics presents students of security with a potentially overwhelming agenda. But what seems problematic at an abstract level may be far less so in practice. And after all, 'it is in the crucible of political practice that critical theories meet the ultimate test of vitality' (Nancy Fraser in Wyn Jones 1995: 299). Analysts must therefore remain sensitive to 'the immediacies of the context that set priorities in particular settings' and openly acknowledge that their choice of referent is a political act

(Falk 1995: 140). Starting points, far from being neutral, have consequences. As Booth and Vale (1997: 335) have argued in relation to southern Africa,

> The definition of the primary security referent(s) in southern Africa is not a value-free, objective matter of 'describing the world as it is'—as it has been falsely characterised in traditional realist theory. It is, as the region's history so tragically shows, a profoundly political act. Whatever definition emerges has enormous implications for the theory and practice of regional security, and not least in terms of identifying threats.

It is the issue of threats and security agendas that occupies the next section.

WHAT IS A SECURITY ISSUE?

As Barry Buzan (1991: 370) correctly observed, the word 'security' remains an incredibly 'powerful political tool in claiming attention for priority items in the competition for government attention ... [This in turn] also helps to establish a consciousness of the importance of issues so labelled in the minds of the population at large'. These powerful political qualities mean that what gets onto and what gets left off different security agendas will reflect the interests of certain individuals and groups over others and thus have significant repercussions.

The security studies literature is replete with analysts claiming that, especially after the cold war, the focus on the military defence of 'the state' was replaced with a 'new', broader range of security issues. But those who talk of the so-called new security issues demonstrate a fundamentally limited understanding of security, even as it relates to the explicitly transnational dimensions of the concept. Poverty, malnutrition, disease, crime, environmental degradation, migration, and so on, as well as war and other forms of violence, have always been security issues for the individuals and groups affected by them. Labelling these issues part of a 'new security agenda' merely highlights the limitations of traditional security theories and how they have lagged far behind the realities of world politics. In particular, they ignore the fact that state security agendas have never been solely about resisting military attack. To take the archetypal example, even during the cold war, whatever the academic experts professed, US officials clearly understood 'national security' as embracing political, economic, ideological, and even developmental dimensions that were inextricably related to the military issues.

With its emphasis on interpretivist methods of understanding the activities of statesmen, the English School's analytical framework is well suited to exploring the intersubjective processes through which certain issues become represented in official discourse as 'threats' to be secured against. To borrow Andrew Hurrell's (1999: 263) formulation, the 'politics of security' need to be scrutinized in order 'to analyse the political processes by which issues come to be defined in terms of threats; identify the actors that are involved in the process of securitization and their relative power; and [remain] alert to whose interests are being served by treating issues as security issues'. In one sense, a significant portion of the diplomatic investigations carried out by English School theorists provides insights into how diplomatic discourse prioritizes certain issues over others—sometimes explicitly invoking the idea of a national security agenda—and how the demands of national, international, and sometimes world security are continually weighed against other concerns, including the search for prosperity and legitimacy, the promotion of human rights, and the benefits of acting in accordance with international law.

Within security studies debate on this topic has been virtually captured by Ole Wæver's notion of securitization. Bull and other English School theorists appear to implicitly share many of the assumptions explicitly articulated by Wæver's theoretical notion of security as a 'speech act'. Specifically, like Wæver, the English School accepts that it is the intersubjective policy-making process conducted by holders of high office that determine what counts as a security issue. Bull would therefore have been quite comfortable adopting a broad understanding of security. Other English School insiders, however, have suggested that 'coercive force and social violence between states or other social groups needs to be understood according to its own distinctive logic and, as such, to remain at the heart of security analysis' (Hurrell 1999: 262).

Wæver's (1995) notion of security as a 'speech act' attempts to reconcile the derivative and intersubjective nature of the concept with a concern to prevent an endless broadening of the intellectual agenda. In later collaborative work the argument developed that to count as a security issue potential threats have to meet strictly defined criteria: 'they have to be staged as existential threats to a referent object by a securitizing actor who thereby generates endorsement of emergency measures beyond rules that would otherwise bind' (Buzan, Wæver, and de Wilde 1998: 5). From this perspective, security is about survival; it is when an issue is depicted as posing an existential threat to a designated referent object. The sentiment invoked is that, 'if we do not tackle this problem, everything else will be irrelevant (because we will not be here or we will not be free to deal with it in our own way)' (Buzan, Wæver, and de Wilde 1998: 24). The crucial ingredient is that a specific audience accepts the claims of the 'securitizing actor'. In other words, there can be 'securitizing moves' without achieving securitization. Successful securitization requires an audience to accept that the breaking of the rules is legitimate in the face of an existential threat and entails three core components: existential threats, emergency procedures, and 'effects on interunit relations by breaking free of the rules' (Buzan, Wæver, and de Wilde 1998: 26). In theory, 'no one conclusively "holds" the power of securitization' but in practice 'the field is structured or biased' in favour of states (Buzan, Wæver, and de Wilde 1998: 31). Curiously, Buzan et al.'s 'defence' of a broad security agenda is followed by a warning:

Although in one sense securitization is a further intensification of politicization … in another sense it is opposed to politicization. Politicization means to make an issue appear to be open, a matter of choice, something that is decided upon and that therefore entails responsibility, in contrast to issues that either could not be different (laws of nature) or should not be put under political control (e.g. a free economy, the private sphere, and matters for expert decision). By contrast, securitization on the international level … means to present an issue as urgent and existential, as so important that it should not be exposed to the normal haggling of politics but should be dealt with decisively by top leaders prior to other issues. (Buzan, Wæver, and de Wilde 1998: 29)

More security is therefore not necessarily 'better'. In fact, 'security should be seen as a negative, as a failure to deal with issues as normal politics' (Buzan, Wæver, and de Wilde 1998: 29). Instead, security analysts should be in the business of 'desecuritization', that is not having issues framed as 'threats against which we have countermeasures' but to move them out of this threat–defence sequence and into the ordinary (and implicitly more cooperative) public sphere (Wæver 1995).

From a CSS perspective, there are at least three problems with this approach. First, by conceptualizing security in terms of human emancipation, CSS challenges the 'us-versus-them' mentality which underpins Wæver et al.'s understanding of securitization (Bilgin, Booth, and Wyn Jones 1998: 148). Once security is conceived in emancipatory terms, securitization ceases to be a necessarily dangerous development. Indeed, securitization may well be very positive given the considerable mobilizing potential of the term security and the fact that leaving problems that many individuals and groups consider threats to their security to be dealt with through normal political channels is a conservative move that privileges status quo interests over those seeking radical change. To give just one example, in the case of the apartheid regime in South Africa, advocating for problems to be solved through 'the normal haggling of politics' (i.e. desecuritization) would have delegitimized the struggles of a majority of the country's citizens to take emergency measures, break the political rules, and effectively resist apartheid oppression. In response to Buzan et al., CSS thus poses the question 'securitization for whom?'

Second, CSS challenges the idea that existential threats can be singled out and dealt with in isolation from other threats and issues. In practice, 'threats' rarely emerge from a single source; the political process of their construction inevitably involves striking a balance between several interrelated issues. As Kenneth Boulding explained in relation to the great issues of war and peace, 'everything has multiple causes and effects, ... the attempt to identify the sole cause of anything is [thus] doomed to frustration' (1979: 47). Combine this insight with a broad (more realistic) understanding of security and threats can soon proliferate. This messier view of threat agendas and a proliferation of equally serious risks challenges the logic of security proposed by Wæver et al. (Huysmans 1998: 501).

Third, once security is understood as an intersubjective concept, acts of securitization quickly proliferate with all kinds of social groups attempting to securitize issues that they regard as engendering insecurity (Bilgin, Booth, and Wyn Jones 1998: 148). CSS accepts that security issues will exist (and acts of securitization occur) wherever human beings, as individuals and groups, feel threatened to the extent that their survival and ways of being are jeopardized. The crucial determinant in deciding what constitutes a security issue is thus the intellectually prior selection of whose security we are talking about and, crucially, who benefits, and who loses out, from particular acts of securitization. The praxeological problem facing analysts and policy-makers alike involves deciding which referents to prioritize and how best to resolve multiple and often competing claims to security. Here, both the English School and CSS agree there can be no doctrinaire answer; it is also necessary to analyse specific historical contexts. Ultimately, however, whereas classical English School thinkers were generally content with preserving order within the society of states, CSS suggests that such conflicts can only genuinely be resolved by encouraging a process of emancipation that does not take international order as the primary value.

WHAT IS TO BE DONE?

Praxeological issues have traditionally maintained 'only a marginal presence in the classical English School literature' (Dunne 2001: 225). Indeed, Bull (1977: 308) suggested that the search for 'solutions' or 'practical advice' was 'a corrupting element in the contemporary study of world politics'. Similarly, the participants of the *Expansion of International Society* project also acknowledged that 'their comparative advantage was in taking a broad brush to the canvass of' international politics (Dunne 1998: 184). More recently, however, English School theorists have expressed considerable interest in whether their ideas 'can provide a moral compass to those in high office facing a choice between competing moral values' (Dunne 2001: 225). Thus, when English School theorists have offered 'practical advice' they have sought to gain a hearing within the corridors of power and the ears of statesmen and diplomats.

But what sort of advice is likely to help provide security and, crucially, are the English School right to suggest it should be given to statesmen? Two issues are especially relevant here. First, does global security require a society of states or can the progressive communities necessary for genuine security be constructed outside (or indeed alongside) international society? And, if so, what are the most appropriate agents to construct progressive communities in world politics?

A serious disjuncture currently exists between the expanding normative ambitions of international society and the political structures on which effective responses continue to depend (Hurrell 1999: 271). It is therefore difficult to be optimistic about the prospects for emancipatory politics and addressing both broad and deep security agendas through existing political structures. Nevertheless, security policies must start from 'here' in order to inch towards 'there'. Since for Bull, the society of states was neither declining nor 'dysfunctional in relation to basic human purposes' (1977: 307), states would and should remain the most important agents of, and framework for, security. Echoing Bull's pluralist defence of international society (and the ethical choices that go with it), Robert Jackson (2000) has argued that the society of states remains the optimal configuration for ensuring global security. But within Bull's 'implicit defence of the states system', he acknowledged that the search for world order, or security for the planet's people, was more fundamental, primordial, and morally prior to the pursuit of order between states. He also recognized the ways in which governments engaged in 'a conspiracy of silence ... about the rights and duties of their respective citizens' to ensure their own coexistence (1977: 308).

At the heart of this issue lies the question of whether a society of (modern, sovereign) states is a prerequisite for world or individual security. Both the English School and advocates of CSS accept that a degree of order is necessary for the provision of security (although the latter are more overtly critical of the prevailing international order). To be secure, as Rothschild (1995: 89) has observed, human beings need the 'predictability and repetitiveness' of a political community. Whereas it is often assumed that the English School saw this as being synonymous with preserving modern international society, there have been renewed attempts within the School to demonstrate the flexibility of its concepts and framework of analysis for thinking about contemporary forms of community that are not based solely on the modern sovereign state (for instance Linklater 1998; Buzan and Little 2000; Diez and Whitman 2002). CSS also envisages that order is possible through stateless forms of relations between communities. According to Booth (2004*b*)

A community is a free association of individuals, recognizing their solidarity in relation to common conceptions of what it is to live an ethical life. Such a community is not essentially defined by territory, though does not exclude living in a common locality. A progressive community recognizes that people have multiple identities, and that a person's identity cannot be sensibly limited to one attribution (except in functional situations such as passport control or public lavatories). Communities recognizing multiple identities celebrate human equality rather than cultural difference.

The fundamental difficulty, of course, lies in building communities that respect outsiders and are capable of devising security policies in cooperation with them rather than against them. But there are historical examples of this type of thinking being put into practice. The obvious parallel to draw here is with the various attempts during the cold war—from non-offensive defence to Gorbachev's 'new thinking'—to think through how security could be achieved without generating insecurity in others. In particular, Olaf Palme's (1982: p. ix) call for 'common security' is still relevant today, particularly the suggestion that protagonists 'must achieve security not against the adversary but together with him. International security must rest on a commitment to joint survival rather than on the threat of mutual destruction'. Such thinking remains evident in, among other places, the multiple calls for states to adopt foreign policies that take multilateralism, dialogue, and cooperation seriously, and in the OSCE's notion of 'cooperative security'.

In a practical sense, modern Africa also provides numerous examples, some positive, some negative, of non-state forms of political community interacting with one another in the search for security. Christopher Clapham (1996), for instance, has highlighted the ongoing development of a 'new international relations of statelessness' in Africa where international organizations, NGOs, and a variety of transnational insurgencies now commonly occupy centre-stage. Similarly, Jeffrey Herbst (2000: ch. 2) has observed how until relatively recently central governments in Africa were able to separate ownership and control of 'their' land. Control of territory was often not contested between central governments because their limited ability to 'broadcast power' combined with the large amounts of open land allowed individuals and groups who felt persecuted by 'their' state to simply move (geographically) to areas beyond its power. And even today, significant numbers of individuals and groups in southern Africa continue to deal with life's insecurities outside of the structures and institutions erected by their local states. As Peter Vale (2003: ch. 6) has argued, ordinary southern Africans have lost faith in, and increasingly bypass, a state system that 'neither delivers security nor satisfies a desire for community'. Consequently, they have found alternative forms of regional intercourse based on religious affiliations, trading associations, musicology, and migration patterns, all of which cross the political borders erected by southern Africa's states. In short, security may require a degree of 'predictability and repetitiveness' but there is no a priori reason why this could not be attained within a world of overlapping networks of political communities other than nation-states. The more fundamental, arguably irresolvable problem is that even progressive communities will have what Bull (1977: 221) called their 'custodians and guarantors' that themselves will require constant scrutiny.

Since states are unlikely to (intentionally) put themselves out of business it is not surprising that many analysts maintain that they represent the most important agents of security, at least in the short term. Initially at least, Bull placed considerable responsibility for international security upon the shoulders of the great powers. Later, however, he described them as 'the great irresponsibles' and voiced his scepticism about the ability of states to act as solidarist agents (Bull 2000: 223). But his work is usually remembered as defending the central role of states as the primary agents of security, a position that finds substantial support within today's English School. Andrew Hurrell (1999: 261 and 270), for instance, contends that it is only states that possess the legitimate coercive capacity necessary to deal with issues such as collective security and humanitarian intervention (see also Dunne 1998: 190).[4]

But while states remain central to the military dimensions of security, their centrality is much less obvious in relation to the concept's non-military dimensions. This has led some English School theorists to argue that while faith in states per se may be misplaced, states of a particular sort, namely, 'good international citizens', can be crucial agents of security for both their citizens and foreigners (see Linklater 1992b; Wheeler and Dunne 1998b). This is a position that some proponents of CSS share. Caroline Thomas (2000: 123), for example, has argued that democratic states have crucial roles to play in ensuring that the institutions and processes of global governance promote rather than threaten human security, especially in the short term.

In response, one might ask why much faith should be placed in purportedly 'good international citizens' that ignore genocide, turn a blind eye to human wrongs committed by their allies, and are content to sit atop an undemocratic global economic order that keeps the majority of the planet destitute and encourages a form of consumerism that is endangering the biosphere? All these strategies of seeking security through states are in essence trying to speak truth—or at least 'moderation' (Dunne 1998: 182)—to power in the hope of altering the behaviour of powerful states. Such strategies have been derided by radical critics of powerful states such as Noam Chomsky (1996: 56–61) as being 'hardly more than a form of self-indulgence' that is often a 'waste of time' and a 'pointless pursuit'. On the other hand, one theme that emerged from the 2001 Oxford Amnesty lectures was the need to take seriously the state's 'potential for helping to solve, as well as create' human wrongs (Owen 2003: 24). But in so doing those who try to speak truth to power risk (often unintentionally) adopting agendas set by the powerful and discussing the problems and issues found therein within the acceptable limits of official discourse (Smith 1997). Some proponents of CSS have therefore suggested that critical intellectuals 'should eschew the temptations of seeking the ears of soldiers and statesmen and should seek instead to aid in the development of counterhegemonic positions linked to the struggles of emancipatory social movements' (Wyn Jones 1999: 6; see also Ray 1993). This position is unlikely to produce dramatic results and is likely to be dismissed as naive and/or utopian by those who see states as an important part of the solution. But this position also has merits. First, it is important to remember that it was international NGOs like Amnesty International not state advocacy that helped turn human rights declarations from platitudes trotted out by the great powers as tools of their cold war foreign policies into a powerful critique of state sovereignty (Ignatieff 2003a: 54–7; see also Ekins 1992). Second, it takes a realistically humble—but not defeatist—view of what can be achieved by social movements given the ideologies and structures that currently dominate world politics (see Evangelista 1999). And as Bull (1977: 94) acknowledged, 'Sometimes it is the struggle for just change itself that creates a consensus in favour of this change that did not exist when the struggle was first undertaken'.

CONCLUSION

A dialogue with the emerging CSS literature can help the English School develop its wide-ranging research agenda and lend credence to the argument that it has a 'profound concern for human emancipation'. This should not be especially difficult since CSS shares many of the assumptions and commitments of the Kantian/revolutionist tradition of English School theorizing and there are considerable areas of overlap between the two approaches, not least in terms of method and agenda.

Both approaches agree that security is a fundamentally important concept for the study of world politics. Both apparently share a commitment to human emancipation, although this was rarely made explicit within the classical English School literature. However, unlike the pluralists in today's English School, CSS explicitly adopts and defends the position that human security is more fundamental than the security of states. Both approaches also emphasize the importance of rigorous historical analysis and remaining sensitive to historical contingency. But where the English School focuses on a top-down version of international history, proponents of CSS suggest that much more work needs to be done cataloguing a bottom-up history of world politics—perhaps akin to Cynthia Enloe's (1989) work focusing on the roles played by women in international political and security structures—that includes listening to the stories and explanations of those currently rendered insecure by the prevailing global order. Finally, both approaches accept that building progressive political communities represents an indispensable part of providing security, although they differ on the forms such community is likely to, or should, take. However, recent work within the English School has contributed to understanding the operation and development of non-state international systems and alternative forms of political community (for instance, Diez and Whitman 2002).

But there are also important differences between the two approaches. First, many proponents of CSS do not share the English School's faith in the ability of states, even the 'good' sort, to eradicate human wrongs. International society has proved indifferent to genocidal slaughter in Rwanda and the silent genocide of poverty and malnutrition responsible for 40,000 deaths daily; it reflects militarist values in its priorities, spending hundreds of billions of dollars on weapons while keeping conflict prevention, peacekeeping, and peacebuilding initiatives woefully underfunded; its great powers have been the most persistent violators of their own norm of sovereignty and international laws; and it is undemocratic and prone to reject attempts at further democratization on the grounds that this would impede effective collective action. CSS is consequently concerned with identifying (and supporting) alternative forms of political agency, the most viable of which currently seems to be transnational social movements committed to cosmopolitan projects.

Second, CSS adopts a far broader ontology than the English School and does not share its preoccupation with relations between states. There are tentative signs that some contemporary members of the English School think it is time to jettison the ontological primacy it attaches to 'the state' (Dunne 2001: 227). Buzan (2001—and Chapter 6, this volume), for instance, has called for a greater engagement with issues of IPE, and Neumann (2001) has stressed the need for the English School to take greater account of NGOs. From a CSS perspective, these would be sensible steps since international society is, as Bull acknowledged, a second order phenomenon inasmuch as the sovereign state and the ideology of nationalism represent specific political forms generated by the capitalist system (see Halliday 1994: 242–3). Proponents of CSS thus recognize the need to situate the study of security within a global capitalist economy and examine how the expansion and operation of this system and its interaction with international society is fundamental to understanding patterns of insecurity (Thomas 2000). Moving beyond a preoccupation with states also opens up a broader agenda than the insecurities generated by the interactions between states, citizens, and foreigners. CSS acknowledges the need to incorporate the class, gendered, racial, and ecological dimensions of insecurity at the heart of its analysis. In doing so, it will catalogue alternative histories and explanations than those provided in the recollections and statements of soldiers and diplomats.

Notes

1. A case could be made that Martin Wight also rejected the narrow and zero-sum nature of realist conceptions of international security (see Wheeler 1996: 125) but the signposts are clearer in Bull's work.
2. I owe this point to Barry Buzan.

3. Booth's notion of anchorage (a metaphor for Frankfurt School-inspired immanent critique) acknowledges that 'Truth' is a product of human beings, a pragmatic truth that, like security, is created intersubjectively. There are, arguably, strong implicit connections here to the idea that the 'something' knowledge should rest on is akin to Habermas' notion of emancipatory cognitive interests discussed in the context of international relations by Richard Ashley (1981).

4. However, if a broad definition of humanitarian intervention is adopted to include non-forcible and non-military elements, states cease to be sufficient or even necessary agents in the process (see Ramsbotham and Woodhouse 1996).

8

Feminism

Jacqui True

According to the English School of International Relations, 'international society' is based on an 'intersubjective agreement among statesmen' about the legitimate interests, rules, and values that pertain at the international level (Little 2000: 408). Portrayed in this way, the concept of international society conveys the implication that world politics revolves around states. However, Hedley Bull—a major contributor to the English School and proponent of international society as an analytical concept—acknowledged that 'it is always erroneous to interpret events as if international society were the sole or dominant element' (1977: 55).

Taken on its own terms, the boundaries of international society are established by the orderly social interactions among states. English School accounts of international society thus focus on what happens to diplomats as representatives of states, in their bilateral interactions with other state representatives, at summits and multilateral meetings. Since women have long been only marginally visible in these public and private worlds of diplomacy, the international society concept has never been developed in ways that can give recognition to women's international presence. More importantly, the concept, as defined, cannot take account of the central role that gender relations play in the maintenance and transformation of the society of states. To the extent that conceptions of gender shape state identities, they also shape and constrain the international consensus among states. Perhaps even more so than the principle of sovereignty, gender norms determine the boundaries of international society; that is, what may be appropriately discussed in diplomatic interactions and what is considered outside the purview of the society of states. This neglect of gender reveals the concept of international society to be neither open nor sufficiently dynamic enough to capture or explain the social sources and dimensions of interstate behaviour, and world politics more broadly. In this respect, a feminist perspective on international society shares many of the same feminist criticisms levelled at realist theories of international relations.

This chapter starts by asking where women are in international society. While observing the absence of women from theories of international society, it argues that women are nonetheless present as actors in diplomatic encounters between and among states, and that gender relations have been an integral part of the evolution and expansion of international society. The chapter then proceeds to account for the conceptual exclusion of gender in English School approaches to international society. It reveals the gender bias behind two core assumptions of international society; that is, that states are the major actors and that domestic politics are irrelevant in the workings of this interstate society. The chapter ends by considering the future viability of the international society concept given its neglect of gender. It is argued that, as a concept, international society risks irrelevance unless it can be revised to fully account for contemporary developments that significantly affect international norms and interstate behaviour.

WHERE ARE WOMEN IN INTERNATIONAL SOCIETY?

For feminist scholars, asking questions such as, 'where are the women?' or 'what is women's experience of this?' represents a critical starting point for examining any framework of international relations. Consequently, this question leads us to ask about other often overlooked or marginalized groups as well.

Martin Wight, one of the founding fathers of the English School approach, acknowledged that international society 'conceals, obstructs, and oppresses the *real* society of individual men and women' (1966*b*: 93; see also Little 1998: 412). But he and other members of the English School assume that 'in so far as the interests of mankind are articulated and aggregated . . . this is through the mechanism of the society of sovereign states' (Bull 1977: 82). An analogy is drawn between the social interaction among individuals in society and the social interaction among states in international society (Buzan 2000: 477), although individuals themselves are not seen to be actors in international society. The questions of who speaks and acts for the state or how inclusive the domestic aggregation of interests is, are not adequately addressed by the international society approach. As Ole Wæver (1998: 109) asks: 'exactly what/where is international society? Is it of the population at large . . . of the state as such, of its decision-makers or a larger elite?' Like realism, the international society approach assumes away such theoretical issues by treating states as a priori, unitary actors in the international realm.

Despite theoretical removal of people from the politics of international society that is a feature of most International Relations theory, feminist scholars put women and men back into the picture. Men are more visible than women in international society since the proxies for states have historically been states*men*—either diplomats or other state representatives—and the typical behaviour of states has been deduced from the behaviour of male individuals.

For early English School scholars the common culture of diplomats constituted the prerequisite for—as well as the substance of—international society. On the face of it, this international culture was developed in and through relationships among agents of the state who also happened to be men. But the gender identities of diplomats are not incidental. Rather, they have helped to forge the common culture through which an international society has developed.

Gender relations are an integral part of the practice if not the theory of diplomacy. International diplomacy has depended upon a patriarchal structure of public and private wherein women, typically spouses and unofficial employees in the private domestic realm, support the men who act on behalf of states, both physically and emotionally, and socially and professionally in their public interstate activities. Sylvester (2002: 197) argues that diplomatic wives have served the causes of international society for the most part without being recognized:

These unpaid servants of national interest create conditions of cosy relational autonomy. For men who incline to reactivity in the diplomatic arena, their wives make the conduct of affairs of state sociable, and they do so not because they are recruited by the state but because the marriage contract carries the private obligations of servants into the public arena of conquerors.

Cynthia Enloe (1989: 96), one of the first scholars to theorize the political role of diplomatic spouses, contends that diplomacy and hostessing have been tightly intertwined since the nineteenth century: 'Diplomacy runs smoothly when there is trust and confidence between officials representing governments which usually have different, if not, conflicting interests'. According to Enloe, it is the role of the diplomatic wife to 'create an atmosphere where men from different states can get to know one another "man to man"'. At public functions, she is often 'her husband's eyes and ears', and the home or ambassador's residence, which is 'the domain of the wife', 'is seen as the place where trust between men can be best cultivated' (1988: 97).

Hedley Bull (1979*b*) made a distinction between the diplomats involved in state to state contacts and who participate in a world diplomatic culture, and the larger urban elite with whom they interact, inter-marry, and from whom come the interest-group pressures on their policies. This distinction is ostensibly gender-neutral but it comes very close to recognizing the gendered structure of international society, and importantly the tension between domestic and international societies that may register at the core of everyday diplomatic life. Ronald Dore (1984: 414) argues that since diplomats come and go, 'the possibilities of fellow-feeling between these wider urban elites of the world becomes important if one is thinking of building sustained commitment to the conventions of an international order'. Indeed, one could interpret Dore's insight to mean that the historical 'fellow-feeling' among diplomatic wives, now spouses (both male and female), could be *as* if not *more* crucial than formal diplomatic exchanges to the reproduction of international society.

The art of diplomacy, most conventional analysts would accept, is as much about managing relationships as it is about 'power politics'. Interpersonal connections and social events taking place in private residences, for example, make up an important part of diplomatic life, and thus, the stuff of international society. Certainly these networks and interactions are difficult to document and study. But they are so taken for granted as the natural infrastructure of everyday diplomacy that scholars of international relations have rarely analysed them as political phenomena. Consequently, the gender politics that support the creation and maintenance of international society have also been overlooked by international relations scholars.

As well as structuring the practices of diplomacy that serve to constitute inter-national society, European gender relations were also integral in the expansion of European international society to the non-European world. In theory, international society has been based on the mutual recognition of the sovereignty of states, which formally precludes one state from interfering in another's sovereign jurisdiction. However, in practice, the expansion of international society involved the imposition of European domestic norms in non-European territories. Historically, European states expanded their authority in colonial territories, incorporating them into a European-centred world order, by diffusing their domestic norms of private enterprise, public administration, kinship, and gender relations (Taylor 1997). Thus, the expansion of Eurocentric international society in the late nineteenth and early twentieth cen-turies was infused by gender politics. These gendered international relations had unintended, often negative, consequences for many women in non-Western countries.

For example, the British Empire practised a kind of 'feminist orientalism', view-ing women in the colonies of Asia, the Middle East, and Africa as 'daughters' who needed to be saved from their own barbaric and backward men (see Burton 1994; Grewal 1996). Colonial rule modernized (and sometimes outlawed) traditional pat-riarchal practices such as sati, purdah, footbinding, and genital mutilation that often oppressed women. But this modernization had the effect of eliminating certain rights available to women under local traditions and ossifying indigenous law in ways often detrimental to women. In spite of the fact that the British outlawed the practice of sati in 1829, the practice has persisted in contemporary times and proven to be very popular in rural provinces of India. In 1987, for instance, a young Rajput widow was deified for sitting on her husband's funeral pyre and being burned alive (Weaver 2000).

Following the Second World War, the American empire played a leading role in the expansion of international society. During the Allied occupation, for example, Americans reconstructed and liberalized the economies of Europe and Japan. They played a central role in the democratization of the German and Japanese political systems and their reintegration into international society. American reform of the Japanese constitution was successful in enfranchising women, although its democratic propaganda was only partially able to break down traditional patriarchal authority.[1] John Dower argues that many Japanese embraced the United States' occupation and its promotion of democratic norms and institutions in their state, and that Japanese women were the first to grasp the benefits of materialism. Less direct but as significant were the informal liaisons between American soldiers and German women, which had far-reaching consequences for the cultural transformation and political re-education of the German population after the experience of fascism (Goedde 1999). The idea that the spread of American influence would improve the lives of foreign women, most recently seen in the American occupation of Afghanistan, 'comprises a consistent trope of American exceptionalism' (Rosenberg 1999: 481).

Traditionally, international society has considered any unjust practice occurring within the borders of a sovereign state as the prerogative of individual states. Yet, in contemporary times this boundary between domestic politics and international relations has become increasingly difficult to sustain, and presents serious challenges to state-centric conceptions of international society. We can see the porousness of state boundaries, for example, in the context of economic globalization and the inequalities it engenders in the spread of environmental degradation and global efforts to avert it, and in the cross-border migration and displacement of peoples (see Linklater 1999).

Moreover, at the same time as state boundaries are becoming less salient, the boundaries of public and private spheres are also shifting. The unequal treatment of women, including many forms of violence against women, has been justified by reference to national, religious, or cultural tradition, and subject not only to the sovereignty defence and norm of non-intervention, but also to gendered norms of privacy that ensured men like states could do as they pleased inside their own 'territories' (private property). 'No social group has suffered greater violation of its human rights in the name of *culture* than women' (Rao 1995: 169). Historically, women's human rights have been excluded from both national and international legal frameworks. They cannot be universal because they are specific to women and yet universal human rights typically excluded the kinds of rights violations that women experience. As Richard Falk (1999*b*: 422) argues, 'the most pervasive forms of injustice are difficult to overcome because their existence is embedded in the deep structure of power and privilege . . . Male domination of structures of authority and decision-making in all sectors of society [and in all states] is so pervasive that it is still treated as nature despite important inroads made by feminism and the global human rights movements'.

Increasingly, however, 'domestic' or 'family violence' is considered to be a violation of women's human rights for which both individuals and states are held responsible under national law and international treaties and agreements. Culture or sovereignty is no longer an adequate defence for acts of violence against women. At the international level, human rights instruments and declarations such the Convention on the Elimination of All Forms of Discrimination Against Women (CEDAW) ratified by 174 states, increasingly acknowledge the gender-specificity of human rights. Since the early 1990s, governments and international institutions have recognized women's human rights by adding gender persecution to its list of forms of political persecution. Canada, for example, was the first state to give asylum to women refugees who fear persecution for not conforming to their society's 'traditions', such as forced marriage, bride-burning, dowry deaths, sexual abuse, domestic violence, genital mutilation, rape, forced sterilization and abortion, practices of purdah, and veiling. Until the Yugoslav conflict in the early 1990s, states and international agencies interpreted the persecution of women in war as a matter of personal privacy and cultural tradition. But through the lobbying of transnational women's movements and the widespread media coverage of rape as an ethnic cleansing war strategy in Yugoslavia and Rwanda, rape is now a war crime under the Geneva Convention Against War Crimes.

European society if not yet international society recognizes gender justice as a domestic condition for international recognition and legitimacy. For example, several Western democracies did not recognize the Taliban government in Afghanistan due to its 'gender apartheid' regime and there was considerable domestic pressure in these states and transnationally to place economic and political sanctions on Afghanistan; the United States has made their bilateral aid to African countries conditional on the passing of legislation against female genital mutilation;[2] and the European Union, for its part, takes a very grim view of states that support child marriage or honour killings of women by failing to prosecute or effectively punish the male kin murderers (*The Economist* 2003). Such practices are considered to be fundamentally 'un-European' and any state harbouring them receives, at best, minimal recognition and no other benefits of reciprocal membership in a society of states. Moreover, it is unlikely that Turkey and Romania, for instance, would be invited to join the European Union—a thicker form of international society[3] as well as common market—while these forms of gender injustice are legitimized by state inaction. Thus, consensus about the appropriate form of gender relations is part of the constitution of a strong international society, premised as it is in most English School accounts, on a common culture.

WHY IS THERE NO GENDER IN INTERNATIONAL SOCIETY?

Given the presence of both women and men, often as partners, in international diplomacy and the importance of European gender norms in the expansion of European international society to the non-Western world, how can we explain the absence of gender from English School accounts of international society? Why have women not been recognized as part of international society and why have gender relations been seen as peripheral in the evolution of the society of states?

In many respects, the failure to include gender analysis in theories of international society stems from the approach's broad agreement with realism on key foundational points that feminists dispute. Foremost among the foundational points on which feminists and international society theorists tend to differ are the assumptions that there is a secure territorial boundary and conceptual distinction between domestic and international politics, and therefore that states act as homogenous units in the international realm.

Not unlike the realist theory of the anarchic international system, the international society approach has been explicitly concerned with comprehending politics between states, ignoring a state's domestic politics. This approach assumes that 'international' politics is a qualitatively different (often inferior) form of politics, distinct and separate from other spheres of political action. Consequently, there is an aversion to the analogy of 'domestic' politics in discussions of international society. But this aversion is compounded in the case of gender politics, which are obscured within domestic politics by a naturalized public–private division that has historically relegated women to the private sphere and considered private sphere matters inherently non-political. Thus, as it has been theorized to date, international society is limited as a concept and as a progressive force for feminists concerned with understanding and transforming gendered structures of inequalities that exist globally, across states, but that are embedded within private spheres of family, community, cultural, and religious tradition.

From a feminist perspective, it is not just that gender is absent in theories of inter-national society, but that the effect of this absence is to deepen women's invisibility and perpetuate gender-based injustices within and across states. It is only through the emergence of a 'world society', in the form of transnational activist networks and global conscientization of gender-based violence, that women have begun to be more readily seen and heard by states and that women's (as well as some excluded men's) security has been put on the international agenda.

Hedley Bull's (1984*b*) analysis of the revolt against the West illustrates how the state-centricity of international society approaches leads to the exclusion of gender. Bull describes five phases of the revolt against the West, in effect, a revolt against Eurocentric international society. The first phase involved the struggle for equal sov-ereignty among subordinate non-Western states; the second phase, the anti-colonial revolution in Western colonies; the third phase, the struggle for racial equality by non-white peoples globally, within minority communities in white states and as majority communities in white-ruled states; the fourth phase concerned the struggle for economic justice in multilateral fora by the group of seventy-seven developing nations; and the fifth and final phase, the struggle for cultural autonomy and self-determination by non-Westerners. Second-wave feminism and women's liberation movements sprung up around the world at approximately the same time as anti-colonial revolutions and black liberation movements. Yet, Bull was silent on this global uprising of women against male domination.

Like race, gender relations are a dimension of struggle and injustice in world politics (see also Vincent 1984*a*). But unlike the struggles of non-Westerners, or non-white men, women's revolts against male power and knowledge have never taken the form of a quest for statehood. Thus, from an international society perspective their struggles are invisible. Only to the extent that groups share Western norms of sovereignty, do their struggles register on the agenda of international relations scholars. Bull's conception of a collective revolt against the West, in effect, recounts a struggle among black and white men for political authority. Historically, this struggle has often played out on—and indeed over—non-Western women's bodies. We need only think of the symbolism attributed to women's dress and conduct, and the physical control of women's place and women's movement in anti-Western movements and states.

IMPLICATIONS OF A GENDER-BLIND INTERNATIONAL SOCIETY

So far this chapter has discussed the presence of women and gender relations in international society, and sought to explain the absence of gender in English School accounts of the evolution of international society. Here I derive implications from the neglect of gender in international society approaches and ask whether a feminist conception of international society is plausible.

For Martin Wight, as well as some more recent members of the English School, international society is predicated on a common culture. For those scholars who do not make this a priori assumption, international society is nonetheless socially constitutive of the shared norms and values among states. An important dimension of the English School research agenda is to examine the expansion of international society beyond its European origins, and to determine whether non-Western states can participate in a society of states founded on European norms and culture. Thus, in order to understand the limits and possibilities of the international society approach, we need to analyse its receptiveness to cultural diversity, including gender diversity, and its responsiveness to cultural conflict, including the conflict over gender norms.

The neglect of gender relations in international society approaches is not trivial; gender relations are an integral dimension of both the cultural diversity and the cultural conflict that shape international society. However, gender does not shape international society in any straightforward way (such as saying that the conflict between women and men shapes the conflict between states). The findings of the World Values Survey provide evidence that demonstrates this conceptual point. In their analysis of the World Values Survey, Inglehart and Norris (2003) found that Western and non-Western states share common values toward many aspects of formal politics and attitudes toward democracy. But the survey reveals that the values of these states diverge sharply when it comes to aspects of informal politics, specifically attitudes toward gender relations, women, and sexuality. It is not that men and women have different views. Indeed, gender differences in values and attitudes were not found to be significant in the worldwide survey. Rather, it is the differences in values/attitudes about gender and sexuality that divide the Western from the non-Western world, and arguably, the norms and boundaries of international society.

The rejection of Western gender relations, specifically gender equality and women's individual rights, by non-Westerners shapes the relations between non-Western and Western states, heightening the possibility of conflict between them. The extension and universality of international society beyond the European or Western milieu is impeded by a clash of cultural norms expressed in the spread of anti-Western, anti-systemic protest and most recently, by the scourge of international terrorism. Attitudes towards women and gender norms are deeply embedded in these new forms of revolt against international society. For instance, the statements of Osama Bin Laden and the diary accounts left behind by the September 11 terrorists clearly indicate that their actions were directed not merely against the West, but against the Western gender identities and relations perceived to be so threatening to their vision of an Islamic and/or pan-Arab culture (see Tickner 2002). The United States' decision to close their military base in Saudi Arabia was partly a response to the Saudi government's request that US female soldiers be veiled in public and not drive or move freely around their country. This diplomatic standoff between the two allies involved irreconcilable differences in their attitudes toward women.

These examples underscore the point that we cannot understand the cultural differences that fuel the conflict among states if we overlook gender as an integral dimension of the international order. A society's attitudes towards gender equality and sexual liberty shape its attitudes towards tolerance, human rights, and democracy and by extension towards international cooperation. Those states/societies with greater gender inequality are also more likely to go to war or to engage in state sanctioned violence (Tickner 1999; Goldstein 2001). By the same token, those states that come closest to gender parity tend also to be more peaceful, more generous aid-donors, and generally 'good citizens' of international society.

In the Middle East, Tessler and Warriner (1997) found that attitudes towards gender equality are good predictors of more pacific attitudes to international conflict. Francis Fukuyama (1998) has suggested that this relationship between gender equality (as revealed by the increasing numbers of women in political power) and pacifism in Western democracies could have detrimental affect on international security in the future. Women leaders and their feminized male counterparts will be no match for 'the surplus of younger hotheaded men' leading states in the larger and poorer part of the world (Africa, the Middle East, and south Asia) (1998: 38).[4] Yet, as Ann Tickner (1999: 11) argues, a critical mass of attitudes within international society favourable to greater equality 'could be the building blocks . . . for a more just and peaceful world in which gender and other social hierarchies of domination . . . are diminished'. A feminized international society might better deliver on the goals of cooperation and security than the statist form of politics founded on the gender-biased assumption of an aggressive, masculine human nature. At present, however, the 'faultline' on gender stands in the way of a truly global international society extending beyond European borders.

TOWARDS A FEMINIST INTERNATIONAL SOCIETY?

Is it possible to integrate feminist insights within the existing English School conceptualization of international society? What would need to be changed? To take up Richard Little's (2000) challenge, could feminism fill some of the gaps in the research programme of the English school? For instance, could it complement the solidarist conception of international society?

To address and incorporate feminist questions, the international society approach would have to take into account the ways domestic societies shape state identities and interests and therefore their membership in the society of states. It would also have to account for how emergent norms in international society reshape the practices and identities of member states. Given the porous nature of the boundaries between domestic and international societies, a revised international society approach would need to investigate the linkages between domestic and international societies and clarify the relationship between those linkages and 'world society'.

The emergence over the past decade or so of feminist approaches in international relations has been hastened not by the actions of states but, more importantly, by the rise of women's movements linked together across states and conscious of their commonalities in world society. Feminists have been pioneers of world society since states have historically provided few avenues for women's organizing or for the articulation of women's gender-specific interests. However, international organizations such as the United Nations have nurtured transnational feminist activism and have helped to place the issues of gender inequality and injustice on the international agenda, and on the agenda of many states.[5] Advocacy networks of women around the world have increased the pressure on individual states to address persistent gender inequities and recognize women's human rights. Indeed, the diffusion of policies and institutional mechanisms to promote gender equality within international organizations and across states has been quite spectacular through the 1990s (see True and Mintrom 2001).[6] As a result of these changes, gender equality and gender justice are increasingly considered legitimate 'standards of civilisation' that underpin the requirements for membership within international society and that increasingly justify the exclusion of some states.

Although undertheorized in English School accounts, the concept of world society suggests the evolution of a global moral consciousness expressed through diverse non-state forms of collective action. The solidarist position within the international society approach recognizes that the emergence of such a world society is a significant, progressive development that need not lead to the weakening of the society of states. Indeed, world society and international society may be mutually reinforcing to the extent that globally connected non-state actors seek to transform international norms and behaviour, but are dependent on individual states and international society to institutionalize and enforce new norms. For example, the global movement to eradicate all forms of violence against women requires states to pass comprehensive national measures to prosecute, monitor, and prevent domestic violence among other things.

While world society and international society can be mutually reinforcing, tensions exist between them (see Neumann 2001). This was revealed by the experience of the 1995 United Nations Fourth World Conference on Women in Beijing which aimed to bring about international change to improve the lives of women. The conference involved participants who were representatives of member states (emblematic of international society) and women's non-governmental organizations and civil society movements (emblematic of world society). At the world meeting, participants resolved contested language in a document that had been prepared in advance at preparatory national and regional meetings. But how well did the conference's participants, agenda, and modes of communication move beyond state-centric politics and foster global cooperation? Three critical responses can be offered.

First, the participants were national representatives who were selected by non-democratic means making them not necessarily representatives of their nation-states. Some national delegations contained non-government organization (NGO) members, but others did not. Thus the official representation of civil society was not global. Second, the agenda for the conference which determined the framing of important questions was set previously in preparatory committee ('PrepCom') meetings.[7] As Abena Busia (1996) notes these meetings were exclusionary because only those who could afford the time and money to participate were the collective authors of the draft language that would be considered at Beijing. Clark, Friedman, and Hochstetler (1998: 17) describe a PrepCom phenomenon in which government representatives tried to exclude NGO participation in the final and most sensitive stages of the negotiations. The narrow (but still large) project of the Beijing Conference was to remove brackets around, or to edit, contested language, such as the word 'gender', and not to introduce new issue areas. Third, lobbyists kept track of NGO allies around the world on various issues and used these sources of knowledge to lobby receptive national delegations. They then relied on sympathetic state representatives (not necessarily from their own countries) to make their arguments in the official conference. However, most NGO activists were situated at the concurrent NGO Forum in Huairou, sixty miles outside Beijing, and were thus not able to gain direct access to the official state forum.

The practices associated with the Beijing women's conference hold importance for the possibilities of a feminist international society; a society of states allied with world society and committed to the normative goals of justice and equality. It comes perhaps closest yet to approximating a form of global dialogue and state consensus.[8] That said, this example shows the real difficulties of achieving this kind of outcome even when the actors involved displayed well-honed political skills at negotiating a normative 'world society' agenda in an interstate context.

CONCLUSION

The goal of this chapter has been to explore the concept of international society and consider how that concept might be expanded to incorporate a gender perspective. Efforts to recognize feminism, to interpret the global rise of the women's movement, and to incorporate gender analysis represent fruitful avenues for proponents of international society. But consideration of how such efforts might proceed serves to raise broader questions about the ongoing viability of the English School approach to international society. We might ask whether the failure to take account of the gendered dimensions of global politics represents an anomaly for the international society approach to international relations or whether it points to a more systematic failure that challenges the theoretical and empirical validity of the concept. Over recent years, feminists and scholars of International Political Economy in particular, have illuminated the shifting public–private boundaries of politics and the increased significance of networks among state and non-state actors in international relations (see Guzzini 2001).

To demonstrate the continuing relevance of the international society approach, members of the English School will have to confront questions that go to the heart of the construction of politics. They will also need to expand the empirical, explanatory scope of the international society approach. Once treated as an anomaly within examinations of international society, gender must now be accorded careful analytical scrutiny. But surely other apparent anomalies now pose challenges for adherents to the English School as well. How far, then, can the concept of international society be amended and revised before it becomes incommensurate with its original formulation and application by founders of the English School? That question takes us beyond the concerns of this chapter. But it is a question that deserves urgent attention.

Notes

1. For a further discussion of the United States' occupation of Japan and Germany see Ikenberry and Kupchan (1990) and Smith (1998). John Dower (1999) argues that many Japanese embraced the United States' occupation and its promotion of democratic norms and institutions, and that Japanese women were the first to grasp the benefits of materialism.
2. Despite its good intentions, United States aid policy has not resulted in the eradication of 'female genital mutilation (FGM)' but in either flagrant resistance to such laws or partial adaptation to them (*The Economist* 1999: 45).
3. The higher standard for membership in the European Union could be compared to the stronger or 'thicker' conception of international society identified by Richard Little in his re-evaluation of the English school literature. Little (1998: 67) makes the distinction between (*a*) societies that are organic and/or rest on a common culture; and (*b*) societies which are multicultural and have developed on a functional and/or contractual basis.
4. See Hudson and Den Boer (2002, 2003) on the international security implications of the surplus of young men in China and India created by the prevailing practice of female infanticide in those countries.
5. The United Nations Decade for Women, 1975–85, CEDAW ('the women's convention') and the related United Nations' four world women's conferences were critical events in the expansion of women's movements globally.
6. For further discussion of the global context of gender equality initiatives, see True (2003).
7. For example, trafficking of women was included under section D, 'Violence Against Women', and not under section A, on poverty, or section F on economic structures.
8. This section draws on a dialogue with Brooke A. Ackerly in a co-authored paper that compares feminist and critical theory approaches to transnational justice (Ackerly and True 2002).

9

Global Environmental Governance

Matthew Paterson

The environment has emerged as a key issue in global politics since the early 1970s. The issues which comprise the so-called environmental crisis—climate change, ozone depletion, deforestation, biodiversity, acid rain, and so on—are widely regarded to have had significant impacts on international politics. On the one hand, they have been the site for the considerable development of international institutions, both quantitatively in terms of the numbers of treaties and the density of negotiations, and qualitatively as the site of much institutional innovation. On the other, they are often regarded to pose very substantial challenges for both conventional forms of politics centred around the international society of states—where many view the principles underpinning that society, notably sovereignty, to be an obstacle to the resolution of environmental problems—and for the conceptual frameworks of international relations which presume that the states-system is the sole or even the principal focus of its study.

At the same time, it would be fair to say that the international society or 'English School' tradition has rarely had much explicit to say regarding the implications of environmental degradation for International Relations.[1] There is a well-known passage in Bull's *The Anarchical Society* (1977: 293–5), but aside from this and some discussions by Robert Jackson and in particular Andrew Hurrell, there is little.[2] This in part reflects both the disciplinary narrowness within which many of us move and the alleged marginality of environmental questions to international relations (Smith 1993; for a critique see Saurin 1996). But it is perhaps a surprise as there are some reasons to suggest that the tradition would have useful insights into the nature of international environmental politics, and into the implications of environment for our overall conceptions of global politics. In particular, contained in the notion of 'international society' is a recognition that the ethics underpinning the actions of states can move beyond simple notions of the 'national interest' towards more cosmopolitan bases for action. At a first look, then, it is a surprise that English School authors have not looked to environmental politics for sources of support for their arguments.

I am grateful to Hidemi Suganami and Alex Bellamy for comments on an earlier version of this chapter.

This chapter attempts to elaborate how such an engagement between international environmental politics and the English School might develop. It begins with an elaboration of Bull's passage on the environment, and then proceeds through a discussion of contemporary accounts of 'global environmental governance'. It concludes that despite the superficial attraction mentioned above, discussions of global environmental governance undermine the image of international society in English School accounts in two principal ways. First, they show that thinking about international society—its norms, the tensions and conversation between the three traditions in English School, and so on—is limited by the lack of understanding of the specifically capitalist character of the states-system. Second, they show that the image in Bull that any alternatives to the states-system tend to founder on the claim that states will not voluntarily cede their authority is misplaced. Practices of global governance are emerging in the environmental field that operate outside the states-system but where states have never given permission in the manner envisaged by Bull and others to be necessary.

BULL ON THE ENVIRONMENT

It is perhaps worth starting with Bull's argument regarding the environment and the states-system. His section, entitled 'Man and the Environment', starts with the statement that 'the states system is today often said to be dysfunctional . . . in relation to the objective which all men [sic] must pursue of living in harmony with their environment' (Bull 1977: 293).[3] He quotes Richard Falk to represent these arguments, quoting Falk's 'four dimensions of planetary danger', of 'the war system', 'population pressure', 'the insufficiency of resources', and 'environmental overload' (Bull 1977: 293, quoting Falk 1971: 8). Such writers, Bull claims, mean that 'meeting them [these environmental threats] . . . will require global unity and global planning, to which the division of mankind [sic] into sovereign states is a standing obstacle' (p. 293).

Bull has three principal counterclaims to these arguments. Before getting to these, he starts with what appears to be a concession to the claims but turns out not to be, but rather a segue into his first argument. He concedes (p. 293) that 'if all men were as willing to co-operate in the pursuit of common goals as the crew of a spaceship, these threats to the human environment would be easier to meet than they are'. He then gives a list of reasons why such levels of cooperation are not possible to achieve, from divergent population and economic policies, to conflict over specific resources, to the export of pollution by some countries, to the erosion of common resources such as the high seas. These read as if it could be accepting the critique: the states-system cannot provide for sufficient levels of cooperation to meet environmental challenges. But Bull does not intend them this way. In his first objection, which follows, he then emphasizes that such lack of cooperation is not due to the 'existence of the system of states but the fact of human disagreement and conflict in the ecological realm itself' (pp. 293–4). That this disagreement and conflict might itself be exacerbated and given institutional form and legitimacy by the institution of state sovereignty is not considered, with such disagreements being assumed to exist independently of such political forms. 'In relation to the human environment . . . it has to be recognised that human conflict has sources that are deeper than any particular form of universal political order', he asserts (p. 294). This is where he brings in Garrett Hardin's 'tragedy of the commons' metaphor (1968), emphasizing its theme of the acceptance of limitations on human freedom (to procreate, produce, consume, etc.) rather than its arguments for the transformation of property rights,[4] to suggest that *any* political order will face similar problems in meeting environmental challenges.

His second objection is that 'the argument we are considering overlooks the contribution that the states system may make to dealing with environmental or ecological threats' (p. 294). His principal claims in this objection are twofold. First, he asserts a standard 'international society' argument, that the states-system is premised on and operates through a set of rules for coexistence between states, such as mutual recognition of each other's right to independent existence, and so on, and thus that 'without such a basis of minimum order it is scarcely possible that common issues of the environment can be faced at all' (p. 294).[5] The second is more pragmatic, and argues that if, as Falk and others claim, the environmental situation requires urgent action, it is then rather perverse to argue for a complete overhaul of global political institutions which cannot be envisaged in such a timescale. He cites a well-known article from the period by Shields and Ott (1974) in support of a statement that 'in the short run it is only national governments that have the information, the experience and the resources to act effectively in relation to these matters' (p. 294).[6]

Bull's third objection is that the anti-states-system argument 'overlooks the possibility that through it [the states-system] a greater sense of human solidarity in relation to environmental threats may emerge' (p. 294). He concedes here that action beyond the states-system is likely 'in the long run' to be necessary to deal with environmental challenges, 'and the functionality of the states system, or of any other form of universal political order, will depend upon the emergence of a greater sense of human cohesion than now exists' (p. 295). But his point here is again an 'international society' one, that the states-system itself helps foster such cohesion, rather than acts as an obstacle to it. 'The states system provides the present structure of the political organisation of mankind, and the sense of common interests and values that underlies it . . . is the principal expression of human unity or solidarity that exists at the present time, and such hopes as we may entertain for the emergence of a more cohesive world society are bound up with its preservation and development' (p. 295).[7]

These three objections—that given the need to restrict human freedoms, any political order (not just the states-system) will have similar problems in achieving this, that the states-system can make many contributions to meeting environmental challenges effectively, and that environmental challenges may increase a sense of human solidarity which would then shape how the states-system responds—are all themselves challengeable, and I will revisit the second and third in the concluding section of this chapter. For the first, it is perhaps worth noting that the assumption that environmental degradation arises out of an 'excess of freedom' is itself highly contestable. More systematic analyses of the causes of environmental degradation rarely sustain such a claim, rooting environmental degradation rather in the dynamics of accumulation, the increasing scale of economic activities, the nature of property rights, and so on (for a survey and extended argument regarding international relations, see Paterson (2000: chs 2 and 3)).

On the few occasions writers associated with the English School take up questions of environmental politics, they act largely as an extension of Bull's argument. Jackson (2000: 175–8) discusses environmental politics in terms of the varied forms of responsibilities that states in international society have. His other three forms—national, international, and humanitarian—correspond to a threefold way of thinking familiar to the English School (realism, rationalism, solidarism) and Jackson suggests that environmental ethics and responsibility are a novel form beyond this framework. This separation of environmental ethics from other cosmopolitan/solidarist concerns is ultimately unconvincing, resting as it does on an assumption that environmental ethics must be non-anthropocentric (i.e. our environmental responsibilities are to 'nature' rather than to each other as human beings). But the more important point is that for Jackson, like Bull, the cosmopolitan ethics which environmental concerns (as well as humanitarian ones) bring about do not translate into persuasive arguments for institutional moves beyond the society of states. Rather they produce a shift towards solidarism as a motive for state action; in Brown's (2001: 428) paraphrase of Bull, also invoked by Jackson (2000: 176), 'states are local agents of the common good'.[8] This discussion occurs in a chapter of Jackson's book on the development of international society in general, and in a passage on the different sorts of responsibility through which this development can be expressed or elucidated. Interestingly perhaps, when he gets to specific proposals for institutional reform in order to set himself up for a defence of the 'global covenant' (which at best is a 'soft-solidarist' account of international society), both environmental degradation itself, and the way that it features as a specific concern driving proposals for institutional change, more or less disappear, gaining only one minor mention in his critique of Falk (Jackson 2000: 382).

In his various discussions of international environmental politics (Hurrell and Kingsbury 1992; Hurrell 1994, 1995), Hurrell similarly tends towards reinforcing Bull's argument resisting the idea that environmental politics means transcending a notion of international society, although he is perhaps more equivocal on the subject. Empirically, Hurrell is explicit that international environmental politics have not in fact produced an 'erosion' of sovereignty (1995: 139), but rather, like Jackson, that they have produced an increased cosmopolitanism in the way that states act. He is worth quoting at length on this:

We have seen a very important change in the character and goals of international society: away from minimalist goals of co-existence towards the creation of rules and institutions that embody notions of shared responsibilities, that impinge heavily on the domestic organization of states, that invest individuals and groups within states with rights and duties, and that seek to embody some notion of the planetary good. (Hurrell 1995: 139, see also pp. 147–8)

Normatively, Hurrell is also quick to defend the independence of states. Like Bull, he argues that another form of global political order is impossible to bring about because states will not cede their authority (Hurrell and Kingsbury 1992: 7–8). But he also makes the stronger normative argument that the state is not simply an empirical fact but also a moral good rather than a necessary evil.

A key theme in Bull's arguments, echoed elsewhere both in English school writers and in contemporary debates in international environmental politics, concerns the nature of what we would now call international governance and the way it interacts with environmental degradation. For Bull, the central point of departure is arguments that environmental degradation requires a 'suprastate' solution because of the extreme collective action problems such degradation purportedly poses. Such arguments (the most well-known are those by Garrett Hardin 1968 and William Ophuls 1977, although Bull's critique focuses on Falk 1971) were prevalent in environmental debates in the 1970s, and leave an ongoing legacy in shaping popular understandings of environmental politics. Bull's argument is designed to refute the claim here and suggest that the states-system, at least in principle, can deal effectively with the environmental crisis.

His key claims are both that the sovereignty of states is both non-negotiable in any case, so for pragmatic reasons environmental protection must be pursued through the states-system rather than through attempts to transcend it, and that state sovereignty is positively beneficial in environmental terms. The important theoretical point in terms of conceptions of international society is that the states-system is not to be understood as an unremittingly competitive realm, where states jealously guard their sovereignty and pursue their interests blind to the consequence beyond their borders. In this sense, Bull's rejection of Falk and others is because of their realist conception of international politics. By contrast, since international politics is to be understood as a *society*, with rules, norms, mutual recognition playing important parts in shaping the interaction between states and constituting their relation to each other, there is no reason in principle to assume that they will not be able to develop new rules, norms, to deal with environmental degradation. Bull emphasizes here the intensification of forms of human solidarity that can emerge within the states-system. In this case, sovereignty becomes positively important as the mode of authority through which states can be expected to keep bargains and implement agreements.[9]

INTERNATIONAL SOCIETY INTERPRETATIONS OF GLOBAL ENVIRONMENTAL GOVERNANCE

Since Bull's arguments, which have had occasional repercussions in environmental debates, environmental debates in international relations have evolved enormously. Many of these debates, especially in the 1990s and beyond, have concerned precisely questions of international or global environmental governance (GEG). These debates have developed considerable sophistication regarding the nature of such governance and how it should be understood theoretically and normatively. These debates are also highly heterogeneous in their understanding of what GEG is, and thus both (*a*) how we reflect on the utility of a conception of international society drawn from the English School; and (*b*) how we attempt to apply such a conception to understand GEG is rather complex. To proceed, I will try to run through a range of current arguments regarding GEG and to discuss their relationship to a notion of international society in the two senses above.[10]

GEG as Programmatic Reform

In policy circles, the most prominent notion of GEG concerns debates about reforming the UN system to meet environmental challenges more effectively. This is most prominent around debates about the establishment of a World Environmental Organisation (WEO, see Biermann 2000, 2001; Newell 2001; Von Moltke 2001; Whalley and Zissimos 2001). As a green version of the debates surrounding the Commission on Global Governance, GEG here is taken to mean a programmatic, reformist orientation to the institutional arrangements in global politics, principally the UN system. Such a conception of GEG informed the run up to the World Summit on Sustainable Development (WSSD, Johannesburg, 2002), with a ministerial-level group meeting on precisely this question: how to reform the UN machinery to deliver more effective environmental governance? In debates within this group, governance was expressed in terms of concerns about the fragmentation of existing environmental agreements into different issue areas, lack of sufficient authority to enforce compliance, and lack of coordination of the various environmental governance mechanisms (see, for example, UNEP 2001, especially paragraphs 15–26). In this sense, the debate has both its own dynamics, in terms of reflections on the adequacy of UNEP, and from the UNCED, the CSD, to coordinate the UN machinery in the direction of sustainable development, and also reflects more general debates about 'UN reform' in the 1990s.

Debates about a WEO reflect what we might call a 'soft suprastatism'. There are arguments for the dysfunctionality of the states-system in environmental terms but a reluctance to draw the full suprastatist conclusions, settling for arguments for more 'authority' to be shifted to global levels. The arguments therefore are structurally similar to those dealt with by Bull, except that because the conclusions are softer, the position actually ends up much closer to Bull. They miss his point about the importance of the intensification of human solidarity, but certainly one might argue that the intensification of institutionalized interaction between states on environmental issues, and the progressive acceptance of internationally negotiated norms, represents in English School terms a shift in the balance away from realism through pluralism to solidarism. The main problem with the WEO debates in the current context is however that they are analytically weak. They focus in wholly normative terms without having much of a coherent concept of 'governance' (it remains very fuzzy term in these debates, and often the debate reduces to a sense simply that whatever governance is, we just need more of it). There is little serious analysis of the nature of environmental challenges and thus the ways political institutions may respond and/or be transformed to respond to them.

GEG as International Regimes

In academic international relations, the dominant account of GEG still perhaps arises out of the neoliberal institutionalist tradition in regime theory. This suggests that 'global environmental governance' refers to little more than the sum of the overlapping networks of interstate regimes and other cooperative arrangements on specific environmental issues. As with Bull, the emphasis here is on regulation at the intergovernmental levels. Key examples of this position are Young (1994, 1997), Vogler (2000), and Haas, Keohane, and Levy (1993). In terms of overall patterns of environmental governance, there is for regime writers little substantive change in the origins, agents, and processes of environmental governance.

As with the international society tradition, neoliberal institutionalism arose out of an observation or claim that international politics, while principally composed of states, is something more than the anarchic free-for-all assumed by realists (for an extensive analysis of the relation between the two traditions, see Hurrell 1993). Theoretically, however, neoliberal institutionalism tends to rely on a rational choice explanation for the emergence of the international regimes that regulate interstate behaviour. Regimes in the environmental field emerge because of the expectations of interaction between states over a long period of time, because states are assumed to behave as absolute-gains rather than relative-gains maximizers, because uncertainty about outcomes means they are likely to choose rules which represent fair outcomes for all parties. Such features also then mean that international institutions and organizations play important roles in facilitating information flows, building trust, and enabling states to find cooperative solutions. There is then a dynamic between these two features, which favours increased institutionalization and thus further cooperation over time. And, of course, the patterns of cooperation over specific issues increasingly intersect with each other. Rules and principles from one regime are borrowed by another, organizations such as UNEP manage several regimes at once, and regimes may be functionally or environmentally interconnected as between climate change and ozone depletion. Collectively, the density of the patterns of regimes are regarded to collectively make up an overarching pattern of global environmental governance (Young 1997).

Neoliberal institutionalist accounts of contemporary environmental governance at a broad level therefore share many similarities with those that could be offered by the international society tradition. There is often emphasis on the viability of the states-system in environmental terms (for instance, Levy, Keohane, and Haas 1993; Young 1997), as made by Bull also. There is an emphasis in the intensification of interaction between states because of increased recognition of common interests and fates, similar to the shift from realism towards solidarism in English School accounts. As a generalization, however, neoliberal institutionalists tend to emphasize the development of interdependence as shaping state interests and thus driving regime development (Keohane 1989), while English School writers tend to be more interested in the normative development of a sense of mutual obligations.

GEG as Multilevel Governance

So far so good for the English School. There are several senses in which both of the accounts of contemporary GEG can be understood in terms of a notion of international society. However there are three other arguments where the perspectives start to diverge widely from international society accounts. The first of these is the notion of 'multilevel governance' associated in particular with pluralist writers such as James Rosenau.[11] Here, the connections begin to collapse, in particular because the assumption of the centrality of states in environmental governance is challenged.

According to this account, global environmental politics interacts with other processes, in particular economic globalization and the emergence of 'global civil society', to produce simultaneous shifts of authority from the state to other spheres of authority, for example at the local and global levels. This approach sees a qualitative transformation in global environmental governance, with both 'sub-statist' and 'supra-statist' processes at play. This account draws from Rosenau (1990, 1992) and is related to work on global environmental governance by Hempel (1996) and Rosenau (1993), as well as a range of writers on multilevel governance (Vogler 2003). The principal point is that global environmental governance refers to the emergence of *multilevel* sites of governance as the result of processes of integration and fragmentation, what Rosenau refers to as 'fragmegration'.

This approach shares some features with the suprastatist argument. In particular, it shares a functionalist account of environmental governance, suggesting (both empirically and normatively) that environmental governance operates on spatial scales commensurate with those of environmental problems or ecosystem 'boundaries'. But rather than suggesting that the implication of this is for a unification of authority at global levels, it suggests a mixed, post-sovereign model of politics with differentiated forms of authority at different spatial levels depending on the features of particular problems and their socio-political dynamics. Thus, we get a localization of many resource management issues, where the responsiveness of locally based initiatives to ecosystem changes is more effective than nation-state based management would be, while we get regionalization of some issues (acid rain) and globalization of others (climate change). The model is not entirely functionalist in this manner, however; it is also the case that the spatial scales being chosen to manage particular issues are also driven by the 'fragmegrating' dynamic of economic globalization.

This account of GEG poses a significant challenge to the English School account of international society. It does, however, have resonance with Bull's notion of new medievalism (1977: 264–76). In particular, it challenges the notion that international politics can be thought of as a society of *states*. It may be a society of sorts, in the sense Bull and others suggest, that it is more than a system and is constituted by rules of mutual recognition, minimal order and solidarity, and so on, but if the multilevel character of GEG is persuasive and taken seriously, then it cannot be thought of solely as a society of states. For Bull, however, the question is not whether or not transnational NGOs exist or whether a variety of levels of governance can be identified, but whether such facts amount to the revision of the view that international politics can still be thought of as principally a society of states or organized according to some other principle (1977: 275), and it would be fair to say that he would be unconvinced by the evidence presented by pluralists developing ideas about global civil society or multilevel governance.

GEG as Deterritorialization

Perhaps a stronger challenge comes from the notion that rather than think of GEG in terms of multilevel governance, we think of it as fundamentally deterritorialized. Rosenau, who emphasizes the emergence of new spheres of authority, notes that some spheres of authority at the global level are distinctly non-territorial in scope. 'Glocalisation' therefore involves not only a change in the spatial scales of governance, where it is remains possible to determine a particular space/place where governance takes place, but also the emergence of patterns of environmental governance that increasingly operate outside a clearly defined space or place. Authority operates in relation to specific sets of practices but not spatially in terms of discretely defined and bounded places as assumed both in the presumption of state centrality and in terms of both suprastatism and the 'levels' focus of multilevel governance approaches.

Well-known examples in this approach are Clapp's (1998) account of the International Organization for Standardization (ISO), and a number of analyses of the Forest Stewardship Council (FSC) (such as Lipschutz 2000/1 and Humphreys 1996). In the former, the ISO,[12] originally an organization where firms and states agree technical product standards, has developed sets of standards for environmental management processes of firms. This has thus had significant effects in terms of preventing state-based regulations regarding such processes, shifting the attention away from environmental outcomes onto firm management processes, and most importantly shifting authority for such governance onto a fairly secretive organization whose decisions are effectively made by some of the largest firms in the world. This has thus significantly affected commodity chains, giving some large firms enhanced control over suppliers (many of whom are in the developing world) by making them conform to ISO14000 standards in order to be able to supply transnational corporations (Clapp 1998).

Regarding the FSC, the dynamics are rather different. Here, the Worldwide Fund for Nature (WWF) established the FSC in response to the failure of states to negotiate an adequate forests management regime, to create an ecolabel for timber products. The scheme, launched in the mid-1990s, has expanded rapidly (albeit with different success in different countries) and significantly affected the practices of forestry companies in many parts of the world. The FSC created a set of ecolabels, and then worked with construction companies and in particular major retailers, to create market pressure on timber firms to attempt to get FSC approval for their products.

In both these instances, governance practices occur and the practices of a range of actors are shaped through patterns of authority and rule-making. But in both, there is no neatly defined spatial scale across which the authority can be said to operate. Rather, practices are affected wherever firms feel either the need to legitimize themselves in environmental terms (for market or political reasons) by gaining ISO14000 accreditation or gain heightened control over suppliers by insisting they get such accreditation, or in the case of the FSC, wherever there are sufficient market pressures for 'sustainable' timber and a market structure which facilitates such consumer power. In this sense, then, the governance is 'deterritorialized'.

Deterritorialized governance tends to be based on transnational networks of actors. Newell (2000) provides the best general account. Newell shows a range of strategies of networked environmental NGOs, to shape corporate and occasionally state behaviour. While there are many differences in strategy, from boycott campaigns to ecolabel schemes to strategic alliances with firms, they all share the feature of attempting to govern corporate behaviour, and to do so in ways many of which have no regard for the territorial boundaries of states. Deterritorialization as a process is embedded in more general accounts of contemporary social change/globalization in terms of the emergent dominance of network forms of social organization—the most prominent general account is Castells (2000). Thus both private business actors and social movements organize themselves in terms of global networks rather than hierarchies, and such networks are able to ignore or bypass hierarchical forms of organization like states and traditional business hierarchies. The Internet is often taken as both the archetype technology of network organization, and a key medium through which business and social movement organization and governance operates.

The challenge to international society accounts of international politics here is obvious, and more severe than that posed by the focus on multilevel governance. Here, the fundamental structure of governance, as based on territorially defined units that govern discrete spaces, and interact in a homogenous way with each other, is called into question.

GEG as Corporate Governance and Governance from Below

But for me (and others) this focus on either multilevel governance or deterritorialization fails to get to the heart of what is going on in GEG. While they both may describe aspects of GEG which are emergent and important, they offer little by way of substantive explanation of such processes. For this, a turn to Global Political Economy is necessary.[13] From this perspective global (environmental) governance involves two contradictory tendencies: a project to centralize economic and political power in a 'globalizing elite' of key transnational firms, banks, and the state managers of the G-7 states; and resistance to these centralizing processes, combined with attempts to govern the practices of states and firms 'from below'. Like for multilevel governance approaches, it is closely associated with processes of global economic governance; unlike those approaches, it offers an explanation for the connections rather than simply asserting a similarity and synchronicity. Like the deterritorialization approach, there is a focus on environmental NGOs; unlike that approach, there is an explanation for this strategy by NGOs and an attempt to situate such strategies in a broader political context.

The first of the twin movements in GEG from this perspective concerns the project of a collectivity of actors making up the neoliberal globalization project, which is engaged in a set of governance activities aimed at achieving a 'new constitutional' settlement 'beyond politics'. Such a project aims to discipline national governments, social movements such as trade unions and environmentalists, as well as individuals, to behave in ways that enable globally mobile capital to pursue its profit-maximization unhindered by 'unnecessary' regulation. This thus involves the centralization of power to a mix of public and private organizations (such as transnational corporations, the WTO, G-7, ISO, and World Economic Forum) where governance is increasingly undemocratic and unaccountable. Global governance operates on behalf of, and is sometimes directed by, transnational businesses that have become the principal actors both nationally (Monbiot 2000) and globally (Korten 1995). The rhetoric of market mechanisms, deregulation, public–private partnerships, codes of conduct, and corporate environmentalism both dominate and constitute global environmental governance. At the same time, environmental questions are a key part of legitimizing such a project, with neoliberals keen to display their environmental credentials through organizations such as the Business Council for Sustainable Development or via the promotion of innovative governance mechanisms such as emissions trading (Chatterjee and Finger 1994; Karliner 1997), and thus this process also entails a shift of environmental questions to the heart of global politics. Specific patterns of environmental governance, be they the operation of interstate regimes, patterns of multilevel or deterritorialized governance, or reform projects such as the proposal for a WEO, can all thus be explained as part of this overall project, and operate in ways which may at times appear to bolster the 'interstate' system, and at others to undermine it.

On the other hand resistance is practised by a variety of actors working against centralization and trying to 'govern' transnational corporations, governments, and global economic institutions (Paterson 1999). Such resistance is often of course, and most spectacularly, in protests at multilateral economic summits, precisely against the project for 'corporate rule' outlined above. But it also is more widespread in terms of the various activities of environmental NGOs outlined in Newell's account discussed above (2000), in movements against biotechnology and 'biopiracy' (Shiva 1996), in movements for economic localization (Hines 2000), in countercultural practices to delegitimize corporate practices and the global institutions which support them (*Adbusters* is the best-known site of such resistance).

This perspective on GEG sits particularly uneasily with English school accounts of international society. To the extent that an international society can be talked about in these terms, its specifically capitalist character should be emphasized in ways which are more or less ignored by English School writers. The nature of the norms that operate between states are specifically those which either directly benefit international capitalist actors (regarding trade, finance, and so on), or which in a more diffuse but definite manner underpin a capitalist economy (mutual recognition, assumptions regarding the relationship between property and sovereignty, and so on). Regarding environmental governance specifically, this perspective emphasizes that even within the confines of the states-system, what the state 'is' and how states interact are principally conditioned by their capitalist character rather than by the features of an 'international society' as envisaged by Bull and others (or for that matter by institutionalists such as Young). The modern state in this view cannot be understood outside its historical emergence alongside capitalism, and the structural nature of the relationship between the state and capital (see for instance Jessop 1990). One of the fundamental purposes of the modern state is to secure the conditions under which capital can pursue accumulation (and at least historically, therefore engender environmental degradation) successfully. But the perspective also explains why increasingly, globalizing economic elites are able to pursue state-based governance when it suits them, but create new forms of governance beyond the states-system if necessary for their purposes, a feature which international society writers find difficult to conceptualize. As a consequence, from this view, Bull's objections to arguments about shifts to a 'new medieval' order, which as noted has resonances with notions of multilevel governance, is misplaced because if the capitalist nature of world order is taken seriously, then the 'either/or' nature of his argument makes little sense; *both* the states-system *and* multilevel (or deterritorialized) governance coexist, as each emerge at different historical points to regulate, promote, and shape capital accumulation and deal with resistance to it.

CONCLUSIONS

A key development when thinking back to Bull's arguments is that for most of the ways of thinking about GEG discussed, especially those it is clear I am more persuaded by, the way of asking the question is quite different to that posed by Bull. Bull asks a rather static question about the adequacy or otherwise of particular political institutions for dealing with environmental degradation. He recounts the apocryphal 'I wouldn't start from here' as an analogy for all of the various objections to the states-system discussed in that chapter, including environmental challenges. 'The doctrine that the states system does not provide the best starting point for the pursuit of world order has something of this quality. The fact is that the form of universal political organization which actually prevails in the world is that of the states system, and it is within this system that the search for consensus has to begin' (Bull 1977: 295–6). His only acceptance of possible change is in terms of the possible increases in human solidarity, which may come about because of dealing with environmental challenges (1977: 294–5).

But what is precisely called into question in many contemporary accounts of GEG is whether or not such an assumption that the only, or even perhaps the prevalent, 'universal political organisation' is the states-system, or at least that there are not tendencies within the global political order which suggest alternatives emerging within contemporary global politics. Rather, many contemporary arguments about GEG do not take the static account of the states-system for granted, and rather ask a question about the ways in which the international system is undergoing changes in forms of governance, and therefore the way in which environmental degradation and its articulation by environmentalists and others are helping to shape such changes, and about the implications of such changes for environmental degradation. In this sense, Bull and the international society tradition share much with realists that system change only could come about through some sort of contractual agreement between states. His rejection of the suprastatist arguments of Ophuls is precisely because he cannot envisage states contracting away their authority.

But in a number of contemporary conceptions of global governance, especially regarding environmental governance, this is rather misplaced, for two principal reasons. First, environmental arguments share much here with arguments in neo-Gramscian and other Marxian International Political Economy (and perhaps most explicitly with Marxist state theory). What Bull and the international society tradition miss, as do realists, neoliberal institutionalists, constructivists, and others, is that to speak of a states-system without thinking about the capitalist character of both the states within it and the broader international economy which structures state authority, legitimacy, resources, and so on, is insufficient. In regard to the particular point here, to miss this is to miss the way that (dominant) states create new governance mechanisms in part in response to, and in part to shape, new patterns of economic interaction, new conceptions of how to promote accumulation, and new interests of dominant fractions of capital. Thus many of the new economic governance mechanisms associated with 'globalisation' (I elide, of course, the various debates about this term) show precisely that Bull was wrong—states do indeed contract out of significant elements of their sovereignty, and do so in important ways concerning both how we think about the nature of international relations in general, and international environmental politics in particular.

Such a focus on the capitalist character of the states-system also involves an explanation of why Bull's second objection to Falk, and the arguments of others who emphasize the potential of states in environmental management, is misplaced. For such a perspective helps to show why environmental degradation is fundamentally and systemically rooted in processes of accumulation, and thus that states, for whom the promotion of accumulation is one of their core functions and legitimating strategies, are systemically bound up with ecologically destructive processes.

Second, many of the governance mechanisms emerging in the environmental field (as well as some in others, although the environmental field is perhaps the principal innovator here), precisely transcend an international society conception of global politics in ways where the question of states contracting to create such new forms is redundant. The forms of governance involved in the FSC are emblematic here. No state has been involved in the generation of a set of ecolabels which nevertheless in a very real sense 'govern' the practices of forest products industries in many places around the world. There may well be some sense of a 'global society', in that the authority of the FSC to regulate forest industries arises in part out of a sense of global solidarity and consciousness among consumers of forest products—norms of mutual recognition and responsibility if you like—but these cannot be regarded in any was as arising out of the states-system in the way that Bull suggests is the only way that such global solidarity can arise.

Thus to revisit Bull's use of the apocryphal story, if one is to ask the question 'what can the international society tradition tell us about global environmental politics?' the answer has to be 'I wouldn't start from here'.

Notes

1. Of course, the converse argument can also be made, that writers wanting to develop ecological–theoretic accounts of global politics have tended to neglect the English School. Laferrière and Stoett (1999), for example, occasionally mention Bull and Wight, but regard them as realists. The English School is also more or less ignored in my own attempts at such theoretical development (Paterson 2000, 2001). But of course the focus here is on the English School, not ecological thought.

2. Tim Dunne's overview (1998) of the English School is good evidence here, containing no references at all to the environment. His review essay on 'new thinking on international society' contains an assertion that recent thinkers have made such connections (2001: 225), but there are no examples developed (while there are ample ones given regarding the field where a similar claim is made about new work developing it, regarding human rights/humanitarian intervention) reinforcing the sense that the field is largely irrelevant for international society writers. Regarding Hurrell and Jackson, both are included in Dunne's list of contemporary members of the School (1998: 22), and I discuss their contributions below.

3. Unless otherwise stated, the page numbers in this section refer to Bull (1977).

4. This as at best a highly tendentious reading of Hardin's argument, if not a complete misreading. To focus only on Hardin's arguments for limitations of freedom is to miss that Hardin's point is precisely that such acceptance of limitations can only come about through different political/property arrangements than open access ones. Freedom and political order are indivisible for Hardin in a way which undermines Bull's attempt to use him.

5. This argument is of course circular, at least when dealt with in relation to the suprastatist arguments. If a global state were brought into being, the issue of mutual recognition becomes irrelevant as the source of global order becomes global state authority not mutual recognition.

6. These arguments about urgency of course pop up in various contexts regarding environmental politics. In this context, it is of course a fair point to make, but worth emphasizing that it has nothing to do with the structural argument about the nature of the states-system that its critics want to make, having only pragmatic force. If, of course, the states-system is so dysfunctional, then whether or not national governments have the information, etc. to act is not the point—the systemic point is that the system makes them behave in ecologically irrational ways, and this point is not challenged by Bull.

7. For more analysis of Bull's defence of the states-system, see Suganami, Chapter 1, this volume.

8. Brown does not give a citation here however to where Bull says this, and Jackson does not acknowledge Bull as a source for this formulation.

9. Related to my main lines of critique below, but not central to them, is a critique of the concept of sovereignty underpinning Bull's argument here. A number of authors reflect Bull's basic argument that environmental challenges can strengthen sovereignty rather than erode it (for instance, Haas, Keohane, and Levy 1993: 415–17; Hurrell 1995: 136–9). But in order to do this, the authors have to 'unbundle' sovereignty into a bundle of rights and responsibilities, which can be traded off against each other, rather than the image of sovereignty as a solid, homogenous edifice as in the classical image adopted by Bull. In this context, Bull's view would make more sense if the constructivist underpinnings of this 'unbundling' of sovereignty were accepted, and thus the arguments in English School writings about a shift from realist to rationalist to solidarist conceptions of international society are expressed in terms of shifts in the meanings of sovereignty, rather than just, for example, in terms of 'responsibility' (Jackson 2000: 175–8). See Litfin (1998*a,b*) on the 'greening of sovereignty'; for another interesting way of thinking about such shifts in the meanings of state sovereignty/responsibility, see Goodin (1990).

10. This section draws on earlier work on GEG, both individually (Paterson 1997, 1999, 2000) and with colleagues (Paterson, Humphreys, and Pettiford 2003).

11. This sense of GEG has brought out some of the more ugly neologisms around. Multi-level governance is tame enough, but 'glocalisation' (Hempel 1996) and 'fragmegration' (Rosenau 1990) are also in widespread use.

12. The ISO is a hybrid international organization with membership from both states and private corporations. It emerged in the mid-nineteenth century to agree technical standards for a range of manufacturing products, to enable international trade. Its role has expanded in the late twentieth century to include standards for management processes and, in the ISO14000 series, environmental management processes.

13. See also Buzan (Chapter 6, this volume) on the relationship between the international society tradition and international political economy (IPE). However, it is probably clear that the conception of IPE here is rather different than that developed by Buzan, arising it does principally out of an (eco-) Marxism as opposed to the liberal economics from which Buzan's account of IPE arises. Fundamentally, I conceive IPE to be about the global development of capitalist society, rather than the international economic interactions (and their interstate managements) of market economies—the ontologies here are fundamentally different. As a consequence the potential conversations between the international society tradition and IPE are rather different, and much more antagonistic. As one example, from the point of view of the conception of IPE here, Buzan's statement that 'liberal international economic orders belong to solidarism' is literally nonsensical, since such an order is precisely about extending capitalist domination across the globe, not about some 'harmony of interests' underpinning Buzan's view. The closest one can get from this conception of IPE to the English School is through the analogous point by Chris Reus-Smit about the increasingly economic character of the 'moral purpose of the state' (1999), Reus-Smit's relatively constructive critiques of the English School (2002) through their conversation with constructivism, and his own analysis of international environmental politics through his notion of the moral purpose of the state (1996).

10

Order and Disorder in World Politics

Roland Bleiker

Order is a rare island, it is an archipelago. Disorder is the common ocean from where island emerge.

(Serres: 1977)

Order is central to the notion of an international society. Without order there can be no society. And without society there can be no civilized life. Or so at least resonates one of the most central themes of the English School, which has recently seen a strong renaissance in international relations scholarship (see the Introduction and Part One of this volume). Two assumptions are thus essential to this tradition of thought: that order does indeed exist in international politics, and that this order is desirable. Both assumptions are, at least to some extent, commonsensical. Of course, some type of order exists, even in an allegedly anarchical post-national realm. Otherwise there would be nothing but endless chaos and conflict. And, of course, order has its positive dimensions, for it provides the basis for stability and the rule of law.

But common sense is not always as commonsensical as it seems, or at least not as unproblematic and value-free. This certainly is the case with English School assumptions about international society. Allow me to present the issue through an unusual foray into neuropsychology. Such a detour may reveal more than a direct look at world politics. Peter Brugger conducted a highly insightful series of studies that demonstrate how the brain seeks to discover rules and patterns even in circumstances where there are only random events. In one of his behavioural tests, Brugger asked forty volunteers to participate in a game. They had to direct a cursor on a screen towards a target and open it as often as possible. Participants did not know that the target could be opened only after a certain period of time had expired—otherwise it simply remained locked. All participants managed to score repeatedly. But instead of simply waiting until the respective time span was over, almost all participants moved their cursors across the screen, searching for a correct route towards the target. Many developed 'highly complex theories about the most efficient ways of reaching [the target].' Only two of the forty participants figured out that there was no correct route, that indeed there was no route at all (Brugger and Graves 1997: 251–72; Brugger 2001: 71).

I strongly suspect that exactly the same is the case in international relations scholarship: that we develop complex theories to visualize the exact outlines of an international society where there are in fact only blurred contours or none at all; that we project far more of ourselves onto the world of world politics than there actually is 'out there'. As a result, we may not only overestimate the existence of order in international relations, but also overvalue its importance. In any case, the relationship between order and disorder is far more complex than the modern practice of dualistic conceptualizing has it. Orders can sometimes be highly unjust, such as in order-obsessed Nazi Germany. Disorder can occasionally be required to promote orders that are more just. Or, perhaps most importantly, disorder can be both the only reality we have and a valuable source of ethical politics. By probing these issues I am not looking for definitive answers. Rather, I would like to pose a few crucial questions about international society. The ensuing ruminations stake no claim to comprehensiveness. There will, for instance, be no engagement with various authors who are central to the English School. Neither will I discuss the controversial issue of who belongs to this tradition and who does not, except to demonstrate how these very discussions are a reflection of the modern compulsion to order the world. Finally, I must admit that I am neither English nor received 'formal' training in the English School. But sometimes a look from the outside can reveal aspects that are difficult to see from within—a premise upon which the contribution of this chapter rests.

ORDERING INTERNATIONAL SOCIETY

The existence of international society, Martin Wight (1991: 30) stressed, is 'a political and social fact', reflected in a variety of phenomena, from predictable diplomatic practices to international law. Scholarship on this issue spans a wide spectrum of ideas, ranging from realism on one end to cosmopolitanism on the other. Extreme realist positions hold that the anarchical nature of the international system does not allow for the emergence of a true society of states: the struggle for power and the need to defend sovereignty is simply too strong. Cosmopolitan traditions, by contrast, focus on either the existence or the desirability of a global sense of solidarity, if not an actual world government. Most contributions to the English School are located somewhere between these extremes. Perhaps best exemplified in Martin Wight's and Hedley Bull's work, the assumption is that even an anarchical international system allows for the existence of rules and patterns. Since the latter account for a relatively high degree of order, one can—and indeed should—speak of an international society (Bull 1977: 23–7; Wight 1991: 14).

One gargantuan task stands out: that of locating manifestations of order and determining what exactly accounts for an international society. Much of English School scholarship falls short on this account, at least according to the numerous critics discussed in this volume. Bull (1977: 8) defined international order as patterned activities that sustain 'the primary goals of the society of states'. But few additional measuring devices are given. This is why Richard Shapcott (2003: 5) stresses the need for a 'more sustained and coherent philosophical articulation'. Robert Jackson (1995: 113), likewise, refers to the need to visualize international society 'not merely as an abstract concept but as an empirical reality'. Perhaps the most explicit critique comes from Martha Finnemore (2001: 509–13), who deplores the remarkable absence of extensive discussions on research methods in the English School. Without such discussions and ensuing rules of evidence, she argues, it becomes very difficult to locate, yet alone analyse international society. Finnemore's critique is convincing, even for someone, as the present author, who eschews positivist falsification methods and assumes, as Tim Dunne (1998: 9) does, that international society and political community can be 'knowable even if they are not observable'. But without clear discussions of method and evidence it becomes difficult to determine the extent to which we superimpose order upon random events, simply because we crave order in a world that appears increasingly complex and chaotic.

A good way into the dilemma of locating order is through a recent practical example. The behaviour of the United States since the inauguration of president George W. Bush in 2002 seems to seriously challenge established patterns of global politics. Some of the ensuing events may even call into question the notion of an international society, for the maintenance of the latter depends heavily on rules, most notably, as Bull (1977: p. xiii) notes, on 'those rules which have the status of international law'. Among the various instruments of order, international law contains some of the most essential and certainly most explicit principles that regulate both the relationship between states and the conduct of world affairs in general. The United States has shown remarkably little respect for these laws and the international institutions that are related to them. Washington withdrew from the Kyoto Protocol on climate change, the Land Mine Ban Treaty, the Biological Weapons Treaty, the Comprehensive Test Ban Treaty, the ABM Treaty, and the newly established International Criminal Court. The US treatment of suspected Al-Qaeda detainees in Afghanistan and Guantanamo Bay is said to violate the Geneva Convention. The same is asserted for the increasingly sweeping surveillance practices within the United States. Perhaps most significantly, the recent war against Iraq violated international law because it lacked a respective resolution from the UN Security Council.

Recent US violations of international law clearly come as a blow to international society. Can one still speak of a meaningful international order if it can be so easily transgressed and replaced with new rules or no rules at all? Bull would undoubtedly answer in the affirmative, pointing out that the element of disorder always looms large and that any legal system gets violated at times. This in itself does not question the system, for without transgressions there would be no need for rules at all (Bull 1977: p. xii, 136). With regard to US behaviour, Bull (1977: 72) would probably stress that each state has different interpretations of existing legal, moral, and operational rules. And Washington did, of course, believe that it fully adhered to the Geneva Convention and that no additional UN Security Council resolution was needed to make the war against Iraq just and legal. This in itself is significant, Bull would point out, for by indicating a just cause, or at least a pretext for war, the respective state is keen to be seen as playing by the rules. The fact that it feels it 'owes others states an explanation of its conduct' is itself indicative of the importance of rules and patterns, even if the state in question violates many of them (Bull 1977: 45, 138).

Following Bull (1977: 137), the task now consists of figuring out whether the rules of international law are sufficiently observed to allow for the existence of an international order. Alternatively, one can go one step further, again with Bull (1977: p. xiii), and contemplate how order may be able to exist independently of international law and international institutions. Consider how a new political order may be emerging, a *pax Americana* so to speak, an order that stands, at least in part, in contradiction to the old body of international laws and institutions. Michael Ignatieff (2003*b*: 24) speaks of a 'global hegemony whose grace notes are free markets, human rights and democracy, enforced by the most awesome military power the world has ever known'. Order would thus emerge from the American-led promotion of certain 'common' interests. The British Prime Minister, Tony Blair, perfectly captured this source of order. He admitted that states act in self-interested ways. But at the same time he stressed that 'our self-interest and our mutual interests are today inextricably woven together' (Blair cited in Cohen 2003: 15). One would be hard pressed to find a better summary of the English School's attempt to demonstrate that common interests make it possible for order to emerge even in an anarchical international system and a world driven by power politics.

The notion of shared interests as a source of global order can be questioned. One can point out, for instance, that the self-interest of the United States and Britain is not necessarily the same as those of many developing countries. One could also draw attention to the possibility of *pax Americana* overreaching itself and thus being on the eve of decline (Kupchan 2003). Or one could, as Janice Bially Mattern (2003: 7) has done, question the very tendency to see order as emerging from either power politics or common interests. These are factors of order, she stresses, not sources. Bially Mattern proposes instead that shared identities are a key source of international order, that, indeed, 'identity is sufficient to impose order upon disorder'. One can see the above described reliance on democracy, market economics, and the rule of law not merely as interests, but as forms of identity too. But that still leaves open the question of whether these values are commonly shared to the point of forming the basis for an international society. Some authors have gone to great length to stress the incompatibility of different cultural traditions. Samuel Huntingdon's *Clash of Civilisations* is probably the most prominent example. The most recent manifestation of this tendency can be seen in Robert Kagan's *Of Paradise and Power* (2003), which popularizes the increasing rift between the United States and Europe that has emerged in 2002 and 2003 over disagreements regarding the legitimacy of the war against Iraq. Kagan sees American and European approaches as fundamentally incompatible. He locates the key differences in a dualism that English school writers (and others before them) identified long ago: the juxtaposition between, on the one hand, a 'Hobbesian' worldview of constant struggle and conflict based on power politics and military might and, on the other hand, a 'Kantian' vision of a world functioning according to rules, norms, and cooperation. The United States, in Kagan's view, subscribes to the 'Hobbesian' paradigm while Europe relies on a 'Kantian' approach. Americans are thus said to be more likely to resort to war while Europeans first explore all other avenues, even if this entails political impotence. But this difference is far less stark than its stereo-typical presentation has it. There is a big middle ground between anarchy and world governance, which is where most politics takes place, as English School writers have convincingly revealed. Furthermore, one can question how serious and lasting the current policy disagreement between the United States and Europe actually is. Bially Mattern is of help here again. She demonstrates how common identities tend to emerge from crises. Although focusing on a now long-past historical event, the Suez Crisis, her analysis is remarkably successful in shedding light on today's situation. In fact, reading her explanation of the breakdown and eventual re-emergence of the US–UK special relationship during the Suez Crisis, one is struck by how relevant the analysis is to present events in global politics. Just as in 1956, current disputes over how to handle the Iraq crisis led to a certain breakdown in traditional security relationships, most notably between the United States and some of its European allies, especially Germany and France. And just as half a century ago, key rhetorical strategies are used to validate one's own narrative and discredit those that compete (consider the terms 'axis of evil' or 'old Europe'). It remains to be seen whether, following Bially Mattern's model of the Suez Crisis, new rhetorical strategies may eventually unlink these 'phrases in dispute' from the 'narrative of betrayal,' thus re-establishing a shared sense of 'we' in the US–European relationship (Bially Mattern 2003: ch. 6). My sense is that this is already happening, and that the respective process is strong enough to establish a common transatlantic identity with regard to many essential issues. But whether a truly global sense of identity can emerge from this rapprochement is an entirely different question. Many states and people in the Arab world, for instance, would undoubtedly question this assumption.

A certain scepticism is thus in order and this scepticism must entail investigating the very values we bring to the study of order. To scrutinize this crucial issue, this chapter leaves the 'real world' for a moment and turns towards examining the assumptions that English School scholars bring to their efforts of locating and understanding international society.

ORDERING KNOWLEDGE ABOUT INTERNATIONAL SOCIETY

'International relations owes much to coincidence', says Bertrand Badie (1999: 7), and adds that we tend to forget this 'as a result of the often mechanic rigour of the social sciences'. Can this be said of the English School as well? Does its quest for knowledge about the international society superimpose order upon random events? Does it create a sense of community where there is in fact only a struggle for power? At first sight such an assumption seems unlikely, for much of English School scholarship has been articulated in opposition to the social scientific rigour that has dominated research on international relations in North America. The respective arguments, often termed as the 'second great debate' in international relations, pitted behaviourists and traditionalists in opposition to each other. It was waged between those who advocated social scientific research methodologies and those, like Bull (1966*a*: 625–38), who defended the value of historical and philosophical investigations.

The English School's refusal to rely solely on scientifically legitimated inquiries makes it a seemingly far more tolerant approach. Barry Buzan (2001: 472) speaks of a 'methodological pluralism'. He even goes as far as arguing that the English School is not simply another paradigm but, instead, 'an opportunity to step outside that game, and cultivate a more holistic, integrated approach to the study of international relations'. My sense is that English School scholarship is far more coherent, and has far more boundaries, than Buzan suggests. Tim Dunne (1998: 6) hints at these boundaries when referring to the English School as a certain 'tradition of inquiry'. But that in itself still suggests an exceptionally broad field of activities, for the methodological contours of the classical English School emerged, as Shapcott (2003: 4) convincingly stresses, as a 'case against the scientific approach rather than a positive statement of what a classical approach actually was'. Of course, English School scholarship is sceptical about an exclusive and unreflective use of scientific methods. Of course, it stresses the need to draw upon historical, philosophical, and legal sources. Of course, it recognizes the legitimacy of supplementing causal and correlational analyses with normative theorizing. In that sense, the English School is indeed very pluralist, certainly more so than most behavioural research. But there is far more order in English School scholarship than either Buzan's 'methodological pluralism' or Dunne's 'tradition of inquiry' suggest. Perhaps it is more appropriate to look at the English School, as Hidemi Suganami (2003*a*: 3) does, as 'a historically constituted and evolving cluster of scholars with a number of plausible and interrelated stories to tell'. But as it is with storytelling: the narrators and their narrations are usually embedded in and perpetuate a very specific set of cultural traditions and values.

The very term 'School' suggest something far more disciplined than the libertarian notion of pluralist tolerance. It evokes established hierarchies, strict rules, timetables, a clearly set curriculum, learning objectives, and recognized basic standards. It involves examinations and punishments to control and enforce these standards and the objectives they seek to measure. Of course, the term English School is only a convenient metaphor, which was in fact coined by a critic who argued for its 'closure' (Jones 1981: 1–13). But in many ways the term School is highly appropriate, for it captures the strong patterns and the need for order that are present underneath the pluralist façade of this tradition of inquiry.

An outsider examining the English School is soon struck by its strict and consistent citational rules, by who needs to be quoted for the scholarly work to count as a contribution to an English School inquiry. The classics are essential: Martin Wight, Herbert Butterfield, Hedley Bull, Adam Watson, and R. J. Vincent. Grotius must make a guest appearance at some stage, even if only fleetingly. And a new body of second- and third-generation writers are currently emerging as citational standards, from Hidemi Suganami to Richard Little, Barry Buzan, Robert Jackson, Tim Dunne, and Nicholas Wheeler, to name just a few. Then there is debate about who should be counted in and who should be left out: whether, for instance, E. H. Carr, C. A. W. Manning, and Andrew Linklater were/are members of the School or not. Such debates run the risk of generating research that revolves around internal disciplinary discussions, as if theorists themselves, rather than the key political challenges of the day, were the proper objects of study (Shapiro 2002: 597). But the practice of adhering to citational conventions is, of course, not unusual. It is standard practice in disciplinary obsessed Western academe. All subfields of politics, from critical theory to postcolonial studies, have their citational policies, even those that advocate pluralist and interdisciplinary methodologies.

But there is also a deeper sense of order in the English School. It manifests itself in two particular ways. First, the respective scholarship displays a strong tendency for reviewing, which has consequences that go far beyond the sense of innocence that is associated with the term. Look at the key journal articles on the subject. They all proceed in a standard and rather predictable manner. Before being able to say anything novel about international society, academic convention has it that the author must first summarize what previous scholars already said about it. This practice is so strong that the flagship journal of the study of international relations in Britain is actually—and very appropriately—called the *Review of International Studies*. On the one hand this practice is commendable, for it contributes to a comprehensive scholarly endeavour. On the other hand it is problematic, for it becomes difficult to advance scholarship that seriously questions the so-established order of knowledge about international society. Since a scholar must first review the existing body of knowledge, there is usually little space left to actually advance original ideas. And even if he or she manages to do so, there are limits to what can be said. Having to present critique or new ideas in reference to existing debates on the subject, confines their impact to the intellectual boundaries that have been established by the initial framing of debates about international society.

A second and interrelated manifestation of ordering that prevails in the English School has to do with the compulsion to structure past and present scholarship into clearly defined categories. The actual categories and their labels keep changing, but not so the need to squeeze every contribution into a preconceived intellectual box. Wight (1991: 31–48), for instance, divided theorists of international relations into realists, revolutionists, and rationalists. Bull (1977: 24) referred to similar contributions as the Hobbesian (realist), the Kantian (universalist), and the Grotian (international-ist) tradition. Contemporary interpreters of these classical texts either rehearse the labels introduced by White and Bull (see Jackson 1995: 114; Little 1995: 16; Buzan 2001: 474–6) or introduce slightly different but equally demarcated labels. Christian Reus-Smit (2002: 487–509), for instance, compares the English School with con-structivism, dividing the former into pluralists and solidarists, and the latter into three axes of debates: 'between sociological institutionalists, Habermasian commu-nicative action theorists and Foucauldian genealogists; between unit-level, systemic, and holistic theorists; and between interpretivists and positivists'.

The practice of reviewing and categorizing is not as unproblematic as it seems. It is, one could say, a modern attempt to bring order and certainty into a world of chaos and flux. It is a desire to squeeze freely floating and thus somewhat worrisome ideas into surveyable categories, to cut off and smoothen the various overlapping edges so that each piece fits neatly into its assigned place. The so-rehearsed standard is inevitably doing injustice to many of the ideas being rehearsed. Consider how Machiavelli, Hobbes, Kant, Grotius, or Pufendorf have come to be presented not as the original and complex thinkers they were, but as convenient labels to designate contemporary schools. Machiavelli and Hobbes, for instance, became ur-and-über-realists, even though many of their texts could easily be used to deconstruct the very core of realist wisdom (or lack thereof). Likewise, all we see rehearsed about Kant is the categorical imperative and the idea of a cosmopolitan government, while the far more complex and challenging *Critiques*, to name just some of his other texts, are being entirely ignored by scholars of international society. In the end, the Machiavelli, Hobbes, and Kant we know indicate far more about the values and political preferences of today's scholars than about the actual ideas that were once advanced by these thinkers. That practices of exclusion emerge from such reviewing practices is evident. We not only project stereotypical images upon far more complex thinkers, ideas, and political practices, but also rehearse and canonize them to the point that we forget the process of abstraction that has taken place along the way.

Can one escape classificatory urges altogether? Could one not simply engage in ordering exercises with caution, knowing that there are clear limits to it, knowing that no category or typology will ever be exhaustive or definitive? Yes, but to do so requires awareness of the dangers that such practices entail, most notably the risk of superimposing ideas and patterns of order upon events that are in reality either different, more complex, or simply random. Such intellectual self-awareness and self-criticism is, however, often lacking from English School scholarship. This in itself is not unusual, for the futile quest for a perfectly ordered world is an essential aspect of modern thought. Jean Baudelaire, in a much-cited passage, drew attention to the recurring quest for certainty in a world of turbulence and chaos. While describing modernity as 'the transient, the fleeting, the contingent,' Baudelaire (1961: 1163) points towards constant attempts to discover underlying patterns behind these ephemeral features. He describes the recurring quest for essences as a desire to 'extract the eternal out of the transient'.

THE VALUE OF ORDER

In view of the long modern compulsion of ordering it is hardly surprising that order is seen by and large as unproblematic and positive. One can say exactly the same about order as Chris Brown (1995*a*: 90) said about the notion of an international community: it is always used in a positive way, never pejoratively, as if order itself would make the world a better place. It is thus also not surprising that English School scholarship treats order not only as an analytical category, but also as a normative goal. Bull (1977: 96, p. xii) is among the few scholars who recognized the problematic dimensions of this double assumption. While introducing his study as a detached scholarly analysis of order as an empirical phenomenon in world politics, rather than a presentation of order as a 'value, goal, or objective,' he acknowledged that the two are difficult to separate:

I have sought to avoid giving a 'persuasive definition' of the term 'order' that would prejudge the question of the value of order as a human goal. On the other hand, I do in fact hold that order is desirable, or valuable in human affairs, and *a fortiori* in world politics.

Few would question that order is desirable and essential. Without order there can be no rule of law, no protection of human rights, no civilized life in general. But order does not necessarily equate with the good life. The recently proliferating anti-globalization movement, for instance, has drawn attention to the undersides of the current neoliberal world order. The merits of this body of knowledge and activism can be debated, but it is far more difficult to dispute that many if not most injustices in life, from domestic abuse to torture, are not the product of disorder, but of unjust orders. The horror of Nazi Germany, or of any authoritarian state, does not stem from absence of order, but from an obsession with order. Indeed, no society is more ordered than present-day North Korea: absolutely everything is regulated and controlled by an omnipresent and paranoid state apparatus. Few commentators would present this form of order as desirable. And yet, order remains an overwhelmingly positive and unproblematized category in scholarship about international society.

Given the problematic but unproblematized dimensions of order, one should reasonably want to inquire into the value not only of existing orders, but also of those that are projected onto the world. The type of normative order that the English School discusses is certainly not value free. If we examine scholarship that has come out of this tradition several clear value traits become visible. Three of them appear particularly distinct: international society is largely presented in Western, masculine, and state-centric terms.

The Western values embedded in English School perspectives on international society are perhaps the most explicit, or at least the most discussed normative dimensions. When surveying several international societies that existed in history, Bull (1977: 16) stressed that they 'were all founded upon a common culture or civilisation'. It is hardly surprising that Western values are identified as the foundation of today's international society. Of course, English School scholars are not the only ones to point out that globalization is above all a process of Westernization, and that it is thus only logical that today's key international institutions and norms contain Western cultural traits (Bull and Watson 1984; Giddens 1990; Latouche 1996). But the issue goes beyond describing an empirical reality, or so at least believes Suganami (2003*a*: 12), who argues that the English School's 'West-centricity is hard to deny'. He locates this tendency in several features, such as insensitivity towards the undersides of the Europanization of the world, the relative lack of engagement with non-Western cultures, or the strong confidence in the values of Western civilization and the resulting fear that other cultures could undermine these values. Jacinta O'Hagan (2002: 115) pursues a similar line of inquiry by stressing that English School scholars tend to privilege the Western experience and its values by using them as a measuring device to judge other societies.

Equally striking, but far less discussed, are the gendered dimensions of the English School (see Jacqui True's contribution, Chapter 8, this volume). The respective scholarship is one of the most male-dominated domains of inquiry, and this even by standards of a discipline that already displays unusually strong masculine traits. All key contributors to the debate are men. Rosalyn Higgins, Claire Cutler, and Jacinta O'Hagan are among the very rare female contributors, but none of them are considered part of the citational canon. And none of them, or any of the men who are part of the canon, have analysed the gendered dimensions of the international society.

A third but not necessarily final value that can be located in English School scholarship is its state-centrism. States are, of course, central actors in international politics, and despite much talk to the contrary, they have not lost this key position (Bernauer 2000). But a great variety of cross-territorial actors and factors, from multinational corporations to media networks and protest movements, are becoming increasingly influential. But apart from a few side-remarks, English School writers have not taken on this issue in a systematic manner. One of the rare exceptions is Margaret Keck and Kathryn Sikkink's study on *Activists Beyond Borders* (1998). But again, their contribution is not recognized as part of the citational canon.

One could discuss in detail to what extent English School scholars are simply describing the Western, masculine, and state-centric nature of the international system, or to what extent they project these values upon practices that are in reality far more complex. Aspects of the latter are certainly involved, but it is not my task here to explore them. Rather, I limit my analysis to demonstrating that the modern compulsion to order tends to make us forget not only that order and disorder are associated with particular values, but also that the relationship between them is far more complex and interrelated than we tend to assume.

THE INTERTWINEMENT OF ORDER AND DISORDER

Just as order tends to be presented as inherently good, disorder is usually seen as inherently bad. 'The most formidable enemy one must face in politics is disorder', writes Alain Joxe (2002: 118, 122). 'Order', he stresses, 'is always necessary because it provides protection'. Again, this is not necessarily wrong, for without order there can, indeed, be no protection. But it is incomplete. Both order and disorder are far more complex phenomena and values. Just as order can be the basis of terror and repression, disorder can provide the opportunity for freedom and justice. Perhaps it is difficult to see this link because Western thought has always revolved around juxtaposing antagonistic bipolar opposites, such as order/chaos, good/evil, or just/unjust. One side of the pairing is considered to be analytically and conceptually separate from the other. The relationship between the bipolar opposites generally expresses the superiority, dominance, or normative desirability of one entity (such as order) over the other (such as disorder). Taoist philosophy is among the traditions of thought that explicitly questioned such dualistic conceptualizing. Instead of thinking in the form of dichotomies, opposites are considered complementary because neither side can exist by itself. Since order, for instance, can only exist and be appreciated by virtue of its opposite—disorder—both form an inseparable and interdependent unit in which one element is absolutely necessary for the articulation of the other. 'Because of the right, there is the wrong, and because of the wrong, there is the right,' Chuang Tzu points out (1963: 182–3). 'Therefore the sage does not proceed along these lines (of right and wrong, and so forth) but illuminates the matter with Nature'.

Let us come back to contemporary world politics in an attempt to illuminate the intertwinement of order and disorder. Look at what happened after the collapse of the cold war order: once the danger of communism had vanished, security had to be articulated with reference to a new *Feindbild*, a new threatening other that could provide a sense of order, safety, and identity at home. Rogue states were among the new threat images that rose to prominence when cold war ideological schism gave way to a more blurred picture of global politics (Derrida 2003). This tendency to order the world intensified after the terrorist attacks on New York and Washington of September 2001. The compulsion to extract the eternal out of an ever-more transient world—to use Baudelairean language—increased dramatically. US foreign and domestic policy sought to re-establish the sense of order and certitude that had existed during the cold war: an inside/outside world in which, according to the words of president George W. Bush (2001), 'you are either with us or against us'. Much like Ronald Reagan's depiction of the Soviet Union as an 'evil empire', the current US reaction to terror is couched in a rhetoric of 'good' versus 'evil'. 'Evil is real', stressed George W. Bush (2002) in his presidential State of the Union address. 'It must be opposed'. What must be stressed as well, though, is that evil here means more than merely 'doing harm or inflicting pain on innocents' (Katznelson 2002: 7). Terrorists are evil because they attack, as did the Soviet Empire, the very foundations of Western (and meanwhile quasi-globalized) order: a form of life based on the principles of liberal democracy and market-oriented capitalism. Few would, of course, question the need and desirability of defending order and democracy from the threat of terrorism. But things are more complex.

The relationship between order and disorder is provocatively explored in a recent monograph by Alain Joxe. By sketching out changes in international politics over the last dozen years, Joxe offers an alternative characterization of the present global system. The picture he paints is grim: it is a world of increasing disorder, of constant conflict, rising inequalities, and lacking ethics. The key for Joxe is that the United States has become an increasingly powerful global hegemon that refuses to take on socio-political responsibility. Traditionally, rulers exchanged obedience for protection. But the United States today, Joxe argues, demands the former without offering the latter. It represses the symptoms of despair while refusing to attack its causes. We thus witness the emergence of a fundamentally new form of empire, one that does not occupy territories, but merely regulates them in two key domains: military and finance. An unprecedented level of military superiority gives the United States the ability to imprint its vision on the world. And this vision includes the promotion of a neoliberal economic order which, according to Joxe, operates without any democratic control or accountability. The result, he stresses, is an empire of disorder: the generation of chaos that cannot be controlled, not even by the hegemon. The hegemon merely regulates disorder by imposing global norms of behaviour. Disorder itself is not new, but today's chaotic world is different, Joxe (2002: 7–94) argues, insofar as disorder is not a transition period to a new order: it is the order itself.

One could easily oppose this or that aspect of Joxe's polemical arguments. Neither US hegemony nor the free-market system nor disorder itself are all repressive and bad. There are many positive dimensions to the post-cold war order, and they need to be examined as much as the negative ones. But the point of this section, as of the previous one, was not to advance a definitive argument. Far more detail and care would be needed to do so. The key, rather, has been to demonstrate, as a preliminary step to the last task of this essay, that order and disorder are far more complex and intertwined than is commonly assumed.

THE VALUE OF DISORDER

Believing that one could advance a balanced scholarly analysis of order was, as mentioned, a keen concern for Bull. And so was his normative commitment to order as a value preference. The same could and should be attempted with disorder: a scholarly take on it that admits, at the same time, to the normative possibility that disorder can have positive dimensions. Bull remains one of the most sophisticated and useful sources in the pursuit of this somewhat controversial endeavour.

An inherent tension between order and justice is a rather normal but often neglected aspect of world politics. Look at recent debates about the wisdom of embarking on a war against Iraq, for they illustrate that two of the most central, widely accepted, and seemingly compatible values of contemporary international society, those of democracy and the rule of law, can at times be incommensurable in practice. A military intervention would violate international law but, so its proponents argue, is essential for upholding the spirit of democracy. Non-intervention, by contrast, would retain the integrity of the international order but only at the expense of inaction in the face of human rights violations against Iraqi people. Some of these assumptions can undoubtedly be challenged, but it would be far more difficult to question the underlying recognition that justice and order often are, as Bull (1984*a*: 18) once put it, 'at loggerheads with one another'. Bull stressed that a conservative position would always put order first, for without order there could be no international society and, indeed, no justice. A revolutionary position, by contrast, would recognize the inherent tension between the present international order and the task of promoting justice. Writing in the late 1970s, Bull noted that many Third World countries were, quite understandably, primarily concerned with issues of justice in the world community, even if promoting it meant having to engender disorder.

Although their normative positions are located at opposite ends, both conservatives and revolutionaries recognize the often incompatible relationship between justice and order. Liberals, by contrast, tend to assume that social change and justice can actually be realized in the context of order. Bull is rather sceptical about this assumption, stressing that it is 'foolish' to expect that order and justice can always be reconciled. He draws attention to the fact that there are moments when 'terrible choices have to be made,' moments when conceptions of justice can be advanced only by 'placing peace and security in jeopardy' (Bull 1984: 18; 1977: ch. 4, esp. 77–8, 86, 93–7).

The values of order and disorder are, then, not as absolute and as diametrically opposed as suggested by dualistic Western thinking patterns. Disorder is certainly not as bad as its reputation has it. There is enough evidence, empirical and conceptual, to back up Bull's suggestion that at times social change can be promoted only at the expense of order. Perhaps a citation from the world of science, somewhat ruthlessly taken out of context, captures this aspect of world politics best. Consider how the so-called Second Law of Thermodynamics states that 'all change is the consequence of the purposeless collapse of energy and matter into disorder' (see Atkins 2003: ch. 4).

One must go one step further: disorder can have positive effects not only as a route towards a more just order, but also as a state of affairs and a value in itself, a possibility that Bull did not contemplate. Consider the countless and continuously spreading new social movements, pressure groups, and other loose organizations that challenge various aspects of local, national, or global governance. The state-centric nature of English School scholarship provides little space to recognize, yet alone appreciate the role of these increasingly important transnational actors. Part of their importance stems from the fact that these movements operate in a rather chaotic way. They come and go. They are neither centrally controlled nor do they all seek the same objective. Some operate on the right end of the political spectrum. Others on the left. Some oppose globalization. Others hail it. Some seek more environmental regulations. Others defend neoliberal free trade. And it is precisely through this lack of coherence, control, and certainty that the respective movements offer a positive contribution to the political, and not only because their activities may contribute to an international society even in the absence of a state-controlled order. These seemingly chaotic activities are perhaps the quintessential aspect of postmodern politics, of local resistance against orders that have become encroaching and unjust (see Walker 1988 and White 1991: 10–12). They embody what William Connolly believes is the key to cultural democratization, perhaps even to a post-national notion of democracy: a certain level of 'productive ambiguity', that is, the commitment to always resist 'attempts to allow one side or the other to achieve final victory' (Connolly 1995: 153–5; White 2000: 106–50). Without such political checks-and-balances, and the disorder they require to exist and thrive, any order will eventually undermine the sense of justice it was originally supposed to promote and protect.

CONCLUSION

The purpose of this chapter was not to bring order into the study of international society. Quite to the contrary; my objective was to muddle things, to blur the distinction between order and disorder, to not only show that both are intrinsically linked, but that each, order and disorder, contains positive and negative components. The stark separation and the opposing values attributed to order and disorder are not a reflection of political realities, but a figment of our imagination, related to the deeply entrenched modern urge to impose order upon an increasingly disorderly world. To problematize order is, of course, not to question its essential role. Without order there can be no rule of law, no justice, no protection of minorities, no civilized life. But disorder too is essential, for without being submitted to periodic scrutiny, orders can easily turn into practices of domination.

The complex relationship between order and disorder must be investigated more thoroughly. Scholars must not halt after asking how much order is 'out there'. They must also ask, as an integral part of this question, to what extent the deeply entrenched modern need for a patterned life may lead them to project order upon a situation which is in reality far more complex, even random. The challenge is to advance such self-reflective and intellectually cautious approaches without falling back into the realist assumption that the international is nothing but an anarchical and chaotic realm, where the struggle for power and superiority suppresses all possibility for order and justice. Bull remains one of the most useful and inspiring sources to theorize this middle ground between realist defeatism and an overzealous cosmopolitan trust in world governance. But to pursue this promising middle ground more effectively, English School scholarship must become far more aware of its own carefully disguised practice of ordering. It must pay attention to how its convention of reviewing and categorizing are part of an ordering drive, and how this very drive may not only project order upon disorder, but also undervalue the important contribution of the latter. Needed, then, is a truly pluralist approach to understanding international society, one that examines the respective phenomenon without resort to established patterns of academic rules and citational standards. Needed is what Pablo Neruda (1978: 294) always admired and aspired to create: 'books without schools and without classifying, like life'.

PART THREE

International Society after September 11

11

(Re)Imagining the Governance of Globalization

Richard Falk

It was the English School that most effectively conceptualized the dual assertions of the anarchical structure of the world political system and of a normative order based on international law, diplomatic prudence, and informal linkages of comity. These ideas were particularly appropriate in the setting of various Westphalian discourses articulating the logic of the state system as a modification of the Machiavellian world-view associated with various forms of realism. Hedley Bull and R. J. Vincent were especially keen to distance themselves from those who advocated more ambitious renderings of the normative dimensions of international relations, either by stressing the promise of international institutions or stretching the coverage of international law to the point of overriding the sovereignty of states and the non-accountability of their official leaders. Such a view of international relations rested the prospects for governance and moderation on the discharge of benevolent managerial roles by the leading states, but within a framework of essential respect for the stability of a pluralist society composed of territorial states whose sovereign status was entitled to a wide margin of respect.

With the rise of transnational economic action, both actors and arenas, and with the multidimensional salience of transnational networks sustained by a variety of information technologies, this essentially Westphalian discourse seems outmoded, or at the very least, in need of being complemented by some post-Westphalian perspectives. This chapter seeks to do this in the context of an evolving critical under-standing of 'globalization', not as cancelling the primacy of the society of states, but in complicating the explication of how politics and authority operate on a global level. I argue that the pluralist tilt of the English School must now be adapted to encom-pass the role of both actors in the global marketplace (trade, investment, currency) and civil society actors (transnational voluntary associations, militant global citizens, and their networks). Notions of power and security were also deeply challenged by the September 11 attacks and the United States' response, initiating an essentially

Portions of this chapter were originally presented as paper at a conference on 'Critical Globalisation' held at UCSB, 1–4 May 2003, and scheduled for publication in a conference volume.

non-territorial war between two actors, neither of which is a state in the generally understood sense of a territorially delimited entity. Of course, the United States is such a state if we cast our gaze upon a world map, but if we construct its global presence in space, oceans, foreign bases, and grasp the global scope of its security zone, it is more useful to abandon the notion of 'state' and signal the rupture by the label 'global state'.

An international society perspective remains illuminating, however, taking account of the continuing absence of centralized authority structures and a globally constituted security system operating within the United Nations. Some readings of American grand strategy attribute a project for world dominance that seeks above all to establish a global security system administered from Washington to the current leadership of the United States. To the extent that an American global empire becomes a reality, it would alter the relevance of a pluralist account of world politics by generating the first historical instance of a solidarist worldview. Such a solidarist world order would be generally viewed as a species of dystopia rather than an idealistic or even utopian response to the alleged chaos and penchant for warfare associated with pluralist experience, which has characterized solidarist thinking in the past. It is the objective of this chapter to consider these solidarist tendencies in contemporary world society within the framework of a reconstituted discourse on globalization.

'GLOBALIZATION' UNDER STRESS

In the 1990s it was evident that 'globalization,' despite objections about the unsatisfactory nature of the term as misleading or vague, was widely accepted as a usefully descriptive and explanatory term: namely, that the world order sequel to the cold war needed to be interpreted largely from an economic perspective and that the rise of global market forces was displacing the rivalry among sovereign states as the main preoccupation of world order. This perception was reinforced by the ascendancy of Western style capitalism, ideologized as 'neo-liberalism' or as 'the Washington consensus', a circumstance reinforced by the collapse of the Soviet Union and the discrediting of a socialist alternative. It seemed more illuminating to think of the 1990s in this light significantly altered by reference to globalization than to hold in abeyance any designation of world politics by continuing to refer to the historical period as 'the post-Cold War'. Some spoke convincingly of this being 'the information age' highlighting the restructuring of international life that was being brought about by the computer and Internet, but such a label seemed less resonant with the wider currents of emphasis on economic growth on a global scale than did the terminology of globalization.

But then came September 11, simultaneously reviving and revolutionizing the modern discourse of world politics, highlighting the severity of security concerns, but also giving rise to doctrines and practices that could not be understood by reference to the prior centuries of interaction among territorial sovereign states. The concealed transnational terrorist network that displayed the capability to inflict severe substantive and symbolic harm on the heartland of the dominant state could not be addressed, or even comprehended, by resorting to a traditional war of territorial self-defence. There was no suitable statist adversary that could be blamed, and then defeated once and for all, although this fundamental and disquieting reality was provisionally disguised by the seemingly plausible designation of Afghanistan as responsible for the attacks by giving safe haven to Al-Qaeda. But with the Afghanistan War producing a 'victory' in the form of the replacement of the Taliban regime and the destruction of the Al-Qaeda infrastructure, it became clear that such a campaign was only marginally related to a 'victory' in this new type of 'war', if by victory is meant the elimination of the threat. For one thing, most of the Al-Qaeda leadership and many among the cadre apparently escaped, indicating the absence of any fixed territorial base or meaningful victory and the US government shifted its focus from the threat of mega-terrorism to the quite different, and essentially unrelated, issue of weapons proliferation in the 'axis of evil' countries. To the extent that globalization is retained as the label, its net must be cast far more broadly. The following section will present this argument by considering the relevance of the September 11 attacks to the reconfiguration of conflict on a global level, as well as to suggest how the quest for a new framework of regulatory authority has changed from the 1990s. At the same time, the central contention of this chapter is that 'globalization' retains its relevance as a descriptive label for the current phase of international relations, but since the events of 2001 it needs to be interpreted far less economistically, and more comprehensively. The final section will consider approaches to global governance, international society, and world society given this altered understanding of 'globalization.'

THE CHANGING GEOPOLITICAL CONTEXT OF GLOBALIZATION AND GLOBAL GOVERNANCE

To set the stage for this extended view of globalization as incorporating the new geopolitics of post-statist political conflict, it is necessary briefly to review the evolution of world politics after the cold war.

The breakdown of the geopolitical discipline of bipolarity that had managed conflict during the cold war era generated a security vacuum that could be, and was, filled in various ways. The Iraqi conquest of Kuwait in 1991 was an initial expression of this breakdown. It would have seemed virtually certain that during the cold war epoch, without the approval of Moscow and Washington, Iraq would not have embarked on a path of aggressive warfare against its small neighbour. The American-led coalition that restored Kuwaiti sovereignty was the mark of a new era being shaped by essentially uncontested American global leadership, seemingly a geopolitical debut for unipolarity in the global security sphere. The fact that the Security Council endorsed the defensive effort, accorded America full operational control of the Gulf War, and endorsed the subsequent ceasefire burdens that Washington insisted be imposed on

Iraq was far more expressive of the actuality of unipolarity than it was a sign of Woodrow Wilson's dream of an institutionalized international community collect- ively upholding the peace. What emerged from the Gulf War more than anything else was the extent to which the Security Council seemed willing to allow itself to be used as a legitimating mechanism for controversial US foreign policy initiatives that seemed to evade the limits on the use of international force contained in both international law and the UN Charter (see Justin Morris' contribution, Chapter 15, this volume).

Another course of action could have been followed, and was seemingly even encour- aged by the first President Bush's rhetorical invocation of 'a new world order' as a means of generating public and governmental support in the United Nations for authorizing a collective security response to Iraqi aggression. Such reliance on the procedures of the Security Council to fashion and supervise a response would have been a genuine expression of the Wilsonian project to shift the locus of authority on matters of international peace and security from the level of the state to that of the world community. But there was no such disposition in the White House at the time of the first Bush administration. Instead, the United States moved to fill the security vacuum by acting on its own to the extent that it deemed necessary, while seeking Security Council approval for the sake of a legitimating rationale whenever it would be forthcoming. The initiation of the Kosovo War under NATO auspices in 1999 made this new American orientation toward law and power clear, and the fact that it was undertaken during the Clinton presidency suggested the bipartisanship of this geopolitical ascendancy in light of the disappearance of the Soviet Union as a state capable of deterring the United States. With the prospect of a Russian and Chinese veto in the offing, the US government avoided the Security Council, while organizing 'a coalition of the willing' under the formal umbrella of NATO, a deliber- ate step away from the multipolarity of independent policy-making in the Security Council. This departure from the discipline of international law and the UN Charter was widely, although controversially endorsed throughout Europe and in the United States (see Independent International Commission 2000 and Glennon 2001). It was justified as an exceptional claim necessitated by the perceived imminence of an ethnic cleansing crisis in Kosovo and against the background of the failure to protect the Bosnian peoples, as epitomized by the 1995 Srebrenica massacre of over 7,000 Bosnian males while UN peacekeepers stood by as disempowered spectators.

The Iraq crisis was a more revealing and consequential departure from the UN framework of restraint with respect to the use of international force in circumstances other than self-defence. Instead of circumventing the Security Council as in Kosovo, the US tried hard to enlist the UN in its war plans, and initially succeed in per- suading all fifteen members of the Security Council to back Resolution 1441, which implicitly accepted the American position that if Iraqi weapons of mass destruc- tion were not found and destroyed by Baghdad's voluntary action or through the UN inspection process, then an American-led war with UN blessing would obtain political backing and international legitimacy. Tensions within the Security Council were mainly concerned with the timing and trigger for an explicit authorization for recourse to war and whether the threshold had been crossed. Evidently concerned that inspection might obviate the case for war, and that the mandate for war might after all not be forthcoming, the United States went ahead on its own in early 2003, inducing a coalition of more or less willing partners to join in the military effort, which produced a quick battlefield victory but a bloody and inconclusive occupation (see Falk 2003*a*).

In an important sense, President George W. Bush was implementing a vision of a new world order, but not the one that his father appeared to favour in 1990–1 or that Wilson pushed so hard for after the First World War. Unlike the Gulf War where the response, which was endorsed by the UN Security Council, was one of collective defence against prior aggression and conquest or the Kosovo War where the military action appeared necessary and justified as humanitarian intervention, the war against Iraq rested on neither a legal nor moral grounding that was persuasive to most governments in the world, was opposed by an incensed global public opinion, and even seemed politically imprudent from the perspective of meeting the Al-Qaeda challenge of transnational terrorism. The 'Bush Doctrine' of pre-emptive war, without a persuasive factual showing of imminent threat, represented a flagrant repudiation of the core international law prohibition of non-defensive force as generally understood, and established a precedent that, if followed by other states, could produce a series of wars and undermine the authority of the UN Charter and modern international law (compare Korb 2003 and Falk 2002). The United States approach filled the security vacuum after the cold war with the unilateralism and lawlessness of hegemonic prerogatives, and seemed to widen even the claimed right of pre-emptive defence by resorting to war in the absence of an imminent threat, and possibly in the absence of any threat whatsoever, thereby extending unilateralism and discretionary recourse to war even beyond the expansiveness of so-called preventive war. For the United States to attack Iraq, at every stage a weak state beyond the reach of its regional status, and weakened further by its exhausting stalemate of the 1980s in relation to Iran, by a devastating defeat in the Gulf War, and by more than a decade of harsh sanctions, involved launching a war without international or regional backing in a context where there was no credible past, present, or future threat.

And by this audacity on the part of the US government, repeatedly justified by the distinctive challenge of global mega-terrorism made manifest in the attacks of September 11, the United States was also reconstituting world order in three crucial respects: seriously eroding the sovereignty of foreign countries by potentially converting the world as a whole into a battlefield for the conduct of its war against Al-Qaeda; discarding the restraints associated with international law and collective procedures of the organized world community in the name of anti-terrorism; re-establishing the centrality of the role of force in world politics, while dimming the lights that had been illuminating the rise of markets, the primacy of *corporate* globalization, and the displacement of statist geopolitics. In effect, the focus on the terminology of globalization and the operations of the world economy were superseded by a novel twenty-first century pattern of geopolitics in which the main adversaries were a concealed transnational network of political extremists and a global state operating without consistent regard for the sovereign rights of normal territorial states (Falk 2003*b*).

For both of these political actors, the framework of diplomacy and conflict that has evolved since the dramatic events of September 11 has important implications for world order. But there are important continuities, as well, that give persisting relevance to the role of the UN and international law. In view of this, it seems far better to deal with the current world by reference to its special novel features as modifying our understanding of world order, rather than claiming a unique set of circumstances that justify the depiction of a new system and the adoption of a new political vocabulary. My view is that despite some merit in this position favouring an entirely fresh language for this early twenty-first century period as compared to the 1990s, it remains advantageous to retain and revise the globalization discourse, especially in light of the continued relevance of global governance as an important focus for inquiry. The worldview associated with the Peace of Westphalia in 1648 and its several centuries of subsequent development in a world order composed of sovereign states is increasingly being treated as obsolete with respect to the resolution of acute transnational conflict.[1] Reliance on the revisionist discourse of globalization seems useful to emphasize the extent to which the crucial dimensions of world history are being addressed with a much diminished role for the boundaries of states. These boundaries continue to identify a significant class of political actors on the world stage, but these actors are no longer appropriately treated as the defining forces shaping the history of our times.

FIVE GLOBALIZATIONS FOR THE TWENTY-FIRST CENTURY

Whether this current rupture with the past is an aberration to be corrected shortly or the new framing of global governance is uncertain. The contours and ideological orientation of globalization and governance are almost certain to remain highly contested and fluid, far more so than during the 1990s, and the future of world order will hang in the balance. The old political language of statism will persist in many formal settings, but it will not illuminate the changing structure of world order nearly as effectively as a revamped reliance on the language of globalization.

Five overlapping approaches to governance can be identified as the structural alternatives for the future of world order. These will be briefly depicted, and a few conclusions drawn. They are: corporate globalization; civic globalization; imperial globalization; apocalyptic globalization; and regional globalization. The emerging structure of world order is a complex composite of these interacting elements, varying with conditions of time and space, and therefore incapable of an authoritative 'construction' as a generalized account of the new reality of the global life world. In other words, many constructions vie for plausibility, but none can be completely prescriptive. The contours and meanings of globalization are embedded in a dialogic process, further complicated by sharply divergent perceptual perspectives and by a bewildering array of shifting contextual elements. We must be content with partial, fluid, tentative formulations of this evolving world order premised on 'globalization'.

Corporate Globalization

In the 1990s, with the resolution of the East/West conflict, the centre of attention shifted to the ideas, arenas, and practices associated with the functioning of financial markets and world trade, as guided by a privileging of capital formation and efficiency. The role of governments was increasingly seen in relation to this dynamic, and to be legitimate political elites had to win the endorsement of private sector elites. Ideological adjustments were made to upgrade markets, privatize a wide range of undertakings previously situated within the public sector, and minimize the role of government in promoting social goals. New arenas of policy formation emerged to reflect this shift in emphasis, giving prominence to the World Economic Forum organized as a gathering of business leaders, but soliciting the participation of the top political figures. Governments and international financial institutions accepted and promoted this economistic agenda, creating arenas designed to facilitate the goals of the private sector, such as the annual economic summit (Group of Seven, then Eight) that brought together the political heads of state of the principal advanced industrial countries in the global North.

In the 1990s there seemed to be a rather neat displacement of the territorial and security features of the state system with the capital-driven concerns of the world economy organized according to the ideology of the free market. It appeared that a new non-territorial diplomacy associated with trade and investment was taking precedence over older concerns with alliances, as well as with friends, enemies, and the security and well-being of the territorial community of citizens. As long as corporate globalization was sustained by impressive growth statistics, even if accompanied by growing indications of persistent massive poverty, widening disparities with respect to income and wealth, and a disturbing neglect of economic stagnancy in sub-Saharan Africa, there was little mainstream questioning directed at the pro-globalization consensus. This consensus was seen as a panacea by important champions of globalization, producing also a drift towards constitutional democracy.

It was only in the wake of the Asian Financial Crisis that began in 1998, and its reverberations in such disparate countries as Argentina, Japan, and Russia, that serious criticism began to produce a controversy as to the future of corporate globalization. In such an atmosphere, the reformist voices of insiders such as George Soros and Joseph Stiglitz began to be heard more widely, lending credibility to the previously ignored leftist critics. And then, in late 1999, the Seattle demonstrations directed at an IMF ministerial meeting signalled to the world the birth of a wide and deep anti-globalization movement deeply opposed to the basic policies associated with the implementation of neoliberalism. The reaction to Seattle finally generated a debate about the effects of globalization, assessing its benefits and burdens and focusing particularly on whether the poor of the world were being victimized or assisted.

During the George W. Bush presidency, despite the focus on global security and the war against mega-terrorism, the US government has dogmatically and unconditionally reinforced its commitment to corporate globalization as the *sole* foundation of legitimate governance at the level of the sovereign state. These policies are being promoted without much fanfare because of the preoccupation with the war/peace agenda, but corporate globalization is being challenged both by the realities of a sharp global recession and by a robust worldwide grass roots movement that has shifted its goals from 'anti-globalization' to 'alternative globalization'.

Civic Globalization

As suggested, the effects of corporate globalization have generated a counter-movement on the level of ideas and practices, which seeks a more equitable and sustainable world economy, although it is not necessarily opposed to 'globalization' as such. That is, if globalization is understood as the compression of time and space as a result of technological innovation and social/economic integration, if people-oriented rather than capital-driven, then support for 'another globalization' best describes the identity of the popular movement. Over the years, civic globalization has clarified its dominant tendencies, although diverse constituencies from North and South, including activist groups mainly concerned with human rights, economic well-being, environmental protection, and global democracy have produced a somewhat incoherent image of what is meant by a people-oriented approach. Civic globalization has been shedding its negative image of merely being against corporate globalization, and can no longer be accurately described as an anti-globalization movement, despite a continuing repudiation of the main tenets of corporate globalization. In the search for coherence and a positive program, there is an increasing disposition to view civic globalization as essentially a movement dedicated to the achievement of global democracy, which includes a major stress on a more participatory, transparent, and accountable process of shaping and implementing global economic policy.

As might be expected, those concerned with the impact of corporate globalization are also deeply disturbed by the American response to the September 11 attacks, and view resistance to 'imperial globalization' (below) as equally important as opposition to corporate globalization. The mobilization of millions to oppose the Iraq War in early 2003 was mainly a phenomenon in the countries of the North, but it attracted many of the same individuals who had earlier been part of the grass roots campaigns associated with opposition to corporate globalization. There is an uncertainty, at present, as to whether anti-war and anti-imperial activism will merge successfully with the struggle for an alternative form of globalization.

Imperial Globalization

Even at the high point of corporate globalization in the mid-1990s, there were a variety of assessments that pierced the economistic veil to discern an American project of global domination (compare Hardt and Negri 2000 and Bacevich 2002).

It was notable that during the 1990s the United States failed to use its global pre-eminence to promote nuclear and general disarmament or to create a more robust UN peacekeeping capability or to address the major unresolved conflicts throughout the world. Instead, the United States government put its energies into the discovery of new enemies justifying high defence spending, perpetuating a network of military bases and regional naval commands, developing its nuclear arsenal, and embarking on an expensive programme for the militarization of space. In retrospect, it seems difficult to deny the charges that US policy, whether or not with full comprehension, was seeking a structure for world order that rested on American imperial authority. True, the apparent priority function of this authority was to make the world safe and profitable for corporate globalization, especially in the face of growing opposition.

The 'election' of George W. Bush as a representative of the radical right in the United States gave an unanticipatedly wide opening to the most ardent advocates of imperial globalization situated within the American policy-making community. September 11 converted the undertaking from one of indirection and closet advocacy in conservative think tanks to that of the most vital security imperative in the history of the country. In the immediate aftermath of the attacks it provided the most powerfully persuasive rationale for United States' global leadership since the cold war era, and it did so in a setting where the absence of strategic and ideological statist rivalry allowed the United States government to project a future world order at peace, and enjoying the benefits of a reinvigorated corporate globalization. As suggested earlier, the anti-terrorist consensus loomed large at first, giving rise to widespread support for the US decision to wage war against Afghanistan, and to dislodge the Taliban regime from control. The move towards war with Iraq disclosed the limits of this global consensus as well as the *diplomatic* limits of American power to induce political support for its project of global dominance. As with Afghanistan, the Iraqi regime was widely deplored by other governments as oppressive and militarist, but unlike Afghanistan, Washington's claim to a right of pre-emption seemed much more connected with its geopolitical expansion, especially in the Middle East, than with a response justified by defensive necessity in relation to the continuing threats posed by the Al-Qaeda network. Indeed, as critics of the Iraq War pointed out during the pre-war debate, the probable effect of the war would be to heighten the Al-Qaeda threat rather than diminish it.

The perception of imperial globalization is a matter of interpretation, as are its probable effects on global governance. The advocates of the new imperialism emphasize its benevolent potentialities, with reference to the spread of constitutional democracy and human rights, and the provision of peacekeeping capabilities that could act far more effectively than what could be achieved by the United Nations (Kagan 1998; Ignatieff 2003*b*). The critics are concerned with arousing a geopolitical backlash in the form of a new strategic rivalry, possibly involving a Sino-European alliance, and about the prospect for a further abandonment of American republicanism at home and abroad under the pretext of responding to the security threats that are present. In this setting, it seems prudent to worry about the emergence of some new oppressive political order that might be most accurately described as 'global fascism', a political fix that has no historical precedent. Of course, the proponents of imperial globalization resent the frictions associated with civic globalization, and despite the claims of support for 'democracy' prefer compliant governmental elites and passive citizenries. Bush 'rewarded' and lavishly praised governments that ignored and overrode the clearly evidenced anti-war sentiments of their citizens, especially Britain, but also Italy and Spain, while 'punishing' those that refused to support recourse to aggressive war against Iraq, including France, Turkey, and Germany.

Apocalyptic Globalization

There is no entirely satisfactory designation for the sort of political stance associated with Osama Bin Laden's vision of global governance. It does appear dedicated to extreme forms of political violence that challenge by 'war' the strongest consolidation of state power in all of human history. Its capability to pose such a challenge was vividly demonstrated on September 11, attacking the United States directly and more effectively than had been done by any state throughout the course of its entire history. The Bin Laden vision also embodies very far-reaching goals that, if achieved, would restructure world order as it is now known: driving the United States from the Islamic world, replacing the state system with an Islamic *umma*, and converting the residual infidel world to Islam, thereby globalizing the *umma*. It is here characterized as 'apocalyptic' because of its religious embrace of violent finality that radically restructures world order on the basis of a specific religious vision, as well as its seeming willingness to resolve the historical tensions of the present world by engaging in a war of extermination of those designated as enemies, including Jews, Christians, and atheists. Since the United States as the target and opponent of Al-Qaeda also expresses its response in the political language of good and evil, but with the moral identities inverted, there seems to be good grounds for the term 'apocalyptic globalization'.[2]

Perhaps this confers on Al-Qaeda an exaggerated prominence by treating its vision as sufficiently relevant to warrant this distinct status as a new species of globalization that approaches the future with its own formula for global governance. At present, the scale of the attacks, as well as the scope of the response, seems to validate this prominence, even though it may seem highly dubious that such an extremist network has any enduring prospect of toppling statism or challenging corporate globalization. As far as civic globalization is concerned, there exists a quiet antagonism, and an even quieter basis for limited collaboration with its more radical counterpart. The antagonism arises because the main supporters of civic globalization regard themselves as secularists, or at least as opponents of extremist readings of any world religion that gives rise to a rationale for holy war. The collaboration possibility, undoubtedly tacit, arises because of certain shared goals, including justice for the Palestinians and opposition to imperial and corporate globalization.

Regional Globalization

As with apocalyptic globalization, the terminology is an immediate problem. Does not the postulate of a regionalist world order contradict trends toward globalization? The language may seem to suggest such a tension, but the intention is coherent, to imply the possibility that global governance may in the future be partially, or even best, conceived by reference to a world of regions. The basic perspective is to view European regionalism as an exploratory venture, which if it succeeds, will lead to imitative behaviour in the other principal regions of the world. What success means in this case is difficult to discern, but undoubtedly includes economic progress, social democracy, conflict resolution in relation to ethnic and territorial disputes, and resistance to, or at least the moderating of, imperial, apocalyptic, and corporate manifestations of globalization. Such regionalizing prospects are highly speculative at this stage, but still worth entertaining, given the dramatic transformations experienced by Europe during the past fifty years, and the difficulties associated with world order alternatives.

Regionalism is conceptually and ideologically appealing as a feasible synthesis of functional pressures to form enlarged political communities and the rise of identity politics associated with civilizational and religious orientations. Regionalism is geopolitically appealing as augmenting the capabilities of the sovereign state without abandoning its centrality in political life at the national level, especially to allow non-American centres of governance to compete economically and to build bulwarks of political resistance to the threats posed by imperial and apocalyptic globalization.

It is also well to acknowledge grounds for scepticism with respect to regional globalization. The disparities in the non-Western regions are so great as to make ambitious experiments in regionalism seem rather utopian for the foreseeable future. Also, the regional frameworks are not entirely congruent with the supposed acknowledgement of civilizational and religious identities. Even in Europe there are large non-Western, non-Judeo-Christian minorities, and in Asia and Africa, the civilizational and religious identities cannot be homogeneously categorized without neglecting the realities of their basic condition of heterogeneity.

CONCLUDING OBSERVATIONS

The basic argument here is that it remains useful to retain the descriptive terminology of globalization in addressing the challenge of global governance, but that its provenance should be enlarged to take account of globalizing tendencies other than those associated with the world economy and the anti-globalization movement that formed in reaction. To remain useful, the discourse on globalization needs to extend its coverage to the antagonism produced by the encounter between the United States and Al-Qaeda, acknowledging its borderless character and the degree to which both antagonists sponsor a visionary solution to the problem of global governance, neither of which seems consistent with the values associated with human rights and global democracy. Moreover, by suggesting an alternative to reliance on statism, the European experiment, in organizing many aspects of political community on a regional basis, is also a potential source of resistance to both imperial and apocalyptic menaces.

Such an appreciation of various globalizations is not intended as a funeral rite for the state system that has shaped world order since the mid-seventeenth century or to deride the achievements of territorial sovereignty in promoting tolerance, reason, and a liberal conception of state/society relations. The state may yet stage a comeback, including a normative comeback, providing most of the peoples of the world with their best hope for blunting the sharp edges of corporate, imperial, apocalyptic, and even regional dimensions of globalization. The recovery of a positive world order role for the state may be further facilitated by collaborative endeavours joining moderate states with the transnational social energies of civic globalization. Such a possibility has already been manifested in impressive moves to support the Kyoto Protocol on climate change, the outlawing of anti-personnel landmines, and especially by the movement to establish the International Criminal Court.

The whole project of global governance has been eclipsed by the events of recent years, especially by the advent of a unilateralist American government in the 2000 presidential elections, followed in 2001 by the unleashing of the borderless war and the deliberate Washington effort to sideline the United Nations. Part of the rationale for reimagining globalization is to encourage a more relevant debate about the needs and possibilities for global governance. That is, suggesting that the world situation is not altogether subject to this vivid clash of dark forces, that constructive possibilities exist, and deserve the engagement of citizens and their leaders throughout the world. Of course, it will be maintained by some commentators that such an undertaking is merely rescuing globalization from circumstances that have rendered the discussions of the 1990s irrelevant to the present.

Returning to the observations made at the outset, the postulate of a decentralized political order composed of many dispersed actors continues to support a pluralist view of world society, but not one that is elegantly simplified by limiting the class of political actors to sovereign states. Beyond this, the integrative characteristics of both the world economy and global civil society, as well as the drive for global empire, give unprecedented weight to more solidarist constructions of the global reality. Indeed, the most responsive rendering would seem to rest upon a creative tension between the two poles of assessment, pluralist and solidarist, associated with the English School. We do not yet have a convincing political language with which to express this new dynamic reality, and so during what might be a long waiting period, the best solution seems to be this presentation of 'complex globalization', a multidimensional view-point that is dialectical in the sense of suggesting the currently anguished interplay of the main contending agents of history. Whether a new coherence will emerge from complex globalization is radically uncertain, although it is plausible to highlight two solidarist candidates for the shaping of the future of world society: the first, associated with the American dominance project; the second associated with the vision of a global democracy that informs the activities of global civil society. An imperial solution for world order would create a negative form of solidarism while a democratic solution would embody a positive form. In either case the pluralist hypothesis is likely to be refuted by the middle of this century. As mentioned in the discussion of *regional globalization* it is at least conceivable that a triumphal regionalism will produce a new pluralism rather than lead to some variant of solidarism as a sequel to the Westphalian era.

The future of world society is being forged on the anvil of complex globalization. It is likely to produce a world order that exhibits a high degree of structural hybridity, combining aspects of pluralist and solidarist organizational ideas. Whether it will be humanly beneficial will depend, above all, on neutralizing apocalyptic and imperial globalization, as well as democratizing corporate, civic, and regional globalization. It is an ongoing historical cosmodrama that is likely to swerve to and fro before arriving at some outcome that is sufficiently stable to give rise to a new generalized account of world society.

Notes

1. For a well-argued realist assessment of some constructivist illusion surrounding the understanding of the Westphalian world order, see Krasner (1999). For detailed depiction see Falk (1998, 1999*a*).
2. I owe my use of 'apocalyptic' in this context to conversations with and presentations by Robert Jay Lifton.

12

The Question of Culture

Jacinta O'Hagan

What is the relationship between culture and international society? This is a question that subtly permeates the work of the English School, the body of scholars in international relations most interested in the formation and functioning of international society. While culture has not always been their primary concern, they invariably take into account its presence and influence in shaping and sustaining the loose community of international society. Assumptions about culture are woven into the discussion of the constitution, maintenance, and purpose of international society. The goal of this chapter is to survey some of the key assumptions about the relationship between culture and international society that can be found in this body of work, and to reflect on the implications of these assumptions for international society in contemporary world politics. Assumptions about this relationship are important because they bring to the fore a key tension within international society. This is the tension between the desire to construct and maintain a universal political and moral order while also respecting and sustaining the political and cultural diversity contained within international society. Furthermore, at their heart, questions about culture and international society force us to address questions of power within that community. These include questions about the extent to which the norms, values, practices, and institutions that comprise contemporary international society are premised upon and project the interests of a dominant culture to which other cultures have come to consent. Or do these norms, values, and institutions provide a platform for communication and interaction that supersedes particular cultural differences. Is modern international society horizontal, as Robert Jackson (2000) suggests, or does it remain hegemonic and hierarchical?

These are matters not just of academic interest but also of political urgency. Events such as September 11 and subsequent terrorist attacks have brought issues of intercultural relations to the fore. They have fuelled debates about whether contemporary world order is inevitably threatened by clashes between cultures. While such debates are often in danger of receding into reductionist understandings of culture and cultural interaction, these acts of violence do raise profound questions about the stability and cohesion of contemporary international society in the context of a plurality of cultures; about the extent to which this cohesion is based upon

perceptions of equity and justice within this society; and about how a more representative and equitable basis might be established. To neglect cultural difference within
international society, and differing cultural perceptions of equity and justice within
that society by assuming that differences between cultures have been transcended
or already managed, is to run the risk of failing effectively to address these issues.
Ultimately such failure may provide a more profound threat to the cohesion of
international society than any single act of violence.

This chapter will first examine ideas among the first wave of English School authors
about the role of culture in the formation of international society. It then considers assumptions about the relationship between culture and international society
to be found among contemporary English School authors. The key issues addressed
here include firstly assumptions about the role culture plays in establishing order
and stability in international society; second, assumptions about the role that key
institutions of international society play in managing the cultural diversity. Third, it
reflects upon assumptions about the relationship between culture and perceptions of
equity and justice within international society. The chapter seeks to draw together
discussion of these three issue areas to reflect on their implications for the functioning
and cohesion of contemporary international society.

CULTURE AND THE FORMATION
OF INTERNATIONAL SOCIETY

The theme of culture has not traditionally been prominent in the writings of
international relations theorists and scholars located in the dominant schools of
realism and neoliberalism. In recent years, the relative neglect of culture in modern
international relations has been rectified by a reawakening interest in the significance
of cultural factors. In particular, critical theoretical and constructivist scholars have
pointed to the importance of culture in contributing to the social constitution of
world politics.[1] However, prior to this resurgence in interest, while the significance
of culture was largely neglected by the main body of the discipline, it was always
tacitly recognized by those reflecting on the nature and constitution of international
society (Walker 1990). For instance, Tim Dunne notes of Martin Wight's essay on
'the theory of mankind' that this essay arguably entails more attention to questions
of cultural encounter than in the rest of mainstream international relations thinking
during the cold war (Dunne 1997: 310). In similar vein, Roger Epp has noted that an
important if long neglected characteristic of the English School is an understanding
of international relations that is less about the structure or 'mechanics' than about the
'diffuse, imprecise domain of culture' (Epp 1998: 49). As Epp suggests, this is manifest
in the interest this literature shows in the historicity of international society, and its
emergence from a process of intercivilizational encounter (Epp 1998). It is also directly
demonstrated in observations by key authors on the role of culture in the formation
and sustaining of international society. Here we find the assumption that a common
culture provides a foundation for unity and a medium that facilitates communication.

Martin Wight remarked that, 'we must assume that a states-system will not come into being without a degree of cultural unity among its members' (1977: 33). Hedley Bull noted that a common feature of historical international societies was that 'they were all founded upon a common culture or civilisation or at least some elements of such a civilisation' (1977: 16). A common civilization facilitates the working of international society in making for easier communication and better understanding between states, thus assisting the evolution of common rules and institutions. It also reinforces the sense of common interests that impels states to accept common rules and institutions with a sense of common values (Bull 1977: 16). For Adam Watson, cultures, in the form of shared civilizational identities, are linked with the common codes of conduct, assumptions, and values that facilitate the cohesion of international society (Watson 1992: 312).

The relationship between culture and the cohesion of international society is a central concern of Bull's (1977: 16, 317). For Bull, common interests and values play an important role in enhancing normative cohesion and shaping the rules and institutions that underpin a society (1977: 3). As noted above, a common culture or civilization may enhance the sense of common interests and values and the definition of these common rules and institutions. This suggests that a common culture may provide the crucial foundation for the consensus on the key norms and institutions that underpin international society. Without consensus, there is a danger of an international society losing its cohesion. This implies that normative cohesion and some measure of cultural homogeneity are linked, and even integral to the continuation of an international society. The question of whether a common culture is a prerequisite for the formation of an international society, or can evolve from the processes that generate an international society, is an issue that is particularly pertinent for contemporary international society and will be addressed below.

But what is meant by 'culture' here? Bull uses the term in three slightly different senses. In some contexts, it refers to culture as the unified modes of thoughts, patterns of behaviour, and preferred norms and values of particular societies (1980: 184). These are 'a society's basic system of values, the premises from which its thoughts and actions derive' (1977: 64). Importantly, he did not see cultures as essentially permanent and indestructible at their core. This allows Bull to envisage the evolution and even synthesis of cultures (1980). Second, he spoke of common cultures, cultures that are shared across particular societies or communities, entailing a common intellectual culture—relating to common language, philosophical or epistemological outlook and common artistic traditions, and a common moral culture—meaning a common religion or moral code. Third, Bull referred to diplomatic culture, meaning that which currently expresses the procedural consensus upon which modern international society is based, 'the common stock of ideas and values possessed by the official representatives of states' (1977: 316). He distinguished diplomatic culture from the international political culture, meaning the intellectual and moral culture of the members of international society. Bull concluded that while in the past European international society was founded upon a common diplomatic and intellectual political culture, such a cultural consensus could only be found at an elite level within contemporary international society (1977: 317). He identified a thin and fragile elite cosmopolitan culture, the culture of 'modernity', equated with a scientific outlook and a process of economic and technological unification. However, while this culture presupposed a particular view of the world, 'it does not bring in its wake any common moral code' (1979: 30). The continued cohesion of international society, he suggested, would require the further evolution of a common, cosmopolitan culture embracing the common ideas and values of both Western and non-Western societies (1977: 317).[2]

Coming towards the end of this first wave of English School scholarship, R. J. Vincent directly addressed issues of culture in world politics and international society. He did this most explicitly in his work on race (1984*a*, *b*) and in his essay on 'the factor of culture in the global international order' (1980). In this essay, Vincent viewed a range of definitions and approaches to the study of culture in world politics. It is significant both in providing a justification for the inclusion of culture in the range of concepts through which we interpret the world, and in providing a useful way of categorizing or thinking about the different approaches to the role of culture in world politics. He noted three dominant approaches to the study of culture in world politics. The first was the extent to which culture affects the stability of the international system. This approach is concerned with the extent to which culture is connected to order, the extent to which it makes society possible. The second approach, or area of inquiry, concerned the relationship between culture and the quality of life: 'It is concerned not with how social life is possible, but with whether it is worth living' (Vincent 1980: 261). This area of inquiry connects culture with the values of justice and liberty, rather than with stability and order. The third approach concerned managing cultural pluralism. It engages with questions of how world order is to accommodate diverse cultures, as well as states, regions, classes, or individuals (Vincent 1980: 262).

The remainder of this chapter considers how these three approaches continue to be reflected in the work of contemporary English School scholars on the relationship between culture and international society. It examines firstly assumptions about the relationship between culture and order, then looks at assumptions about the management of international society in the context of cultural diversity; and finally at assumptions about the ethics of contemporary international society in relation to perceptions of equity and justice. The chapter argues that the three approaches that Vincent outlined remain deeply salient to debate and analysis of the role of culture in contemporary international society. They return us to a central tension within international society, that between the pursuit of order and justice. Debate about the relationship between cultures in international society takes on different dimensions and meanings depending upon which of these norms is prioritized. This chapter argues that there is a tendency, particularly among pluralist scholars, to see the institutions of international society as enhancing order through managing cultural pluralism in an acultural arena. However, recognition of cultural differences and of the extent to which cultural perspectives are built into existing institutions and structures must be more fully acknowledged if we are to find a way to continue to negotiate the consensus that is critical to the cohesion of international society.

ASSUMPTIONS ABOUT CULTURE IN
THE CONTEMPORARY ENGLISH SCHOOL

Culture and Order

The first approach to the study of culture outlined by Vincent focuses on the issues of order and stability: it returns us to the central question raised by Bull in his classic work *The Anarchical Society*, how is order maintained in an international system that comprises a plurality of sovereign political communities? Bull's response was that order is maintained through consensus upon the functioning of certain norms, rules, and institutions by which members of the system consent to a measure of self-regulation. A key question is: how do these common norms, rules, and institutions come about? And to what extent do they emerge from a common culture? As noted above, there is consensus amongst scholars of the English School that some measure of common culture is necessary to the proper functioning of an international society, but to what extent is it assumed that a common culture is a prerequisite to the formation of such a society?

Barry Buzan has argued that within the works of Wight and Bull we find very different positions on the functioning of culture in the formation of an international society. Buzan applies Ferdinand Tönnies' sociological distinction of *gemeinschaft* and *gesellschaft* to analysing these different approaches (also see Chapter 2, this volume). A *gemeinschaft* is a community stemming from a sense of common sentiment, experience, and identity. A *gesellschaft* is a contractual and constructed community that can be made from an act of will. It is a community constructed without pre-existing cultural bonds through, for instance, processes of intense interaction (Buzan 1993: 333). From this perspective, an international society can emerge when the density of interaction induces some measure of mutual accommodation and recognition (Buzan 1993: 334).

Buzan suggests that Wight's conception of contemporary international society leans towards the *gemeinschaft* model. Wight's vision was that international society developed in subsystems in which the 'units shared significant elements of culture, especially religion and language' (Buzan 1993: 333). He sees Bull's vision of international society, in contrast, leaning towards the functional *gesellschaft*. Bull saw international society emerging from 'a common desire for order as a minimum condition for the evolution of international society' (Buzan 1993: 334). Common needs and interests may generate common rules which, over time, may generate common 'modes of thought, patterns of behaviour and preferred norms and values' that could give rise to a common culture (Bull 1979a: 184). This observation equates with a more generally held view of Bull's vision of international society as an instrumentalist one, focusing on it as a practical association rather than a purposive one (Nardin 1983; Chakrabarti Pasic 1996; Hurrell 1998; Wheeler and Dunne 1998*a,b*).

However, as observed above, Bull—like Wight and Watson to some degree—recognized that some form of common culture is necessary to the smooth functioning of an international society. In practice, the majority of historical international societies identified in this literature have been based on a common societal culture (Watson 1992) though as Buzan notes, the sample here is too small to determine whether this is the rule.[3] The one major exception is modern international society. Modern international society is unique in two respects. First, it is global in reach: preceding international societies were largely regionally focused. Second, it is multicultural: preceding forms of international society largely comprised intracivilizational relations. Contemporary international society, then, is distinct in having a significant intercivilizational dimension. Its foundations, however, lie in the relative cultural homogeneity of European international society. Its origins lie in the 'habitual intercourse of independent communities, beginning in the Christendom of Western Europe' (Wight 1966*b*: 96). It is initially within the context of Christendom that a sense of common identity and differentiation from those outside the community evolved. Christendom provided the elements of common norms and values that facilitated the growth of interaction in the first place and the foundations for a society of initially Christian states (Bull 1977: 29). Within Christendom there emerged a set of standards, assumptions, and expectations of conduct different to those that applied to interaction outside of this. It also, to an extent, provided factors of differentiation that were initially a barrier to the admission of new members (Wight 1977; Bull 1980: 177; Watson 1984*b*, 1992: 216–18). As the Christian society of states evolved into a European international society, those factors of differentiation evolved to encompass both implicit and explicit criteria such as race and the standards of governance encapsulated in the phrase 'the standard of civilisation' (Bull 1984*a*: 122; Gong 1984; Vincent 1984*a*).

The initial expansion of international society, in a geographical context, occurred with the admission of territories and societies that had strong cultural links with Europe. What is interesting here is that interaction between European international society and non-European societies did not automatically produce the expansion of this society, in the manner of Buzan's *gesellschaft*. For instance, contact between Portugal and the Netherlands and the civilizations and societies of Asia did not automatically result in the incorporation of these civilizations into international society (Watson 1992: 222). The Ottoman Empire was a substantive political community on the fringes of European international society and one with which Europe had extensive interaction. Yet this community was not incorporated into the society until 1856, when it was included as an unqualified member of the European states-system in the Treaty of Paris that concluded the Crimean War.[4] Its entry marked the evolution of European international society from a culturally homogeneous community—in the sense that all its members were European and Christian—to a heterogeneous, multicultural one.

Buzan is perhaps correct to argue that as it became multicultural, modern international society shifted from being predominantly a *gemeinschaft* to being a *gesellschaft*. This raises the question: how was this unique transition effected? For Buzan the medium for this transition is the density of interaction. As Chakrabarti Pasic (1996) points out, however, this is a somewhat thin explanation because it ignores the historical and social context within which the transition occurs. It also neglects the distribution of power within these interactions that shape the outcomes. This is power, not just in the sense of the exercise of material power, but also in the sense of ideational and institutional power, the power to set standards and establish norms and codes of interaction. Buzan notes, but Chakrabarti Pasic further highlights, the significance of the European imperial legacy, in addition to capitalism and the Church, as vehicles for the expansion of the European world system through their capacity to establish shared-culture systems (Chakrabarti Pasic 1996: 95). Imperialism as a cultural complex facilitated the transmission of the European and Western ideas, norms, perceptions, and structures that comprised imperial culture, but also laid the foundations for a global international society. However, there is, here, something of a paradox: the expansion of the reach and influence of Europe and the growth of interaction between European states and other political communities initially expanded the scope of the international *system*, but this did not automatically expand the international *society* per se. Indeed, the expansion of the European colonial and imperial relations with non-Europeans saw the establishment of an order quite distinct from the Westphalian order (Keene 2002). It was in fact the withdrawal or retreat of the direct influence and power exercised through imperialism, and the political recognition of the political autonomy of non-Western societies via decolonization, that marked the true expansion of international society. In this respect, Buzan is correct in identifying sovereignty as the focus of a common identity, which is essential to the formation of any form of political community. However, to end the discussion of sovereignty as the mark of a common identity is to end the discussion too soon. What happens to the element of culture here? Does it simply become irrelevant, contained and domesticated within the territorial boundaries of the state, but removed from practical interaction of international society?

Managing Cultural Pluralism

For pluralist authors such as Robert Jackson, culture does not become irrelevant. Like Bull, he sees political and cultural diversity as a basic feature of international society. Cultural plurality is a factor within the international system that has to be managed if order is to emerge. For Jackson, the institutions and procedures of international society—in particular international law and diplomatic practices— become the means through which political and cultural diversity is transcended and managed. Jackson refers to these discourses as underpinning the 'global covenant' of international society.

Jackson argues that diplomatic dialogue is made possible by moral and legal ideas and a corresponding normative vocabulary. Normative discourse in international relations operates by reference to certain assumptions and expectations concerning justified and unjustified conduct. However, this does not require that people 'must necessarily share deeper assumptions regarding social morality or political culture that are characteristic of particular civilisations' (2000: 24). In fact he argues that a normative dialogue of world politics is possible to the extent that it is divorced from the values of particular civilizations—such as that of the West, east Asia, or the Muslim world (Jackson 2000: 1). For Jackson, the expansion of international law and diplomatic practice indicate the way international society can accommodate numerous and diverse political systems: 'the global covenant enable state leaders to relate to one another, to co-exist with each other, to cooperate with each other without sacrificing their political independence, and the domestic values and life-ways upheld by it' (2000: 23). The global covenant provides a common language for cross-cultural interaction. In so far as this society is based on a common culture, Jackson is suggesting, as did Bull, that international society has seen the evolution and transmission of a common elite culture that provides the adhesive and lubricant for the establishment of functioning of international order.

But is this unifying cultural framework simply Western culture writ large? Jackson acknowledges that modern international society has its foundations in the political culture of European peoples, but argues that this has become globalized and further humanized so that it has evolved beyond the initial Western-centric order from which it emerged (2000: 12). The adoption of European discourses of diplomacy and inter- national law has provided common codes of respect and recognition and common expectations permitting a global political dialogue across cultures. This covenant, though rooted in the particular civilization of post-medieval Europe, now serves 'as a bridge between the diverse cultures and civilisations of the contemporary world order', providing 'a channel for normative discourse and dialogue' between the community of independent states rooted in different cultures and civilization (2000: 24–5) Signi- ficantly then for Jackson, the norms of the global covenant are a response to diversity and a means of achieving a unity of political order that respects this cultural diversity. The global covenant is an arrangement that has evolved in an increasingly intercon- nected and interdependent world, not because of a common intellectual and moral culture, but because of the absence of such a common culture:

Civilisation used to be a barrier to the political conversation of humankind. That is no longer so. The global covenant has made it possible for the political people of the world to rise above their own civilisational parochialism in dealing with one another. (Jackson 2000: 25)

Like Bull, Jackson's understanding of international society, and of the means through which it expanded, is essentially instrumental and pragmatic in that international society emerges as a means to deal with political and cultural pluralism. In a 1988 article, Chris Brown appeared to endorse this understanding of international soci- ety as a promising way of accommodating cultural diversity, noting that the state, while issuing from the West, is now the accepted universal framework and suggesting that once states mutually agree to rules for the conduct of relations between them, then differences in their cultural make-up cease to matter (Brown 1988: 345; Keal 2003: 153).

There are perhaps two issues for reflection here: first, do the rules and institutions of international society represent a genuine pluralist consensus or an expression of cultural hegemony?[5] A second related question is, to what extent does there remain an implicit or perceived hierarchy between cultures within international society based upon the history of its evolution, and on continuing inequalities of material, institutional, and ideational power and influence with this global community? Is it true to say that these are now embraced and have become acultural or do they continue to imbue Western societies with a degree of ideational and institutional power? Bull believed that the future of international society was likely to be determined by the preservation and extension of a genuine cosmopolitan culture, embracing the ideas and values of societies as well as elites, and non-Western as well as Western societies (1977: 317). Has this occurred?

Equity in International Society: a Horizontal or Hierarchical Cultural Order?

Jackson describes the global covenant as a horizontal community, inclusive rather than exclusive, and based on a pluralist ethic of state sovereignty; of self-determination; and of non-intervention (2000: 14). Within his work is perhaps the quintessential expression of the concept that culture as that which is best contained within the political entity of the state.[6] Brown has elsewhere argued that the pluralist perspective implicit in such an analysis and articulated by Jackson:

Is constructed out of the belief that the institutions of international society, properly understood, can have an appeal divorced from their political and geographical points of origin. In other words, if the argument is to succeed it needs to be shown that institutions such as diplomatic and customary international law can be defended as practices which all members of international society must obey, where the strength of 'must' is divorced from considerations of power, culture or history. (Brown 1995*b*: 191)

Can the institutions of modern international society be divorced from these considerations of history, culture, and power? As noted above, there is little or no dispute that historically the political structures, institutions, and norms that form the core of international society emerged from European origins and are culturally based on Western philosophies and experiences. In Martin Wight's work, there is a suggestion that Western values did not just initiate international society as a practical association, but are critical to its ongoing constitution as a meaningful entity. Indeed he states at one point that the Whig or constitutional tradition of moderation and prudence that he associates with Western values is the only tradition within which international society can be conceptualized as a meaningful entity (Wight 1991: 30–49).

In relation to considerations of power, Bull made the important observation that Western dominance of the evolving international system and society was premised not just on its technical and material power, but also on its command of intellectual and cultural authority, and of the rules and institutions of international society, facilitating the moulding of that society to mirror Western institutions and values. As Bull himself put it, 'the rules and institutions of international society at the end of the nineteenth century, by contrast with those that are recognized today, appear to have been made by Europeans, to arise out of their experience' (1980: 179). These included the institutions of the sovereign state, entailing the norms of sovereignty, equality and reciprocity, and international law. With reference to international law, Bull notes: '[t]he international legal rules ... were not only made by European and Western powers, they were also in substantial measure, made *for* them' (Bull 1984a: 217). While the willingness and capacity of Western states to exercise direct imperial domination over other societies ebbed during the twentieth century, the norms and institutions which formed the foundation of international society became a vehicle whereby important elements of Western political culture became universalized. Therefore, in important respects, other societies came to be constituted as political communities and to function within the context established by the West. In Buzan's terms, the norms and institutions of the West effectively provide the vehicle for the expansion of a European *gemeinschaft* into a multicultural *gesellschaft*.

In important respects, therefore, the evolution of international society represen-ted the evolving hegemony of the West in terms of the projection of institutional and ideational power. Was this then a hierarchical society, or did Western hege-mony provide a framework within which cultural difference was not only tolerated but equally respected? Edward Keene has argued that a much neglected dimension of the study of European international society is how it evolved in conjunction with the expansion of relations between Europeans and non-Europeans. Keene argues that through this process of interdependent evolution two separate orders were estab-lished. Within European international society an order was established based on the principle of the tolerance of diversity and cultural difference—though this was a tol-erance of differences contained within the context of a common European cultural heritage. Outside of this 'family of nations', however, the order that was constructed promoted the value of 'civilisation', entailing the promotion of forms of material devel-opment and concepts of good governance (Keene 2002). Within this order the concept of imperial paramouncy rather than sovereign equality was legitimated. Worth noting here is not only the development of a concept of civilizational hierarchy in European thinking during the period of the evolution European international society, but also the interdependence between the evolution of this society and the construction of an order based on these hierarchical conceptions. This suggests that the evolution of international society is historically embedded in a broader process of the creation of cultural hierarchies.[7]

Paul Keal also suggests that while this was a society that evolved to encompass a plurality of cultures, it did not treat all cultures with equal respect and value. Keal's work traces the evolution of different criteria upon which 'admission' to international society was granted, shifting from that of religion, to the perception of the capa-city to apply reason, to that of the 'standard of civilisation'. Embedded within these standards of differentiation were the criteria of race and culture. In tracing the evolving and mutually constitutive relationship between international law and international society, Keal demonstrates that 'non-Europeans were conceptualised in ways that dehumanised them and represented their cultures as inferior'. He goes on to draw out the ramifications of this for the structure of international society:

By creating the concept of 'rational' and 'civilised' beings that were essentially European, and placing this above other conceptions of what it was to be fully human, Western theory not only denied cultural pluralism was a problem, it also imposed European (or Western) values as universal standards. (Keal 2003: 152)

This suggests that international society is not simply based on norms and institutions drawn from European and Western cultural and historical experiences, it is also premised on a history of the systematic devaluation of other cultures. Viewed in this way, international society as a historical entity appears less as a horizontal, pluralist community in which all cultures are accorded equal respect, and more a 'totalizing discourse' in which broader cultural diversity is neglected, and difference is absorbed, contained, and its meaning eliminated.

The work of Keene and Keal suggests, therefore, that the evolution of international society was based on a history of the differential treatment of non-European cultures, rather than a tradition of according other cultures mutual respect. Did this undermine international society's capacity to provide a framework of unity in the context of cultural diversity as attitudes to non-European cultures changed? While Bull was cognizant of the unequal power relations which had underpinned the expansion of modern international society, and was concerned about the future cohesion of that society, he firmly advocated that the Western states-system had provided what was to date the first effective universal political system; it was for him 'the principal expression of human unity or solidarity that exists at the present time' (1977: 295). For Bull this solidarity had been achieved by the willingness of non-Western societies to embrace the Western norms and institutions (1984*b*: 124, 1984*c*). This implies solidarism based upon consensus. Andrew Hurrell (1998), however, usefully distinguishes between *consensual* and *coercive* solidarism (see the Conclusion, this volume). In reflecting on the adoption of the norms and institutions of European based international societies by non-Western societies, it is valid to ask, under what conditions was this consensus obtained? To what extent was access to particular resources or benefits conditional on the acceptance of particular politics? In his discussion of Bull and Watson's account of the expansion of international society, Sanjay Seth notes from a postcolonial perspective that

The process by which an international order, first confined to Europe, came to be globalised is a story of pillage, exploitation, violence, doctrines of racial superiority, and resistance of various sorts. Little of the conflict, drama and fundamental inequality of this is captured in the bland phrases of Bull and Watson, or indeed in most accounts of the origins and spread of the contemporary state system of states. Phrases like 'embraced', admitted' and 'joined' function precisely to elide the realities of imperialism and colonialism, to make the globalisation of Europe sound consensual rather than coercive, amiable rather than bloody. (Seth 2000: 221)

The fundamental condition that pertained for most non-Western societies was that admission to international society was obtained through processes of decolonization that entailed the removal of the right of colonial or imperial authorities to directly intervene in the affairs of that society. Acceptance of the norms and institutions of international society was the condition for self-determination in the context of a tradition of European imperialism.

Seth goes on to argue that for the colonized to have asserted themselves through nationhood and the institutions of the state was not an escape from but rather a continuation, even an intensification, of a moral-epistemological and political sub-ordination to the West. As he notes, the nation-state is not an empty vessel but already has content; it presupposes certain forms of selfhood and community (2000: 221). It is not, therefore, a neutral institution devoid of culturally informed assumptions. Furthermore, for Seth, the privileging of the nation-state in international society and international relations theory generally is problematic in that it codifies and contains all difference in the vessel of national difference. It leaves little space for recognizing the legitimacy of alternative forms of political community (2000: 225). This again raises significant and continuing questions about the extent to which cultural difference, expressed in alternative visions of political community, has been truly recognized and respected within modern international society, and the extent to which international society may continue to reproduce forms of cultural hierarchy in contemporary world politics.

THE RELEVANCE OF CULTURE IN CONTEMPORARY INTERNATIONAL SOCIETY

Culture, Order, and Cohesion

To what extent are these issues of the cultural heritage of international society relevant to contemporary international society? These issues matter on two fronts; first, that of maintaining the cohesion of international society on which order is premised; and second, in relation to maintaining an ethical order. This may further impact upon the cohesion and stability of the order. As Richard Shapcott argues, if the ethics of practical association are contested, for instance by demands for reform from the Global South, then they may no longer be a guarantee of order (Shapcott 1994: 69). Furthermore, it may be argued that for the cohesion of international society to be maintained, that society needs to be, and be perceived to be, a genuinely plural association, in the sense that people of various cultures feel equally recognized and valued. Current trends in politics suggest that there is a significant element within the global polity who feel that the society does not recognize or treat them fairly.

As noted above, Bull argued that the cohesion of international society depended upon the existence of consensus about common interests and values that provides the foundations for the society's common rules and institutions (Bull 1977: 315). Even at the time of writing *The Anarchical Society*, Bull feared that this necessary consensus had shrunk. Other authors related to the English School such as Adda Bozeman further expressed these concerns. In an eerie precursor to Huntington's later 'Clash of Civilisations' argument, Bozeman argued that the international system is 'as meaningful as the concepts that compose it. Such concepts are solid if they are equally meaningful in different local orders that are encompassed by the international system'. She suggested that Western concepts of law and individuality were not easily comprehended by, nor suited to, other cultures (Bozeman 1984; Shapcott 1994). Bozeman further argued the modern world polity was witnessing a re-emergence of precolonial cultures and identities, 'a plurality of diverse political systems, each an out-growth of culture specific concepts'. Consequently, there was no globally meaningful system (Bozeman 1984: 404).

For his part, Bull oscillated between optimism and pessimism regarding the consequences of the burgeoning heterogeneity of the global international society (Dunne 1998: 148). He took consolation in the extent to which postcolonial societies had sought to achieve equality and independence through participation in the institutions of the existing international society rather than seeking to overthrow this society (Bull 1984*b*: 124; 1984*c*). However, he also feared that the core Western values upon which that society had been constructed had been absorbed only superficially and were increasingly under challenge from non-Western peoples. Tensions that were emerging between the West and non-Western societies on normative issues and interpretation of values—in particular tensions in relation to concepts of and demands for justice—threatened to undermine the consensus crucial to the cohesion of international society (Bull 1984*b*, *c*; Alderson and Hurrell 2000: 13). Recent debates about human rights, democracy, the management of the environment, economic equity, migration, and the role of religion in governance among others seem to bear further witness to Bull's concerns.[8]

Bull was concerned that these challenges to consensus would grow stronger as non-Western powers grew in strength and autonomy. However, in the years since Bull wrote these remarks, the discrepancy between Western and non-Western power in fact has grown larger. While growth and development has occurred in sectors of the South, inequalities in terms of wealth, economic, and military resources have increased. Persisting impoverishment, the perceived lack of autonomy in the face of market forces and of powerful international institutions, and the growth of corruption and conflict in many non-Western societies have all been profound sources of disquiet and disgruntlement with regard to the current distribution of power and resources in the current global polity. The growing interconnectedness of international society highlights and enhances differences, gaps, and inequalities as much as it highlights and enhances commonalities and diffusion of ideas and institutions. This may have profound consequences both for stability and order in international society, and for perceptions of the moral value of that society.

While in the 1960s and 1970s, discontent with such inequalities were expressed through the vehicle of nationalist and Marxist movements, in the latter part of the twentieth century alternatives to Western models of politics, economy, and society were sought and advocated. Issues of cultural identity and of hegemony resurged in world politics, aggravated by discrepancies in the distribution of material and institutional power between societies of different cultures. This became most prominent in the 'Asian values' debate in the 1990s, and in the rise of Islamist movements, particularly in the Middle East and throughout Asia. While not necessarily representing the voices of the majority of those in non-Western societies, such movements have nevertheless presented a profound and at times violent challenge to the structures, assumptions, and norms of contemporary international order and thus the cohesion of international society. They also challenge us to think more deeply about not only the efficacy, but also the morality of contemporary international society that sustains and manages this order.

In considering the cohesion of international society, Barry Buzan suggests that levels of commitment to the global international society vary across societies. He suggests the level of commitment to the shared norms and values of the society becomes progressively thinner as one spirals out from the society's centre, a centre which we might observe is essentially composed of European and Western societies. For Buzan this is represented in the 'uneven development of international society' into 'concentric circles of commitment' (Buzan 1993: 345). His analysis suggests that international society becomes progressively more a pragmatic than a purposive association, and less cohesive as one moves away from its cultural and historic centre. Writing in the early 1990s, Buzan alluded to 'pariah states' on the fringes of international society, those whose commitment to the norms and institutions of that society was minimal (Buzan 1993: 349). Today we might usefully expand this conception of those on the fringes of international society to include non-state actors such as terrorist organizations who see the current society as illegitimate and supporting an oppressive hegemonic order privileging Western concepts and values, and Western dominated structures and institutions. While it would be grossly inaccurate to argue that terrorist organizations represent the majority in non-Western cultures, particularly in terms of their chosen methods of achieving their political goals, they do represent an element within the contemporary international system that have said powerfully that they will not abide by the rules and norms of interaction and behaviour of the current international society (see Richard Devetak's contribution, Chapter 13, this volume). They argue that the inequalities of power within today's international system justify their utilization of tactics that, for instance, target civilians.[9] The employment of these tactics resulted in a resurgence of mass impact terrorism in the late 1990s and early 2000s in the Middle East, South-east Asia, Europe, and Africa, as well as the stunning attack on the World Trade Centre in September 2001. In many cases 'Western' targets were the principal objective.[10] The attack on the headquarters of the UN mission to Iraq in August 2003 appeared to continue this trend. This attack had the added symbolic impact of attacking an institution that is perhaps the principal embodiment of contemporary international society.[11]

The violence wrought by these attacks undermines the stability of the current international order by perpetrating harm, contributing to a sense of insecurity within communities, and exacerbating tensions and suspicions between communities. It may also contribute to a redefinition of the rules and norms of that order.[12]

This could well undermine rather than enhance order in the sense of stability and the minimization of conflict within international society.

Kai Alderson and Andrew Hurrell (2000: 69) make the important point that in reflecting on issues of cultural diversity, it is important to consider how far these issues reflect differences in national histories, in social and economic circumstances, and political contexts, rather than in cultures per se. At the same time, it is important to be aware of the degree to which cultural identity and cultural difference come to be perceived as associated with differences not only in values and perspectives, but also in the distribution of power and resources more generally, alerting us again to the importance of 'managing' cultural pluralism to the stability of international order and of international society.

An Ethical Order?

The terrorist attacks of this period highlighted once again the relationship between cultural diversity and the management of order through the structures of international society. However, they also raise a further significant question with regard to the cohesion of international society: can a society that does not share a consensus on the ethics and morality of the international order maintain its cohesion? Is the current international society perceived to be a just society? This returns us to questions about the study of culture that asks not how is social life possible, but is it worth living? It focuses attention on issues of justice, morality, and liberty rather than stability (Vincent 1980: 262). A central question becomes: does this society provide an order that is perceived as just by peoples of different cultures? Does it provide equal recognition and respect for all cultures within that society?

As Andrew Hurrell has so clearly articulated, a central dilemma for international society is the tension between the quest to establish a universal order while also respecting and even protecting cultural diversity. There are at least two elements to this dilemma that relate to the ethical premises of a universal order. First, what ethical depth might such an order entail? For Terry Nardin, international society is a practical association 'of independent and diverse political communities each devoted to its own ends and to its conception of the good often related to one another by nothing more than the fragile common thread of diplomacy' (Nardin 1983: 19). Conceptions of ethics and morality emanate from within the political and cultural community while international society provides a mechanism for coexistence. This, argues Brown, forces Nardin to 'conceive of coexistence as possessing a positive value in itself, independent of the values tied up in the forms of life it protects' (1995b: 191). As Brown notes, this suggests we can escape from the dilemma of plurality and universality by describing a very thin normative basis for international society which would not cover matters of domestic jurisdiction except in some extreme circumstance, such as genocide. Authoritative rules would not be established in 'inappropriate' areas of domestic jurisdiction: this would include areas such as human rights and distributive justice. Is such an order feasible? Contemporary international society in fact appears to be moving in the opposite direction of extending further into areas of domestic jurisdiction. As Hurrell observes, the normative ambitions of international society appear to be spreading and cooperation increasingly involves rules that involve domestic structures of state, investing individuals with rights and seeking to embody notions of the common good, be that in human rights or standards of governance (1998: 24). Furthermore, would such a thin normative code be desirable or ethically meaningful for individuals within international society (1995: 193)? Such a thin normative basis of international society would exclude much on the grounds of the need for tolerance, but how would ordinary citizens view this (Brown 1995*b*: 193)?

The dilemma of the ethical premises of a universal order also raises the question of the genuine universality of such an order. Do cultures stand in equal relationship to one another, or is international society in practice the projection of the hegemony of a dominant culture, but one so deeply embedded within the structures and institutions of the society that this hegemony becomes invisible? As discussed above, for Robert Jackson, the 'global covenant' is a neutral framework for managing cultural and political pluralism, one that recognizes 'otherness'. As further noted above, Keal (2003) and others have argued that, historically, international society evolved through processes through which cultural difference was codified and treated as symptomatic of inferiority: 'Otherness' may have been recognized, but it was not respected (Todorov 1984; Blaney and Inayatullah 1994). Furthermore, Jackson's understanding of contemporary international society assumes perhaps a degree of tolerance and even respect for difference which may not be as encompassing as Jackson seems to suggest. Brown, for instance, argues that ultimately the doctrine of human rights is ethically bounded and essentially an intolerant doctrine. Jackson argues that the quintessential values underpinning modern, global international society are those of liberty and self-determination (2000: 361). Yet, a key debate in contemporary international society is the extent to which that society is prepared to tolerate non-liberal modes of governance and non-liberal societies which refuse to conduct their internal affairs according to 'new "global" norms' (Hurrell 1998: 31). My argument here is not to advocate the abandonment of certain norms or ethical positions within international society, but to argue that it is important to raise questions about how these normative and ethical positions were reached, and the extent to which they represent a genuine consensus rather than a hidden hierarchy of ideational and institutional power that might ultimately undermine both the efficacy of the norms and the cohesion of international society.

NEGOTIATING CULTURAL PLURALISM: THE DILEMMA

At the outset, we noted that R. J. Vincent identified three areas of enquiry in exploring the 'factor of culture' in world politics: the relationship between culture and order, the relationship between culture and the quality of social life, and the management of cultural pluralism. In certain respects, while these are three separate realms of inquiry, they are intertwined. The perceived morality and justice of that order may influence the normative cohesion of international society, and the degree of commitment to the structure of order it supports. A lack of commitment to that order or the collapse of normative cohesion can contribute to the instability and undermine order. Therefore, the management of cultural pluralism is intrinsic to both order and the morality of the society. This chapter has argued that, while the pluralist perspective argues in favour of and even presumes the existence of a universal order that encompasses but stands above the cultures that comprise international society, there is a perception, both within the academic community and in the broader political community, that the society evolved in the context of political and cultural hierarchy and retains elements of this legacy. If this is the case, how then do we negotiate a more level playing field? How do we go about achieving a broader consensus? How do we attain the common cosmopolitan culture that Bull suggested was vital to international society's future?

The answer provided by scholars such as Andrew Linklater and Richard Shapcott is through processes of dialogue, which provide 'a route to achieving understanding between the representatives of different cultural standpoints' (Keal 2003: 154). 'The legitimation of international norms', argues Shapcott, 'requires legitimate and just procedures and processes for achieving agreement, procedures that are not only inclusive but also just in themselves' (Shapcott 2000: 165). Linklater and Shapcott both address the conditions and terms under which such dialogue should take place in order to maximize inclusiveness and enhance the possibility of attaining outcomes that all parties would feel equally committed to. In pursuit of the extension of international society to a more cosmopolitan and inclusive community, Linklater draws on the work of Jürgen Habermas to outline a theory of discourse ethics through which areas of consensus might be expanded. Discourse ethics is premised upon the belief that 'norms cannot be valid unless they command the consent of everyone whose interests stand to be affected by them' (Linklater 1996a: 85–6). This consent can only be achieved through an unconstrained dialogue between equals, in which no person or moral community can feel excluded in advance. In this context, he argues, universalism is wedded to multiculturalism (Linklater 1998: 91–2). This dialogue, therefore, requires that the parties to the dialogue are capable of reflection on their own starting points and positions to see how these reflect personal and cultural biases, as well as remaining open to the positions and arguments of others. Discourse ethics, argues Linklater, is a form of dialogue that seeks to empower rather than simply tolerate difference (1998: 96).

Shapcott draws his model of dialogue from the philosophical heremeneutics of Hans Georg Gadamer. Shapcott's proposal is for 'conversations' the goal of which is not to defeat arguments or assimilate the position of the other, but to generate understanding and a shared horizon of meaning (Shapcott 2000: 162–3; 2001). While acknowledging that it is necessary to be cautious about whether such conversations will necessarily lead to consensus, Shapcott remains confident that these 'models of conversation' provide the possibility for legitimizing norms of global governance among the members of international society (Shapcott 2000: 165).

As Keal notes, discourse ethics requires that moral actors should

> Think from the standpoint of the other and recognise that their own beliefs are a reflection of their own experiences and therefore partial . . . Dialogue based on thinking from the standpoint of others offers the prospect of identifying universal values, which all parties can accept and which are not open to the objection of being merely the values imposed by dominant actors. (Keal 2003: 155)

This is attractive as a means of shoring up the normative cohesion of international society on the basis of a genuine cross-cultural dialogue. However, the challenges to establishing these conditions for dialogue or conversation are many. The first is to secure the participation of relevant parties. This requires all relevant parties to recognize that differences in perspective exist and are salient. This is a problem perhaps with Jackson's position. He recognizes differences, but does not appear to view them as salient to the structure and institutions of international society. Rather, he views the universal order that international society provides as already managing these differences. Second, though perhaps related to this point, there must be a recognition that parties to dialogue may enter that dialogue not only with different perceptions of the present, but also with different understandings of history. The memories of the past can provide a powerful barrier to constructing the conditions of trust that may be necessary to the construction of alternative futures.

A third consideration that must be acknowledged for the establishment of dialogue is that, in order to critique domination, violence, and systemic inequality (Linklater 1998: 106), all parties to conversation or dialogue must necessarily acknowledge inequalities of power, both past and present, that have shaped the contours of international society, including material, institutional, and ideational power. Finally, the parties to the dialogue must surely be representative of a broad spectrum of domestic societies, not simply representing the voices of political and cultural elites. In other words, there must also be some representation of the voices of 'societal culture' if the dialogue is to result in a consensus that has practical and ethical resonance.

It could be argued that a minimum order is required to create the conditions for this dialogue to occur. Dialogue requires some modicum of stability and some basic rules of engagement. From Jackson's perspective, it may be argued that it is this very minimum degree of order that 'the global covenant' already provides. This returns us to the question of whether securing a minimal order is a prerequisite for and therefore supersedes justice. In considering the conundrum of precedence between order and justice, Kai Alderson and Andrew Hurrell have observed that the issue is rarely a stark choice between order and justice: 'rather it is a question about how order and justice are related *within* different, and often conflicting, conceptions of world order' (2000: 64). Alderson and Hurrell go on to note that in Bull's work, and in contemporary thinking on this issue, there is a shifting sense of what a minimally acceptable order would comprise. Considerations of what would comprise a minimal degree of order for the establishment of intercultural dialogue about international society cannot be divorced from normative perceptions of justice To presume that the normative basis of order has already been mutually established is to neglect key elements of the problems that currently threaten to unsettle that order.

CONCLUSION

Considerations of culture have been intrinsic to conceptions of international society put forward by the English School. Within this body of work, culture has been discussed as a central foundation of the common norms and values that ultimately underpin order in international society. Yet, the institutions of international society have also been viewed as providing the means through which to manage the challenges of political interaction among culturally diverse communities in what has become a heterogeneous, multicultural society. There is, however, an important body of thought within this school concerned with the degree to which contemporary international society is, and is perceived to be, based on a just and ethical order, in that it is an order which respects and represents the cultures it encompasses in equal measure. Contemporary international society evolved in a context of hierarchical perceptions of culture, and inequalities in the distribution of power and influence among cultures. While some are confident that this hierarchical structure has now been superseded, signs of discontent in the contemporary political environment suggest this confidence may be misplaced. The reconstitution of international society in a form perceived as ethical and just by the plurality of communities and cultures it encompasses is critical to its ongoing cohesion. A number of commentators have suggested that this can only be achieved through dialogue. However the conditions of acknowledgement and representation this requires present a formidable challenge to even the establishment of such a dialogue. Equally challenging is the central task that such a dialogue would confront: to continue to grapple with the dilemma of seeking a moral consensus that continues to respect the ethic of difference. This is a daunting task. However, the first necessary step in meeting these challenges is to recognize that the continued cohesion of international society requires that this dilemma be confronted rather than resting on the assumption that the job of managing cultural pluralism has already been done.

Notes

1. See, for instance, Barnett (1999); Blaney and Inayatullah (1994); Campbell (1998); Chan, Mandaville, and Bleiker (2001); Falk (1990); Grovugui (1996); Katzenstein (1996*b*); Lapid and Kratochwil (1996); Neumann (1999); Rae (2002); Reus–Smit (1999); Salter (2002); Weldes et al. (1999); Wendt (1999); Walker (1990).
2. Bull did suggest that a future cosmopolitan culture could emerge, based on the discussion of common concerns such as the environment, nuclear weapons, and population problems (Bull 1977: 317; 1984*c*: 14).
3. As Buzan notes, Watson's survey of international societies identifies eleven historical cases (Buzan 1993: 333).

4. Both Bull (1984*b*: 123) and Watson (1990) treat inclusion in this major peace conference as marking the Ottoman Empire's inclusion as a full and unqualified member of the European states-system. As Bull notes, at the Congress of Vienna in 1815 only European powers were included.

5. In this context, the concept of hegemony is used to indicate a relationship among a group of societies, the cornerstone of which is the adoption of a dominant set of ideas promoted by a leading power (Cox 1996; Cronin 2001).

6. Indeed Jackson notes that one of the most fundamental concerns of international society over the past 350 years has been 'to confine religious and ideological *weltanshauungen* within the territorial cages of national border' (Jackson 2000: 368).

7. Keene goes on to argue that in the twentieth century, as European international society evolved to a global society, it has sought to continue to pursue and reconcile both goals of tolerance and civilization, thus generating the tensions alluded to at the outset of this chapter between the tolerance of diversity and the imperative of a universal, progressive order (Keene 2002: ch. 5).

8. As Hurrell notes, while there has been progress in the articulation of norms relating to human rights, democracy, liberal economics, and sustainable development, underlying and deep divisions remain. The consensus on core values and how they should be promoted remains fragile (1998: 30–1).

9. For instance, on trial and subsequently convicted for involvement in the bombing of a nightclub in Bali in October 2002 in which 202 Indonesians and foreigners died, Amrozi stated:

   There will be more bombs until the Westerners are finished. How can I feel sorry? I'm very happy because they attack Muslims and are inhuman because they are brutal. With their brutality, I don't feel sorry. You can see from their behaviour, they come here, Americans, Jews, and their lies, they want to colonise, not just for play. Terrorism is ordered by Allah in the Koran. (Reproduced in ABC Radio National, 2003)

   Similarly, Muslims were called to *jihad* against 'Americans and their allies, civilians and military . . . in any country in which it is possible to do so' in the now famous *fatwa* '*Jihad* against Jews and Crusaders', issued by Osama bin Laden with several other Islamist leaders as the World Islamic Front Statement (Bin Laden 1998).

10. Although in each case heavy casualties were also inflicted upon the domestic population. In addition, the use of mass impact terrorist attacks was also becoming more evident in other sites of conflict and tension, such as India and Israel.

11. Whether this symbolism was intended, or whether this attack was perpetrated on the UN mission because it was staffed by a substantial contingent of Westerners and a 'softer target' than more heavily guarded US institutions, is unknown at time of writing. However, the attack did consciously target the Head of the UN mission and the Secretary General's Special Envoy to Iraq and UN High Commissioner for Human Rights, Sergio Vieira de Mello.

12. An example of this is the articulation by George W. Bush's administration of a doctrine of self-defence that entails pre-emptive action against potential rather than actual attack (Bush 2002; National Security Council 2002). Such a norm, if widely adopted, would radically alter the rules of contemporary international society. It could alter the premises for intervention and the use of force, and ratchet up the implications of threat perceptions.

13

Violence, Order, and Terror

Richard Devetak

Of course, the element of disorder looms as large or larger in world politics than the element of order.

(Bull 1977: p. xii)

Many of the most important issues in world politics today involve actors and processes outside international society. The advent of globalization and the rise of multinational corporations, non-governmental organizations, refugees, transnational criminal networks, and global terrorist groups add further complexity to the challenges of maintaining international order. This chapter focuses on the challenge global terrorism poses to international society's order.

Hedley Bull's study of threats to international order, it will be suggested, provides a useful starting point for an examination of terrorism's impact on international society. Three further aspects of Bull's work on international society will be drawn upon: his recognition that the use of violence by non-state actors is by no means unusual in world politics; his argument that the 'revolt against the West' has the potential to unleash destabilizing violence; and his understanding that international society may be threatened by unchecked hegemons as much as global terrorists. It will be argued that terrorism's globalization of violence marks the latest element of disorder in an international society that has the capacity to absorb and pacify violence of both sanctioned or unsanctioned kinds. In fact, in the end the major threat to international society may lie in how hegemonic states react to terrorism. Having said this, neither Bull nor other English School thinkers paid much attention to terrorism. However, because terrorism always acts upon political order, either to preserve or disrupt it, Bull's perspective has particular cogency since order is one of his central themes.

I would like to thank Tim Dunne for several valuable conversations during the course of writing this chapter, and Alex Bellamy, Scott Burchill, Peter Lentini, Emma Renowden, and Richard Shapcott for insightful and constructive feedback on earlier drafts.

TERRORISM AND THE ENGLISH SCHOOL

Terrorism is not a new phenomenon. It has been around in one form or another for millennia (Gearty 1997: ch. 1; Halliday 2002: 76). International or global terrorism is not particularly new either. At least since the nineteenth century terrorism has had an international dimension as anarchist and socialist revolutionaries flowed regularly across national borders embracing the idea of 'the propaganda of the deed', exploding bombs and assassinating state officials to provoke insurrection (Townshend 2002: 54–60). Significantly, however, international relations theorists of all persuasions have paid little attention to it as an international phenomenon.[1] This is certainly the case with the leading theorists of international society.

The 1970s witnessed several thousand terrorist incidents (Mickolus 1980: pp. xiv–xxx), many of which had an international dimension to them. Radical political movements such as the Red Brigades in Italy, the Baader–Meinhof gang in Germany, and the Weathermen in the United States used violence to pursue anarchist and anti-capitalist agendas, albeit largely within national borders. Other movements, however, focused global attention on self-determination issues. Both the substantive issues and the media coverage were international in scope. The Irish Republican Army (IRA) and the Basque terrorist group *Euzkadi to Askatasuna* (ETA—'land and liberty') were actively engaged in terrorist violence throughout the 1970s, as were the Palestine Liberation Organization (PLO). The PLO's murder of Israeli athletes at the 1972 Munich Olympics demonstrated terrorists' capacity and will to operate beyond national borders. Indeed, aircraft hijacking was one of terrorists' favoured tactics during the 1970s (Rapoport 2001: 421). Furthermore, governments such as Libya, Iraq, and Syria employed terrorists in other countries as foreign policy instruments (Rapoport 2001: 421). The 1970s was also a period in which states, through multilateral institutions, negotiated several treaties to outlaw and combat terrorism.[2]

In spite of these developments, Hedley Bull's *The Anarchical Society*, a wide-ranging structural and functional analysis of international society and its prospects, has almost nothing to say about terrorism. In fact, the word 'terrorism' itself does not appear on its pages. When discussing aircraft hijackings and diplomatic kidnappings, Bull (1977: 268–70) preferred to speak in more general terms of 'private international violence'. In an earlier article where he does use the word terrorism, Bull (1971) refers to it as a form of internationalized 'civil violence'. Other members of the English School also paid little attention to the impact of terrorist activity on international society.[3] This can hardly have been an oversight. Bull and other international society theorists most likely formed the judgement that terrorism was a peripheral issue and therefore could be omitted from sustained discussion. At least two reasons seem likely.

First, the English School's starting point is the system of states with the sovereign state as its fundamental unit. Indeed, Martin Wight (1966a: 17) associates the study of international relations straightforwardly with the 'tradition of speculation about relations between states'. As a consequence of this state-centrism, the actions and interactions of transnational actors who traverse state borders, such as multinational corporations (MNCs) and non-governmental organizations (NGOs), generally come in for short shrift. Having said this, the English School certainly does not deny the existence or importance of such actors. However, they are sceptical of the extent to which they directly shape or reshape world orders.

Second, the English School's scant treatment of terrorism may also indicate a resistance to presentism, a resolve 'to escape from the *Zeitgeist*', to use Wight's (1991: 6) words. Bull generally sought to confine enquiry to 'enduring issues of human political structure ... and to avoid consideration of the substantive issues of world politics at the present time' (Bull 1977: p. xiii). This statement should not be taken as a wilful denial of contemporary realities. Rather, it reflects an attempt to 'acquire perspective' (Wight 1991: 6) by adopting an historical and interpretive attitude; historical in the sense that it views history from the perspective of the *longue durée*, and interpretive in the sense that shared or intersubjective understandings constitute the identities, interests, and norms that shape international politics. Overemphasizing the importance of actors and events in the present is one of the forms of ahistoricism that the English School generally tries to avoid, the other being the realist view that nothing ever changes.

Most likely, English School thinkers judged terrorism to be a passing phase with few lasting consequences for international society. Certainly, the English School was sceptical of arguments predicated on the assumption that profound change is just around the corner. See, for example, Bull's (1977: chs 10–11) scepticism towards the view that the growth of interdependence and the rise of transnational organizations were threatening the survival of the states-system. However, it should be noted that while Bull (1977: 276) rejected the view that the states-system was in decline, he did recognize that it was under increasing pressure as a result of new normative and material forces, including transnational organizations.[4] Bull (1977: 276) also acknowledged that the states-system, while primary, is only part of a 'wider political system' that includes actors both above and below states. But Bull dispelled the inference that this is historically novel or unique. Indeed, he says it has always been the case that non-state actors have interacted with international society (Bull 1977: 281).

TERROR, TERRORISM, AND TERRORISTS

Like most key political concepts, terrorism is an essentially contested term. Indeed, more often than not 'terrorism' functions as a political label rather than analytical concept (Crenshaw, quoted in Betts 2002: 19). That is to say, it is a term of opprobrium generally used to delegitimize one's enemy by condemning their methods. In fact, 'to call an act of violence a "terrorist act" is not so much to describe it as to condemn it' (Gearty 1997: 11). For as Townshend (2002: 3) says, almost no group voluntarily adopts the label 'terrorist'; it is instead 'applied to them by others', generally by enemy governments.

At the most general level, terrorism is a form of political violence. This is a view accepted across the political and theoretical spectrum. The US State Department defines terrorism as 'politically motivated violence perpetrated against noncombatant targets by subnational groups or clandestine agents, usually intended to influence an audience' (quoted in Tilly 2002).[5] The problem with this definition is that it concentrates on the actors rather than the act: the terrorists who 'perpetrate' the acts, the victims who are 'targeted', and the audience struck with fear. Of course, terrorism will always involve perpetrators, targets, and audiences. But this approach lacks analytical utility, even if it offers political utility, by excluding state terrorism. It shifts too quickly and disingenuously from being a definition of terrorism to being a designator of terrorists. This is a partisan political act that functions to erase the term's history, not something we normally expect of definitions.

There are some analytical issues that ought to be resolved straight away. It is important not to elide the distinction between the act of terrorism and the actors as the State Department definition does. If we start from the proposition that terrorism is a method, then terrorists are simply those actors who employ the methods of terrorism. As Richard Betts (2002: 20) says, 'terror is a means, not an end in itself. Terror tactics … are a use of force designed to further some substantive aim'. Similarly, Ken Booth and Tim Dunne (2002: 8) aver that terrorism is not an ideology but a method. If we take this as our starting point, then states are just as capable of employing terrorist methods as non-state actors. Indeed, as has frequently been pointed out, states are much more significant producers of terror than non-state groups (Gearty 1997: 54; Booth and Dunne 2002: 9; Halliday 2002: 48).

This approach to the question of definition has the advantage of separating terror from its agents. It allows us to recognize acts of terror whether committed by states, individuals, or groups. It thus marks a significant improvement on those definitions that refuse to acknowledge the capacity of states to employ terror as a political strategy. At the same time, it does not imply that states are simply legitimized forms of terrorism. Rather than reduce all states to terrorism, it is better to follow Ghassan Hage (2003: 71) and argue that terrorist organizations are groups committed to using terrorism as a central or sole political practice. States, while they may employ terrorism, sometimes systematically, do not rely on it exclusively.

Having said this, it still remains unclear what marks terrorism as a method. What precisely is involved in making terrorism a tactic or strategy of politics? For this, we might turn to Edmund Burke. He suggested that terror is the emotional affect felt by the mind when excited by intense ideas of pain or death (1987).[6] In other words, terror is the feeling caused by fear; it makes one shake or tremble with dread. To use terror as a political tactic or strategy then is to generate ideas of overwhelming fear by directing violence against selected targets. Terrorism, broadly understood, refers to the systematic use of violence to eliminate opposition and create a general climate of fear for political reasons. In the following section we look at some of the ways the cultivation of fear through violence has been put to political ends both by the state and against the state, inflicting physical and psychological damage on the enemy.

STATE AND NON-STATE TERRORISM

The word 'terror' first appeared in the English language before the end of the eighteenth century to describe the revolutionary Terror that gripped France in 1793–4 (Townshend: ch. 3). On 5 September 1793, the new French Republic's Constituent Assembly declared 'the Terror' the order of the day (Furet 1989). This is not to say that the Terror began on that precise date. At least since the storming of the Tuileries Palace in the summer of 1792, the revolutionary leadership had been resorting to violent attacks that prefigured the Terror. Henceforth, however, the revolutionary government of the Republic would build its rule on the basis of fear by *systematically* liquidating its adversaries. As François Furet (1989: 144–5) explains, the Terror 'was a massive repression organized from above … with the intention of destroying not only the rebels but the population, farms, crops, villages, and anything else that had served the "brigands" as shelter'. Thousands were killed in the name of the new French nation as a result of the Terror.

The Terror eventually became a *system* of government insofar as it was not simply a random, arbitrary use of violence and repression, but its institutionalization. It became an organized mode of repression and domination to stave off threats to the revolutionary government; a 'systematisation of the exceptional', to use Colin Lucas's (1994: 73) words. It gave rise to a government of fear in two senses: it was a paranoid, fearful government, and a government that sought to cultivate fear everywhere. Anxiety, fear, and vengeance were central to the strategy of the Terror. As Timothy Tackett (2001: 575) argues, the drift towards a 'terrorist mentality' was a result of genuine threats to the revolution being interpreted in increasingly exaggerated and irrational ways. This heightened the urgency of dealing with suspected enemies quickly and ruthlessly, suspending the rule of law and fair trials in favour of swift punishment of opponents. The revolutionaries, of course, defended their resort to violence in terms of defending the achievements of the revolution, namely, liberty and equality.[7] Their violence, they claimed, was as nothing compared to the violence and tyranny of the *Ancien Régime*. Regardless of attempts at justification, it is important to note that the Terror depended on a perception of dangerously omnipotent and omnipresent enemies. As Furet (1981: 54) put it, 'the Revolution invented formidable enemies for itself, for every Manichean creed needs to overcome its share of eternal evil'.

Of course revolutionary France is not the only example of a state systematically using murderous violence to cultivate fear for political reasons. The totalitarian regimes of the twentieth century generally adopted similar measures, including Nazi Germany, Stalin's Soviet Union, Pol Pot's Cambodia, and Saddam Hussein's Iraq. Terrorism has also been adopted as a tactic by repressive military juntas such as those in Chile, Argentina, and Peru to name just a few. Fred Halliday (2002: 73) aptly refers to these types of terrorism as 'terrorism from above'; Townshend (2002: ch. 3), following Eugene Walter, refers to it as the 'regime of terror'. Common to all these examples of state terror is a profound and often irrational fear that leads to violent acts of repression and retribution systematically carried out in the name of security and survival.

The second type of terrorism issues from below. In the latter half of the twentieth century it was this 'terrorism from below' (Halliday 2002: 75) that was most readily and commonly associated with terrorism. In fact, in most Western capitals terrorism is by definition a form of political violence 'from below', as the US State Department definition shows. In contrast to state terrorism, which seeks to maintain and strengthen the state's power, terrorism from below can be understood as an act of subversive political violence, usually aimed at delegitimizing, destabilizing, and destroying the state. For a variety of reasons the state is perceived as illegitimate. For the anarcho-communist movements of the 1970s, such as the Red Brigades and Baader–Meinhof, the state was simply an undemocratic tool of the capitalist ruling classes; for groups seeking national liberation, from the Algerian *Front de Libération Nationale* (FLN) to the IRA and PLO, the state represented foreign domination; and for right-wing movements, such as US militia groups or Jewish messianic militants, the state or nation's existence is being traduced by liberal-minded governments. In any case the state is perceived as an enemy because it represents an intolerable betrayal of a people or class.

When small non-state actors pit themselves against states like this they set up an asymmetrical confrontation. In fact, as both Richard Betts (2002: 24) and Audrey Cronin (2002/3: 51) point out, terrorism is the perfect example of asymmetrical conflict. Large, immobile, solid, organized, coercive apparatuses versus small, mobile, furtive, dispersed, coercive 'groupuscules'.[8] These groupuscules focus all their energies on bringing down or sending home their vastly more powerful state enemy. Most importantly, they are committed to the systematic use of violence to defeat and eliminate their declared enemy. The political end, whatever it may be, is believed to justify the application of deadly and unconventional force.

In pursuing their political end, such groups are deprived of the massive arsenals of weapons and armed forces integral to the states against which they fight so they must be resourceful and improvise with whatever instruments of violence they can get their hands on. More important than the military hardware though is the tactical use made of their military assets. They cannot confront the enemy directly; instead, they launch surprise attacks at its vulnerable points. The aim is to disorient and destabilize the enemy state, in the hope that it will lead to collapse or withdrawal. Such are the tactics of guerrilla warfare also. Indeed, there are several tactical similarities between terrorism and guerrilla operations. As Richard Betts argues, in both cases the weaker actors depend on their ability to blend into their environment unnoticed, whether civil society or the natural landscape. By so doing they maximize the ability to strike enemy targets suddenly and unexpectedly and then blend back into their surroundings undetected (Betts 2002: 28).

To summarize, 'terrorism from above' generally uses violence to maintain an extant domestic political order, whereas 'terrorism from below' uses violence to challenge it. It should be obvious that both forms of terrorism pose a threat to human life and strain the bonds of trust within civil society by disrupting the orders of everyday life.

The threat to civil society will however depend on the intensity and regularity of the violence and the extent to which civilians are targeted and harmed.

VIOLENCE AND TERROR AS THREATS TO ORDER

International order is the central preoccupation of the English School (see Vincent 1990; Dunne 1998; Linklater 2001; Suganami 2002*a,b*). Underpinning this preoccupation is the premise that order is a fundamental precondition of social existence. This premise has a long pedigree. Many of the foundational works of modern political thought were prompted by a concern to limit or reduce violence so as to achieve an ordered political existence. For example, the governing theme of Hugo Grotius's *De Iure Belli ac Pacis* (1925), written during the transnational religious violence of the Thirty Years' War, was that the preservation of social order requires restraints on violence. Distressed by the way men rushed to arms for slight or non-existent causes, Grotius developed an argument that while war was not in itself contrary to the laws of nature, it had to be strictly regulated by the law of nations (*ius gentium*).

Thomas Hobbes's *Leviathan* was likewise 'occasioned by the disorders of the present time' (1968: 728). In particular, he believed that moral and theological matters were fuelling the flames of violence. In his words, the 'most frequent prætext of Sedition, and Civill Warre' proceeds from the 'difficulty ... of obeying at once, both God, and Man' (1968: 609). He continues that the fanatical obsession with salvation and the spreading of 'phantasticall and false Doctrines' in God's name merely served the purpose of 'private ends'. His solution was the establishment of a supreme political authority, the sovereign state, which would effectively expunge private morality (namely, religion) from the public realm and bring to an end the tension between the Word of God and the word of the sovereign. Hobbes sought to neutralize religious conflict by moving moral and theological matters from the public to the private realm, and establishing order as the primary political value. For both Grotius and Hobbes the solution to violence is to establish a minimal moral basis for rules of coexistence (see Tuck 1987; Pasquino 1996). This applies at both the domestic and international levels. The same mode of thinking underpins the English School's understanding of international society.

Two points about Bull's conception of order are important here. First, Bull (1977: 4–5) asserted that any society requires the promotion of three basic goals if order is to be sustained: security against violence, observance of agreements, and stability of property. According to Bull (1977: 6) they form the 'elementary or primary conditions of social existence'. At the level of international society these goals translate into the laws of war, the principle of *pacta sunt servanda*, and the mutual recognition of sovereignty (Bull 1977: 16–20). These do not aim to eliminate conflict and violence, but to limit it and mitigate its worst effects. More than simply regulate international conduct, they have the constitutive effect of making sovereign states legitimate actors.

Second, contra Hobbes, order can exist in the absence of an orderer, and society in the absence of a sovereign; they arise out of common interests, rules, and institutions

(Bull 1977: 53 *ff.*). This is an important element of the argument because it opens up the possibility that ordered societies can be achieved not just without an orderer but also without the constant recourse to violence. States internalize rules and norms about appropriate conduct, including those pertaining to the legitimate use of force. For the English School this points to the civilizing influence of dialogue and non-violent agreement in international politics (Watson 1982). This of course contrasts with the outlook of terrorists who reject dialogue in the belief that violence is the only means of resolving a specific conflict (Booth and Dunne 2002: 8–10).

Orders are always established against threats; they are intended to contain threats or hold them at bay. Of course, the nature of the threat changes over time; there are different intensities and sources of threat. In his collaboration with Adam Watson, Bull identified several threats in the twentieth century to the order established by international society. To begin with, Bull and Watson (1984) identified the emergence of a universal international society and its consequent diminution of European dominance as a threat to international order. They took the view that with the twentieth century's development of a universal international society, states were less united by a common interest in maintaining the extant framework of rules and institutions. The 'ligaments' of international society, to use a Burkean term, seemed to be fraying under the pressures of expansion: increased membership, cultural diversity, and uneven economic development. This gave rise, among other things, to the phenomenon of 'quasi-states', as Bull and Watson called them, which lack the capacity to exercise power and authority over their territory and are sovereign states only in name.

Bull and Watson surmised that the rise of quasi-states, created through the rush to decolonize, has had the effect of weakening international society's cohesion by virtue of their inability to enforce either domestic or international rules. This has become a particularly important phenomenon since the latter years of the twentieth century, not least because, as Robert Rotberg (2002) points out, these quasi- or 'failed states' seem to be an enabling condition of terrorism. The instability, violence, and bloody conflict that flourish within the borders of quasi-states make them the perfect incubators for the growth and export of terrorism, as experience in Afghanistan shows (Halliday 2002: ch. 1; Kaldor 2002; Rotberg 2002). While Bull and Watson (1984: 433) acknowledged that several factors originating in the West, such as ideological rivalry, the scars of two World Wars, nuclear weapons, and globalization, also enervated international society, they placed special emphasis on the 'revolt against the West' as a threat to international society.

Five themes mark the revolt against the West: the struggle for sovereign equality, the anticolonial revolution, the struggle for racial equality, the demand for economic justice, and the revolt against Western values (Bull 1984*b*: 220–3). The first four themes draw upon Western notions of justice and equality, and reject the exclusionary criteria of membership informing international society's European origins. The last theme however poses a grave threat to international society because it can potentially take the form of a rejection of the very procedural principles upon which consensus can be reached and order built. This is an important factor in understanding and assessing the threat terrorism poses to international society. Indeed, as we shall see below, there are good reasons for viewing the September 11 terrorist attacks and the Bali Bombing within the framework of the 'revolt against the West' as Scott Burchill (2002) and Andrew Linklater (2002) have argued. There is also however a broader and longer-term historical context in which to understand and assess the threat of terrorism: the persistence of what Bull (1977: 268) calls 'private international violence'.

Bull (1977: 268–70) reminds us that the exercise of violence by non-state actors has been an enduring aspect of international relations. Because of the pacification of modern societies and the largely successful monopolization of the legitimate instruments of violence by sovereign states, it is easy to forget that for several centuries, from 1300 to 1900, the instruments of violence were dispersed among various actors, both public (state) and private (non-state). Indeed, for a long time states in fact encouraged 'private international violence' because non-state actors often did the bidding of states. Eventually, however, states began to disarm the pirates, privateers, mercenaries, and merchants so as to monopolize the instruments of violence.

Perhaps the most important instances of non-state violence were the mercantile companies established in the sixteenth century to engage in long-distance trade and to help states settle and build colonies and to facilitate trade. Governments delegated significant powers to these prototypical multinational corporations such as the Dutch East India and Hudson's Bay companies. In faraway regions they were given extensive powers, including the rights to 'raise an army or a navy, build forts, make treaties, make war, govern their fellow nationals, and coin their own money' (Thomson 1994: 35). These large mercantile companies were in many senses extensions of the state and, consequently, the source of much conflict.

Piracy provides an example of non-state violence with striking parallels to terrorism (Bull 1971: 34; Keohane 2002). Pirates were rather like privateers except that they generally acted without state authorization, or if they did have a 'letter of marque' did not restrict themselves to fighting in times of war only. This complicated the distinction between privateer and pirate somewhat. Indeed, examples such as Henry Morgan, who, quite to the pleasure of England, raided and pillaged Spanish settlements in the mid-seventeenth century, suggest that one person's pirate is another's privateer (Thomson 1994).

Other examples of piracy also posed problems. The corsairs of the Barbary Coast presented a particular problem for European powers because of the unconventional authority under which they operated. First, it was unclear whether the Barbary powers (of Morocco, Algiers, Tunis, and Tripoli) were under the suzerain power of the Sublime Porte or constituted independent states (Mössner 1972: 206; Thomson 1994: 45).[9] Second, it remained unclear whether the pirates acted under authorization of their hosts. Third, there was the issue of whether the Barbary Powers were to be dealt with under the law of nations or were barbarians outside the 'standard of civilisation'. Vattel (1916: Book III, ch. 4, §68), for instance, took the latter view, insisting that a nation attacked by pirates 'is not under any obligation to observe towards them the rules belonging to formal war; it may treat them as outlaws'. Grotius (1925: Book III, ch. 3, §§ 2–3) advances a similar view. Although he allowed for 'private war' as a means of defending rights where legal recourse was unavailable, he condemned brigands and pirates for being little other than associations for wrong-doing. His view was that unlike enemy states (*hostis*), or private enemies (*inimicus*), pirates and brigands were designated as 'enemies of mankind' (*hostes humani generis*), and therefore were subject to a different set of rules. Grotius did however retain the category of 'private war', as opposed to 'public war' between sovereign states, to justify private trading companies using violence in defence of shipping routes and the despoliation of rivals.[10]

These examples suggest that 'private international violence' has a very long and politically significant history. The histories of the state-building process and the expansion of European international society would be incomplete without a proper accounting of the ways non-state violence were deployed on behalf of European powers. Before states had the resources and capacity to monopolize the instruments of legitimate violence, they were content to exploit the coercive capabilities of non-state actors. It was perhaps a kind of state-sponsored terrorism as Thomson (1994: 23) suggests. Eventually, however, states began to perceive the damaging effects of allowing non-state violence to continue—privateering degenerated into piracy, mercenaries dragged their employers into unwanted wars, and merchant companies directed violence against each other and against their own states (Thomson 1994: 43)—and set about delegitimating and disarming non-state actors.

Placing terrorism in the context of private international violence reminds us of the historical 'normality' of non-state violence and continuities with the present. Violence instigated by non-state actors may be as endemic to international relations as war among sovereign states. Certainly states have for centuries been willing to exploit non-state violence for statist ends. For example, states have continued to sponsor non-state violence, with countries such as Libya, Syria, and Afghanistan, among others, funding, sheltering, and employing terrorist groups at different times. There are also historical continuities in the political use of religion to justify non-state violence against enemy states, as we shall see in the following section; and questions persist about how best to categorize and treat non-state actors who use violence to pursue their goals. A hotly contested political issue in America's 'war on terrorism' is the status and treatment of prisoners, both Taliban and Al-Qaeda, captured and detained in Guantanamo Bay (Hurrell 2002*b*: 192; Roberts 2002).

However, for all the continuities in 'private international violence' across history, it is important to remember differences. Modern terrorism might be a form of 'private international violence' but it has very different means and ends to early modern examples of non-state violence. While pirates may have inspired fear, generally the fear extended no further than to seafarers; nor was fear instrumental to their purposes. By contrast, the spread of fear is instrumental to the political purposes of terrorism. Furthermore, mercenaries, merchants, privateers, and pirates never made violence their sole practice; it was generally employed haphazardly and only whenever required, not systematically. The following section outlines key characteristics of one contemporary form of 'private international violence', the so-called 'new terrorism'.

RISE OF THE 'NEW TERRORISM'

While terrorists believe the end justifies the means, in the past they have tended to place limits on violence directed at civilians. Terrorist groups such as the IRA and PLO, for example, have always been at least partly concerned with legitimizing their campaigns to both domestic and international publics. They have wanted to exploit domestic fears and win over public sympathy wherever possible. Radical left wing–anarchist movements such as the Red Brigades aimed their violence at political targets. For this reason, as Brian Jenkins (1975: 15) noted, 'terrorists want a lot of people watching and a lot of people listening and not a lot of people dead'. They have wanted to delegitimize particular states; targeting civilians directly with violence would only have delegitimized their cause. Hence, they preferred to select political and military targets and to disrupt, rather than destroy, everyday life.

This may have been the case with traditional forms of terrorism, but it has been suggested that the 'new terrorism' does not abide by this thinking. Instead, it is said to aim at causing death and destruction on a massive scale. Steven Simon and Daniel Benjamin (2000 and 2001–2) argue that the 'new terrorism' began in 1993 with the first attempt to destroy the World Trade Centre in New York. This was followed by the Oklahoma City bombing in 1995, the Tokyo underground sarin gas attacks of 1995, the East Africa bombings of 1998, the September 11, 2001 attacks on New York and Washington, and the Bali Bombing of October 2002. They were 'harbingers of a new and vastly more threatening terrorism' intended to produce mass casualties (Simon and Benjamin 2000: 59). Simon and Benjamin (2000: 66) identify four developments that mark the advent of the 'new terrorism':

- Religious motivation;
- Greater lethality of attacks;
- Greater technological and operational competence;
- Desire to obtain weapons of mass destruction (WMD).

Religious Motivation

From Ramzi Yousef's 1993 bombing of the World Trade Centre, through Yigal Amir's assassination of Israeli Prime Minister Yitzhak Rabin in 1995, to the first female 'suicide bombing' of Jerusalem in 2002 by Waffa al-Edress, several acts of political violence since the 1990s have been accompanied by what Cronin (2002/3: 38) calls 'hyperreligious motivation'. In these and other cases the perpetrators believe that their acts of violence are justified by religious injunction. To understand the source of this violence we need to follow Fred Halliday by focusing on the fundamentalism, Islamic or otherwise, of these groups.

Fundamentalism combines two elements in asserting absolute, unquestionable grounds of authority: the appeal to God's Word and holy texts, and their dogmatic, literal, and violent application to social and political life (Euben 2002*b*: §9; Halliday 2002: ch. 2). There is an intimate connection between fundamentalism and intolerant, anti-democratic doctrines and attitudes. Fundamentalists express contempt for those who are different, or, in extreme cases, a will to silence or eliminate those who do not conform (infidels and apostates).

This blend of selective and dogmatic interpretation of sacred texts with political doctrines of intolerance and elimination informs Al-Qaeda. As its founding statement says, quoting from The Qur'an: 'fight and slay pagans wherever ye find them, seize them, beleaguer them, and lie in wait for them in every stratagem [of war]'. The statement then issues a *fatwa* about the religious duty of *jihad*: 'The ruling to kill the Americans and their allies—civilians and military—is an individual duty for every Muslim who can do it in any country in which it is possible to do it' (quoted in Halliday 2002: 217–8).

For fundamentalists, the violent struggle to remake the world is a duty. As Roxanne Euben (2002a: 9) argues, 'in the hands of contemporary Islamic "fundamentalists", *jihad* is ... a form of political action in which ... the pursuit of immortality is inextricably linked to a profoundly this-worldly endeavour—the founding or recreation of a just community on earth'. The same can be said of Jewish messianic militants and puritanical Christian Patriots. So for all their exalted otherworldliness, as Halliday (2002: 55) remarks, fundamentalists have rather mundane, sublunary aspirations of social and political upheaval.

Greater Lethality of Attacks

Fundamentalists share a Manichean worldview characterized by the battle between good and evil.[11] In this life-and-death struggle there can be no constraints imposed on efforts to ensure victory against evil. Secular laws and modern humanist values are rejected as irrelevant by religious fundamentalists prepared to use violence (Simon and Benjamin 2000: 67; Cronin 2002/3: 41).

This 'new terrorism' has 'no discrete set of negotiable political demands' (Simon and Benjamin 2001–2: 5). No accommodation or conciliation is conceivable when one or both sides in the conflict seek the elimination of the other. The enemy is conceived as an implacable and irreconcilable foe. Terrorist groups like Al-Qaeda aim to eliminate rather than persuade their enemy; they do in fact want a lot of people dead, to invert Jenkins's view (Simon and Benjamin 2000: 71). This is what accounts for the increased lethality of their attacks and creates the impression of an infinite and 'total' war. Dialogue, which has been a central aspect of international society and its 'civilizing' ambitions for centuries, is simply rejected. In this way, terrorist groups deliberately alienate themselves from the rules and norms of international society, most especially those regarding restrictions on the use of force.

Greater Technological and Operational Competence

The September 11 attacks revealed the existence of a global terrorist network of skilled and highly committed agents. Al-Qaeda may have been built up by Osama Bin Laden but it remains unclear whether 'he is in any conventional sense in charge of it' (Smith 2002: 50). The point here is that Al-Qaeda is not a hierarchical structure. It does not operate with a pyramidal command and control structure of conventional organizations. Instead, it is a 'decentralised and transnationally dispersed network', as Deibert and Stein (2002: 2) put it. To borrow from Deleuze and Guattari (1987: ch. 1), Al-Qaeda is organized rather like a 'rhizome'; that is to say, it resembles the tangled underground roots and shoots of couch grass. 'Rhizomatic' organizations or networks are decentred and non-hierarchical with multiple intersecting lines of connection and communication between nodes.

One of the characteristics of flat, flexible, 'rhizomatic' networks is that individual units can operate with a significant degree of autonomy, often without other units in the network being aware of its activities or even existence (Simon and Benjamin 2001/2: 9–10; Deibert and Stein 2002: 7). More importantly, if one or more nodes of the network is disconnected or destroyed, the rhizome as a whole does not die; it simply generates new nodes. This type of set-up allows for a better 'swarming' capacity, as John Arquilla and David Ronfeldt (2003) call it, where small, dispersed, and manoeuvrable units strike like bees in coordinated, pulsing strikes. It makes life extremely difficult for large, hierarchical actors, as groups like Al-Qaeda and Jemaah Islamiah are demonstrating to international society today.

It is important to note here that despite the anti-modern rhetoric of Al-Qaeda and other fundamentalist terrorist groups, they are deeply implicated in modern processes of globalization. Their activities take full advantage of the technologies afforded by modern industrialized societies including travel, communications, computers, information, and global finance. The same conditions that enable individuals, multinational corporations, and non-governmental organizations to move relatively freely across state borders also allow terrorists and other transnational criminal organizations to do the same.

This suggests that more attention needs to be paid to what Carolyn Nordstrom (2000) calls 'shadow' networks, the vast, transnational webs of power and exchange that exist outside the formal institutions of states and markets that trade in drugs, arms, prostitution, and people. Wilfully defying the laws and borders of states, these mobile and elusive extraterritorial actors exist in something like a global 'frontierland', to use Bauman's (2002) term. Terrorism is just the most lethal type of transnational criminal activity in the frontierland created by globalization. Like other actors in this frontierland, terrorists have learned how to exploit modernity's technological developments. The case of global terrorism is distinguished however by its pursuit of political rather than private economic ends, and by its redirection of modern society's forces back upon itself. Also, whereas transnational criminal organizations seek to evade confrontation with the enemy, global terrorist networks are designed to take the fight to the enemy wherever he happens to be on the planet.

Desire to Obtain Weapons of Mass Destruction

The will to increase the lethality of attacks lends itself of course to a desire to acquire weapons of mass destruction; it is simply a corollary of the objective to create mass death and destruction. This is what President Bush refers to as 'the perilous crossroads of radicalism and technology'.[12] Launching and delivering accurate nuclear missiles is prohibitively expensive at present for all but the wealthiest and most determined of states. However, unsophisticated, yet still highly destructive, chemical and biological weapons can apparently be built with minimal know-how and financing. This has given rise to a fear of what Ehud Sprinzak (1998) calls 'superterrorism'. In terms of conventional warfare these weapons may be unnecessarily cruel and baleful; but for those who make no discrimination between combatants and non-combatants, and whose ends are unconstrained by secular limitations on force, these weapons are simply useful tools for inflicting massive harm on an enemy.

NEW TERRORISM'S IMPACT ON INTERNATIONAL SOCIETY

There are three ways in which the 'new terrorism', especially the most virulent form of Islamic fundamentalism, poses a challenge to prevailing political orders. First, it challenges prevailing principles of international legitimacy (Wight 1977: ch. 6). Instead of having political communities constituted on the basis of secular, humanist, democratic, and human rights principles, Islamic fundamentalism seeks to create theocratic states like Afghanistan's Taliban regime that use the Word of God to steer their 'terror from above'. The 'peace' sought by these fundamentalists is not grounded on toleration and coexistence, but on the expunging of non-believers to establish a *Dar-al-Islam* (House of Islam) informed by what has perhaps opportunistically been called 'Islamo-fascism'. This 'religionised' politics, to use Mark Juergensmeyer's (2002: 29) term, of course, reverses the Hobbesian solution by granting the Word of God primacy over the word of the sovereign. It also challenges historic monopolies claimed by the modern state over 'morally sanctioned killing' (Juergensmeyer 2002: 35) and the instruments of violence. As Bull and Vincent independently observe, this violates international society's rule that only sovereign states have the authority to resort to force against an enemy, and then only according to the laws of war (Bull 1971: 31–2; 1979c: 117; Vincent 1986b: 2–3).

Second, the 'new terrorism' challenges the procedural rules and institutions of international society by rejecting secular principles of dialogue and coexistence in favour of fundamentalist doctrines of silencing and eliminating others. Fundamentalist groups like Al-Qaeda resolutely believe that the *Dar-al-Islam* cannot be built without violence and the elimination of the enemy. They reject ideas of dialogue and consent because they rest on a willingness to negotiate and reach agreement on the basis of secular rules of communication and argumentation. Dialogue also presupposes a willingness to listen to others, a capacity for critical self-reflection, and a reciprocal openness to reconsider political claims or demands so that coexistence may continue. Clearly, these values are at odds with attempts to silence and eliminate others that characterize fundamentalisms and terrorism.

Global terrorism's violent interruption of 'ordinary, everyday international life' (Vincent 1986*b*: 2) threatens to place 'an intolerable strain' on international society (Bull 1971: 36) by breeding fear and mistrust among states and publics. However, this strain will only become intolerable for international society if the agents of the 'new terror' have the technological and organizational competence to inflict sustained physical and psychological damage on their declared enemies over time. Until then they will be a deadly threat to individuals but not to the fundamental rules and principles of international society.

Third, the 'new terrorism', as exemplified by Al-Qaeda at least, challenges the global distribution of power, namely, US and Western hegemony. As misconceived as its ideas are, Al-Qaeda sees America as the paradigmatic case of Western evil and seeks to deny them any presence or power in the Islamic world. It has been suggested that Al-Qaeda's strategy of antagonizing the United States is intended to 'bring to the surface the great war' (Juergensmeyer 2002: 40), a war that pitches the empire of good against the empire of evil, truth against tyranny. Terrorists typically feel vindicated when states react violently to acts of terror, lending further persuasiveness to their narratives of a powerful tyrant's evils, and justifying their exhortations to violent *jihad*.

It may be instructive to understand the 'new terrorism' as part of the 'unfinished revolt against the West' (Burchill 2002; Linklater 2002). Previous phases of the revolt have resulted in violence, especially the anticolonial revolutions. But even these revolts did not reject modern Western values entirely. This contrasts however with the latest phase which is characterized by a rejection of values thought to be central to Western modernity. The 'new terrorism' signals a clear rejection of what is seen as the Western path to modernity. Putting aside the problems of attributing unity to modernity, we can safely say that insofar as principles of dialogue, consent, toleration, freedom, democracy, and human rights animate modern conceptions of international legitimacy, they are resolutely and violently rejected by the Islamic fundamentalists who see these values and their associated political cultures as threatening. It is important though not to present this conflict simply as a clash between Islam and the West. Fred Halliday (2002: 46) makes the vital point that at the heart of the conflict lies a violent clash *within* the Muslim world between secular reformists and religious fundamentalists.

In these ways, the 'new terrorism' of Al-Qaeda marks a departure from the forms of 'private international violence' that were integral to the development of modern international relations. It also marks a departure from the 'old terrorism' in terms of its increasingly global scope and intention to take the fight to the enemies wherever they may be. Having said this, the capacity of the 'new terrorism' to overturn the prevailing principles of international legitimacy, the rules and institutions of international society, or US hegemony is profoundly limited by the overwhelming power and legitimacy of international society itself. None but the fundamentalists themselves would be willing to consent to their preferred political order. Global terrorism's threat to international society therefore should not be overstated.

Indeed, the primary threat to international society may not come from global terrorism itself, but from the great powers' reaction to it, as both Bull (1971: 31–2) and

Vincent (1986*b*: 2) recognized. Tim Dunne (2003) has observed that the United States is increasingly placing itself outside the rules, norms, and institutions of international society, prompting him to speculate on whether US foreign policy is developing into a 'revolt against the institutions of international society'. In its statements about the 'axis of evil', America is arrogating to itself the authority to decide rightful membership of international society, an authority historically drawn from international society's collective judgement. And in its advocacy of more elastic notions of self-defence and pre-emption, the United States appears to have embarked on what Michael Byers (2003) describes as a unilateral attempt to change the 'generally applicable rules' of international law. As Bull (1984*a*: 14) argued, when states 'set themselves up as the authoritative judges of the world common good, in disregard of others', they become 'a menace to international order'.

CONCLUSION

Hedley Bull was always aware of the limitations imposed on understanding world politics exclusively through the structures of international society. He averred that 'it is always erroneous to interpret international events as if international society were the sole or the dominant element' (Bull 1977: 51). The states-system, in his view, is part of a wider system of social and economic exchange that includes the world economy and world society. Bull may not have spent much effort elaborating the nature of this relationship but his brief comments suggest it is a mistake to assess terrorism's impact on international society as if it were removed from these wider systems and from the changing dynamics of politics (1971: 29).

Perhaps Bull's (1977: 254–5) image of a 'new medievalism' is apt in capturing not just the emergence of multitiered, overlapping powers and authorities, criss-crossing loyalties, and universal society in an era of globalization and global governance, but also the permanent presence of non-state violence and insecurity. Bull's (1971: 31) conjecture about the potential 'return to medieval ideas of private violence' also finds confirmation in Mary Kaldor's (2002) observation that the restructuring and diversification of modes of violence today resembles that of the premodern period. In the same way that 'private international violence' functioned as something like a hinge between the social, political, and mercantile systems of early modern Europe, global terrorism today functions at the intersection of world society, the states-system, and the world economy in what Bauman (2002) suggestively calls the 'planetary frontierland'.

In this respect, global terrorism is simply another, albeit more directly violent, aspect of the intensifying global flows that are transforming the character of modern political life. Like 'private international violence', it is a reminder of the difficulties states confront in acquiring or maintaining a monopoly over the instruments of violence. The persistence of 'private international violence' in the form of terrorism also suggests that asymmetrical conflicts between different types of actors with vastly different capacities are an enduring feature of international relations. In these respects,

Booth and Dunne (2002: 13) are no doubt correct to say that September 11 is only the latest chapter in 'the historic rivalry between states and non-state actors'.

Bull was right to say that disorder always threatens international society. This is so for two reasons at least: first, because political orders are generally fragile things; second, because violence, both sanctioned and unsanctioned, seems an ineradicable aspect of political life. Not all violence, of course, leads to disorder. Bull (1977: 188) was aware of the way violence could be used to maintain or restore international order. Even terrorism can be used as a method of maintaining order, as the example of the French Terror showed. Indeed, there are interesting parallels between the French Terror and the United States' current 'war against terrorism' insofar as both are organized around a Manichean creed of good versus evil, the 'systematisation of the exceptional', the perception of dangerously omnipresent enemies, and the cultivation of fear and vengeance. By suspending the rules and institutions of international society and rejecting principles of dialogue to secure international order, the 'war against terrorism' looms as a significant threat to international society.

Neither individual states nor international society can control activities in the global 'frontierland'. Nor can international society make any guarantees about the security of individual states; susceptibility to violence, whether sanctioned or unsanctioned, cannot be eliminated. Like any political order, that established by international society will always be open to internal and external threats since politics allows for no foreclosure on the possibility that opponents of the prevailing order will resort to violence. But insofar as international society maintains and strengthens the rules and institutions that promote dialogue and consent, it will improve the chances that coexistence among different cultural, religious, and political societies can occur without resort to violence and terror.

Notes

1. James Der Derian's work stands out as an important exception in recent international relations theory. See his *Antidiplomacy* (1992).
2. The *Convention for the Suppression of Unlawful Seizure of Aircraft* (1970), the *Convention for the Suppression of Unlawful Acts against the Safety of Civil Aviation* (1971), the *Convention on the Prevention and Punishment of Crimes against Internationally Protected Persons, including Diplomatic Agents* (1973), the *European Convention on the Suppression of Terrorism* (1977), and *The Convention against the Taking of Hostages* (1979) all appeared during the decade.
3. Although R. J. Vincent (1986*b*) wrote an introduction and conclusion to an edited collection on terrorism.
4. Notwithstanding what Bull wrote in a letter to Shaie Selzer, editor at Macmillan, in November 1975. See Alderson and Hurrell (2000: 7).
5. It should be noted that different arms of the US government employ different definitions of terrorism. For example, a rather better definition than the State Department's was offered in the 1984 *US Army Operational Concept for Terrorism Counteraction*. It defined terrorism as 'the calculated use of violence or threat of violence to attain goals that are

political, religious, or ideological in nature ... through intimidation, coercion, or instilling fear' (quoted in Chomsky 2002: 128).

6. Terror, variously described by Burke (1987: 58 and 64) as the 'ruling principle' or 'common stock' of the sublime, is enhanced by the sublime power of darkness, vastness, infinity, and uncertainty, among other things.

7. For a very good account of the tension between the discourse of rights and liberty and the practice of extreme violence against people and property, see Colin Lucas (1994).

8. Townshend (2002: 68) uses this term.

9. Mössner tells us that after 1688, when Pasha Ismael, the Sultan's delegate, was sent home, the Barbary Powers considered themselves sovereign. Even before then, however, it was not uncommon for European rulers to treat with the Barbary powers.

10. For Grotius's justification of Dutch traders' violence against Portuguese and Spanish merchant traders, see his treatise on the law of the prize, *De Iure Pradae Commentarius*. See also the very useful accounts in Tuck (1999: ch. 3) and Keene (2002: ch. 2).

11. It is worth mentioning that the crusading mentality of President Bush also grows out of a Manichean worldview. As Euben (2002*b*: §5) says, Bush and Bin Laden's rhetoric are mirror images of each other. James Der Derian (2002*b*: §15) has rightly pointed to another identification between Bush and Bin Laden: they may be ideological foes, but they are epistemological friends.

12. George W. Bush, 'President Bush Delivers Graduation Speech at West Point', 1 June 2002, at www.whitehouse.gov/news/releases/2002/06/print/20020601-3.html.

14

Justice and Coercion

Terry Nardin

In discussing international relations we often speak loosely of policies, practices, or states of affairs as just or unjust. Sometimes this signals a legal judgement, sometimes a moral one, and sometimes merely a judgement that what is being judged is desirable or undesirable. It is not surprising that politicians, journalists, and citizens should use the word 'justice' loosely, but we expect scholars to do better. Yet, the academic literature on international justice is disappointingly eclectic. If the contents of some recent books can be taken as evidence, the scope of justice includes the use of armed force, human rights, the rights of indigenous peoples, humanitarian intervention, war crimes, the international criminal court, self-determination, isolationism, protectionism, immigration, toleration, economic inequality, international taxation, global warming, peacemaking, confederation, imperialism, political realism, and cultural relativism (C. Jones 1999; Robertson 1999; Shapiro and Brilmayer 1999; Coates 2000; Pogge 2001; Moellendorff 2002). As the author of a recent study of twentieth century views of international justice observes, 'in the latter half of the century, justice came to be defined in astonishingly broad terms' (D. Jones 2002: 234). If there is a common thread linking these themes in a coherent theory of justice, it is not evident.

For a coherent discussion of international justice we might look within particular traditions of inquiry. One such tradition is the 'international society' approach assessed in this book. International relations, according to this approach, consists of transactions and relationships between members of a society of states constituted and regulated by norms, and this implies judgements of conduct as just or unjust according to those norms. Starting with the publication of Hedley Bull's *The Anarchical Society*, writers on international society have paid attention to 'justice'. But neither Bull nor those who have taken up the themes of his landmark book are especially clear about what they mean by it. In part this is because Bull's key concept was not justice but order. He regarded order and justice as in tension with one another and was, moreover, inclined to give priority to order, not as the superior value but as the more objective concept. Order is patterned activity and it is patterns that are

This chapter was written during my tenure as a fellow of the Center for 21st Century Studies at the University of Wisconsin-Milwaukee.

the proper subject of historical and other kinds of systematic scholarship. Justice, in contrast, is an ideal and therefore nothing but an idea, a label for competing and ultimately arbitrary values and judgements (Bull 1977: 97). In retrospect this looks like a superficial judgement, but it has been an influential one. It did not lead Bull to think that nothing can be said about justice—on the contrary, he devotes a chapter to the theme of 'order versus justice' in which he rehearses the familiar distinctions between formal and substantive justice, reciprocal and distributive justice, justice for states versus justice for individuals, and so forth, before arriving at the standard realist view that order is the condition for realizing justice and other values. And he does not substantially alter this conclusion in the often-cited Hagey Lectures, delivered in 1983, in which he considers Third World justice claims against the West—claims which, given their revolutionary character, he doubts are easily reconcilable with the demands of order (Bull 2000: 227). Because 'order' is still his central concept, Bull is reluctant to theorize justice. Such reluctance remains characteristic of the international society approach (Jackson 2000; Foot, Gaddis, and Hurrell 2003: 11 and 29). Justice is contentious and therefore cannot be defined; the best we can do is to describe alternative perspectives on it. The incoherence of this scepticism becomes clear, however, if we ask, what is the 'it' that different people (or social classes, countries, civilizations, etc.) view differently? A coherent theory of international justice cannot evade the question of definition.

Another source of incoherence in discussions of justice within the international society approach, as well as in the wider literature, is the influence of globalization on how we think about international affairs. The justice debate has shifted from international relations to the world viewed as a unity—from 'international society', the society of states, to 'global society', a society whose members are human beings, not states. The publication of books with titles like 'cosmopolitan justice' and 'global justice' signals this shift. The international society approach treats the distinction between international and cosmopolitan justice, somewhat obscurely, under the labels 'pluralism' and 'solidarism'. For Bull, cosmopolitan justice is a myth because the global society—the universal solidarity—it postulates does not exist, and he simply dismisses the arguments of 'self-appointed spokesmen' of the global common good (Bull 1977: 85). International society is composed of a multiplicity of diverse states and is therefore pluralist. But here again one feels that there is more to be said—that the theorists of global justice, the 'solidarists', have at least this on their side, that the idea of a society of states implies a body of shared norms in virtue of which it is a society at all, and that this implies at least a 'thin' solidarity as the basis for its pluralism. Nor is it easy to refute the solidarist claim that the rights of states must be connected in some way to the rights of the persons who compose them and whose good would seem to be the moral point of having states at all. Bull implicitly acknowledges all this when he observes that growing interdependence, new common challenges, and the expression of a cosmopolitan moral consciousness in the idea of human rights must be seen as foreshadowing an emerging global common good. But in his late as well as early writings, Bull insists that the cosmopolitan society implied by such concerns exists only as an ideal (Bull 1966: 63; 2000: 221). If justice between states is unreal, global justice is doubly unreal. Other theorists of international society challenge this conclusion (Wheeler 1992; 2000: 33–51). A coherent account of justice in world affairs will have to clarify the relationship between international and global justice.

JUSTICE AS COERCIVELY ENFORCEABLE MORALITY

One way to define justice and thereby to delimit a coherent area of inquiry is to ask which moral principles are properly enforceable. Which of these principles justify coercion? Which are so important that they should be turned into enforceable *law*? The main argument of this chapter is that we gain coherence if we link the word 'justice' to prescriptions that can with moral justification be made legally authoritative and, if need be, coercively enforced, and that also justify coercion in the absence of law or even, in extreme cases, in violation of law.

The aim of political deliberation, as it is widely understood, is to determine which principles or rules should be laws—which rules should govern the conduct of members of a legally defined community, which rules a community can rightly insist that its members observe. 'Justice' is an important, perhaps the supremely important, concern in political deliberation, so defined. It identifies conditions that it would not be morally improper to make legally binding and to enforce. If the community in question is a society of states, a community whose legally recognized members are states, arguments about justice are about which moral rights and duties of states fall within the proper scope of international law. If the community is a global one governed, actually or ideally, by a comprehensive system of world law, concern with justice will be concern with the proper content of that law. No matter how the relevant community is defined, debates about justice are debates about which moral rights and duties may be coercively enforced by being incorporated into a relevant body of law.

My suggestion, then, is that the connecting thread in a coherent theory of justice in world affairs is the question of which moral rules are properly part of international or global law, or which might, as in the case of humanitarian intervention, justify coercion where laws and institutions are morally deficient or ineffective. The moral tradition that underlies the legal traditions of the modern world, including the tradition of international law, provides a clear, though contested, answer to this question. Coercion is justified to prevent some persons from using others coercively for their own ends. As one interpreter of this tradition puts it, coercion is justified when it is 'a hindrance to a hindrance of freedom' (Kant 1991: 134). One way to rescue discussions of international justice from imprecision, equivocation, and inconsequence, then, is to recover the narrower sense of justice represented by Kant's suggestion— also made around the same time by Fichte and itself the product of a tradition of natural law theorizing that goes back through Pufendorf and Hobbes to Grotius and beyond—that it entails the right or authority to use coercion. Principles of justice in this sense are principles that can be enforced by each person in a state of nature and that can become the coercive laws of a civil society without infringing anyone's legitimate freedom (Kant 1991: 134–5; Fichte 2000: 87–9).

'Justice', on this view, is not a synonym for 'morality'. Rather, it identifies one kind of moral concern among others. It is a concern with what people owe to one another as persons—not as citizens of this or that state or as members of this or that community, but simply as human beings. There are at least three elements in this definition we should notice.

First, it links justice with *universal* morality, not with the moral customs or laws of particular communities. The principles on which justice rests are those that are binding on everyone and can in principle be known by anyone. When philosophers like Kant say that these principles can be known by reason, they mean to assert that they cannot be derived from a merely empirical description of customs or laws. They rest on a deeper view of the kind of normative order appropriate to human beings. A long tradition has identified this normative order as the sphere of 'natural' or 'rational' or 'universal' or 'common' morality.

Second, the definition of justice as what people owe to one another implies that justice is *social*. It concerns my duties to others, not to myself.

Third, the definition identifies justice with *duty*. To be just to others is to give them 'their due'—that is, what is morally due to them and therefore what we have a moral duty to do (or avoid doing) to or for them. Justice is about actions that others have a right to expect from us, not merely those they would like us to perform, or that it would be good or desirable that we perform. The word 'justice', on this view, identifies those aspects of morality that are about duty and excludes those that are not: selflessness, self-respect, temperance, courage, friendship, generosity, charity, and other moral virtues or practices that are not usually thought of as involving duties. These virtues or practices are desirable and praiseworthy, perhaps, but they are not morally obligatory. Nor can they be properly enforced, as such, by law, though selfish or intemperate conduct may be legally constrained if it is harmful to others. Justice, then, is not about what is merely desirable or praiseworthy but what is morally required. It is about 'what morality compels us to do' (Swift 2001: 12) and, by implication, what we are at least sometimes rightly compelled to do (Kant 1991: 134).

Implicit in this view of justice as related to duty, then, is a link between justice and coercion. The word 'justice' marks out, inside the larger realm of morality, those things people can be compelled to do if they neglect or refuse to do them. But that link is somewhat loose because it is hard to specify precisely where the line between permissible and impermissible coercion should be drawn. That a conclusion is morally compelling, for example, does not mean that people should be forced to behave according to it. This question of the boundaries of permissible coercion is at the heart of debates about war, humanitarian intervention, and international redistribution. It is also central to political theory in general, for the state is a non-voluntary association in the sense that its laws are authoritative for those who fall within their jurisdiction and can be coercively enforced in cases of noncompliance. The idea of the state as an institution aimed at securing justice depends upon this link, however we understand it, between justice and coercion. A just state is one that succeeds in transforming morality into law and it is therefore of utmost importance that a state not enact laws that are contrary to morality. Nor, though this is more controversial, should it make and enforce laws that advance particular views of desirable public policy even when these views are not morally objectionable, for it is not the proper business of a government to force those it governs to cooperate in promoting ends that are not their own ends, unless respect for the moral rights of others demands such cooperation.

The understanding of morality that this view of justice presupposes is a limited one. The demands of morality, though universal, are nevertheless minimal. Morality is sharply distinguished from desirability. Many things are desirable or good, according to one or another view of human flourishing. But it is not the business of morality to further such views. Morality does not rest on a conception of what is good for human beings but on the premise that a human being is a thinking creature capable of forming and acting on its own ideas of what is desirable or good. There are of course theories of morality that dispute this, but those theories do not do a good job of accounting for the widely shared conviction that to be moral is to treat other people as thinking, choosing beings with lives of their own. This means that we should refrain from imposing our own conceptions of the good on them and, above all, abstain from treating them as things we can use for our own purposes while ignoring theirs.

The principles of this familiar morality were discerned by Socrates, Confucius, Jesus, and other sages and systematized by Aquinas, Kant, and other philosophers. Its precepts are embedded in Christian, Jewish, and Muslim ethics, entwined with and often distorted by particularistic religious ideas. But morality can be detached from these ideas. It is not itself religious even though religion has been one of its vehicles.

Morality, so understood, is universal—an understanding vividly expressed in the Stoic idea of the moral community of all human beings, the universal polis (*cosmopolis*, from which we get the word 'cosmopolitan'). Today the idea of universal morality finds expression in the idea of 'human rights', though the expression is often carelessly used to denote ideals that go beyond what is required to respect human beings as free persons. Because it prescribes duties that are binding on all human beings, this morality has been called a 'common morality' that transcends the mores of particular peoples. The label is fine provided one keeps in mind that 'common' here means universally applicable, not universally recognized—that anyone's conduct can be judged by this morality, not that everyone in fact grasps those precepts or acknowledges their validity. I believe that the principles of common morality are in fact widely recognized, but their moral authority does not stand or fall with this recognition. Slavery is unjust and *was* unjust even when many throughout the world did not see it that way.

This universal or common morality can be seen as a tradition but the force of its precepts derives from reasoned argument, not received authority. It is a critical morality that provides a standpoint from which to judge not only actions but local moral practices and institutions. And though many have claimed religious or scientific foundations for it, common morality can be given a thoroughly pragmatic or postmodern interpretation as a social construction resting on a single unprovable assumption: that human beings are free intelligences equally entitled to enjoy their inherent capacity to choose.

Let us take a closer look at this assumption. It can be analysed into the following elements.

The first element is agents—thinking, choosing beings who are 'intelligent' in the sense that they can use language to form concepts and make arguments. This does not mean that human beings always think or choose intelligently (rationally, reasonably), much less 'correctly', nor does it depend on drawing a sharp line between thinking and feeling, reason and emotion.

The second element is wants—conditions desired by or repugnant to human beings. Human beings are 'rational creatures'—animals with the capacity to reason but also with appetites, desires, dislikes, and the rest (though it understands people as rational creatures, common morality does not commit itself to the theory of 'rational choice', as that theory is understood by economists and political scientists).

The third element is actions—the choices people make to satisfy wants or to avoid or alter unwanted situations. These may be their own wants or those of others—friends, partners, compatriots, etc.—for whom they are acting.

The fourth element is equality—recognizing other human beings as 'persons', that is, as thinking, feeling, choosing agents like oneself.

The fifth element is respect—a non-instrumental attitude toward other persons, recognizing other human beings, individually or collectively, not merely as a 'means' to satisfy one's wants but as 'ends' in themselves. Like the ability to reason, this recognition is something people have to learn and which some acquire more successfully than others.

The sixth element is approval and disapproval of actions according to recognized standards—a way of distinguishing not between what is wanted and what is not wanted but between what is proper and improper according to such standards—between right and wrong in contrast to what is merely desirable or undesirable.

Taken together, these elements or presuppositions generate a moral system—the system of morality that, because it constitutes a common world of moral judgement and conduct, I am calling 'common morality'. What are the main properties of this system?

The first property of common morality is that, unlike the laws and customs of particular peoples, it is binding on all human beings. One way to put this is to say that all natural persons are members of a notional inclusive community of human beings and that common morality is the 'law' (even if unenforceable) of this community. Human beings are related not only in transactions and cooperative enterprises, but also as members of a human community constituted and governed by common standards of right and wrong. These standards apply both to actions and to the laws and customs of every particular, less-than-universal, community. A morally justifiable system of positive law is one that does not affront common morality.

The second property of common morality is that it rests on the human capacity for reasoned argument, not on custom, contract, or legislation (human or divine). Though it may seem outrageous in an age of cultural sensitivity, the claim that common morality is knowable means that everyone is capable of understanding it. Anyone can (in principle) grasp its basic ideas—agency, action, respect, rights—and the precepts they imply, even though there may be cultural obstacles to be overcome and mistakes are possible. We can correct our moral understanding by examining whether moral precepts are consistent with one another and with the premises on which they rest. Moral reasoning is interpretive, not deductive or computational. It requires judgement, leaves room for disagreement, and is compatible with a plurality of moral vernaculars and cultural understandings.

A third property of common morality is that its precepts are obligatory constraints on choice, not recommendations. They are 'rules of the game', not maxims of skill. Rules prescribe duties by distinguishing permissible from impermissible acts. These duties can be negative (like the duty to avoid harm) or positive (the duty of beneficence). Negative duties are usually expressed as prohibitions, such as the rule that forbids us to treat other human beings as objects (by killing or enslaving them to satisfy wants of our own, for example). Such prohibitions are always binding and for that reason have been labelled, *inter alia*, 'absolute', 'categorical', 'unconditional', 'exceptionless', and 'perfect'. Positive duties, in contrast, are for the most part indefinite, conditional, or 'imperfect'. Because wants are never entirely satisfied, there is always more to do. For this reason, there must be limits on beneficence.

Some of these limits are prudential. For example, for a beneficent act to be a duty, one must be able to perform it at reasonable cost. In the absence of contractual or other special obligations, there is no duty to help someone if doing so requires more than one can reasonably afford. This is an uncertain standard but not so uncertain as to bar all criticism—for example, of affluent states with miserly foreign aid budgets. Prudential limits on beneficence are needed to preserve the premise that human beings are persons with their own wants and projects. Without such limits we would always be at the call of others, without lives of our own. We would be little more than vehicles for satisfying the wants of others. This does not mean there are no duties of beneficence or that performing these duties is never compulsory. 'Bad Samaritan' laws illustrate the view that failing to assist others is, at least sometimes, a crime—that in some cases the moral duty to provide assistance is coercively enforceable and therefore a matter not of charity but of justice.

There are also moral limits on the manner in which we perform positive duties. We may do things we see as desirable for ourselves or for others, and we are sometimes required to do such things, but only if we can do them in morally permissible ways. To wrong others in pursuing good ends is to violate the fundamental principle of respect. In contrast to utilitarianism or political realism, which are consequentialist systems in which ends justify means, in common morality it is never permissible to pursue a good end by prohibited means.

A word on terminology is in order here: 'consequentialism' identifies the view that it is what happens as a consequence of an act, not an act's relationship to rules, that determines its rightness. Consequentialist systems are outcome-oriented or teleological. They construe goodness as a desirable condition of affairs and right conduct as success in producing that condition and therefore as a kind of expediency. Common morality, in contrast, is duty-oriented, at least to the extent that it requires us to respect certain moral constraints in our efforts to produce good outcomes: we may not seek to realize a good end by impermissible means. It does not bar us from considering consequences, but it is incompatible with the view that consequences are the criterion of moral right and wrong. This is an important distinction. Confusion arises because the word 'consequentialist' is used both for a kind of reasoning—reasoning about costs and benefits, which common morality permits within moral limits—and for a system of ethics, antithetical to common morality, according to which the costs and benefits of action are all that matter.

Because common morality is not outcome-driven, its defence does not require a theory of basic human goods like that articulated by Aristotle, adopted by Aquinas, and defended by recent Catholic thinkers belonging to the school sometimes labelled 'the new natural law' (Finnis 1980; Finnis, Boyle, and Grisez 1987: 275–84). Kantian moral theory begins with freedom and for this reason is criticized by moral philosophers who argue that a number of basic goods must be considered in acting and that freedom or autonomy is merely one of these goods. From the Kantian perspective, this is a mistake. Freedom is a postulate of morality, not its goal. Adopting a substantive theory of the good puts moral theory on the slippery slope towards consequentialism. The new natural lawyers are ardent anti-consequentialists, but their theory, by proposing knowledge, friendship, religion, and other 'basic values' as universal, obscures the distinction between 'good' and 'right'. In doing so, it moves towards judging conduct in terms of an intention to realize such goods as the outcome of action, even though its defenders insist that these goods are realized in how one acts and not as a consequence of one's actions. One way to make this point is to say that Catholic moral philosophy sees morality as a comprehensive guide to life based on a substantive or 'thick' theory of the good. Kant's theory of morality, which rests on the postulate of human freedom or agency, does not rest on a substantive theory of the good. Some philosophers say that common morality implies a 'thin' theory of the good, but that is misleading because, strictly speaking, it does not postulate any substantive goods. Agents, not theorists, determine what is desirable or good.

Justice, I have suggested, concerns those parts of common morality that it is not improper to enforce, for example, by incorporating them into positive law. Underlying this understanding of justice is the premise that our choices can bring us into conflict with one another. Because we often 'will' (that is, desire and seek to bring about) incompatible states of affairs, a society needs rules for reconciling our divergent wills. And what we call 'justice' is determined by such rules insofar as they respect the equal claims of every person to do what he or she chooses. If the principles of justice are those that impartially reconcile conflicting wills, the relationships it governs are those in which one person's actions infringe the rights—the morally justifiable liberties— of another. People often act in ways that make other people worse off. But they have acted unjustly only if what they do wrongly injures others by violating their rights. In such cases they can be coercively prevented from doing those things.

Justice includes standards of praise and blame as well as standards of right and wrong. We hold people responsible for their actions and think they can justly be punished if they deliberately or negligently harm others. Beyond that, the motives from which one acts, though morally important, are usually irrelevant to justice: motives are internal and private but justice concerns actions and their effects on other persons. Common morality has standards for judging motives and therefore for judging character and virtue. Mostly, however, these standards fall outside the scope of justice because they cannot or should not be enforced.

Justice, then, entails the right to use coercion. And the moral basis of this right should by now be clear. Human beings are thinking, choosing beings—'agents', in the jargon of philosophy—and if they are to exercise their agency they need to be protected against interference with that exercise. They have the right to defend themselves against force and fraud. They also have the right to live under laws that protect them from being used, against their will, to satisfy the wishes of other human beings. In civil societies the right to use coercion to defend one's rights or the rights of others is transformed into the authority of the state to defend individual ('natural' or 'human') rights. Coercion by the state, through the medium of enacted and effective law, is morally justified to protect those rights. Finally, where the state is tyrannical, where its laws are unjust, people may be justified in coercively defending themselves and others against violations of their rights. The casuistry required to work out the implications of these principles in particular situations is necessarily complex and contested. But, speaking philosophically rather than practically, this is the moral logic of 'justice' in human affairs.

COERCION AND INTERNATIONAL JUSTICE

The traditional view of justice in international relations is that it concerns justice between states. This view assumes that morality applies not only to natural persons but also to states. There are two things to notice here.

First, states can be morally legitimate. One way human beings exercise agency is by joining with others in institutions. These include marriages, contractual relationships, non-coercive ('voluntary') associations of all kinds, and states (understood as coercive or non-voluntary associations). Provided their rules and activities are not substantially unjust, institutions must be regarded as morally legitimate because they spring from individual choices to associate and to be associated. This important point is sometimes overlooked by those who assume not only that existing states are morally illegitimate but also that no state *could* be legitimate (except perhaps the global state of the cosmopolitan moralist's utopian imagination). States—coercive associations ruled by laws and having procedures for making, interpreting, and enforcing laws— enable human beings to coexist within a framework of common rules. That, at least, is their moral rationale. A state is morally legitimate only in so far as it serves this end. Because a state is a coercive association, its moral legitimacy depends on having laws that regulate the coexistence of those within its jurisdiction, thereby protecting their rights as free individuals. The laws of a morally legitimate state do not mobilize its citizens in the pursuit of a collective purpose but are concerned only to protect their moral rights. Citizens are morally obligated to respect the laws of a morally legitimate state—a legitimacy that depends on its laws not being substantially unjust.

A state of this kind has the moral right to exist and the authority to govern, and other states must respect its independence. No theory of international justice can ignore the rights of morally legitimate states—political sovereignty and territorial integrity (Walzer 1977: 61)—for these rights are grounded on the moral rights of persons. And no theory of international justice can ignore the implication of this moral fact, which is the existence of a world of states (Rawls 1999). A society of states is no less legitimate, morally speaking, than a cosmopolitan or world society.

Second, the view that morality applies to states assumes that states are artificial persons. How does this work? Institutions with procedures for making collective choices can be said to deliberate, decide, and act. Such institutions can be said to exercise agency, just as natural persons exercise agency. A committee, corporate board, or legislative body makes decisions and these decisions can be judged to be morally right or wrong. States, then, can be understood as artificial persons, at least for some purposes. And this means that the world community is a community of natural *and* artificial persons—a community of human beings with human rights and of states with sovereign rights.

It follows that a theory of international justice must take account of transactions and relationships involving a variety of natural and artificial persons

1. between states;
2. between states and international organizations—alliances, confederations, supranational regulatory or judicial institutions—that are themselves associations of states;
3. between the government of a state and that state's own citizens—relations constrained by human rights;
4. between the government of one state and the citizens of another, as in the case of immigration, asylum, refugees, and humanitarian action;
5. between private persons or associations across state boundaries, that is, in the arena of 'transnational relations'.

I cannot discuss what morality implies for all these relationships. But let me briefly discuss a few of them to illustrate the view I have been exploring: that international justice must be understood as involving coercively enforceable moral principles.

One (unsurprising) implication of this view is that common morality is at the core of just war theory. It also explains why just war theory is superior to both pacifism and political realism. Common morality forbids us to use other persons coercively to achieve our ends. Coercing others fails to respect their nature as agents—persons pursuing their own self-chosen purposes—unless its aim is to restrain those who are forcing their purposes on others. It follows that we can use force to defend our rights and to defend the rights of others. It is morally permissible to use force to thwart the violent. And we can apply these principles to states, understood as artificial persons with rights that can be violated and defended. Doing so generates the logic of *jus ad bellum* and humanitarian intervention. States must also respect moral constraints on the use of armed force, taking care, for example, to avoid gratuitous injury. Fleshing out the implications of these concerns for interstate relations gives us the *jus in bello* principles of proportionality, non-combatant immunity, and due care.

Common morality has similar implications for nuclear deterrence, terrorism and counter-terrorism, and the use of economic sanctions. It explains why such practices, insofar as they are directed at people who are not themselves engaged in unjust violence, are morally suspect. It explains the unease that both the author of *Just and Unjust Wars* and his readers feel when he defends deliberate attacks on non-combatants, like the Allied bombing raids on German cities between 1940 and 1943, as a necessary response to a supreme emergency (Walzer 1977: 255–63), for this is a clear case of pursuing good ends by impermissible means. There are arguments for such expedients but they are not arguments from common morality.

Another area in which common morality has implications for international affairs is that of moral responsibility. It distinguishes the rules guiding conduct from those that determine whether persons who act wrongly can be held responsible for their behaviour. Persons can be blamed and sometimes punished for wrongdoing. For example, an issue in judging war crimes is whether an act judged to be criminal is a voluntary act for which the agent is culpable. Can a soldier who commits a war crime in ignorance of the law or under duress be excused from blame? Common morality is rather stingy in granting such excuses. And it does not confuse an excuse with a justification. Furthermore, because it regards artificial persons as agents, common morality permits judgements of responsibility when one state commits aggression against another or injures its nationals. The principles governing such judgements are reflected, no doubt imperfectly, in the international law of state responsibility, which concerns issues of liability and compensation in the treatment of aliens, the expropriation of foreign property, and the regulation of transnational pollution.

The ethics of using armed force, controversial though it sometimes is, is relatively well understood. It has a clarity that is lacking in debates about international distributive justice. If the argument of this chapter is sound, much of the incoherence in these debates comes from their failure to link the ideas of justice and coercion. Justice gets confused with charity and with desirable social policy. In common morality, in contrast, justice *is* linked to coercion. Unjust conduct warrants a coercive response—not necessarily a response involving armed force but one that is designed to restrain the wrongdoer. Many of today's theories of global distributive justice, in contrast, reflect ethical ideals that go far beyond the minimal but still demanding prescriptions of common morality—certainly beyond prescriptions that can justifiably be enforced. For example, it is unlikely that common morality can be made to yield a principle of distributive justice like that once advocated by Peter Singer, who urged the citizens of developed countries to give away nearly all their assets to ameliorate famines. Nor does it support John Rawls's difference principle, which holds that material inequalities are morally permissible only if they advantage the least well off. This principle has been applied to global affairs by Charles Beitz (1979) and Thomas Pogge (1989), among others, though interestingly not by Rawls himself.

Moralists like Singer and Pogge appeal to our unease at the gross inequalities that exist between the richest and poorest inhabitants of the earth. But their efforts to draw a clear line between just and unjust inequalities are arbitrary and spuriously precise (Mapel 1989). We can condemn those who enjoy luxuries while others starve without appealing to an unqualified principle of material equality or a global difference principle.

Singer tries to undermine our intuitive sense that it is proper to give attention to those we regard as close to us by suggesting that such partiality can be indefensible, as in the case of racism (Singer 2002: 153–67). But it does not follow that because racism is immoral all partiality is immoral. What is wrong is racist partiality, not partiality itself. Institutional duties can modify natural duties, creating morally justifiable partialities. To the general ('natural') duties of morality we must add the special ('institutional') duties that spring from family ties, from morally legitimate promises, contracts, and property rights, and from civil society and positive law. Special duties do not override the general (common) morality. If I contract with you to murder someone, you are not morally bound to carry out the deed, for that contract is itself morally impermissible. But if special or institutional duties can be legitimate, it is a mistake to claim that my duties to people in general are the same as my duties to people with whom I am associated in morally legitimate relationships. Morality supports no such principle of unqualified impartiality.

Morality does, however, contain an indeterminate principle of beneficence on which we can ground redistributive duties. There are forceful statements of this principle in the common moral tradition, such as the passage from Aquinas, cited by Singer, that 'whatever a man has in superabundance is owed, by natural right, to the poor for their sustenance' (Singer 2002: 185). But this passage will not bear the construction Singer puts on it—that our natural duty to assist the global poor overrides our duties to those who are closer to us. The superabundance Aquinas refers to is what is left after we have made adequate provision for maintaining our lives, health, households, and professions, for paying our debts and educating our children, and so forth. I mention this not to assist you in rationalizing your luxuries but simply to suggest that impartiality cannot be reduced to a formula. The principle of beneficence, which takes account of institutional duties and special obligations, is radical enough, as anyone who reads the relevant writings of Aquinas—illuminatingly glossed by Finnis (1998: 188–96)—will soon discover. And people can with moral justification be coercively required to observe that principle when their assistance is urgently required in emergencies or by morally justified schemes of redistributive taxation.

But it seems clear that we do not have the same duty to assist people with whom we are not institutionally related as we do those with whom we do have an institutional relationship—our children, neighbours, colleagues, or fellow-citizens. The idea that we should 'care for' (Singer's term) those to whom we are specially connected more than we care for others is not equivalent to the view that 'whites should care more for, and give priority to, the interests of other whites' (Singer 2002: 163). Whites do not have *morally legitimate* special or institutional duties to other whites, as such.

To care for others is, above all, to respect them as persons. And the first thing this principle of respect requires is that we not interfere with their choices, which means that we cannot coerce them without just cause. Caring for others by *assisting* them is a very different matter. I have an absolute or 'perfect' duty to refrain from using violence against you. But my duty to assist you in pursuing your own ends is much more limited and it cannot be precisely specified. It is an 'imperfect' duty.

Singer, like other consequentialists, does not distinguish perfect from imperfect duties (as that distinction is understood by theorists of common morality). The ethical system he defends, utilitarianism, is based on happiness or preference satisfaction—not on respecting the rights of persons but on satisfying their wants, not on justice but on well-being. For utilitarians, morality, as a social practice, is an instrument for producing desirable states of affairs. And impartiality—bootlegged into utilitarianism from common morality as a mutilated version of the principle of respect—is reinterpreted as requiring that one person's interests should not count for more than another's. Even if we grant this doubtful premise, it does not follow that my own interests cannot be more important *to me* than the interests of other persons. There is no reason why I should give your interests equal weight with mine or with the interests of those to whom I owe special duties. But I must assist you if you are in a desperate situation and only I can help.

If people are starving, we have a duty—imperfect, to be sure, but still a duty—to assist them. This duty may not fall on us directly, but if (for example) our government taxes us to fund an international relief effort, thereby coercively interfering with our freedom to dispose of our wealth as we choose, such interference cannot in principle be said to be unjust. Some of our resources are owed, as a matter of justice and not merely as charity, to the relief of the poor, and what is justly owed can be coercively taken if it is not given voluntarily.

The argument that the rights of states rest ultimately on the same moral ground as the rights of individuals—an argument that is the premise of any sound theory of political and international morality—is nicely illustrated by the logic of humanitarian intervention. Though legal positivists and political realists sometimes disagree, moralists are inclined to argue that state sovereignty and international law (the UN Charter, for example) have no more than provisional authority. As one recent writer on humanitarian intervention puts it, 'states that massively violate human rights . . . forfeit their right to be treated as legitimate sovereigns, thereby morally entitling other states to use force to stop the oppression' (Wheeler 2000: 12–13). This judgement is supported by common morality. When large numbers of people are being murdered, deported, or enslaved, we should assist them if we can. We must not stand idly by the blood of our neighbours. We not only have a moral right to intervene forcibly to stop the massacre but a duty to do so if its victims cannot be protected in any other way and we are in a position to act effectively and at reasonable cost to ourselves. In other words, the non-intervention principle, which derives from the idea of state sovereignty and is part of the institutional structure of the states-system, here gives way before the natural duty of assistance to those who are victims of atrocity and whose situation is desperate (Nardin 2002).

Those who argue that international law should not recognize a right, much less a duty, of humanitarian intervention usually do so on prudential rather than moral grounds. They understand the moral considerations supporting humanitarian intervention, but they think it dangerous to give those considerations legal force. Legitimizing the use of armed force by states to protect human rights, they fear, will provide legal cover for aggression and further rend the already worn fabric of international order. Disagreements on this subject do not necessarily mean that there is a fundamental moral difference between 'pluralists' who defend sovereignty as the pillar of international 'order' and 'solidarists' who want to limit sovereignty in the name of universal 'justice'. That dichotomy caricatures a far more nuanced debate.

Some would strictly construe the UN Charter as limiting the lawful use of armed force by states to self-defence or to interventions specifically authorized by the Security Council, defending this reading on prudential as well as on legal grounds. Others think that international law has changed in the six decades since the Charter was adopted and that it now permits armed intervention in certain cases. There is, they argue, an evolving body of customary international law governing the use of armed force in humanitarian crises. That the international community has not protested or the Security Council not condemned certain interventions is presumptive evidence for new rules that would permit intervention in similar situations. There is, in short, an emerging consensus that coercive intervention to protect human rights is sometimes lawful. Some argue that this consensus should now be codified as a legal right of humanitarian intervention in certain carefully specified circumstances; others that codification is premature and that the consensus should be allowed to develop incrementally.

Those who want to preserve the non-intervention principle, even in human rights catastrophes, sometimes argue that the best solution is simply to violate the law in such cases. Just as Walzer defends violating the laws of war in supreme emergencies, they defend violating the non-intervention principle in situations of 'extreme necessity' (Franck 2003: 212) or 'supreme humanitarian emergency' (Wheeler 2000: 13). In such cases, the law may be violated (or, some prefer to say, 'overridden' or 'suspended') while the emergency lasts.

Adjectives like *extreme* necessity or *supreme* emergency signal that we are no longer in a normal, normatively constrained situation, one that is governed by clear rules about the use of force. We are now in an abnormal, normatively unconstrained situation in which our choices are discretionary, guided by prudential rather than by moral or legal considerations. We are in the realm of what Carl Schmitt calls the 'sovereign exception', a realm of decision beyond the laws governing decisions in normal situations (Agamben 1998; Scheuerman 1999).

How, given this distinction between normal and emergency situations, should we view humanitarian crises? Is humanitarian intervention a normal—a well-understood and regularized—exception to rules of non-aggression, non-intervention, and self-defence, an exception already included in or implied by those rules? Or is it a 'sovereign exception' that permits states to override the normal rules?

Walzer takes the first path, treating humanitarian intervention as one of several well-understood exceptions to the non-intervention principle, itself an expression of the basic rights of political sovereignty and territorial integrity that states are presumed to have. It is an exception that can be specified and incorporated into the rules governing relations between states. States have a right to govern themselves without interference, *provided* their governments do not grossly abuse the rights of those they govern. This judgement is founded on common morality. Humanitarian intervention is an exception to the non-intervention rule in the same way that killing in self-defence is an exception to the rule against killing—a revision of imprecise statements of the rule, one that should be understood as *part of* the rule itself when properly stated.

For Wheeler and Franck, in contrast, a humanitarian crisis creates an exceptional situation not governed by normal rules. Armed intervention (by states acting individually or collectively outside the authority of the United Nations) is not permitted by international law. It is always an emergency action. Franck thinks that international law should not be revised to permit it because doing so would open the door to abuse—to aggression masquerading as humanitarian intervention. The decision to intervene is best left to the discretion of states, subject to a retrospective judgement of its propriety by the international community, whose members constitute a 'jury' permanently convened to ascertain whether such actions are justified.

This is a reasonable position with respect to positive international law. But it does not make sense with respect to the morality of humanitarian intervention. We cannot say that necessity justifies setting aside moral constraints without bringing morality itself into question. There is, in other words, an important distinction between making exceptions to positive law and making exceptions to morality. In the past, one might have said that only God can authorize exceptions to morality, morality being 'his law'. In the Middle Ages moralists recognized a principle of reason of state according to which a sovereign might suspend positive law for the good of a community. But they did not think that a sovereign might suspend God's law, nor did they believe that a sovereign could override the natural or moral law. No sovereign can have such authority, for morality is a matter of reason, not will, and cannot be altered by human legislation. Machiavelli is shocking not because he suggests that positive law may be set aside for the sake of the public good, but because he suggests that a ruler might also disobey the moral law. The modern doctrine of reason of state, which reflects his view, therefore goes far beyond recognized medieval doctrine. The modern political realist is either a sceptic who simply evades the problem by denying the existence of moral rules to be overridden, or a consequentialist who admits that moral rules exist but insists that their authority is merely instrumental. If observing those rules endangers the community, they need not be observed.

The view of humanitarian intervention that common morality supports does not need such arguments. One state may violate the legal rights of another by intervening if the latter is grossly abusing the rights of others, not excluding its own subjects.

There is no need to invoke the concept of 'supreme humanitarian emergency' because in such cases intervention can be justified *within* common morality.

CONCLUSION

One can reach some of these conclusions by other routes. What, then, is the contribution of common morality to the debate on international justice? There are many answers to this question in this chapter and I will not recapitulate them. Instead, let me close by making the following more general points.

First, because it is a rational reconstruction, common morality has been purged of principles whose jurisdiction is merely local. A clear grasp of common moral principles can help distinguish which parts of a given communal ethic are binding universally and which bind only members of that community. It helps us to see that most ethical systems express a view of the good life that goes far beyond the demands of common morality. People may choose to live a Christian life, for example, but common morality does not require that they make that choice. We cannot assume, however, that common morality is compatible with all ways of life. Its principles permit us to condemn certain practices, no matter how ancient, treasured, or sacred they may be within a given community. It offers a framework within which other ways of life are constrained to proceed. To flesh out the complicated issues of civil and international life, one must look at the moral and legal practices of particular communities. These practices are constrained by common morality but they are not determined by it.

Second, because it is a moral system, common morality is more than an aggregate of unrelated principles. As a rational system of precepts and postulates, common morality is coherent and robust. This makes it a powerful tool for answering moral questions. Moral arguments are often confused because the grounds on which they rest are not made explicit or are mistakenly understood. Moralists often fail to distinguish moral arguments from people's preferences or prejudices. They confuse morality with religion, science, custom, or law. Or they reason in a haphazard 'all-things-considered' way to conclusions that reflect received opinion or the reasoner's private epistemology. Common morality can sustain a claim to universality that religious moralities cannot. And unlike its main secular rivals, utilitarianism and political realism, it does not offend the basic right of equal human freedom and the corollary duty of respect. For these and other reasons, it is an indispensable voice in discussions of international justice. This is not to say that politics consists merely in applying its principles. Politics is deliberative, not deductive or demonstrative. The more complicated and institutional the question, the more complex and uncertain are the interpretations and judgements required. Making moral judgements is straightforward, if ever, only in the simplest cases. In politics and international affairs, moral reasoning is always discursive and persuasive, never a matter of proof.

Third, common morality challenges the view that the principles of interpersonal and international morality are radically different. Such a view can be found in the realist argument that international relations is a realm of necessity to which moral principles do not apply, or that it is governed by a special ethic of 'prudence' or 'responsibility'. It can also be found in the argument that though international morality may be thin or minimal, the morality that governs relationships within a community rests on a thick theory of the good. From the standpoint of common morality, the claim that civil society is constituted by a shared teleology is an antiliberal misreading of the civil condition.

Fourth, a just state enforces only laws that are compatible with common morality. More comprehensive or demanding moral practices, religious or secular, may be enforced against persons who have voluntarily chosen to be members of the communities whose practices they are, but those persons must be free to leave such communities if they wish. Because a state is a coercive community, one whose members are not free to leave in the same way that a person might leave a church, commune, or other voluntary association, it cannot legitimately enforce moral prescriptions that go beyond those of common morality without infringing on the basic right of persons to pursue their own self-chosen purposes. The question of 'justice' is the question of which constraints—which laws—are morally justifiable. Debates about global justice, if they are to be about justice properly so-called, and not about other concerns, must confine themselves to the question of the actions that persons or governments can legitimately be compelled to perform, the prescriptions that can rightly be imposed as law. Though I have not argued it here, I believe a case can be made within common morality for taxation to support certain kinds of international aid, especially that aimed at averting humanitarian catastrophes and, beyond that, ensuring the conditions of agency for human beings everywhere.

Finally, the conception of justice considered in this chapter implies the continued relevance of international society. A sound solidarist or cosmopolitan theory of justice will base itself, implicitly if not explicitly, on common morality. But it will not deny the moral significance of civil society—society constituted and regulated by laws. And as long as there is more than one such society there will be an international, not a global, civil order. Cosmopolitan justice does not require a world without states. States remain important in an age of globalization because they are legal communities; transnational groups or 'networks' (Castells 2000) are not. The question of justice, then, is the question of which moral considerations are properly a matter of coercive law, within and between states. The central tension in international society is not between order and justice but between just and unjust coercive orders.

The current literature on international justice abounds with academic theories. But few of those contributing to this literature have undertaken to explore the implications of our common moral tradition for international affairs in an era of globalization. One of the tasks of political theory today is to understand, and perhaps recover, that tradition.

15

Normative Innovation and the Great Powers

Justin Morris

International society is a purposive entity through which its membership, under the helmsmanship of the great powers of the day, pursue collective goals and enshrine shared values. For some, contemporary unipolarity and the exercise of US omnipotence pose a greater threat to international society than did the bipolarity of the cold war which preceded it (Dunne 2003; Glennon 2003; Weiss 2003). The global distribution of power is indeed crucial in determining the shape and changing nature of international society, but while it may be more or less conducive to normative development, it cannot determine its content. The cold war period witnessed the globalization of international society and the entrenchment of the prohibition of the use of force. These were crucial developments, but thereafter normative innovation was prevented by the ideological discord and strategic exigencies of the day. In the post-cold war era the normative basis of international society has been radically amended as the Western powers, led by the United States, have sought to ensure that member states comply with a domestic model which reflects more closely their particular liberal democratic values and beliefs. Unipolarity has facilitated these advances, but the ability of the United States and its allies to remould international society nevertheless remains circumscribed by the extent to which they are able to elicit support for the normative changes they propose. Since no society can be sustained through coercion alone, and since great powers have a clear interest in perpetuating a society which reflects the values and goals which they promote, it follows that a prudent course of action will be to accept the limitations which this imposes. The ongoing conflict in Iraq, in both its build-up and prosecution, demonstrates the nature of the compromise demanded.

I would like to thank Nicholas Wheeler and Colin Tyler for advice and comments given on earlier drafts of this chapter.

THE NORM INNOVATION IN INTERNATIONAL SOCIETY

In his classic text, *The Anarchical Society*, Hedley Bull's focus of study is international order, by which he means not simply the absence of conflict which may result from a balance of power—the basic realist understanding of the term—but something more specific. For Bull the term 'order' denotes:

[N]ot *any* pattern or regularity in the relations of human individuals or groups, but rather a pattern that leads to a particular result, an arrangement of social life such that it promotes certain goals or values ... [and 'international order' a] pattern of activity that sustains the elementary or primary goals of the society of states, or international society. (Bull 1977: 4 and 8)

Rejecting the idea that a complete understanding of world politics can be gained from study focused exclusively on structure and power, Bull presents a complex picture in which the element of international society competes with a 'Hobbesian' element characterized by 'war and struggle for power among states' and a 'Kantian' element of 'transnational solidarity and conflict, cutting across the divisions among states'. In his repudiation of the argument, based upon the domestic state analogy, that international anarchy precludes society (because there is no central authority to enforce society's rules), Bull states:

The ... weakness of the argument from international anarchy is that it is based on false premises about the conditions of order among individuals and groups other than the state. It is not, of course, the case that fear of a supreme government is the only source of order within a modern state: no account of reasons why men are capable of orderly social coexistence within a modern state can be complete which does not give due weight to factors such as reciprocal interest, a sense of community or general will, and habit or inertia. (1977: 48)

Hence, to the extent that states can be said to form an international society at any given place and time, they do so because the majority of them identify with common values and conceive themselves to be bound by rules which facilitate the pursuit of shared objectives. International society does not, anymore than does domestic society, require unanimous acceptance of its underpinning values and goals, but it does necessitate a sufficiently broad consensus among its membership to ensure that its existence can be preserved against the acts of recalcitrant states. This enforcement role may be shared among the membership, but it is most likely to fall disproportionately to the great powers of the day, hence Bull's identification of these states as an institution of international society and the requirement that they be counted among its adherents (pp. 200–29). Coerced compliance must, however, be the exception rather than the rule, for the ultimate sustainability of international society is dependent upon the internalization of its constituent norms by its members.

Scholars such as Alexander Wendt and Ian Hurd provide useful insights into how states internalize norms through coercion, calculations of self-interest, and/or legitimization (Hurd 1999; Wendt 1999: 246–312). While analytically distinct, in practice these modes of compliance are unlikely to be either mutually exclusive, distinct, fixed over time, or, indeed, necessarily clear to the actor. Coercion involves an asymmetric power relationship in which one actor is, through the exercise of power, forced to comply with a rule. In this case neither the content of the norm in question nor the institution for which it stands are relevant to the state; it is merely the norm's status as a behavioural parameter and its enforcement through the application of external power which are of consequence. In contrast, self- rather than external restraint induces compliance where calculations of self-interest motivate compliance, though as with coercion, the content of the norm and its institutional role are irrelevant, since compliance is motivated solely by the advantageous outcome in which it results. It follows that were no such advantage to accrue, the norm would be disregarded. Consequential advantage is crucial to distinguishing between these two modes of compliance, for while both centre upon prudential calculations, in the case of coercion, the state acquiesces for fear of punishment but finds itself, by way of contradistinction, ultimately disadvantaged by doing so. Finally, where compliance results from the perception that a norm is legitimate, either in its content or by virtue of the institution which it serves, it is motivated neither by fear of punitive sanction by others nor by self-interest (as defined above) but rather by the belief that the norm is of intrinsic value and hence its observance and general standing form a constituent element of the state's interests and identity. At this level of internalization, interest is defined by way of reference to the norm itself rather than by consideration of the beneficial or detrimental consequences of compliance; interest and obligation are as one. In this case, while the state is 'interested' in the sense that it pursues goals, it does so within behavioural parameters which are internally driven and hence non-compliance is the exception to the rule (Henkin 1979: 9–88).

Preceding the issue of norm compliance is that of norm establishment. Within the context of international society at least two models present themselves. One model involves a process whereby agents seek to promote norms which incorporate behavioural precepts which they consider appropriate and derisible. Finnemore and Sikkink term such agents 'norm entrepreneurs', though the attendant connotations of risk and commercial gain makes this terminology somewhat problematic. 'Norm innovators' would appear more appropriate (and will be used hereafter) since it removes the implication of self-interest inherent in the common usage of the term entrepreneur, but these semantic concerns apart, their identification of this role and the process of norm 'emergence', 'cascade', and 'internalization' is useful in understanding international society and the manner in it has evolved over time (Finnemore and Sikkink 1998: 894–906). According to this model, norm emergence is a directed process in which norm innovators promote, perhaps in competition with others, and always within an existing normative context, a given norm or set of norms. Cascade involves a gradual process of socialisation until 'a critical mass of states . . . become norm leaders and adopt new norms, [at which point] the norm reaches a threshold or tipping point' (p. 901). Crucially, at this point the norm becomes 'the norm' in the sense that it is the common practice against which expectations are generated and actions judged. Ultimately the process reaches a point of internalization, whereby 'norms may become so widely accepted that they are internalized by actors and achieve a "taken-for-granted" quality that makes conformance with the norm almost automatic' (p. 904).

In contrast to this directed model of norm establishment, the second model suggests a more organic process whereby particular modes of behaviour become enshrined in social life by way of convention. Such conventions are not negotiated, but rather develop over time as practices which reflect a general sense of common interest. Through a mechanism akin to the economists' 'invisible hand' or the naturalists' natural selection, social practices arise through the development of reciprocal relationships which become increasingly dispersed and, with the passage of time, increasingly embedded. The inculcation of such practices elevates their status from that of instrumental behaviour to social norm, instilling it with value rather than simple utility. This account of how norms become established suggests a slower, less dynamic process of norm establishment in which the utilitarian roots of social practices become lost in the mists of time. Moreover, it depicts a society which, rather than being purposive, is acephalous in nature. This does not appear to be the vision of international society which Bull (or most subsequent English School scholars) had in mind, since international society's great powers are specifically vested with responsibility for its helmsmanship and preservation, but there is no inherent contradiction in accepting that *some* social practices develop in this manner. The scope for such developments is, however, limited. The eighteenth century Scottish philosopher David Hume famously used the analogy of two men rowing a boat to help explain how conventions could arise through a process of coordination in the absence of communication or promise. Hume's oarsmen may have managed, without discussion, to coordinate their strokes and established the most effective means of propelling their boat, but had they been part of a much larger crew aboard a Roman galley, then the hortator, exhorting the oarsmen to pull to the beat of his drum, would have proved an indispensable element in the ship's workings. This analogy provides one further insight into international society, for despite Hollywood's cinematic depiction of the galley's oarsmen as slaves motivated by the slave-master's lash, in fact the majority were highly skilled professionals who needed no such motivation. So it is that within international society the role and the limits of power are most evident, for though the great powers are predominant in defining its content and extent, the continuance and cohesion of its normative content ultimately dependent on internalization by others. This process may initially be dependent upon a relatively high degree of coercion, but over time requires that compliance comes increasingly to be motivated by considerations of self-interest and ultimately legitimacy.

To suggest that international society's development is, in significant part, directed by the great powers gives rise to a further fundamental question: what motivates the normative innovations they seek to introduce? The stock-in-trade answer to this question is that states are motivated to act by instrumental concerns, seeking to develop norm structures which best suit their own interests. This approach is problematic, first, because it is commonly based on the false premise that evidence of a vested interest disproves the existence of non-instrumental, normative behaviour—that, for example, the presence of oil negated concerns over the rule of law during the 1990–1 Gulf Conflict—and second, because it is based upon an assumptive methodology. To demonstrate that states seek to introduce (or indeed comply with) norms because they consider them, or the resultant order, legitimate is notoriously difficult, but it is no more a non-falsifiable proposition than is that of the realist who explains behaviour in terms of coercion and/or self-interest. Ian Hurd is correct when he states:

> It is unreasonable to use the difficulty of proving any one motivation to justify the retreat to the default position [i.e. Realism] that privileges another, without requiring similar proof. . . . We have no better reason to assume coercion [or self-interest] than to assume legitimacy. (1999: 392)

In regard to both norm innovation and compliance, it is at the very least plausible and consistent to argue that behaviour is motivated by a belief that benefit will accrue to the state *and* because the values embodied in the norm in question are of intrinsic value. In the case of norm innovation, states, and most particularly the great powers, will be motivated to reproduce at the international level the values enshrined in their domestic political cultures. Insofar as these values are themselves held by a sufficiently broad base of domestic society to be valuable and true, their reproduction beyond the state so as to enrich the lives of others is best understood as a normative (though still 'interested') rather than *self*-interested act.

A more subtle formulation of the instrumental versus non-instrumental debate is found in E. H. Carr's critique of the normative developments of the inter-war period in which he argued not that states use the language of principles and legitimacy as a cloak for the policies of *realpolitik*, but rather that such rationalizations are '*unconscious* reflexions of national policy based on a *particular* interpretation of national interest at a *particular* time' (Carr 1946: 87, emphasis added). Yet even this formulation fails to capture the nature of the dynamic involved in norm innovation, exaggerating the room for manoeuvre available to states by suggesting that the backdrop for such actions is a blank canvass. In practice, as Finnemore and Sikkink note, 'new norms never enter a normative vacuum but instead emerge in a highly contested normative space where they must compete with other norms and perceptions of interest' (1998: 897).

Success in this contest requires not only the advocacy of a norm acceptable to others, but also the generation of perceptions of fidelity. In this regard normative inconsistency is a liability, particularly in the case of states associated with the existing normative structure. The greater the extent to which states are seen to be attempting to instigate changes to a norm structure so as to accommodate their short-term policy objective, the greater the degree to which others are likely to perceive their actions as instrumentally driven. Attempts to justify actions taken contrary to the prevailing norm structure by reference to alternative codes of conduct will serve to undermine both the existing structure and the ability to build new ones in the future. Hence, while norm structures are sufficiently flexible to accommodate change, their malleability is finite. Attempts to introduce radical change, or repeated change over a short period of time, are likely to incur greater opposition. In seeking to amend the normative content of international society states must advocate and seek support for their proposal, but in so doing, they will encounter opposition from those who wish to see alternative modifications and/or those who support the status quo. All parties to the contest will be motivated by a complex combination of instrumental and non-instrumental factors and the actions of all will have material implications which may, in extremis, include military conflict. It follows that the great powers are the most likely to prevail in this endeavour, but their material strength and the distribution of power within which they operate only makes normative innovations more or less possible; it does not account for the content of the change sought. It follows that, in a world of increasing unipolarity, international society has recommenced its normative march.

THE NORMATIVE DEVELOPMENT OF INTERNATIONAL SOCIETY

It has been suggested above that international society is a purposive entity which embodies prevailing values and through which states act in association to achieve shared goals. These values and goals, adapted over time, determine the criteria applied to membership of the society of states, the relationship between the collective and individual members and intermember relations, and are reflected in the normative structures relating to recognition, collective intervention, and the uni- or multilateral use of force. In its earliest phases Christianity provided the somewhat vague criteria for membership and 'Just War' theory an even looser 'regulatory' framework for intervention and conflict (Bull 1977: 24–38; Meyer and McCoubrey 1998). The culmination of the Thirty Years War and the ensuing secularism, positivism, democratic constitutionalism, and industrialization which through the eighteenth and nineteenth centuries came increasingly to influence European affairs, marked a shift in the underlying foundations of international society and its perception of exceptionalism. Of these developments Bull notes that

As the sense grew of the specifically European character of the society of states, so also did the sense of its cultural differentiation from what lay outside: the sense that European powers, in their dealings with one another were bound by a code of conduct that did not apply to them in their dealings with other and lesser societies. (1977: 33–4)

It was the challenge to this homogenous notion of European exceptionalism, coupled with changing material circumstances, which brought about the twentieth century's evolution in international society. The Third Reich may have posed the most direct threat to international society, as well as to Europe's sense of moral worth and certainty, but it was the alternative value structure and sense of identity ushered in by the Russian Revolution which would prove to have the most profound implications for much of latter half of the century, effectively reducing international society to a mere modus vivendi. This loss of normative unity was coupled with a major shift in the world's material centre of gravity. The demise of European imperialism and the rise of alternative centres of power such as the United States and post-Meiji Japan undermined Europe's leadership and the values for which it stood. Russia's defeat at the hands of Japan in 1902 shattered the impression of European superiority and invincibility, while the growing industrial and eventually military strength of the United States slowly transformed its claim to exceptionalism and challenge to European ideals (embodied in its sense of 'Manifest Destiny', the Monroe Doctrine, and the Roosevelt Corollary) into an increasingly global reality. The decline of Europe's great imperial powers, hastened by the destruction of the First and Second World Wars, was accompanied by the inevitable loosening of their grip on the reins of international society, but though their claims to great power status came in material terms to be succeeded and far surpassed by the United States and Soviet Union, the ideological (as opposed to merely material) confrontation between the cold war superpowers prevented their assuming its leadership.

That the post-1945 world was one of great power rivalry did not differentiate it from that which went before, for to varying degrees such competition is an integral part of international life. Such competition had, however, previously taken place between states striving for pre-eminence *within* international society, rather than between champions of wholly divergent visions *of* international society. There was, for example, a continued recognition throughout Europe's intrareligious wars of the fifteenth century of the distinction between the Christian and non-Christian worlds and similarly, the constitutional tensions of post-Napoleonic Europe never questioned its exceptionalism. Where states, such as Napoleonic France and Nazi Germany, sought domination rather than mere leadership, they were opposed by the collective ranks of international society and defeated. Hence pluralism has been an ever-present element of international society, but it has existed within a sphere of mutual recognition and shared identity, as evidenced by the Treaty of Westphalia and more specifically between the great powers in the presence of the Holy Alliance within the Congress/Concert of Europe. The normative discord of the cold war reduced this to such an extent that international society became little more than an agreement to differ and pluralism, in the guise of self-determination, became its *raison d'être*. The morality of international society thus came to be premised on the assumption that states would fulfil their domestic obligations towards their citizens— through the provision of security and welfare—and the provisos that they abide by the norms of non-aggression and non-intervention in their external behaviour (Jackson 1990: 265–7). Through a normative framework conducive to this arrangement the benefits of self-determination, proclaimed as *the* intrinsic good of cold war international society, could accrue to all, but in the absence of any agreement regarding the domestic responsibilities of states, intrastate behaviour was deemed *ultra vires* and the avoidance of interstate conflict assumed paramount importance.

The United Nations system was the most obvious embodiment of this normative framework. The Charter's Article 2(3)/(4) provisions constituted a more restrictive application of the non-use of force rule than any before, limiting the right of all states to use force to cases of individual or collective self-defence in response to an armed attack. Moreover, this rule, in conjunction with the Article 2(7) prohibition of collective intervention through the auspices of the United Nations in the domestic affairs of member states, established a framework within which states could not, whether uni- or multilaterally, UN-authorized or otherwise, act to impose on others their particular view of the 'good life'. The exception to this came in the Chapter VII enforcement mechanism, which empowered the UN's Security Council to take action necessary to maintain or restore international peace or security, irrespective of whether the threat posed was intra- or interstate in origin. Though the Security Council's obligation to act in the face of such a threat was absolute, its discretion in determining such a circumstance in practice provided unfettered room to manoeuvre. The veto power granted to the five permanent members of the Council (China, France, UK, US, and Soviet Union) gave these states both an accentuated say in this process of determination and a constitutional safeguard against being the target of UN policing. In sum, therefore, the Charter provided a potential mechanism through which recalcitrant members of international society could be coerced into abiding by its rules, though this did not extend to the permanent Council members and could not operate amidst the superpower disagreement which characterized cold war politics.

The UN Charter not only laid down new rules for existing members of international society; in its *travaux préparatoires* and through specific provisions such as those contained in Chapters XI and XII, lay the seeds of a process of decolonization which would see it expand to a global level. Reflecting a lack of great power consensus beyond the fact that the territorially defined state should be the basic political unit through which people should be able to determine their own futures, the UN's *Declaration on Independence for Colonial Counties and Peoples* (UN General Assembly Resolution 1514(XV), 14 December 1960) declared that 'inadequacy of political, economic, social or educational preparedness should never serve as a pretext for delaying independence'. Independence, and with it membership of international society, was now an unconditional right of territorially defined 'peoples', the status so conferred being dependent neither upon a newly independent state's ability to meet internal obligations to its citizens through the provision of security and welfare, nor upon an ability to defend itself from external threats. The theoretical conception of the state which demanded the performance of such tasks had, to greater or lesser degree, always been something of a fiction, but decolonization constituted the ultimate repudiation of such criteria as prerequisites for membership of international society (Jackson 1998). The events of succeeding decades suggest that the lack of internal and external competence demonstrated by the vast majority of states to emerge from this process was a significant causal factor in the conflict which blighted the developing world, but preferable approaches are not readily evident and but for the chosen course, decolonization would have been a far more protracted process, if it had taken place at all.

So, in an era of normative discord between the great powers, the UN system, in its establishment and subsequent (mis-)application, was a compromise which, to varying degrees, served the normative *and* instrumental goals of the great majority of international society's members. Neither the passage of time nor cynicism should cloud the fact that few of those involved in initiating a system aimed at reducing recourse to force in international relations can have remained unmoved by the carnage of the two World Wars. The destructive potential of modern weaponry, never more clearly demonstrated than by the nuclear strikes on Hiroshima and Nagasaki, could only serve to stress further the unacceptability of war as a normal means of international intercourse. Coincidental with this view of war, limiting the use of force served far more instrumental purposes. For the United States, the rapidly emerging military and economic superpower, a more peaceful and orderly world held the potential for global rebuilding and with it trade. This process was likely, at least in the long term, to be economically beneficial as well as conducive to securing allies for what was, by this time, the almost inevitable confrontation with the Soviet Union. Soviet interests were also well served by a curtailment of the use of force. No victorious power (and arguably no state at all) had suffered more in terms of material or lives than the Soviet Union and as such it was, at the end of the Second World War, in no position to challenge the United States militarily. Efforts had at this time to be directed towards rebuilding and consolidating Soviet influence in Eastern Europe. As such, a system founded on the principles of non-use of force, inviolability of borders, and territorial integrity was a significant boon. A desire to maintain extraterritorial possessions also provided the United Kingdom, and to a lesser extent France, with vested interests in the new UN system. At the time unaware of how the decolonization process would play out, as a normative support for their significantly diminished material power it appeared to harbour within it significant potential as a means by which empire could be maintained.

A similarly complex combination of normative and instrumental factors can be identified in considering the motives of the key architects of decolonization. From the outset the matter of non-self-governing territories had been one of considerable contention between the sponsoring powers, not least in terms of whether there should be a predetermined end point in the management of such territories—namely, independence—and whether preparedness for such an outcome should be measured against specified empirical criteria. The final Charter provisions were the inevitable product of compromise, but as the 'wind of change'—as British Prime Minister Harold Macmillan was later to famously term it—blew stronger and more rapidly than any had envisaged, their actual content proved less important than the basic notion which they enshrined (Goodrich and Hambro 1946: 226–56; White 1999; Springhall 2001). For once the United States and Soviet Union were united in their advocacy of decolonization, though they diverged markedly in terms of ideological underpinning and ulterior motives. The former was built by people driven to seek greater freedom than that offered by the states of Europe and as such the idea that others should have the right to determine their own futures was a central tenet of its guiding political culture. Soviet political culture was no less imbued with anti-imperialist sentiment, though under Stalin's leadership one may justifiably question the true motivation behind the Soviet Union's support for self-determination. That both had much to gain the process is also clear; a spate of newly independent states was likely to provide rich pickings for each as they sought new clients to further their cause in the global contest with the other, while the dismantling of the

European empires would inevitably prove a significant nail in the coffin of potential great power competitors, most notably Britain.

Even this most cursory discussion of the origins of these key elements of the UN system demonstrates the interplay between the instrumental and non-instrumental factors that motivated its founders. During the decades to come, cold war imperatives would see in its application greater emphasis being placed on the former at the expense of the latter, though in a rapidly expanding world of sovereign states, each nursing often conflicting political ambitions, the degree of order maintained is remarkable. This is not to suggest that either the UN system was the cause of order or that conflict was absent from interstate affairs. Even the UN's most ardent supporters must concede that, at least in the most strategically sensitive areas of the world, cold war bipolarity, with its attendant danger of escalation and ultimately mutually assured destruction, provided the strongest constraints on superpower activity. And within recognized spheres of influence both the United States and the Soviet Union demonstrated a willingness, where necessary, to resort to force in their dealings with client states so as to ensure order and subservience, employing normative rhetoric as a meagre disguise for the imperatives of *realpolitik*. Beyond such regions the cold war more often than not fed, rather than reduced conflict, as either side supported client states in an attempt to prevent the other gaining ascendancy in the global competition. Africa in particular provided an arena of intra- and interstate conflict, fuelled by the cold war dynamic. The incidence of conflict notwithstanding, the UN system had a profound impact on Africa and other former colonized areas of the world, a key factor in their transformation to regions of territorially defined, sovereign states. Though conflict raged, it was for state control rather than territorial conquest. The sovereign state was confirmed as the unassailable political unit through which people were to exercise their right of self-determination, and though the superpowers sought and gained political influence, assisting many domestic political elites in their corruption of the system to their own narrow ends, delivery from colonial subjugation, at least potentially, offered a better future. Though decades would pass before even the most rudimentary realization of this potential, with the lives of many deteriorating rather than improving, this remained a significant step in the evolution of international society.

Elsewhere, for many states recourse to force was rejected not only because of cold war considerations but because their interests were better served by maintaining peaceful relations which facilitated and promoted trade and broader commercial concerns. For the Euro-Atlantic community and others who practised or sought to develop market economics, war was a counterproductive, highly destabilizing, and hence detrimental condition. In similar vein the cold war protagonists' acceptance of the notion that material superiority should not be employed for the purpose of territorial expansion was motivated in significant part by the fact that territorial possession in the form of overseas empire was likely to be far less beneficial than fostering in the new members of international society a particular economic, social, and/or political culture. Empire was not just an outmoded idea, it offered a far less efficient way of extending global influence and control. For the United States in particular, economic and social neoimperialism, global 'coca-colonization', was to prove the key to success, allowing it to emerge as the most powerful state on earth while simultaneously extending to others the capitalist and (to a lesser extent) liberal democratic practices at the core of its own political beliefs and identity. It is, perhaps, somewhat ironic, that in a world obsessed by military relations it was the benefits, potential, and allure of this system, rather than military victory, which ultimately did most to end the cold war and bring down the Soviet Union. This point notwithstanding, it was the cold war and for many the requirements of international market economics which did most to suppress interstate conflict in the decades following the United Nations' establishment. The UN system was not without impact however, for, irrespective of actual motives, it provided a fundamental normative reference point for political debate throughout the cold war. As memories of global conflict faded, the cold war provided an umbrella under which the UN system and the values enshrined therein laid down its roots in international politics. As international relations entered a new phase it was deemed less acceptable than ever before to use force to resolve international differences other than in the manner prescribed by the UN system itself.

INTERNATIONAL SOCIETY AFTER THE COLD WAR

The end of the cold war brought with it a palpable relaxation in global political and military tensions, a radically altered global distribution of power, and, as liberal democracy began to emerge as the benchmark against which other value systems were to be judged, it heralded a seismic shift in the global normative landscape. If not quite the 'end of history' professed by some (Fukuyama 1992), liberal democracy provided the unifying ideology among those states, led by the United States, which assumed an unassailable position of leadership within international society. 'The West' now stood without material equal and though it could not claim to act *qua* international society, as a norm innovator of unparalleled influence its values would profoundly shape its future. Paradoxically, the end of superpower confrontation also released many (often well armed) state and substate actors from the material and political constraints which had for forty years militated against war and hence ushered in a more disorderly world than that which had gone before. Much of this conflict was intrastate in nature, with the parties to it paying scant regard to established rules of war. Women, children, and other non-combatants were often targeted with a level of brutality deliberately intended to maximize suffering and instil fear. That such atrocities were often the resort of recognized governments acting in a desperate attempt to maintain their power in the absence of superpower patronage only exacerbated matters. An ever-present element of the media diet, these violations of human and political rights struck at the heart of liberal democratic ideals. In the absence of the cold war constraints which had reasonably justified inaction, Western governments found themselves under immense domestic pressure to 'do something' in the face of such suffering, with their failure to do so only giving succour to those who questioned the sincerity with which their purported liberal ideals were held. Yet, even in the post-cold war era action would not be cost free. In a world of norm-ative flux it would engender international friction; it would result in loss of life for which governments would have to account domestically and internationally; and it would generate fiscal costs at a time when electorates demanded 'peace dividends'. The resultant tensions raised difficult questions for Western governments as they sought to mould international society to reflect their own values. Irrespective of the prevailing power imbalance, too coercive an approach would risk destroying, rather than reshaping, the very object of their efforts, while too tentative an approach risked a closing of the window of opportunity provided by the end of the cold war and the successful prosecution of the 1990–1 Gulf Conflict.

Newly independent states, primarily those which emerged from the break-up of the Soviet Union and the implosion of Yugoslavia, were accepted into international society on the basis that they accepted the new values enshrined in the liberal demo-cratic model. Such conditionality was a clear break with cold war practice, but since recognition was a long-established discretionary right of states, this was seen as a relatively benign change in practice which could not, in any case, be contested and which was essential to the substantiation of the latest evolution of the society of states. The effective retrospective application of new rules to existing members was, however, more contentious. Where existing members committed acts or omissions— relatively commonplace during the cold war—which resulted in extreme human suffering, these would now attract international censure which on occasion would instigate redress through military intervention. Where sufficient international sup-port could be garnered, the Western powers sought to act through the auspices of the United Nations, to realize their normative ambitions, though given the costs and complexities involved action was inevitably selective. Sometimes it met with limited success (e.g. Somalia, Yugoslavia). Sometimes it was belated (e.g. Rwanda, Yugoslavia). Where it occurred without UN authority it pushed the bonds of inter-national society to breaking point (e.g. Kosovo). But none of these factors controvert the normative basis of the actions taken. Most significantly, while debates regard-ing ulterior motives, volitionality, and the appropriateness and efficacy of different response strategies continue, what had been established by the end of the twentieth century was that no state could claim carte blanche in the manner it treated its people. Irrespective of differing social, religious, and political cultures, very few were willing to argue that policies leading to mass slaughter, mutilation, and displacement were acceptable. Pluralism, the rationale of a cold war world in which the most powerful members of international society could do little more than agree to disagree, was no longer to be interpreted as a free licence in domestic affairs. Such issues were now the legitimate concern of international society (Wheeler 2000; Chesterman 2001).

The move to a situation in which the protection afforded by sovereignty and the principle of non-intervention was, at least potentially, conditional upon maintain-ing certain minimum standards of human rights constituted a major change in the nature of international society. It was a development which had been facilitated by a coincidence of factors: a pattern of global power distribution conducive to change; the proliferation of democratic governments more receptive to change of the type proposed; and active advocacy of a new normative structure by states in a position of overwhelming power. As dictatorships around the world began to crumble in the absence of superpower support, this normative amendment came increasingly to be accepted as a tenet of international society, but however widespread its acceptance, some remained opposed to both its content and the manner in which had been brought about. Even explicit UN authorization did not put the new post-cold war practice beyond reproach, for though the discretion vested in the Security Council provided a sound legal basis for consideration of and intervention in human rights matters, broader issues of legitimacy were raised by those who perceived a hijacking of the organization for more instrumental purposes. Such concerns were not totally without foundation. In the absence of alternative sponsors, the West was able to generate high levels of international compliance through offers or denial of economic and/or diplomatic patronage. This it used to pursue policies which were beneficial in assuaging domestic concerns and replicating beyond its borders particular values and practices, at times paying little heed to cultural differences. Even in this new era accusations of cultural insensitivity rang normative alarm-bells around international society, offending, according to those making such claims, against both the idea of a world of sovereign states and the liberal beliefs of those responsible for the change in international practice. Nevertheless, given the nature of the contested values and practices in question, such charges proved an inadequate foil to rising humanitarian sentiment, in part because those critical of the new interventionary agenda often appeared to have an even weaker claim to normative probity, but also because it was premised on a corruption of both sovereignty and liberalism, historically only sustainable in the case of the former because of the exigencies of the cold war and not at all in the case of the latter (Parekh 1999; Kymlicka 2001).

In practice, the objections of some of the potentially most obstructive opponents of the new Western international agenda, such as Russia, China, and India, were tempered by their desire to attract investment and to participate more fully in a global economic system dominated by the West. The level of compliance which this ensured, coupled with the impossibility of employing coercive measures against states of such power, resulted in an uneasy normative truce, with active engagement being identified as the most appropriate means of developing greater acceptance of international society's new values. Deprived of other poles to which to gravitate, the majority of international society embraced or acquiesced to the Western project, but some, such as Iran, North Korea, and most notably Iraq, remained steadfast in their opposition and thus reaffirmed in their pariah status. Non-democratic and unwilling to abide by basic human rights, these states were said by US President Bush in his 2002 State of the Union Address to constitute an 'axis of evil', accused of sponsoring terrorism and seeking to develop and proliferate weapons of mass destruction (WMD). This was not a universally shared characterization, but to the significant extent that it did constitute the basis of consensus, this did not extend to the question of how international society should respond to such behaviour. Limited military intervention in the face of gross human suffering may by now be due careful consideration, but to use force in pursuit of more expansive objectives was for many a step too far. Led by the

United States, those seeking to promote the Westernization of international society and a more proactive approach to ensure it, countered that to limit intervention only to the alleviation of gross human suffering offered no more than a short-term palliative; what was required was the removal of the source of such problems. For most, however, 'regime change' constituted an unacceptable crossing of the normative Rubicon.

This was the dilemma faced by the Bush administration, stung into action by the terrorist attacks of 11 September 2001. In its initial response to the strikes the United States succeeded in building an extensive coalition—extending beyond its usual Western allies to include Russia, China, and major regional actors such as India and Pakistan—to help in the 'war on terror'. Sympathy with the United States and a fear of the threat posed by the global terror network Al-Qaeda to the state system provide a partial explanation for this support, but more instrumental concerns regarding a desire not to alienate the United States in its moment of need and the free licence it provided to indulge more punitive tendencies in dealing with domestic dissidents also played a part. Whatever the combination of factors that provided the impetus for states to support the United States initially, the issue of Iraq was to shatter the consensus within international society, and even within its leading Western clique. Though there was extensive agreement, as evidenced by the Security Council's unanimous support for Resolution 1441, that Iraq was failing to meet its international obligations regarding WMD, the appropriate means by which to respond to this remained a matter of discord. Opposed by France, Russia, and China (all veto bearing members of the Council) among many others, the United States was unable to secure explicit Security Council authorization for military action and unlike NATO action in Kosovo, it could not here plausibly argue that authorization was being blocked by vetoes cast in the face of broader international backing, nor that force was to be employed in support of broadly accepted international norms.

Opposition to action in Iraq was motivated by a complex combination of factors. Most obviously there was suspicion that, despite its protestations to the contrary, the United States was motivated primarily by concerns over oil, geostrategic calculations, and the desire to finish business left undone. The lack of evidence to support the claim that Iraq was seeking to develop WMD and the desire of the UN inspectors charged with determining the matter to be given more time to fulfil their task were further factors. Having failed to exhaust all pacific means to resolve the crisis, many viewed proposed US military action as that of a vengeful post-9/11, unrestrained, extreme administration unconcerned about the loss of lives of non-nationals, the United Nations, or the rule of law. Case-specific, legal, and evidential concerns were exacerbated by doubts over whether a secular Ba'athist regime such as Saddam Hussein's, assuming it had WMDs, would wish to proliferate them to a fundamentalist Islamic organization such as Al-Qaeda and whether, therefore, military action would prove a counterproductive strategy in terms of the wider 'war on terror'. These are matters of considerable import, but it is the longer-term normative implications of action in Iraq which are likely to have the most far reaching ramifications. Radicalized by the events of 9/11 and bolstered by the international support it was able to muster, the United States acted in the absence of UN or widespread international sanction. The Bush administration sought to justify its actions in terms of the right of individual and collective self-defence, but in keeping with its 2002 *National Security Strategy*, claimed not a right of *pre-emptive* strike—arguably an inherent right of states within the UN system in accordance with Judge Webster's famous dictum that there existed 'necessity of self-defence, instant, overwhelming, leaving no choice of means, and no moment for deliberation . . .'—but more radically a right of *preventive* action, allowing action to be taken even where the exact nature of the threat is yet to materialize. In so doing it argued not that its actions conformed to the prevailing normative framework, but rather that this normative framework required amendment so as to reflect the political, material, and technological realities of the twenty-first century (Wheeler 2004). The United States sought to act not as outlaw, but as norm innovator.

The danger inherent in such an approach is clear. In attempting to bring about a further evolutionary step in the development of international society, allowing for the removal of regimes which steadfastly refuse to accept its rules and which pose a threat to others, it threatened to undermine the very thing on behalf of which it sought to act. In seeking to redefine the right of self-defence, an inherent right of states necessarily exercizable without prior UN sanction which is already subject to abuse, the United States raised the spectre of a further endangering of international peace and security. Moreover, that in both the *National Security Strategy* and subsequent rhetoric there was much to suggest that the United States viewed the right of preventive action as being exclusively available to itself and its allies ill served its purpose, since it reinforced the view that acknowledging such a right would constitute for the self-appointed chosen few the granting of a free licence to use force outside of UN auspices. Even US allies such as the United Kingdom, Australia, and Spain balked at advocating such normative developments, instead justifying their actions as being in accordance with and support of previous UN resolutions. The questions remain however; should international society adopt a more interventionary agenda to ensure compliance with standards of good governance beneficial to all, and if so, how is this to be operationalized without jeopardizing its very existence?

CONCLUSION

To see the Bush administration as a norm innovator rather than an outlaw is to appreciate the true implications of the recent conflict in Iraq. At least in the hands of its so-called neoconservative elements, its desire to bring about normative change is driven by an idealist view of the relationship between citizen, state, and international society rather than by *realpolitik*. Contrary to stereotypical depictions of left and right, realist and idealist, its policies combine Wilsonian aspirations regarding democracy and self-determination with what is, for many, an inherently contradictory willingness to coerce unilaterally those who oppose it. The current global distribution of power is most conducive to this project, but it is facilitative rather than determinative of recent developments. Material accounts of international relations cannot explain current

US foreign policy objectives, nor international relations more generally, because they are essentially normative. For this reason, current US foreign policy and responses to it can only be understood within the broader context of the evolution of international society.

As stressed throughout this chapter, international society is a purposive entity, the normative content of which is, to a significant degree, determined by the great powers of the day. During its Christian and later European phases its shared objectives were underpinned and strengthened by the prevailing perception of exceptionalism. In these contexts the normative innovations brought about by the great powers were essentially introverted in nature, in that they impacted upon the behaviour of the great powers themselves as well as a limited number of lesser powers with which they shared their defining identifying criteria. Hence, though norm innovation was a 'top-down' process, the amenability of the less powerful members of international society subject to it was enhanced by this shared sense of identity. Neither a sense of exceptionalism nor shared identity could survive the globalization of international society which resulted from decolonization. The consequent loss of normative direction was intensified by the divisions of the cold war and for the next four decades non-use of force and the protection of unlimited pluralism would become the rationale of the society of states. The end of the cold war, with the attendant collapse of bipolarity, reintroduced the prospect of normative development. Seizing on this, the Western powers drove forward an agenda which would, within a relatively short period of time, see dominant attitudes to sovereignty and the use of force change such that the former was no longer a shield behind which states could grossly violate the human rights of their citizens without the potential threat of collective intervention.

Beyond this, however, sovereignty remained intact. Provided states observed their international obligation not to use force and did not offend against the most basic of human rights, their internal affairs, at least with regard to the prospect of collective military intervention, remained sacrosanct. This was the normative balance which US-led action in Iraq disturbed. Long after issues specific to the conflict have been resolved, its longer-term legacy (besides that relating to the not unconnected matter of the 'war on terror') will lie in its implications for the relationship between individual members and international society as a whole, the legitimate role of the great power(s) and the use of force. Unipolarity has allowed international society to address questions disbarred by the imperatives of the cold war. The dominance of liberal democracy inclines it to do so. Should regimes that remain steadfastly unresponsive to the wishes and needs of their people be tolerated? And to what extent is the answer to this question conditional upon the intent and ability of such regimes to threaten others? The imposition of such a condition would constitute a less radical departure from the current normative position, adding an interstate proviso to an intrastate concern, and thereby maintaining the privileging of the state over the individual. The linking of these issues is not without merit, since regimes dismissive of their domestic obligations are likely to be similarly disposed internationally, but it is an ultimately unsatisfactory compromise, for as Bull noted in his Hagey Lecture, 'what is ultimately important has to be reckoned in terms of the rights and interests of the individual persons of whom humanity is made up, not the rights and interests of the states into which these persons are now divided' (1984*a*: 13).

Nevertheless, the linking of inter- and intrastate obligations provides a strategically sound transit-point in the competition to shape the normative content of international society, more palatable to those secure in the status quo. The United States rationalized its goal of regime change in Iraq by reference to self-defence because, even in a radically redefined form, such an explanation is, by virtue of its interstate basis, less threatening to a society of sovereign states. The terminal point of this process must, however, be the recognition that the privileges inherent in state sovereignty are qualified by considerations of good government per se.

Having identified this normative position, the question of how it is to be cascaded throughout international society remains. What was viewed as most malign in recent US action was the willingness to act in the absence of UN sanction or broad international support, for this illustrated a view of the relationship between the hyperpower and the other members of international society which was unacceptable to the vast majority of the latter. Unipolarity made such an approach feasible, but it was counterproductive and despite the allusions to self-defence, undermined rather than advanced international society. Power is a crucial factor in bringing about normative change, but it must be seen to be employed on behalf of, rather than at the expense of, international society. With regard to issues as fundamental as those at hand, cascading is likely, even in conditions of unipolarity, to be a prolonged process in which the likelihood of achieving legitimization is increased by refraining from provocative action. The United States and those who support its normative venture must, therefore, embrace the multilateral platform offered by the United Nations and in so doing accept its inherent limitations. A normative code which allows international society to act collectively against states which eschew accepted principles of good government remains an aspiration which, while unipolarity prevails, the Western powers should pursue, but in so doing they must accept that coercive enforcement is a means of last resort, the inappropriate use of which is likely to weaken rather than strengthen their cause.

Conclusion: Whither International Society?

Alex J. Bellamy

At the outset of this book, I outlined three alternative visions of the future of the English School approach to world politics. There were those who described it as an underexploited resource that international relations scholars ought to make greater use of. At the other end of the spectrum, some scholars called for the School's closure or even denied that such an approach existed, arguing that it is too indistinct to make it a worthwhile category. Somewhere between these two poles, many realist and constructivist writers argued that the approach offered valuable insights about world politics but that its central ideas needed further refinement. It seems clear from the previous fifteen chapters, many of them written by scholars who do not identify themselves with the English School, that the case for closure or for arguing that the School does not exist is a weak one. Even those who criticize the approach's preoccupation with order, lack of explanatory theory, or inability to accommodate the many planes of political interaction that characterize contemporary world politics, acknowledge that, nevertheless, there is a degree of value and insight to be gleaned from it. In particular, English School writers thought about international relations as a set of social practices some time before such ideas became common within the discipline of international relations.[1] What is more, from the outset the approach insisted upon the importance of normative analysis—assessing the possibility for collective action, shared purposive goals, and acknowledging the problem that in world politics actors face competing moral claims.[2] All these issues remain at the heart of the theory and practice of contemporary international relations.

Undoubtedly the central question that has preoccupied English School theorists and their critics in the past, and will continue to do so in the future, is 'what is international society like?' To date, the English School has addressed this question via two principal means. The first is the debate between pluralists and solidarists discussed in the introduction and referred to in many of the chapters. Some writers ask whether international society is moving from a pluralist one characterized by

I am grateful to Marianne Hanson, Paul Williams, and especially Sara Davies for their helpful comments on earlier drafts of this chapter.

the predominance of sovereignty and the principles of territorial integrity and non-interference to a more solidarist one. Nicholas Wheeler, for instance, identified a subtle shift in that direction in the emerging norm of humanitarian intervention (Wheeler 2000), though others argued that any shift was limited to particular parts of the world (Western Europe, see Bellamy and Kroslak 2001) while others still denied that there had been a shift (Chesterman 2001). Importantly, there was also debate about whether international society *should* develop greater solidarist tendencies. Solidarists argue that such development is vital if international society is to fulfil its ethical promise and enhance human security. Pluralists, however, continue to share Hedley Bull's scepticism and to argue that, given a lack of global consensus about human rights and competing claims about redistributive justice, any move towards a more solidarist world order risks destabilizing international order. Echoing E. H. Carr and Hedley Bull, pluralists argue that undermining the rules of coexistence that underpin international society and permit diverse societies to live side-by-side to promote what can only ever be a particularist conception of the good is ethically as well as pragmatically undesirable (see Jackson 2000). Within this frame of reference, there is little agreement about either what contemporary international society is, or what it ought to be. Within its present terms of reference, the pluralism–solidarism debate seems to have reached something of an impasse though it does help to illuminate many of the important issues of the day (see Bellamy 2003*b*).

An alternative way of thinking about the nature of contemporary international society is the three traditions idea pioneered by Martin Wight. Each tradition tells us something different about world politics, and taken together help illuminate the degree of ongoing debate in international society and the choices that confront state leaders. The realist tradition emphasizes the state's primary responsibility to its citizens, questions the existence of 'cross-cultural moral truth', and is sceptical about humanitarian justifications for intervention. The rationalist tradition draws attention to the rules and norms that govern international society. It suggests that state leaders ought to abide by those rules, as failure to do so could undermine the fabric of international society. Finally, there is the revolutionist tradition. This tradition emphasizes a global responsibility to protect people in peril wherever they may live. It shows that there is common agreement about a basic floor of humane governance and insists that state practice indicates an emerging consensus on the idea that sovereignty should be suspended when that floor is transgressed (Vincent 1986*a, b*). It feeds a powerful discourse emanating from the media, non-governmental agencies, and politicians demanding that 'something be done' about suffering in the world (Bellamy 2003*a*). According to the three traditions perspective, international society is caught in a struggle between three different moral and political codes, each of which exert powerful influences upon state leaders.

As Robert Jackson (1995) pointed out, each tradition could be thought of as a layer of responsibility confronting state leaders. Realism refers to a leader's primary responsibility for the welfare of citizens. In contractarian terms, a state can be under-stood as having a contract to secure its own citizens. Rationalism refers to a state's responsibility to abide by international law, and its constitutive rules in particular. If we take seriously the claim that modern states and contemporary international society are mutually constituted then there is a very strong imperative for states to abide by the core principles of law. We should not underestimate the importance of Bull's insight that states have a vested interest in the maintenance of international society and hence in the preservation of its constitutive rules. Finally, Jackson takes revolutionism in its benign form to refer to the idea that states, particularly liberal states, feel a sense of moral responsibility for the welfare of individuals across borders. From this perspective, then, international society is a site of perpetual contestation between three levels of responsibility that confront state leaders.

Although both of these perspectives contribute to our understanding of world politics and illuminate important questions, such as the relationship between domestic, international, and global responsibilities and the moral value of order, many of the contributors to this volume have aired disquiet about these pictures of international society. To put it bluntly, too much is left out of our conception of international society for it to make sense of much other than certain questions about state-to-state relations. Indeed, there is little surprise that the issue that has prompted most debate about the nature of contemporary international society has been the question of the legitimacy of humanitarian intervention. This 'fits' neatly into the English School view of the world for two principal reasons: the main protagonists in this debate are states and the debate is one of order versus justice, or more accurately sovereign rights versus human rights.[3] Once we move away from issue areas that fulfil these two criteria, English School conceptions of international society—from both ends of the spectrum—begin to look less convincing. Matthew Paterson demonstrated that patterns of global environmental governance, which are often non-state based and multilayered, expose the ontological narrowness of international society traditionally conceived. To put it more simply, international society as currently conceived has very little to say about the political and social patterns that Paterson identifies, let alone helping us to explain or understand such patterns. Many other chapters highlighted similar problems (in addition to Paterson, see Chapters 6, 7, 8, and 10 by Buzan, Williams, True, and Bleiker, respectively). To remain relevant, therefore, our understanding of international society needs to develop in at least four ways: first, the relationship between international society and world society requires further elaboration; second, there is a need for further reflection about the structures that underpin international society; third, the pluralism–solidarism debate needs rethinking; finally, if not a theory of causation, we certainly need a better understanding of the drivers and dynamics of change in international society than we have presently. I will briefly examine these suggestions in more detail.

FOUR CHALLENGES

International Society and World Society

Several chapters in this volume (notably those by Little and Reus-Smit, Chapters 2 and 4, respectively) focused on the relationship between the international society of states and world societies composed of individuals and groups who directly identify and cooperate with individuals and groups in other places. Other chapters (notably those by Williams, True, and Paterson, Chapters 7, 8, and 9, respectively) complained that international society, conceived as a society of states, is too narrow to accommodate the needs of human emancipation, the fact of gendered identity, or the governance of the global environment. There can be no doubt that today there is little utility in thinking about world politics in terms of a society of states alone. This raises the important question of whether the English School is attempting to construct a grand theory of everything in world politics or whether it is merely trying to explain one aspect of it (state-to-state relations). In many ways, the English School's founding fathers avoided this problem by insisting that international society was only one of three elements that comprised world politics, with the revolutionist or Kantian strand incorporating civil societies and non-state actors.

There remain, however, three important problems with this perspective. First, the majority of non-state actors in world politics are neither revolutionists nor Kantians. Many of them are transnational business organizations that support and strengthen the underlying economic structures of international order. Second, contemporary 'international' and 'world' societies are not easily separable domains. Are global environmental or trade summits that comprise state and non-state agencies features of the 'international' or the 'world society'? Third, maintaining the division means that international society will continue to be seen as constituted on one plane, that of state-to-state relations. As many of the contributors to this volume have suggested, we need a multilayered account of international society to make sense of contemporary world politics.

While it certainly seems appropriate to conceptualize international society and world society as different realms when we are studying periods prior to the global expansion of international society, the capitalist economic system, and the international legal system, and world society remains a useful vehicle for interrogating the global and transnational processes that create change in world politics, the distinction is becoming less useful today. When thinking about contemporary international society, it is perhaps much better to follow Barry Buzan in asking whether it is necessary and justified to exclude particular actors from our worldview. It seems to me that there is no reason why regional organizations, business groups, non-state organizations, civil society movements, human rights activists, and others could not (and should not) be incorporated *within* our conception of international society rather than as an adjunct. Or, alternatively, why our understanding of state-to-state relations embedded with the idea of international society could not be incorporated within a new concept of world society. This would mean conceiving international society as constituted on vertical as well as horizontal planes and as a much more complex collection of actors, institutions, and rules than we have hitherto acknowledged. It would also mean developing a more diffuse theory of power that developed constructivist ideas about the relationship between its material and ideational forms. Such a move would mark a significant step away from Bull's conception of international society, but just as his theory was a product of his time so must ours be. It may be time, therefore, to eschew the international society–world society divide in favour of a conception of either international society or world society that incorporates different types of actors operating at different levels. At very least, there is a need for a careful and expansive articulation of the relationship between the two domains. As Buzan demonstrated when he attempted to incorporate the economic sector, our understanding of international society is enriched not discredited by such revisions.

The central danger with such an approach is that by broadening the scope of study, the concepts lose their analytical usefulness. However, as many of the chapters in this volume have pointed out, the concept of international society that we use today does not, by itself, provide a useful vehicle for exploring state-to-state relations in a variety of policy domains. We do not have to argue that the English School should provide a 'theory of everything' in order to call for revisions to the concept of international society. However, in order fully to comprehend the values, interests, and influences on state policy in the international sphere—and to maintain international society's usefulness as a way of understanding the behaviour of states—there is a need to reformulate the concept of international society and rethink its relationship with world society.

The Structures of International Society

International society is characterized at root by its anarchical structure. Many English School theorists would concur with Alexander Wendt's (1992) injunction that while anarchy may be a 'fact', the logic that flows from it is indeterminate. Indeed, many early international society theorists saw their primary role as trying to elucidate the manner in which the logics of anarchy changed over time. Thus, for instance, in a brief study of the balance of power, Martin Wight demonstrated that through history, the balance had taken nine, quite different, forms (Wight 1966c).

One of the central questions posed by many of the chapters in this volume is whether the fact of anarchy and the interstate institutions and norms designed to deal with that fact do constitute the basic structures of international society. The suggestion here is that they do not, and that there are other underlying structures and forces that the international society approach needs to incorporate into its account of world politics. In particular, it needs to take account of the role of capitalist modes of production and the forces of neoliberal economics. Today, most states have a capitalist economic system. International interaction has grown exponentially in the past few decades largely as a result of the spread of market economies and the growth of international trade. If we were to include global economic norms of behaviour into our account of international society, our picture of the world would look much more solidarist. As Barry Buzan pointed out, if we include the economic sector in our understanding of international society it becomes apparent that there is a much higher level of agreement and cooperation between states and societies and much more in the way of shared values and interests than has generally been recognized by English School writers. Moreover, what we consider to be the constitutive norms of international society begin to change somewhat. When we add the panoply of global economic governance that has sprung up in the twentieth century to our worldview, the central importance of sovereignty, territorial integrity, and the principle of non-interference become much less central. Increasingly, states and economic institutions interfere on a regular basis with the domestic economies of other states. Moreover, ideas such as the importance of free trade and the privatization of state industries and forces such as the flow of investment capital come to compete with more established ideas. When we acknowledge the presence of these forces in world politics, the pluralism–solidarism debate and the dispute about the appropriate balance of order and justice in international society become less central. That is not to say they should be dismissed, however. On the contrary, there are important debates to be had about the value of economic justice and the potential peace that a world of capitalist democracies may bring.

However, we need to do more than simply add a new collection of issues and actors to our understanding of international society if we are to meet the challenge fully. There is also a need to understand that the fact of capitalism is every bit as important as the fact of anarchy when it comes to constituting particular types of international society. We do not have to be Marxists to understand that the mode of production and exchange can have important consequences for the creation, per-petuation, and—sometimes—demise of international societies. The emergence of the Westphalian system in Europe was as much (if not more) a product of the cent-ralization of bureaucratic power to meet the needs of industrialization as it was a product of the peace treaties that brought a century of war in Europe to a (tem-porary) end. As Paterson and Williams implied, we need to understand economics not just as a sector of world politics in need of examination (though it is important that we do this too) but to understand that a particular form of economics—cap-italist and neoliberal—provides an underlying ideational structure for international society.

There are, of course, many structures that underpin international society that have yet to be fully acknowledged and explored. In particular, the cultural and gendered structures that shape world politics were brought to the fore alongside capitalism in this volume. As O'Hagan pointed out, Hedley Bull's idea that the culture of international society is a neutral diplomatic culture needs to be prob-lematized. It is important to understand that the types of actors considered legitimate in international society, the appropriate modes of behaviour, and even the com-monly used methods for interaction were shaped by particular cultural predilections. As Martin Wight (1966b) recognized, international societies are more stable and enduring when they are predicated on a common culture. We need to ask, there-fore, whether the culture that underpins contemporary international society is a genuinely shared one or whether it merely reflects the cultural preferences of the powerful.

The answer to this question, as O'Hagan points out, is not a simple one. On the one hand, it is clear that important aspects of international society's founda-tions are indeed Western in origin and were often transmitted globally via coercive rather than consensual means. For example, as Roland Paris argued, contemporary peacebuilding missions are not manifestations of non-political, non-ideological, non-cultural international managerialism. Instead

> One way of thinking about the actions of peacebuilders is to conceive of liberal market democracy as an internationally-sanctioned model of 'legitimate' domestic governance. Peacebuilders promote this model in the domestic affairs of war-shattered states as the prevailing 'standard of civilization' that states must accept in order to gain full rights and recognition in the international community. (Paris 2002: 650)

On the other hand, however, it would be a major simplification to suggest that today's international society is simply the European system writ large. Through the processes of colonization and decolonization, non-Western ideas and interests were incorporated into the structures of international society to some degree. Sometimes, these ideas used the language of European international society. For instance, we noted earlier that Southeast Asian states created a regional international society predicated on the rigid application of pluralist ideas. On closer inspection, however, the 'ASEAN way' is a combination of positive law drawn from European international society and the distinctly Southeast Asian ideas of *musyawarah* (consultation) and *muafakat* (consensus) which reputedly emerged from Javanese village traditions (Acharya 2001: 68). Similarly, the idea that 'liberalism', 'democracy', 'self-determined statehood', and 'sovereign' independence are Western impositions overlooks the extent to which such ideas existed and were fought for in the colonial world.

It is therefore important to recognize the existence of the cultural structures that underpin international society and to interrogate them. We need to understand what those structures are and how they frame interaction between different cultural groups; and whether and how they prioritize certain forms of knowledge and particular experiences of the world over others. Indeed, it is well worth echoing O'Hagan and pointing out that if international society is to be a 'meeting place' for different cultures, it is important to ensure that the means of communication allow for difference. To date, English School writers have tended to assume that these problems are overcome by a shared diplomatic culture. In light of O'Hagan's chapter, however, it is fair to say that international society has not, as yet, resolved this problem.

A third type of structure that underpins international society are structures of gendered identity. To date, as Jacqui True pointed out, English School theorists have been utterly silent on the issue of gender. However, as an important part of national identity, gender has played—and continues to play—a number of important roles. First, different ideas about gendered identity shape states' perceptions of each other and hence frame important aspects of international behaviour. True recounts many instances of Western and non-Western states arguing about the appropriate role of women in society. Domestic gender structures therefore play an important role in shaping how states relate to one another. Second, acknowledging the fact that most International Relations theory excludes women, asking 'where are the women?' (Enloe 1989) promises to offer a radically different picture of international society, contributing more to our understanding of the relationship between international society and world society and perhaps adding weight to the idea that the distinction between the two is becoming less meaningful. Finally, taking gender seriously requires a rethinking of the boundary between the public and the private, the international and the domestic. To date, English School scholarship has tended to focus on the public/international realm and has said little about the contribution of the private/domestic realm. This tendency, True rightly emphasizes, is in need of reversal.

One of the central claims of this volume, therefore, is that our theories of international society need to acknowledge the variety of social, economic, and cultural structures than underpin world politics. In particular, although actors make the world we live in, it is important to recognize that the international spaces in which they operate are not void of ideological and cultural norms and rules. To paraphrase Karl Marx, people make history but not in the circumstances of their own choosing. If it is to remain at the fore of debates about international relations, our conception of international society needs to recognize that there is more underpinning world politics than the fact of anarchy and the shared need to fulfil certain goals of social life.

The Pluralism–Solidarism Debate

It is the question of what type of international society we live in that is at the heart of debates within the English School. The idea that we need to rethink the relationship between international society and world society and acknowledge the socio-economic structures that also underpin international society has important consequences for the pluralism–solidarism debate. As I noted earlier, several writers have already suggested that the debate has reached an impasse. Indeed, in recent years the debate has focused almost exclusively on the question of humanitarian intervention (Wheeler 2000; Bellamy 2003*b*). Nevertheless, the debate does remain an important vehicle for evaluating the many competing claims and ideas within international society. If it is to progress, however, the debate needs to be recast to allow it to say useful things about the many other important international issues that shape our world today. At the outset, it is important to reiterate Buzan's insight that incorporating the economic sector alone dramatically shifts the balance of the debate. To date, solidarists have found it virtually impossible to demonstrate anything other than the faintest recognition that sovereign rights may be trumped in cases of supreme humanitarian emergency. We are asked, for example, to take cold comfort from the fact that during the 1994 genocide in Rwanda no state argued that intervening to halt the genocide was forbidden by the sovereignty principle. Once we add in the economic sector, however, the task for pluralists becomes much harder. Within the World Trade Organization, for example, sovereignty arguments play a small role when compared to neoliberal economic arguments, particularly for the least powerful members of international society.

Of course, the trumping of sovereignty by the shared values of neoliberal economics would have done very little to rescue imperilled Rwandans. The significant point here is that there is not one type of solidarism but many. In recent English School debates about humanitarian intervention and human rights, solidarism has been taken, almost exclusively, to mean shared agreement about liberal human rights. However, Bull himself did not always describe solidarism a solely consisting of agreement about human rights and justice. In its simplest form, a solidarist society is any society that takes on agency to pursue its collective goals. This involves two moves that imply the 'thickening' of a society's relations. First, the society needs to move beyond the identification of practical rules designed to manage relations between its constituent units, towards agreement about the identification and pursuit of collective goods. That is, the substantive goals (beyond coexistence) that the society as a whole agrees are goods worth pursuing. Second, the society needs to develop forms of collective agency able to accomplish those purposive goals (the terminology is Terry Nardin's, 1983). These goals need not relate to human rights, and need not be ethically or intuitively appealing. The key feature that distinguishes a solidarist from a pluralist society is its purposive content: a solidarist society has purposive content while a pluralist society is a purely practical association.

Once we acknowledge the idea that there are different types of solidarism, we are confronted with two further questions. First, how do different types of solidarism emerge and how do they come to unite diverse societies in pursuit of a common purpose? Second, what different types of solidarism can we identify, how do they relate to one another, and how do they influence international society? In relation to the first question, Andrew Hurrell has already begun to conceptualize different types of solidarism based upon their different processes of emergence. As I noted earlier, Hurrell identified 'consensual' and 'coercive' forms of solidarism (Hurrell 1998: 31). According to Hurrell, the difference emerges because: 'there may well be conflict over the political processes and institutional procedures by which those [solidarist] values are to be promoted' so that 'moves towards coercive solidarism have been, and are likely to remain, an important source of tension' (Hurrell 1998: 31). The first type is made up of shared values that all members agree to because they are cognisant with their moral and political codes. Thus, for instance, although the 1949 Geneva Conventions governing conduct in war was very much a product of Western jurisprudence, many of its central components were elements of a more commonly held form of morality.[4] For example, the idea of non-combatant immunity that is central to the Conventions has antecedents in most of the world's major ethical codes (see Lepard 2002). The second type of solidarism is made up of those common ideas and values that are more directly imposed on others, sometimes by the use of force and economic measures. Thus, for instance, the British Empire in the early twentieth century may be conceived as a form of solidarist community predicated on common values and ideas. Those values and ideas, which revolved around the so-called 'standard of civilisation', were created in London and enforced by the Empire's agents.

The idea of consensual and coercive forms of solidarism is an important one that provides a very useful starting point for a reconsideration of the pluralism–solidarism debate. However, it is worth noting that in all but the most extreme of cases it is difficult, if not impossible, to draw a line between 'consensus' and 'coercion'. In the absence of Habermasian-style dialogic encounters, it is impossible to know where consensus is the product of truly shared belief and where it is the product of the exercise of power. After all, as Reus-Smit demonstrated in his chapter, the power of ideas may be just as important in shaping action as material power. In most cases, therefore, trying to understand where particular types of solidarism come from involves a subtle blend of consensus and coercion, ideas, and material power. In future, English School theorists will need to think much more carefully about how different types of solidarism emerge. To do that effectively, they will need to employ their pluralistic methods: for example, historical sociology may help us understand the emergence of the material forces that give certain ideas material weight; and constructivism has much to offer in helping to explain where ideas come from and why certain ideas become norms in particular epochs (see Crawford 2002).

The second task that springs from the idea that there is not one but many types of solidarism involves identifying and charting the different types. At the outset, we need to recognize that not all types are morally appealing. As Richard Falk pointed out in his chapter, today there are many different visions of globalization competing for prominence. Falk argued that the George W. Bush administration has its own vision of a form of global solidarism—a world community bound together by liberal democracy and neoliberal economics. On finding that the world is not actually like this and that many of Bush's dearest held principles are actually contested, the administration may attempt to create such a world through economic, political, and social means, and even the use of force where it deems it necessary. This presents the danger that in trying to recreate international society in its own image, the United States may undermine that society's constitutive rules. Interestingly, in the post-September 11 world, perceived rule-breaking by the United States has led many states and regions to reaffirm their faith in the constitutive rules of international society.

It is useful to think about the different types of solidarism that exist today. Undoubtedly the most powerful form of solidarism is that of neoliberal economics (see Buzan's Chapter 6). Domestic polities and societies are conditioned by liberal ideas about the mode of production, the proper relationship between state and society, and the role of foreign trade. States who do not conform to these norms pay heavy costs, even when norm-compliance may also carry significant and negative consequences. It is evident from the work of contemporary solidarist writers such as Tim Dunne and Nicholas Wheeler that there is a slowly emerging human rights solidarism.[5] States are expected to uphold the rights of their citizens and may face punitive measures if they fall below the baseline of humane governance. This form of solidarism also includes a commitment to democratization and is predicated on the liberal peace idea: the notion that democratic states do not wage war with each other.

A third type of contemporary solidarism revolves around the defence of the state. As Richard Devetak demonstrated in his chapter, the state's monopoly of legitimate violence—the bedrock of international order—is under increasing threat from a variety of groups who are competing with states for the loyalty of social groups. The most obvious manifestation of these threats is the threat of terrorism. Of course, Hedley Bull argued that states share a common interest in the preservation of the society but today's international society is to a large extent designed to promote cooperation to protect itself. International society is no longer merely an egg-box protecting the constituent units from smashing against each other. Today, the constituent units work together in order to preserve the egg-box itself. The rules and norms of behaviour that constitute a pluralist international society do not simply 'exist'; they are manufactured and policed by powerful members of the society. Thus, as I discussed earlier,

UN peacekeeping and humanitarian intervention in failed states may be considered to be forms of police action designed to maintain international society in regions where its constituents are threatened by the forces of fragmentation (Paris 2002).

A fourth type of contemporary solidarism are the different religious fundamentalisms trying to recreate the world in their own image. These are reminiscent of the 'apocalyptic' forms of globalization identified by Richard Falk and also the more malign variants of 'revolutionism' that troubled Martin Wight. These types of solidarism are attempting to reorder international society by replacing a pluralist society of states with a global state organized along religious lines. They are directly opposed to the other three types and are today engaged in a war with forces trying to preserve the current international society. This battle transcends and subverts state boundaries, taking place within states like Indonesia and Pakistan where government forces confront religious zealots.

There are therefore at least four different types of solidarism operating in contemporary international society, though this is by no means an exhaustive list. Sometimes, different solidarisms cohabit comfortably with each other, such as neoliberalism, human rights, and statist based solidarisms. There are tensions between even these types, however. The prerogatives of state power sometimes impede the neoliberal trade agenda, particularly when the protection of the agricultural, manufacturing, and defence sectors in North America and Western Europe are at stake. The economic inequalities caused by neoliberalism make it much more difficult to provide human security and a decent standard of living for at least a third of humanity. The third type demonstrates that revolutionism and irredentism are not things of the past. These types attempt to overthrow international society and replace it with a new world order based upon religious precepts. To remain at the forefront of the contemporary study of world politics, international society needs to explain and understand these global forces, the relationship between them, and the role they play in world politics.

The Drivers and Dynamics of Change

A fourth challenge that English School writers need to confront is that of understanding and explaining the drivers and dynamics of change in international society. As Suganami pointed out in Chapter 1, international society theorists have shed very little light on *why* international societies emerge and change, and beyond recognizing the agency of actors, identifying what the key causal variables are. These questions have tended to be overlooked because the School's commitment to methodological pluralism eschews the idea that global change can be reduced to the interplay of a few key variables, such as the number of powers in a balance of power. Instead, it is suggested that our understanding of the drivers and dynamics of change can be furthered by thorough theoretically informed empirical study. It is only quite recently, however, that much of this type of work has been undertaken, though the potential value of methodological pluralism has been quick to reveal itself. For instance, several writers have begun to explore important questions about the historical emergence of international society and to identify some of the factors that prompt the creation and demise of international societies (such as Buzan and Little 2000; Keene 2002). Using a method reminiscent of Martin Wight's 'three traditions', Buzan and Little were able to distinguish between weak and strong types of international system and to hypothesize about the impact that these different types of systems had on weak and strong states through history (Buzan and Little 2000: 413–14).

To help our understanding of contemporary international society, Nicholas Wheeler's path-breaking work on humanitarian intervention (2000) provides an excellent account of the evolution of humanitarian norms and the values and interests that prompt states to react in particular ways to 'supreme humanitarian emergencies'. For further explanation about the origins and role of international norms, however, we need to look to constructivist ideas (see Reus-Smit's contribution, Chapter 4, this volume). If the English School is to meet the challenge of identifying the causes of change in world politics that has been laid by realists and constructivists, much more empirical study is needed along the lines suggested above. What Parts Two and Three of this book help to demonstrate, though, is that the scope of our empirical studies needs to be broadened to include questions of gender, culture, the environment, the global economy, race, religion, and the rule of law to name just a few.

Under the guise of methodological pluralism, the English School can adopt at least three types of method aimed at uncovering the drivers and dynamics of change in international society. First, following Wheeler, we can use the critical tension between pluralist and solidarist conceptions of international society as a starting point for addressing the limits of political community within particular historical epochs. Second, taking Roger Spegele's search for a teleological account of history, we can explore the relationship between the 'reasons' for particular actions (something that may be ascertained in a variety of ways) and the 'causes'. Finally, although English School writers have dismissed scientism, contemporary scholars can build upon Andrew Linklater's ideas about the methodological implications of the three traditions (see the Introduction) in order to bring empirical, hermeneutic, and critical or emancipatory methods to bear on a particular issue. Using combinations of these three interrelated approaches, advocates of the international society approach can build theoretically informed empirical knowledge about the world which—while avoiding the absolutist claims of scientific approaches to the subject—can shed important light upon the drivers and dynamics of change in international society.

CONCLUSION

English School approaches to international relations therefore confront at least four major challenges. Above all, the School needs to move beyond the introspection that has characterized much of its scholarship in the past decade. On the one hand, its writers need to embrace pluralism more fully in their methodologies and to engage in dialogue with the other major traditions of thought within the discipline. On the other hand, however, the approach needs to yield more in the way of empirical analysis of contemporary international society. In that sense, it is important to either think more carefully about the relationship between international society and world society or, as I suggested earlier, to erase the distinction and replace it with a wider and deeper concept of either international society or world society that is able to accommodate the wider range of actors and issues that inform contemporary world politics. After all, the crucial test in international relations' marketplace of ideas is not so much the theoretical sophistication of a particular perspective but its ability to shed light on our current predicament.

Notes

1. Though such ideas were evident in North American sociological and political thought on international relations at the turn of the twentieth century. See Schmidt (1998).
2. Although Bull repeatedly warned against making practical normative statements in the form of policy advice it is important to bear two points in mind. First, in Bull's broad historical studies, normative questions about the relative weight given to individual well-being and the well-being of states were at the fore. Second, despite his own warnings, Bull did in fact offer normative policy advice on innumerable occasions. See, for instance, Bull (1975).
3. According to Christian Reus-Smit, sovereignty and human rights are interdependent on one another. See Reus-Smit (2001c).
4. The idea of 'common morality' is explored in Terry Nardin's contribution, Chapter 14, this volume.
5. According to Bull, the idea of racial equality was one early manifestation of solidarism.

Bibliography

ABC Radio National (2003), The Media Report: 22 May 2003 — Managing Terror in the Media, www.abc.net.au/rn/talks/8.30/mediarpt/stories/s859473.htm.

Acharya, A. (2001), *Constructing a Security Community in Southeast Asia: ASEAN and the Problem of Regional Order* (London: Routledge).

Ackerly, B. A. and J. True (2002), 'Transnational Justice: A Feminist Development of Critical International Relations Theory'. Annual Convention of the International Studies Association, New Orleans, March.

Adler, E. (1997), 'Seizing the Middle Ground: Constructivism in World Politics', *European Journal of International Relations*, 3(3): 319–63.

—— and M. Barnett (eds.) (1998), *Security Communities* (Cambridge: Cambridge University Press).

Agamben, G. (1998), *Homo Sacer: Sovereign Power and Bare Life* (Stanford: Stanford University Press).

Alderson, K. and A. Hurrell (eds.) (2000), *Hedley Bull on International Society* (London: Palgrave).

Alexandrowicz, C. H. (1967), *An Introduction to the Law of Nations in the East Indies: Sixteenth, Seventeenth and Eighteenth Centuries* (Oxford: Oxford University Press).

Almeida, J. (2003), 'Challenging Realism by Returning to History: The British Committee's Contribution to IR Forty Years On', *International Relations*, 17(3): 253–72.

Alston, W. P. (1996), *A Realist Conception of Truth* (Ithaca: Cornell University Press).

Anheier, H., M. Glasius, and M. Kaldor (2001), 'Introducing Global Civil Society', in H. Anheier, M. Glasius, and M. Kaldor (eds.), *Global Civil Society 2001* (Oxford: Oxford University Press), pp. 3–22.

Arquilla, J. and D. Ronfeldt (2003), *Swarming and the Future of Conflict* (Santa Monica: RAND).

Armstrong, D. (1993), *Revolution and World Order: The Revolutionary State in International Society* (Oxford: Clarendon Press).

Archer, M. (1995), *Realist Social Theory: The Morphogenetic Approach* (Cambridge: Cambridge University Press).

Ashley, R. (1981), 'Political Realism and Human Interests', *International Studies Quarterly*, 25(2): 204–36.

—— (1984), 'The Poverty of Neorealism', *International Organization*, 38(2): 225–86.

Atkins, P. (2003), *Galileo's Finger: The Ten Great Ideas of Science* (Oxford: Oxford University Press).

Audi, R. (1999), *Cambridge Dictionary of Philosophy*, 2nd edn. (Cambridge: Cambridge University Press).

Bacevich, A. J. (2002), *American Empire: The Realities and Consequences of US Diplomacy* (Cambridge, MA: Harvard University Press).

Baczko, B. (2002), 'The Terror Before the Terror? Conditions of Possibility, Logic of Realisation', in Keith Baker (ed.), *The French Revolution and the Creation of Modern Political Culture: The Terror* (New York: Pergamon Press).

Badie, B. (1999), *Un Monde sans Souveraineté: Les États entre Ruse et Responsibilité* (Paris: Fayard).

Balcer, J. M. (1995), *The Persian Conquest of the Greeks 545–450 BC* (Konstanz: Universitatverlag Konstanz).

Banks, M. (1984), 'The Evolution of International Relations Theory', in M. Banks (ed.), *Conflict in World Society: A New Perspective on International Relations* (London: Harvester Wheatsheaf).

Barkin, S. J. and B. Cronin (1994), 'The State and the Nation: Changing Norms and the Rules of Sovereignty in International Relations', *International Organization*, 48(1): 107–30.

Barnett, M. (1999), 'Culture, Strategy and Foreign Policy: Israel's Road to Oslo', *European Journal of International Relations*, 5(1): 5–36.

Bartelson, J. (1995), *A Genealogy of Sovereignty* (Cambridge: Cambridge University Press).

Baudelaire, J. (1961), 'Le Peintre de la Vie Moderne', in *Oeuvres Complètes* (Paris: Gallimard).

Bauman, Z. (2002), 'Reconnaissance Wars of the Planetary Frontierland', *Theory, Culture and Society*, 19(4): 81–90.

Beitz, C. R. (1979), *Political Theory and International Relations* (Princeton: Princeton University Press).

Bellamy, A. J. (2003a), 'Humanitarian Intervention and the Three Traditions', *Global Society*, 17(1): 1–20.

—— (2003b), 'Humanitarian Responsibilities and Interventionist Claims in International Society', *Review of International Studies*, 29(3): 320–41.

—— (2003c), 'International Law and the War Against Iraq', *Melbourne Journal of International Law*, 4(3): 497–520.

—— (2004), *Security Communities and their Neighbours: Regional Fortresses or Global Integrators?* (London: Palgrave-Macmillan).

—— and D. Kroslak (2001), 'The Dawning of a Solidarist Era? The NATO Intervention in Kosovo', *Journal for the Study of Peace and Conflict*, 5: 37–53.

—— and M. McDonald (2004), 'Securing International Society: Towards an English School Discourse of Security', *Australian Journal of Political Science*, 39(2): 307–30.

—— and P. Williams (2004), 'What Future for Peace Operations? Brahimi and Beyond', in A. J. Bellamy and P. Williams (eds.), *Peace Operations and Global Order* (London: Frank Cass), pp. 183–212.

Berlin, I. (1953), *The Hedgehog and the Fox* (New York: Simon & Schuster).

Bernauer, T. (2000), *Staaten im Weltmarkt: Zur Handlunsfähigkeit von Staaten trotz Wirtschaftlicher Globalisierung* (Opladen: Leske und Budrich).

Bernstein, S. (2001), *The Compromise of Liberal Environmentalism* (New York: Columbia University Press).

Betts, R. (2002), 'The Soft Underbelly of American Primacy: Tactical Advantages of Terror', *Political Science Quarterly*, 117(1): 19–36.

Bhaskar, R. (1979), *The Possibility of Naturalism* (Brighton: Harvester).

Bially Mattern, J. (2003), *Ordering International Politics: Identity, Crisis, and Representational Force*, manuscript, February.

Biermann, F. (2000), 'The Case for a World Environment Organization', *Environment*, 42(9): 22–31.

—— (2001), 'The Emerging Debate on the Need for a World Environment Organization', *Global Environmental Politics*, 1(1): 45–55.

Bilgin, H. P. (2000), *Regional Security in the Middle East: A Critical Security Studies Perspective*, Ph.D. Thesis, University of Wales, Aberystwyth.

Bilgin, P., K. Booth, and R. Wyn Jones (1998), 'Security Studies: The Next Stage?', *Nação e Defesa*, 84(2): 131–57.

Bin Laden, O. (1998), 'Jihad against the Jews and Crusaders: World Islamic Front Statement', in Y. Alexander and M. S. Swetnam (eds.), *Usama bin Laden's al-Qaida: Profile of a Terrorist Network* (Ardsely, NY: Transnational), pp. 32–5.

Blaney, D. and N. Inayatullah (1994), 'Prelude to a Conversation of Cultures in International Society? Todorov and Nandy on the Possibility of Dialogue', *Alternatives*, 19(1): 23–51.

Blaug, R. (1999), 'The Tyranny of the Visible: Problems in the Evaluation of Anti-Institutional Radicalism', *Organisation*, 6(1): 33–56.

Booth, K. (1991), 'Security and Emancipation', *Review of International Studies*, 17(3): 313–26.

—— (1995), 'Human Wrongs and International Relations', *International Affairs*, 71(1): 103–26.

—— (1997), 'Security and Self: Reflections of a Fallen Realist', in K. Krause and M. C. Williams (eds.), *Critical Security Studies: Concepts and Cases* (London: UCL Press), pp. 83–119.

—— (1999), 'Three Tyrannies', in T. Dunne and N. J. Wheeler (eds.), *Human Rights in Global Politics* (Cambridge: Cambridge University Press), pp. 31–70.

—— (ed.) (2004a), 'Realities of Security', *International Relations*, 18(1) (Special Issue): 5–8.

—— (ed.) (2004b), *Critical Security Studies and World Politics* (Boulder, CO: Lynne Reinner).

—— and T. Dunne (2002), 'Worlds in Collision', in Booth and Dunne (eds.), *Worlds in Collision: Terror and the Future of Global Order* (Basingstoke: Palgrave), pp. 1–26.

—— and P. Vale (1995), 'Security in Southern Africa: After Apartheid, Beyond Realism', *International Affairs*, 71(2): 285–304.

—— and —— (1997), 'Critical Security Studies and Regional Insecurity: The case of southern Africa', in K. Krause and M. C. Williams (eds.), *Critical Security Studies: Concepts and Cases* (London: UCL Press), pp. 329–58.

—— and N. J. Wheeler (1992), 'Contending Philosophies about Security in Europe', in Colin McInnes (ed.), *Security and Strategy in the New Europe* (London: Routledge), pp. 3–36.

Boulding, K. (1979), *Stable Peace* (Austin: University of Texas Press).

Bozeman, A. (1984), 'The Future of International Society in a Multicultural World', in H. Bull and A. Watson (eds.), *The Expansion of International Society* (Oxford: Clarendon Press), pp. 387–406.

Brown, C. (1988), 'The Modern Requirement? Reflections on Normative International Theory in a Post-Western World', *Millennium: Journal of International Studies*, 17(2): 339–48.

—— (1994), '"Turtles All the Way Down": Antifoundationalism, Critical Theory, and International Relations', *Millennium: Journal of International Studies*, 23(2): 213–36.

—— (1995a), 'International Political Theory and the Idea of World Community', in K. Booth and S. Smith (eds.), *International Relations Theory Today* (Cambridge: Polity Press), pp. 90–109.

—— (1995b), 'International Theory and International Society: The Viability of the Middle Way', *Review of International Studies*, 21(2): 183–96.

—— (1997), *Understanding International Relations* (Basingstoke: Macmillan).

—— (2000), 'Cultural Diversity and International Political Theory; From the Requirement to 'Mutual respect'?', *Review of International Studies*, 26(2): 199–213.

—— (2001), 'World Society and the English School: An "International Society" Perspective on World Society', *European Journal of International Relations*, 7(4): 423–41.

Brugger, P. (2001), 'Das paranormale Gehirn: Was der Umgang mit Zufällen über den Glauben verrät', *Neue Zürcher Zeitung*, 29 November.

Brugger, P. and R. E. Graves (1997), 'Testing versus Believing Hypotheses: Magical Ideation in the Judgement of Contingencies', *Cognitive Neuropsychiatry*, 2.

Bull, H. (1966a), 'International Theory: The Case for a Classical Approach', *World Politics*, 42(4): 361–77.

——(1966b), 'The Grotian Conception of International Society', in M. Wight and H. Butterfield (eds.), *Diplomatic Investigations: Essays in the Theory of International Politics* (London: Allen and Unwin), pp. 51–73.

——(1966c), 'Society and Anarchy in International Relations', in H. Butterfield and M. Wight (eds.), *Diplomatic Investigations* (London: Allen and Unwin), pp. 35–50.

——(1969), 'International Theory: The Case for a Classical Approach', in K. Knorr and J. N. Rosenau (eds.), *Contending Approaches to International Politics* (Princeton: Princeton University Press), pp. 20–38.

——(1971), 'Civil Violence and International Order', *Adelphi Papers*, No. 83, pp. 27–36.

——(ed.) (1975), *Asia and the Western Pacific: Towards a New International Order* (Melbourne: Thomas Nelson for the AIIA).

——(1977), *The Anarchical Society: A Study of Order in World Politics* (Houndmills: Macmillan).

——(1979a), 'The Third World and International Society', *The Yearbook of World Affairs, 1979* (London: Stevens and Sons for the London Institute of International Affairs), pp. 127–45.

——(1979b), 'Human Rights and World Politics', in R. Pettman (ed.), *Moral Claims in World Affairs* (Basingstoke: Macmillan), pp. 79–91.

——(1979c), 'The State's Positive Role in World Affairs', *Daedalus*, 108(4): 112–23.

——(1980), 'The European International Order', in K. Alderson and A. Hurrell (eds.) (2000), *Hedley Bull on International Society* (Basingstoke: Macmillan), pp. 175–200.

——(1984a), *Justice in International Relations* (Waterloo: University of Waterloo, 1983–84 Hagey Lectures).

——(1984b), 'The Revolt Against the West', in H. Bull and A. Watson (eds.), *The Expansion of International Society* (Oxford: Clarendon Press), pp. 217–28.

——(1984c), 'The Emergence of a Universal International Society', in H. Bull and A. Watson (eds.), *The Expansion of International Society* (Oxford: Clarendon Press), pp. 117–26.

——(1991), 'Martin Wight and the Theory of International Relations', in M. Wight (ed.), *International Theory: The Three Traditions* (Leicester: Leicester University Press/Royal Institute of International Affairs), pp. ix–xxiii.

——(2000), 'Justice in International Relations', in K. Alderson and A. Hurrell (eds.), *Hedley Bull on International Society* (London: Palgrave), pp. 206–45.

——and A. Watson (eds.) (1984), *The Expansion of International Society* (Oxford: Clarendon Press).

Burch, K. (1994), 'The "Properties" of the State System and Global Capitalism', in S. Rosow, N. Inayatullah, and M. Rupert (eds.), *The Global Economy as Political Space* (Boulder, CO: Lynne Rienner), pp. 37–60.

Burchill, S. (2002), 'Understanding the Revolt Against the West', *Australian Financial Review*, 22 November.

Burke, E. (1987), *A Philosophical Enquiry into the Origin of Our Ideas of the Sublime and the Beautiful* (Oxford: Basil Blackwell).

Burton, A. (1994), *Burdens of History: British Feminists, Indian Women and Imperial Culture, 1865–1915* (Chapel Hill: University of North Carolina Press).

Burton, J. W. (1972), *World Society* (London: Cambridge University Press).

Busia, A. P. A. (1996), 'On Cultures of Communication: Reflections from Beijing', *Signs: Journal of Women in Culture and Society*, 22(1): 204–10.

Bush, G. W. (2001), 'You are Either With Us or Against Us', CNN, 6 November.

—— (2002), Remarks by the President at 2002 Graduation Exercise of the United States Military Academy, West Point, New York, www.whitehouse.gov.newsrelease/2002/06/print/20020601-3.html.

Butterfield, H. (1929), *The Peace Tactics of Napolean, 1806–1808* (Cambridge: Cambridge University Press).

—— (1939), *Napoleon* (London: Gerald Duckworth).

—— (1950), *Christianity and History* (New York: Charles Scribner's Sons).

—— (1951), *History and Human Relations* (London: Collins).

—— (1955), *Man on his Past* (Cambridge: Cambridge University Press).

—— (1957), *George III and the Historians* (London: Collins).

—— (1960), *International Conflict in the Twentieth Century: A Christian View* (London: Routledge and Kegan Paul).

—— (1968), *The Whig Interpretation of History* (London: G. Bell and Sans).

—— (1971), *The Historical Novel: An Essay* (Cambridge: Cambridge University Press).

—— (1979), *Herbert Butterfield: Writings on Christianity and History*, edited by C. T. McIntire (New York: Oxford University Press).

—— (1981), *The Origins of History* (London: Eyre Metheun).

—— and M. Wight (eds.) (1966), *Diplomatic Investigations: Essays in the Theory of International Politics* (London: Allen and Unwin).

Buzan, B. (1983), *People, States and Fear: The National Security Problem in International Relations* (Brighton: Wheatsheaf).

—— (1991), *People, States and Fear: An Agenda for International Security Studies in a Post-Cold War Era*, 2nd edn. (London: Harvester Wheatsheaf).

—— (1993), 'From International System to International Society: Structural Realism and Regime Theory Meet the English School', *International Organization*, 47(3): 327–52.

—— (1999), 'The English School as a Research Program', paper presented at the annual conference of the British International Studies Association, Manchester.

—— (2001), 'The English School: An Underexploited Resource in IR', *Review of International Studies*, 27(3): 471–88.

—— (2004), *From International to World Society? English School Theory and the Social Structure of Globalisation* (Cambridge: Cambridge University Press).

—— and R. Little (1994), 'The Idea of "International System": Theory Meets History', *International Science Review*, 15(3): 231–55.

—— and —— (1996), ' Reconceptualising Anarchy: Structural Realism Meets World History', *European Journal of International Relations*, 2(4): 403–38.

—— and —— (2000), *International Systems in World History: Remaking the Study of International Relations* (Oxford: Oxford University Press).

—— and —— (2001), 'The "English Patient" Strikes Back: A Response to Hall's Mis-Diagnoses', *International Affairs*, 77(4): 943–6.

—— and O. Wæver (2003), *Regions and Powers: The Structure of International Security* (Cambridge: Cambridge University Press).

——, C. Jones, and R. Little (1993), *The Logic of Anarchy: Neorealism to Structural Realism* (New York: Columbia University Press).

——, O. Wæver, and J. de Wilde (1998), *Security: A New Framework for Analysis* (Boulder, CO: Lynne Rienner).

Byers, M. (2003), 'Pre-emptive Self-defence: Hegemony, Equality and Strategies of Legal Change' *Journal of Political Philosophy*, 11(2): 141–90.

Callahan, W. (forthcoming), 'Nationalizing International Theory: Race, Class and the English School', *Global Society*.

Campbell, D. (1998), *National Deconstruction: Violence, Identity, and Justice in Bosnia* (Minneapolis: University of Minnesota Press).

Carr, E. H. (1946), *The Twenty Years' Crisis 1919–1939: An Introduction to the Study of International Relations* (Basingstoke: Macmillan).

—— (1960), *The New Society* (Basingstoke: Macmillan).

—— (1987), *What is History?* (London: Penguin).

Castells, M. (2000), *The Rise of the Network Society*, 2nd edn. (Oxford: Basil Blackwell).

Cederman, L.-E. (1997), *Emergent Actors in World Politics: How States and Nations Develop and Dissolve* (Princeton: Princeton University Press).

Cerny, P. G. (2000), 'Political Agency in a Globalizing World: Towards a Structurationist Approach', *European Journal of International Relations*, 6(4): 435–63.

Chakrabarti Pasic, S. (1996), 'Culturing International Relations: A Call for Extension', in Y. Lapid and F. Kratochwil (eds.), *The Return of Culture and Identity in International Relations Theory* (Boulder, CO: Lynne Rienner), pp. 85–104.

Chan, S., P. Mandaville, and R. Bleiker (2001), *The Zen of International Relations: International Relations Theory from East to West* (Basingstoke: Palgrave).

Chatterjee, P. and M. Finger (1994), *The Earth Brokers: Power, Politics and World Development* (London: Routledge).

Chesterman, S. (2001), *Just War or Just Peace? Humanitarian Intervention and International Law* (Oxford: Oxford University Press).

Chirac, J. (2003), 'Iraq War Undermined UN', CNN Report, 23 September 2003, www.cnn.com/2003/US/09/23/sprj.irq.annan.

Chomsky, N. (1996), *Power and Prospects: Reflections on Human Nature and the Social Order* (London: Pluto Press).

—— (2002), 'Who are the Global Terrorists?', in K. Booth and T. Dunne (eds.), *Worlds in Collision: Terror and the Future of Global Order* (Basingstoke: Palgrave), pp. 128–37.

Chuang Tzu (1963), 'The Chuang Tzu', translated by W. T. Chan, in *A Source Book in Chinese Philosophy* (Princeton: Princeton University Press).

Clapham, C. (1996), *Africa and the International System: The Politics of State Survival* (Cambridge: Cambridge University Press).

Clapp, J. (1998), 'The Privatization of Global Environmental Governance: ISO 14000 and the Developing World', *Global Governance*, 4(3): 295–316.

Clark, A. M., E. J. Friedman, and K. Hochstetler (1998), 'The Sovereign Limits of Global Civil Society: A Comparison of NGO Participation in Global UN Conferences on the Environment, Human Rights, and Women', *World Politics*, 51(1): 1–35.

Clark, I. (1989), *The Hierarchy of States: Reform and Resistance in the International Order* (Cambridge: Cambridge University Press).

—— (2003), 'Legitimacy in a Global Order', *Review of International Studies*, 29(5): 75–95.

Clausewitz, C. van (1976), *On War*, ed. and trans. M. Howard and P. Paret (Princeton: Princeton University Press).

Coates, T. (ed.) (2000), *International Justice* (Aldershot: Ashgate).

Cohen, E. E. (2000), *The Athenian Nation* (Princeton: Princeton University Press).

Cohen, W. I. (2003), 'I'm Shocked!' *Times Literary Supplement*, 28 March.

Coll, A. R. (1985), *The Wisdom of Statecraft* (Durham: Duke University Press).

Collingwood, R. G. (1956), *The Idea of History* (Oxford: Oxford University Press).

Connolly, W. E. (1995), *The Ethos of Pluralization* (Minneapolis: University of Minnesota Press).

Copeland, D. C. (2003), 'A Realist Critique of the English School', *Review of International Studies*, 29(3): 427–41.

Cox, M. (2003), 'Editor's Introduction', *International Relations*, 17(3): 251–2.

Cox, R. (1986), 'Social forces, States and World Orders: Beyond International Relations Theory', in R. O. Keohane (ed.), *Neorealism and its Critics* (New York: Columbia University Press), pp. 126–53.

—— (1994), 'Global Restructuring', in R. Stubbs and G. Underhill (eds.), *Political Economy and the Changing Global Order* (Toronto: McClelland and Stewart).

—— (1996), 'Gramsci, Hegemony and International Relations: An Essay in Method', in R. W. Cox and T. Sinclair (eds.), *Approaches to World Order* (Cambridge: Cambridge University Press).

Crawford, N. C. (2002), *Argument and Change in World Politics: Ethics, Decolonization and Humanitarian Intervention* (Cambridge: Cambridge University Press).

Cronin, A. K. (2002/03), 'Behind the Curve: Globalisation and International Terrorism', *International Security*, 27(3): 30–58.

Cronin, B. (2001), 'The Paradox of Hegemony: America's Ambiguous Relationship With the United Nations', *European Journal of International Relations*, 7(1): 103–30.

Davidson, D. (1980), 'Actions, Reasons, and Causes', in D. Davidson (ed.) *Essays on Actions and Events* (Oxford: Oxford University Press), pp. 3–19.

De Grieff, P. and C. Cronin (eds.) (2002), *Global Justice and Transnational Politics* (Cambridge, MA: MIT Press).

Dehio, L. (1962), *The Precarious Balance: The Politics of Power in Europe 1494–1945* (London: Chatto and Windus).

Deibert, R. J. and J. Gross Stein (2002), 'Hacking Networks of Terror', *Dialog-IO*, Spring, 1–14, accessed at http://mitpress.mit.edu/journals/INOR/Dialogue_IO/diebert.pdf.

Deleuze, G. and F. Guattari (1987), *A Thousand Plateaus: Capitalism and Schizophrenia* (Minneapolis: University of Minnesota Press).

Derrida, J. (2003), *Voyous* (Paris: Galilée).

Dessler, D. (1989), 'What's at Stake in the Agent-Structure Debate?', *International Organization*, 43(3): 441–73.

Der Derian, J. (1992), *Antidiplomacy: Spies, Terror, Speed, and War* (Oxford: Blackwell).

—— (ed.) (1995), *International Theory: Critical Investigations* (London: Macmillan).

—— (2002a), '*In Terrorem*: Before and After 9/11', in K. Booth and T. Dunne (eds.), *Worlds in Collision: Terror and the Future of Global Order* (Basingstoke: Palgrave), pp. 101–17.

—— (2002b), 'The War of Networks', *Theory and Event*, 5(4): accessed at http://muse.jhu.edu/journals/theory_and_event/v005/5.4derderian.html.

Deutsch, K. et al. (1957), *Political Community and the North Atlantic Area* (Princeton: Princeton University Press).

Diez, T. and R. G. Whitman (2002), 'Analysing European Integration: Reflecting on the English School', *Journal of Common Market Studies*, 40(1): 43–67.

Dore, R. (1984), 'Unity and Diversity in World Culture', in H. Bull and A. Watson (eds.), *The Expansion of International Society* (Oxford: Clarendon Press), pp. 407–24.

Dower, J. (1999), *Embracing Defeat* (New York: W. W. Norton).

Dunne, T. (1995*a*), 'The Social Construction of International Society', *European Journal of International Relations*, 1(3): 367–89.

—— (1995*b*), 'International Society—Theoretical Promises Fulfilled?', *Cooperation and Conflict*, 30(2): 125–54.

—— (1997), 'Colonial Encounters in International Relations: Reading Wight, Writing Australia', *Australian Journal of International Affairs*, 51(3): 309–23.

—— (1998), *Inventing International Society: A History of the English School* (London: Macmillan, St. Anthony's Series).

—— (2001), 'New Thinking on International Society', *British Journal of Politics and International Relations*, 3(2): 223–42.

—— (2002), 'After 9/11: What Next for Human Rights?', *International Journal of Human Rights*, 6(2): 93–101.

—— (2003), 'Society and Hierarchy in International Relations', *International Relations*, 17(3): 303–20.

—— and N. J. Wheeler (2004), '"We the Peoples": Contending Discourses of Security in Human Rights Theory and Practice', *International Relations*, 18(1): 9–23.

Economist, The (1999), 'Is it Crime or Culture? Female Genital Mutilation', February 13, p. 45.

—— (2003), 'An UnEuropean Habit: Honour Killings in Turkey', 28 June–4 July, p. 53.

Ekins, P. (1992), *A New World Order: Grassroots Movements for Global Change* (London: Routledge).

Enloe, C. (1989), *Bananas, Beaches and Bases: Making Feminist Sense of International Politics* (London: HarperCollins).

Epp, R. (1998), 'The English School on the Frontiers of International Relations', *Review of International Studies*, 24(Special Issue): 47–63.

Euben, R. (2002*a*), 'Killing (For) Politics: *Jihad*, Martyrdom, and Political Action', *Political Theory*, 30(1): 4–35.

—— (2002*b*), 'The New Manichaeans', *Theory and Event*, 5(4): 7–12.

Evangelista, M. (1999), *Unarmed Forces: The Transnational Movement to End the Cold War* (Ithaca: Cornell University Press).

Falk, R. (1971), *This Endangered Planet: Prospects and Proposals for Human Survival* (New York: Random House).

—— (1990), 'Culture, Modernism, Postmodernism: A Challenge to International Relations', in J. Chay (ed.), *Culture and International Relations* (New York: Westport), pp. 267–79.

—— (1995), *On Humane Governance* (Cambridge: Polity Press).

—— (1998), *Law in an Emerging Global Village: A Post-Westphalian Perspective* (Ardsley, NY: Transnational).

—— (1999*a*), *Predatory Globalisation: A Critique* (Cambridge: Polity Press).

—— (1999*b*), 'The Pursuit of International Justice: Present Dilemmas and an Imagined Future', *Journal of International Affairs*, 52(2): 409–31.

—— (2002), 'The New Bush Doctrine', *The Nation*, 275(3): 12.

—— (2003*a*), 'What Future for the UN Charter System of War Prevention?' *American Journal of International Law*, 97(3): 590–9.

—— (2003*b*), *The Great Terror War* (Northampton, MA: Olive Branch Press).

Fierke, K. M. (2002), 'Meaning, Method and Practice: Assessing the Changing Security Agenda', in S. Lawson (ed.), *The New Agenda for International Relations* (Cambridge: Polity Press), pp. 128–44.

Fichte, J. G. (2000), *Foundations of Natural Right*, edited by Frederick Neuhauser (Cambridge: Cambridge University Press).

—— (1996*a*), *National Interests in International Society* (Ithaca: Cornell University Press).

—— (1996*b*), 'Norms, Culture, and World Politics: Insights from Sociology's Institutionalism', *International Organization*, 50(2): 325–47.

—— (2001), 'Exporting the English School?', *Review of International Studies*, 27(3): 509–13.

—— and K. Sikkink (1998), 'International Norm Dynamics and Political Change', *International Organization*, 52(4): 887–917.

Finnis, J. (1980), *Natural Law and Natural Rights* (Oxford: Oxford University Press).

—— (1998), *Aquinas: Moral, Political, and Legal Theory* (Oxford: Oxford University Press).

——, J. M. Boyle Jr., and G. Grisez (1987), *Nuclear Deterrence, Morality and Realism* (Oxford: Oxford University Press).

Fodor, J. A. (1990), *A Theory of Content and Other Essays* (Cambridge, MA: MIT Press).

Foot, R. (2000), *Rights Beyond Borders: The Global Community and the Struggle Over Human Rights in China* (Oxford: Oxford University Press).

——, J. L. Gaddis, and A. Hurrell (eds.) (2003), *Order and Justice in International Relations* (Oxford: Oxford University Press).

Foucault, M. (1987), 'Nietzsche, Generalogy, History', in M. Gambon (ed.), *Interpreting Politics* (Oxford: Blackwell), pp. 221–40.

Franck, T. M. (2003), 'Interpretation and Change in the Law of Humanitarian Intervention', in J. L. Holzgrefe and R. O. Keohane (eds.), *Humanitarian Intervention: Ethical, Legal, and Political Dilemmas* (Cambridge: Cambridge University Press), pp. 204–31.

Freedman, L. (2001), 'The Third World War?', *Survival*, 43(4): 61–88.

Fukuyama, F. (1992), *The End of History and the Last Man* (London: Penguin).

—— (1998), 'Women and the Evolution of World Politics', *Foreign Affairs*, 77(5): 24–41.

Furet, F. (1981), *Interpreting the French Revolution*, translated by E. Foster (Cambridge: Cambridge University Press).

—— (1989), 'Terror', in F. Furet and M. Ozouf (eds.), *A Critical Dictionary of the French Revolution*, translated by Arthur Goldhammer (Cambridge, MA: Belknap Press of Harvard University Press), pp. 234–43.

Gearty, C. (1997), *The Future of Terrorism* (London: Phoenix).

Giddens, A. (1971), *Capitalism and Modern Social Theory* (Cambridge: Cambridge University Press).

—— (1990), *The Consequences of Modernity* (Stanford: Stanford University Press).

Gill, S. (1996), 'Globalization, Democratization, and the Politics of Indifference', in J. H. Mittelman (ed.), *Globalization: Critical Reflections* (Boulder, CO: Lynne Rienner), pp. 205–28.

Gilpin, R. (1981), *War and Change in World Politics* (Cambridge: Cambridge University Press).

—— (1984), 'The Richness of the Tradition of Political Realism', *International Organization*, 38(2): 287–304.

Glennon, M. J. (2001), *Limits of Law, Prerogatives of Power: Interventionism After Kosovo* (New York: Palgrave).

—— (2003), 'Why the Security Council Failed', *Foreign Affairs*, May/June: 16–35.

Goedde, P. (1999), 'From Villains to Victims: Fraternization and the Feminization of Germany, 1945–1947', *Diplomatic History*, 23(1): 1–20.

Goffman, Daniel (2002), *The Ottoman Empire and Early Modern Europe* (Cambridge: Cambridge University Press).

Goldfischer, D. (2002), 'E. H. Carr: a "Historical Realist" Approach for the Globalisation Era', *Review of International Studies*, 28(4): 697–717.

Goldstein, J. (2001), *War and Gender* (Cambridge: Cambridge University Press).

Goodin, R. E. (1990), 'International Ethics and the Environmental Crisis', *Ethics and International Affairs*, 4(1): 90–105.

Goodrich, L. M. and E. Hambro (1946), *Charter of the United Nations: Commentary and Documents* (Boston: World Peace Foundation).

Gong, G. (1984), *The Standard of 'Civilization', in International Society* (Oxford: Clarendon Press).

Gonzalez-Pelaez, A. (2003), *Basic Rights In International Society: R. J. Vincent's Idea of a Subsistence Approach to the Practical Realisation of Human Rights*, Ph.D. Thesis, CSD, University of Westminster.

Grader, S. (1988), 'The English School of International Relations: Evidence and Evaluation', *Review of International Studies*, 14(1): 29–44.

Grewal, I. (1996), *Home and Harem: Nation, Gender, Empire and the Cultures of Travel* (Durham, NC: Duke University Press).

Grotius, H. (1925), *The Law of War and Peace*, translated by F. Kelsey (Indianapolis: Indiana University Press).

Grovugui, S. N. Z. (1996), *Sovereign, Quasi-Sovereign, and Africans: Race and Self–Determination in International Law* (Minneapolis: University of Minnesota Press).

Guzzini, S. (2001), 'Calling for a Less "Brandish" and Less "Grand Reconvention"', *Review of International Studies*, 27(3): 495–501.

Haas, P. M., R. O. Keohane, and M. A. Levy (1993), *Institutions for the Earth: Sources of Effective Environmental Protection* (Cambridge: MIT Press).

Hage, G. (2003), '"Comes a Time We are All Enthusiasm": Understanding Palestinian Suicide Bombers in Times of Exigophobia', *Public Culture*, 15(1): 65–89.

Hall, I. (2001), 'Still the English Patient? Closures and Inventions in the English School', *International Affairs*, 77(3): 931–42.

—— (2002), 'History, Christianity and Diplomacy: Sir Herbert Butterfield and International Relations', *Review of International Studies*, 28(4): 719–36.

Hall, R. B. (1999), *National Collective Identity: Social Constructs and International Systems* (New York: Columbia University Press).

Halliday, F. (1992), 'International Society as Homogeneity: Burke, Marx, Fukuyama', *Millennium: Journal of International Studies*, 21(3): 435–61.

—— (1994), *Rethinking International Relations* (Basingstoke: Macmillan).

—— (2002), *Two Hours that Shook the World: September 11, 2001: Causes and Consequences* (London: Saqi Books).

Hardin, G. (1968), 'The Tragedy of the Commons', *Science*, 162: 1243–8.

Hardt, M. and A. Negri (2000), *Empire* (Cambridge, MA: Harvard University Press).

Haslam, J. (1999), *The Vices of Integrity: E. H. Carr 1892–1982* (London: Verso).

Held, D., A. McGrew, D. Goldblatt, and J. Perraton (1999), *Global Transformation: Politics, Economics and Culture* (Cambridge: Polity Press).

Hempel, L. (1996), *Environmental Governance: The Global Challenge* (Washington, DC: Island Press).

Henkin, L. (1979), *How Nations Behave: Law and Foreign Policy* (New York: Columbia University Press).

Herbst, J. (2000), *States and Power in Africa: Comparative Lessons in Authority and Control* (Princeton: Princeton University Press).

Hines, C. (2000), *Localization: A Global Manifesto* (London: Earthscan).

Hobbes, T. (1968), *Leviathan* (Harmondsworth: Penguin)

Hobden, S. and J. M. Hobson (eds.) (2002), *Historical Sociology of International Relations* (Cambridge: Cambridge University Press).

Hoffman, M. (1987), 'Critical Theory and the Inter-Paradigm Debate', *Millennium: Journal of International Studies*, 16(2): 231–49.

Holsti, K. J. (2002), 'The Institutions of International Politics: Continuity, Change, and Transformation', paper presented at the ISA Convention, New Orleans, March.

Homer-Dixon, T. (2002), 'The Rise of Complex Terrorism', *Foreign Policy*, 128: 52–62.

Honig, J. W. (2001), 'Warfare in the Middle Ages', in A. V. Hartmann and B. Heuser (eds.), *War, Peace and World Orders in European History* (London: Routledge), pp. 113–26.

Hopf, T. (1998), 'The Promise of Constructivism in International Relations Theory', *International Security*, 23(1): 171–200.

Howard, M. (1999), 'When are Wars Decisive? *Survival*, 41(1): 126–35.

—— (2002), 'What's in a Name? How to Fight Terrorism', *Foreign Affairs*, 81(1): 8–13.

Hudson, V. M. and A. M. Den Boer (2002), 'A Surplus of Men, A Deficit of Peace: Security and Sex Ratios in Asia's Largest States', *International Security*, 26(4): 5–38.

—— and —— (2003), *Bare Branches: The Security Implications of Asia's Surplus Male Population* (Cambridge, MA: MIT Press).

Humphreys, D. (1996), *Forest Politics: The Evolution of International Cooperation* (London: Earthscan).

Hurd, I. (1999), 'Legitimacy and Authority in International Politics', *International Organization*, 53(2): 379–408.

Hurrell, A. (1993), 'International Society and the Study of Regimes: A Reflective Approach', in V. Rittberger (ed.), *Regime Theory and International Relations* (Oxford: Oxford University Press), pp. 49–72.

—— (1994), 'A Crisis of Ecological Viability—Global Environmental Change and the Nation-State', *Political Studies*, 42(2): 146–65.

—— (1995), 'International Political Theory and the Global Environment', in K. Booth and S. Smith (eds.), *International Relations Theory Today* (Cambridge: Polity Press), pp. 129–52.

—— (1998), 'Society and Anarchy in International Relations', in B. A. Roberson (ed.), *International Society and the Development of International Relations Theory* (London: Continuum), pp. 17–42.

—— (1999), 'Security and Inequality', in A. Hurrell and N. Woods (eds.), *Inequality, Globalization, and World Politics* (Oxford: Oxford University Press), pp. 248–71.

—— (2001), 'Keeping History, Law and Political Philosophy Firmly Within the English School', *Review of International Studies*, 27(3): 489–94.

—— (2002a), 'Foreword to the Third Edition: *The Anarchical Society* 25 Years On', in H. Bull (ed.), *The Anarchical Society* (Basingstoke: Palgrave), pp. vii–xxiii.

—— (2002b), '"There are no Rules" (George W. Bush): International Order after September 11', *International Relations*, 16(2): 185–203.

—— and B. Kingsbury (eds.) (1992), *The International Politics of the Environment* (Oxford: Clarendon Press).

Hutto, D. D. (1999), *The Presence of Mind* (Amsterdam: John Benjamins).

Huysmans, J. (1998), 'Revisiting Copenhagen: Or, On the Creative Development of a Security Studies Agenda in Europe', *European Journal of International Relations*, 4(4): 479–505.

Ignatieff, M. (2003a), 'Human Rights, Sovereignty and Intervention', in N. Owen (ed.), *Human Rights, Human Wrongs* (Oxford: Oxford University Press), pp. 52–87.

Ignatieff, M. (2003*b*), 'The Burden: With a military of Unrivaled Might, the United States Rule a New Kind of Empire. Will this Cost America its Soul—or Save it?' *New York Times Magazine*, 1 January, 22–7, 50–3.

Ikenberry, J. and C. Kupchan (1990), 'Socialization and Hegemonic Power', *International Organization*, 44(3): 292–314.

Independent International Commission (2000), *The Kosovo Report: Conflict, International Response, Lessons Learned* (Oxford: Oxford University Press).

Inglehart, R. and P. Norris (2003), *Rising Tide: Gender Equality and Cultural Change Around the World* (New York: Cambridge University Press).

International Commission on Intervention and State Sovereignty (ICISS) (2001), *The Responsibility to Protect* (Ottawa: ICISS).

Jackson, R. H. (1990*a*), 'Martin Wight, International Theory and the Good Life', *Millennium: Journal of International Studies*, 19(2): 261–72.

—— (1993), 'Armed Humanitarianism', *International Journal*, XLVIII: 579–606.

—— (1995), 'The Political Theory of International Society', in K. Booth and S. Smith (eds.), *International Relations Theory Today* (Cambridge: Polity Press), pp. 110–28.

—— (1996), 'Is There a Classical International Theory?', in S. Smith, K. Booth, and M. Zalewski (eds.), *International Theory: Positivism & Beyond* (Cambridge: Cambridge University Press), pp. 203–18.

Jackson, R. H. (1998), 'Boundaries and International Society', in B. A. Roberson (ed.), *International Society and the Development of International Relations Theory* (London: Continuum), pp. 156–72.

—— (2000), *The Global Covenant: Human Conduct in a World of States* (Oxford: Oxford University Press).

—— and G. Sorensen (1999), *Introduction to International Relations* (Oxford: Oxford University Press).

Jackson, R. J. (1990*b*), 'The Political Theory of International Society', in K. Booth and S. Smith (eds.), *International Relations Theory Today* (Cambridge: Policy, 1995).

James, A. (ed.) (1973), *The Bases of International Order: Essays in Honour of C. A. W. Manning* (Oxford: Oxford University Press).

—— (1993), 'System or Society?', *Review of International Studies*, 19(3): 269–88.

Jenkins, B. (1975), 'International Terrorism: A New Mode of Conflict', in D. Carlton and C. Schaerf (eds.), *International Terrorism and World Security* (London: Croom Held), pp. 10–25.

Jepperson, R. L., A. Wendt, and P. J. Katzenstein (1996), 'Norms, Identity, and Culture in National Security', in P. J. Katzenstein (ed.), *The Culture of National Security: Norms and Identity in World Politics* (New York: Columbia University Press), pp. 33–75.

Jessop, B. (1990), *State Theory: Putting Capitalist States in Their Place* (Cambridge: Polity Press).

Johnston, A. I. (1995), *Cultural Realism: Strategic Culture and Grand Strategy in Chinese History* (Princeton: Princeton University Press).

Johnston, P. (1989), *Wittgenstein on Moral Philosophy* (London: Routledge).

Jones, C. (1999), *Global Justice: Defending Cosmopolitanism* (Oxford: Oxford University Press).

Jones, D. V. (2002), *Toward a Just World: The Critical Years in the Search for International Justice* (Chicago: University of Chicago Press).

Jones, R. E. (1981), 'The English School of International Relations: A Case for Closure?', *Review of International Studies*, 7(1): 1–13.

Joxe, A. (2002), *Empire of Disorder*, translated by A. Hodges (New York: Semiotext(e)).

Juergensmeyer, M. (2002), 'Religious Terror and Global War', in C. Calhoun, P. Price, and A. Timmer (eds.), *Understanding September 11* (New York: The New York Press), pp. 43–57.

Kagan, R. (1998), 'The Benevolent Empire', *Foreign Policy*, 111 (Summer): 24–35.

—— (2003), *Of Paradise and Power: America and Europe in the New World Order* (New York: Knopf).

Kaldor, M. (2002), 'Beyond Militarism, Arms Races and Arms Control', in C. Calhoun, P. Price, and A. Timmer (eds.), *Understanding September 11* (New York: The New York Press).

Kampfner, J. (2003), *Blair's Wars* (London: Simon and Schuster).

Kant, I. (1991), *Kant's Political Writings*, 2nd edn. edited by H. Reiss (Cambridge: Cambridge University Press).

Kapstein, E. B. (1999), 'Does Unipolarity Have a Future?', in E. B. Kapstein and M. Mastanduno (eds.), *Unipolar Politics: Realism and State Strategies After the Cold War* (New York: Columbia University Press), pp. 464–90.

Karliner, J. (1997), *The Corporate Planet: Ecology and Politics in the Age of Globalization* (San Francisco: Sierra Club Books).

Katzenstein, P. J. (1996*a*), *Cultural Norms and National Security: Police and Military in Postwar Japan* (Ithaca: Cornell University Press).

—— (1996*b*), *The Culture of National Security: Norms and Identity in World Politics* (New York: Columbia University Press).

—— (1999), *Tamed Power: Germany in Europe* (Ithaca: Cornell University Press).

Katznelson, I. (2002), 'Evil and Politics', *Daedalus*, 131(1): 7–11.

Keal, P. (2003), *European Conquest and the Rights of Indigenous Peoples: The Moral Backwardness of International Society* (Cambridge: Cambridge University Press).

Keck, M. and K. Sikkink (eds.) (1998), *Activists beyond Borders: Advocacy Networks in International Politics* (Ithaca: Cornell University Press).

Keene, E. (2002), *Beyond the Anarchical Society: Grotius, Colonialism and Order in World Politics* (Cambridge: Cambridge University Press).

Kennedy, P. (1989), *The Rise and Fall of the Great Powers: Economic Change and Military Conflict from 1500–2000* (London: Fontana).

Keohane, R. O. (1988), 'International Institutions: Two Approaches', *International Studies Quarterly*, 32(4): 379–96.

—— (1989), *International Institutions and State Power: Essays in International Relations Theory* (Boulder, CO: Westview Press).

—— (2002), 'The Globalisation of Informal Violence, Theories of World Politics, and the "Liberalism of Fear"', *Dialogue-IO*, Spring: 29–43, accessed at http://mitpress.mit.edu/journals/INOR/Dialogue_IO/keohane.pdf.

Knorr, K. and J. N. Rosenau (eds.) (1969), *Contending Approaches to International Politics* (Princeton: Princeton University Press).

Korb, L. (ed.) (2003), *A New National Security Strategy in an Age of Terrorists, Tyrants, and Weapons of Mass Destruction* (New York: Council on Foreign Relations).

Korman, S. (1996), *The Right of Conquest: The Acquisition of Territory by Force in International Law and Practice* (Oxford: Clarendon Press).

Korten, D. (1995), *When Corporations Rule the World* (London: Earthscan).

Krasner, S. D. (1999), *Sovereignty: Organised Hypocrisy* (Princeton: Princeton University Press).

Kratochwil, F. (1989), *Rules, Norms, and Decisions: On the Conditions of Practical and Legal Reasoning in International Relations and Domestic Affairs* (Cambridge: Cambridge University Press).

Kratochwil, F. (2000), 'Constructing a New Orthodoxy? Wendt's "Social Theory of International Politics" and the Constructivist Challenge', *Millennium: Journal of International Studies*, 29(1): 73–101.

—— and J. G. Ruggie (1986), 'International Organization: A State of the Art on the Art of the State', *International Organization*, 40(4): 753–75.

Krause, K. and M. C. Williams (eds.) (1997), *Critical Security Studies: Concepts and Cases* (London: UCL Press).

Kupchan, C. A. (2003), *The End of the American Era: US Foreign Policy and the Geopolitics of the Twenty-First Century* (New York: Knopf).

Kymlicka, W. (2001), *Politics in the Vernacular: Nationalism, Multiculturalism and Citizenship* (Oxford: Oxford University Press).

Laferrière, E. and P. Stoett (1999), *Ecological Thought and International Relations Theory* (London: Routledge).

Lapid, Y. (1989), '"Quo Vadis" International Relations? Further Reflections on the next stage of International Relations Theory', *Millennium*, 18(1): 77–88.

—— and F. Kratochwil (eds.) (1996), *The Return of Culture and Identity in International Relations Theory* (Boulder, CO: Lynne Rienner).

Larsen, M. T. (ed.) (1979), *Power and Propaganda: A Symposium on Ancient Empires* (Copenhagen: Copenhagen University Press).

Latouche, S. (1996), *The Westernization of the World*, translated by R. Moorris (Cambridge: Polity Press).

Lawson, S. (ed.) (2002), *The New Agenda for International Relations* (Cambridge: Polity Press).

Legro, J. W. and A. Moravcsik (1999), 'Is Anybody Still a Realist?', *International Security*, 24(1): 5–55.

Lepard, B. (2002), *Rethinking Humanitarian Intervention: A Fresh Legal Approach Based on Fundamental Ethical Principles in International Law and World Religions* (University Park: Pennsylvania State University Press).

Levy, M., R. Keohane, and P. Haas (1993), 'Improving the Effectiveness of International Environmental Institutions', in P. M. Haas, R. O. Keohane, and M. A. Levy (eds.), *Institutions for the Earth: Sources of Effective Environmental Protection* (Cambridge, MA: MIT Press).

Ling, L. H. M. (2002), *Postcolonial International Relations: Conquest and Desire between Asia and the West* (Basingstoke: Palgrave Macmillan).

Linklater, A. (1990), *Beyond Realism and Marxism: Critical Theory and International Relations* (Basingstoke: Macmillan).

—— (1992a), 'The Question of the "Next Stage" in International Relations Theory: A Critical-Theoretical Point of View', *Millennium: Journal of International Studies*, 21(1): 77–98.

—— (1992b), 'What is a Good International Citizen?', in P. Keal (ed.), *Ethics and Foreign Policy* (Canberra: Allen and Unwin), pp. 21–43.

—— (1996a), 'Citizenship and Sovereignty in the Post Westphalian State', *European Journal of International Relations*, 2(1): 77–103.

—— (1996b), 'Rationalism', in S. Burchill et al. (eds.), *Theories of International Relations* (London: Macmillan), pp. 93–118.

—— (1998), *The Transformation of Political Community: Ethical Foundations of the Post-Westphalian Era* (Cambridge: Polity Press).

—— (1999), 'The Evolving Spheres of International Justice', *International Affairs*, 75(3): 473–82.

—— (2001), 'Rationalism', in S. Burchill et al. (eds.), *Theories of International Relations* (Basingstoke: Palgrave), pp. 103–28.

—— (2002), 'Unnecessary Suffering', in K. Booth and T. Dunne (eds.), *Worlds in Collision: Terror and the Future of Global Order* (Basingstoke: Palgrave), pp. 303–12.

—— and H. Suganami (forthcoming), *The English School of International Relations: A Contemporary Reassessment* (Cambridge: Cambridge University Press).

Lipschutz, R. (2000/1), 'Why Is There No International Forestry Law? An Examination of International Forestry Regulation, both Public and Private', *UCLA Journal of Environmental Law and Policy*, 19(1): 155–82.

Litfin, K. (1998*a*), 'The Greening of Sovereignty: An Introduction', in K. Litfin (ed.), *The Greening of Sovereignty* (Cambridge, MA: MIT Press), pp. 1–27.

—— (ed.) (1998*b*), *The Greening of Sovereignty* (Cambridge, MA: MIT Press).

Little, R. (1995), 'Neorealism and the English School: A Methodological, Ontological and Theoretical Assessment', *European Journal of International Relations*, 1(1): 9–34.

—— (1998), 'International System, International Society, World Society: A Re-evaluation of the English School', in B. A. Roberson (ed.), *International Society and the Development of International Relations Theory* (London: Pinter), pp. 59–79.

—— (2000), 'The English School's Contribution to the Study of International Relations', *European Journal of International Relations*, 6(3): 395–422.

—— (2003), 'The English School vs. American Realism: A Meeting of Minds or Divided by a Common Language', *Review of International Studies*, 29(3): 443–60.

Lowith, K. (1949), *Meaning in History* (Chicago: University of Chicago).

Luard, E. (1990), *International Society* (Basingstoke: Macmillan).

Lucas, C. (1994), 'Revolutionary Violence, the People and the Terror', in K. Baker (ed.), *The French Revolution and the Creation of Modern Political Culture: The Terror* (New York: Pergamon Press), pp. 57–79.

Makinda, S. M. (1997), *Hedley Bull and International Security* (Canberra: Australian National University, Dept of International Relations Working Paper No. 1997/3).

Mann, M. (1986), *Sources of Social Power Volume 1: A History of Power from the Beginning to A.D. 1760* (Cambridge: Cambridge University Press).

Manning, C. A. W. (1962 [1975]), *The Nature of International Society* (London: Macmillan for the LSE), 2nd edition [1975].

Mapel, D. (1989), *Social Justice Reconsidered: The Problem of Appropriate Precision in a Theory of Justice* (Urbana: University of Illinois Press).

Mayall, J. (1982), 'The Liberal Economy', in J. Mayall (ed.), *The Community of States: A Study in International Political Theory* (London: George Allen & Unwin), pp. 121–53.

—— (1984), 'Reflections on the "New" Economic Nationalism', *Review of International Studies*, 10(4): 313–21.

—— (1989), '1789 and the Liberal Theory of International Society', *Review of International Studies*, 15(2): 297–307.

—— (1990), *Nationalism and International Society* (Cambridge: Cambridge University Press).

—— (2000), *World Politics: Progress and its Limits* (Cambridge: Polity).

McCarney, J. (2000), *Hegel on History* (London: Routledge).

McKinlay, R. D. and R. Little (1986), *Global Problems and World Order* (London: Pinter).

McSweeney, B. (1999), *Security, Identity and Interests: A Sociology of International Relations* (Cambridge: Cambridge University Press).

Mele, A. R. (1997), *The Philosophy of Action* (Oxford: Oxford University Press).

Meyer, J. W., J. Boli, G. M. Thomas, and F. O. Ramirez (1997), 'World Society and the Nation-State', *American Journal of Sociology*, 103(1): 144–81.

Meyer, M. A. and H. McCoubrey (eds.) (1998), *Reflections on Law and Armed Conflicts: The Selected Works on the Laws of War by the late Professor Colonel G. I. A. D. Draper OBE* (The Hague: Kluwer).

Mickolus, E. F. (1980), *Transnational Terrorism: A Chronology of Events 1968–1979* (Westport, CT: Greenwood Press).

Miller, J. D. B. (1990), 'The Third World', in J. D. B. Miller and R. J. Vincent (eds.), *Order and Violence: Hedley Bull and International Relations* (Oxford: Clarendon Press), pp. 65–94.

Mink, L. (1978), 'Narrative Form as a Cognitive Instrument', in R. H. Carney and H. Kozicki (eds.), *The Writing of History* (Madison: University of Wisconsin Press).

Moellendorff, D. (2002), *Cosmopolitan Justice* (Boulder, CO: Westview Press).

Molloy, S. (2003), 'The Realist Logic of International Society', *Cooperation and Conflict*, 38(2): 83–99.

Monbiot, G. (2000), *The Captive State: The Corporate Takeover of Britain* (London: Macmillan).

Moravscik, A. (1997), 'Taking Preferences Seriously: A Liberal Theory of International Politics', *International Organization*, 51(4): 513–54.

Morgenthau, H. (1948), *Politics Among Nations* (New York: Knopf).

Mössner, J. M. (1972), 'The Barbary Powers in International Law (Doctrinal and Practical Aspects)', *Grotian Society Papers*, pp. 197–221.

Nagel, T. (1986), *The View From Nowhere* (New York: Oxford University Press).

Nardin, T. (1983), *Law, Morality, and the Relations of States* (Princeton: Princeton University Press).

—— (2002), 'The Moral Basis of Humanitarian Intervention', *Ethics and International Affairs*, 16(1): 57–70.

National Security Council (2002), The National Security Strategy of the United States of America, September 2002, www.whitehouse.gov/nsc/nss.pdf.

Neruda, P. (1978), *Memoirs* (London: Penguin Books).

Neufeld, M. (1993), 'Interpretation and the "Science" of International Relations', *Review of International Studies*, 19(1): 39–61.

Neumann, I. B. (1996), *Russia and the Idea of Europe: A Study in Identity and International Relations* (London: Routledge).

—— (1999), *The Uses of the Other: The 'East' in European Identity Formation* (Minneapolis: Minnesota University Press).

—— (2001), 'The English School and the Practices of World Society', *Review of International Studies*, 27(3): 503–7.

Newell, P. (2000), 'Environmental NGOs, TNCs, and the Question of Governance', in Va. D'Assetto and D. Stevis (eds.),*The International Political Economy of the Environment* (Boulder, CO: Lynne Rienner), pp. 85–107.

Newell, Peter (2001), 'New Environmental Architectures and the Search for Effectiveness', *Global Environmental Politics*, 1(1): 35–44.

Nietzsche, F. (1998), *Beyond Good and Evil*, edited by M. Faber (Oxford: Oxford University Press).

Nordstrom, C. (2000), 'Shadows and Sovereigns', *Theory, Culture and Society*, 17(4): 35–54.

Norman, A. P. (2001), 'Telling It Like It Was: Historical Narratives on their Own Terms', in G. Roberts (ed.), *The History and Narrative Reader* (London: Routledge), pp. 21–41.

O'Hagan, J. (2002), *Conceptualizing the West in International Relations* (Houndmills: Palgrave).

Onuf, N. (1994), 'The Constitution of International Society', *European Journal of International Law*, 5(1): 1–19.

—— (1989), *A World of Our Making* (Columbia: University of South Carolina Press).

—— (2002), 'Institutions, Intentions and International Relations', *Review of International Studies*, 28(2): 211–28.

Onuma, Y. (2000), 'When was the Law of International Society Born? An Inquiry into the History of International Law from an Intercivilizational Perspective', *Journal of the History of International Law*, 2: 1–66.

Ophuls, W. (1977), *Ecology and the Politics of Scarcity* (San Francisco: W. H. Freeman & Co.).

Osiander, A. (1994), *The States System of Europe 1640–1990: Peacemaking and the Conditions of International Stability* (Oxford: Clarendon Press).

Owen, N. (2003), 'Introduction', in N. Owen (ed.), *Human Rights, Human Wrongs* (Oxford: Oxford University Press), pp. 1–25.

—— (ed.) (2003), *Human Rights, Human Wrongs* (Oxford: Oxford University Press).

Palme, O. (1982), 'Introduction', in *Independent Commission on Disarmament and Security Issues, Common Security: A Blueprint for Survival* (New York: Independent Commission on Disarmament and Security Issues).

Parekh, B. (1999), 'The Logic of Intercultural Evaluation', in J. Horton and S. Mendus (eds.), *Toleration, Identity and Difference* (Basingstoke: Macmillan), pp. 264–94.

Paris, R. (2002), 'International Peacebuilding and the "Mission Civilsatrice"', *Review of International Studies*, 28(4): 637–56.

Pasquino, P. (1996), 'Political Theory, Order, and Threat', in Ian Shapiro and Russell Hardin (eds.), *Political Order* (New York: New York University Press), pp. 62–75.

Paterson, M. (1997), 'Institutions for Global Environmental Change: Sovereignty', *Global Environmental Change*, 7(2): 175–7.

—— (1999), 'Globalisation, Ecology, and Resistance', *New Political Economy*, 4(1): 129–46.

—— (2000), *Understanding Global Environmental Politics: Domination, Accumulation, Resistance* (London: Macmillan).

—— (2001), 'Green Politics', in S. Burchill, R. Devetak, and A. Linklater (eds.), *Theories of International Relations*, 2nd edn. (London: Palgrave).

——, D. Humphreys, and L. Pettiford (2003), 'Conceptualizing Global Environmental Governance: From Interstate Regimes To Counter-Hegemonic Struggles', *Global Environmental Politics*, 3(2): 1–10.

Peyrefitte, Alain (1993), *The Collision of Two Civilisations: The British Expedition to China in 1792–4* (London: Harvill).

Pogge, T. W. (1989), *Realizing Rawls* (Ithaca: Cornell University Press).

—— (2001), *Global Justice* (Oxford: Basil Blackwell).

Price, J. J. (2001), *Thucydides and Internal War* (Cambridge: Cambridge University Press).

Price, R. (1994), 'Interpretation and Disciplinary Orthodoxy in International Relations', *Review of International Studies*, 20(2): 201–4.

—— (1997), *The Chemical Weapons Taboo* (Ithaca: Cornell University Press).

—— (1998), 'Reversing the Gun Sights: Transnational Civil Society Targets Land Mines', *International Organization*, 52(3): 614–44.

—— and C. Reus-Smit (1998), 'Dangerous Liaisons? Critical International Theory and Constructivism', *European Journal of International Relations*, 4(3): 259–94.

Rae, H. (2002), *State Identities and the Homogenisation of Peoples* (Cambridge: Cambridge University Press).

Rao, A. (1995), 'The Politics of Gender and Culture in International Human Rights Discourse', in J. Peters and A. Wolper (eds.), *Women's Rights/Human Rights: International Feminist Perspectives* (New York: Routledge), pp. 167–75.

Ramsbotham, O. and T. Woodhouse (1996), *Humanitarian Intervention in Contemporary Conflict* (Cambridge: Polity Press).

Rapoport, D. (2001), 'The Fourth Wave: September 11 in the History of Terrorism', *Current History*, December: 419–24.

Rawls, J. (1999), *The Law of Peoples* (Cambridge, MA: Harvard University Press).

Ray, L. (1993), *Rethinking Critical Theory: Emancipation in the Age of Global Social Movements* (London: Sage).

Reeves, J. (1921), 'International Society and International Law', *American Journal of International Law*, 15(3): 361–74.

Rengger, N. (1992), 'A City Which Sustains All Things? Communitarianism and International Society', *Millennium: Journal of International Studies*, 21(3): 353–69.

——(2000), *International Relations, Political Theory and the Problem of Order* (London: Routledge).

Reus-Smit, C. (1996), 'The Normative Structure of International Society', in F. Osler Hampson and J. Reppy (eds.), *Earthly Goods: Environmental Change and Social Justice* (Ithaca: Cornell University Press), pp. 96–121.

——(1997), 'The Constitutional Structure of International Society and the Nature of Fundamental Institutions', *International Organization*, 51(3): 555–89.

——(1999), *The Moral Purpose of the State: Culture, Social Identity and Institutional Rationality in International Relations* (Princeton: Princeton University Press).

Reus-Smit, C. (2000), 'In Dialogue on the Ethic of Consensus: A Reply to Shapcott', *Pacifica Review*, 12(3): 305–8.

——(2001*a*), 'The Strange Death of Liberal International Theory', *European Journal of International Law*, 12(3): 573–94.

——(2001*b*), 'Constructivism', in Scott Burchill, Richard Devetak, et al. (eds.), *Theories of International Relations*, 2nd edn. (London: Palgrave-Macmillan).

——(2001*c*), 'Human Rights and the Social Construction of Sovereignty', *Review of International Studies*, 27(4): 519–38.

——(2002), 'Imagining Society: Constructivism and the English School', *British Journal of Politics and International Relations*, 4(3): 487–509.

Reynolds, S. (1997), 'The Historigraphy of the Medieval State', in M. Bentley (ed.), *Companion to Historiography* (London: Routledge), pp. 117–38.

Richardson, J. L. (1990), 'The Academic Study of International Relations', in J. D. B. Miller and R. J. Vincent (eds.), *Order and Violence: Hedley Bull and International Relations* (Oxford: Clarendon Press), pp. 140–85.

Riley-Smith, J. (2001), 'The Crusading Movement', in A. V. Hartmann and Beatrice Heuser (eds.), *War, Peace and World Orders in European History* (London: Routledge), pp. 56–73.

Risse, T. (2000), '"Let's Argue!": Communicative Action in World Politics', *International Organization*, 54(1): 1–39.

——(2002), 'Transnational Actors and World Politics', in W. Carlsnaes, T. Risse, and B. A. Simmons (eds.), *Handbook of International Relations* (London: Sage), pp. 255–74.

Roberson, B. (ed.) (1998), *International Society and the Development of International Relations Theory* (London: Pinter).

Roberts, A. (1993), 'Humanitarian War: Military Intervention and Human Rights', *International Affairs*, 69(3): 429–49.

—— (2002), 'Counter-Terrorism, Armed Force and the Laws of War', *Survival*, 44(1): 7–32.

Robertson, G. (1999), *Crimes against Humanity: The Struggle for Global Justice* (New York: Penguin).

Rosenau, J. N. (1990), *Turbulence in World Politics: A Theory of Change and Continuity* (Princeton: Princeton University Press).

—— (1992), 'Governance, Order, and Change in World Politics', in J. Rosenau and E.-O. Czempiel (eds.), *Governance Without Government: Order and Change in World Politics* (Cambridge: Cambridge University Press), pp. 1–29.

—— (1993), 'Environmental Politics in a Turbulent World', in R. D. Lipschutz and K. Conca (eds.), *The State and Social Power in Global Environmental Politics* (New York: Columbia University Press), pp. 71–93.

Rosenberg, E. (1999), 'Consuming Women: Images of Americanization in the "American Century"', *Diplomatic History*, 23(3): 479–97.

Rosenberg, J. (1994), *The Empire of Civil Society: A Critique of the Realist Theory of International Relations* (London: Verso).

Rotberg, R. (2002), 'Failed States in a World of Terror', *Foreign Affairs*, 81(4): 127–40.

Rothschild, E. (1995), 'What is Security?', *Daedalus*, 124(3): 53–98.

Ruggie, J. G. (1983), 'Transformation and Continuity in the World Polity: Toward a Neorealist Synthesis', *World Politics*, 35(2): 261–85.

—— (1993*a*), 'Territoriality and Beyond: Problematizing Modernity in International Relations', *International Organization*, 47(1): 139–74.

—— (ed.) (1993*b*), *Multilateralism Matters* (New York: Columbia University Press).

—— (1998), *Constructing the World Polity: Essays on International Institutionalization* (London: Routledge).

Said, E. (1994), *Representations of the Intellectual* (London: Vintage).

Salter, M. B. (2002), *Barbarians and Civilization in International Relations* (London: Pluto Press).

Saurin, J. (1996), 'International Relations, Social Ecology and the Globalisation of Environmental Change', in M. Imber and J. Vogler (eds.), *Environment and International Relations* (London: Routledge), pp. 77–98.

Sayer, A. (2000), *Realism and Social Science* (London: Sage).

Scheuerman, W. E. (1999), *Carl Schmitt: The End of Law* (Lanham, MD: Rowman and Littlefield).

Schmidt, B. C. (1998), *The Political Discourse of Anarchy: A Disciplinary History of International Relations* (New York: State University of New York Press).

Scholte, J. A. (2000), *Globalisation: A Critical Introduction* (Basingstoke: Macmillan).

Sehon, S. R. (1994), 'Teleology and the Nature of Mental States', *American Philosophical Quarterly*, 31(1): 63–72.

Serres, M. (1977), *Hermes IV: La Distribution* (Paris: Éditions de Minuit).

Seth, S. (2000), 'A "Postcolonial World"?', in G. Fry and J. O'Hagan (eds.), *Contending Images of World Politics* (London: Macmillan), pp. 214–26.

Shapcott, R. (1994), 'Conversation and Coexistence: Gadamer and the Interpretation of International Society', *Millennium: Journal of International Studies*, 23(1): 57–83.

—— (2000), 'Solidarism and After: Global Governance, International Society and the Normative 'Turn' in International Relations', *Pacifica Review*, 12(2): 147–65.

Shapcott, R. (2001), *Justice, Community and Dialogue in International Relations* (Cambridge: Cambridge University Press).

—— (2003), 'Defining a Classical Approach: IR as Practical Philosophy', manuscript, January.

Shapiro, I. (2002), 'Problems, Methods and Theories in the Study of Politics, or What's Wrong with Political Science and What to do About it', *Political Theory*, 30(4): 569–619.

—— and L. Brilmayer (eds.) (1999), *Global Justice* (New York: New York University Press).

Shields, L. and M. Ott (1974), 'The Environmental Crisis: International and Supranational Approaches', *International Relations*, 4(6): 584–607.

Shiva, V. (1996). *Biopiracy: The Plunder of Nature and Knowledge* (Boston: South End Press).

Simon, S. and D. Benjamin (2000), 'America and the New Terrorism', *Survival*, 42(1): 59–75.

—— and —— (2001), 'The Terror', *Survival*, 43(4): 5–18.

Singer, P. (2002), *One World: The Ethics of Globalisation* (New Haven: Yale University Press).

Smith, S. (1989), 'Paradigm Dominance in International Relations', in H. Dyer and L. Mangasarian (eds.), *The Study of International Relations: The State of the Art* (London: Macmillan).

—— (1991), 'Mature Anarchy, Strong States and Security', *Arms Control*, 12(2): 325–39.

—— (1993), 'Environment on the Periphery of International Relations: An Explanation', *Environmental Politics*, 2(4): 28–45.

—— (1997), 'Power and Truth: A Reply to William Wallace', *Review of International Studies*, 23(4): 507–16.

—— (2002), 'Unanswered Questions', in K. Booth and T. Dunne (eds.), *Worlds in Collision: Terror and the Future of Global Order* (Basingstoke: Palgrave), pp. 48–59.

——, K. Booth, and M. Zalewski (eds.) (1996), *International Theory: Positivism & Beyond* (Cambridge: Cambridge University Press).

Smith, T. (1998), 'The International Origins of Democracy: The American Occupation of Japan and Germany', in T. Skocpol (ed.), *Democracy, Revolution and History* (Ithaca: Cornell University Press).

Spegele, R. D. (1987), 'Three Forms of Political Realism', *Political Studies*, 35(2): 189–210.

—— (1996), *Political Realism in International Theory* (Cambridge: Cambridge University Press).

Springhall, J. (2001), *Decolonization Since 1945* (Basingstoke: Palgrave).

Sprinzak, E. (1998), 'The Great Superterrorism Scare', *Foreign Policy*, 112: 110–24.

Spruyt, H. (1994a), 'Institutional Selection in International Relations: State Anarchy as Order', *International Organization*, 48(4): 527–58.

—— (1994b), *The Sovereign State and Its Competitors: An Analysis of Systems Change* (Princeton: Princeton University Press).

Stamnes, E. (2004), 'Critical Security Studies and the United Nations Preventive Deployment in Macedonia', *International Peacekeeping*, 11(1): 161–81.

—— and R. Wyn Jones (2000), 'Burundi: A Critical Security Perspective', *Peace and Conflict Studies*, 7(2): 37–55.

Starr, C. G. (1986), *Individual and Community: The Rise of the Polis 800–500 BC* (New York: Oxford University Press).

Steans, J. (1998), *Gender and International Relations* (Cambridge: Polity Press).

Strange, S. (1988), *States and Markets: An Introduction* (London: Pinter).

Strong, T. B. (1988), *Friedrich Nietzsche and the Politics of Transfiguration* (Berkeley: University of California Press).

Suganami, H. (1983), 'The Structure of Institutionalism: An Anatomy of British Mainstream International Relations', *International Relations*, 7(5): 362–81.

—— (1996), *On the Causes of War* (Oxford: Clarendon Press).

—— (1997), 'Narratives of War Origins and Endings: A Note on the End of the Cold War', *Millennium: Journal of International Studies*, 26(3): 631–49.

—— (1999), 'Agents, Structures, Narratives', *European Journal of International Relations*, 5(3): 365–86.

—— (2001), 'Alexander Wendt and the English School', *Journal of International Relations and Development*, 4(4): 403–23.

—— (2002a), 'The International Society Perspective on World Politics Reconsidered', *International Relations of the Asia-Pacific*, 2(1): 1–28.

—— (2002b), 'On Wendt's Philosophy: a Critique', *Review of International Studies*, 28(1): 23–37.

—— (2003a), 'Beyond the English School', paper presented at the 2003 Annual Convention of the International Studies Association, University of Birmingham, 15–17 December.

—— (2003b), 'British Institutionalists, or the English School, 20 Years On', *International Relations*, 17(3): 253–72.

Swatuk, L. A. and P. Vale (1999), 'Why Democracy is not Enough: Southern Africa and Human Security in the Twenty-first Century', *Alternatives*, 24(2): 361–89.

Swift, A. (2001), *Political Philosophy: A Beginners' Guide for Students and Politicians* (Cambridge: Polity Press).

Sylvester, C. (2002), *Feminist International Relations: An Unfinished Journey* (Cambridge: Cambridge University Press).

Tackett, T. (2001), 'Interpreting the Terror', *French Historical Studies*, 24(4): 569–78.

Taylor, P. (1997), 'What's Modern about the Modern World System?', *Review of International Political Economy*, 4(3): 270–86.

Tesdike, B. (1998), 'Geopolitical Relations in the European Middle Ages: History and Theory', *International Organization*, 52(2): 325–58.

Tessler, M. and I. Warriner (1997), 'Gender, Feminism and Attitudes toward International Conflict: Exploring Relationships with Survey Data from the Middle East', *World Politics*, 49(2): 250–81.

Thomas, C. (2000), *Global Governance, Development and Human Security: The Challenge of Poverty and Inequality* (London: Pluto Press).

Thomson, J. (1994), *Mercenaries, Pirates and Sovereigns: State-Building and Extraterritorial Violence in Early Modern Europe* (Princeton: Princeton University Press).

Tickner, J. A. (1992), *Gender and International Relations: Feminist Perspectives on Achieving Global Security* (New York: Columbia University Press).

—— (1995), 'Re-visioning Security', in K. Booth and S. Smith (eds.), *International Relations Theory Today* (Cambridge: Polity Press), pp. 175–97.

—— (1999), 'Why Women Can't Rule the World: International Politics According to Francis Fukuyama', *International Studies Review*, 1(3): 3–11.

—— (2002), 'Feminist Perspectives on 9/11', *International Studies Perspectives*, 3(4): 333–50.

Tilly, C. (1990), *Coercion, Capital and European States AD 990–1990* (Oxford: Basil Blackwell).

—— (2002), 'Violence, Terror, and Politics as Usual', *Boston Review*, 27(3), accessed 6 March 2003, at http://bostonreview.mit.edu/BR27.3/tilly.html.

Todorov, T. (1984), *The Conquest of America: The Question of the Other*, translated by R. Howard (New York: Harper Perennial).

Townshend, C. (2002), *Terrorism: A Very Short Introduction* (Oxford: Oxford University Press).

Toynbee, A. J. (1954), *A Study of History*, Vol. 9 (Oxford: Oxford University Press).

True, J. (2001), 'Feminism', in S. Burchill, Andrew Linklater et al. (eds.), *Theories of International Relations*, 2nd edn. (Basingstoke: Palgrave), pp. 231–76.

—— (2003), 'Mainstreaming Gender in Global Public Policy', *International Feminist Journal of Politics*, 5(3): 368–96.

—— and M. Mintrom (2001), 'Transnational Networks, and Policy Diffusion: The Case of Gender Mainstreaming', *International Studies Quarterly*, 45(1): 27–57.

Tuck, R. (1987), 'The "Modern" Theory of Natural Law', in A. Pagden (ed.), *The Languages of Political Theory* (Cambridge: Cambridge University Press), pp. 99–122.

—— (1999), *The Rights of War and Peace: Political Thought and the International Order from Grotius to Kant* (Oxford: Oxford University Press).

Underhill, G. (2000), 'State, Market, and Global Political Economy: Genealogy of an (Inter-?) Discipline', *International Affairs*, 76(4): 805–24.

UNEP (2001), Open-Ended Intergovernmental Group Of Ministers Or Their Representatives On International Environmental Governance, First Meeting, New York, 18 April 2001, Report Of The Chair. Document UNEP/IGM/1/3, 21 May. Available online at www.unep.org/IEG/WorkingDocuments.asp.

Vale, P. (1996), 'Regional Security in Southern Africa', *Alternatives*, 21(2): 363–91.

—— (2003), *Security and Politics in South Africa: The Regional Dimension* (Boulder, CO: Lynne Rienner).

van Aardt, M. (1993), 'In Search of a More Adequate Concept of Security for southern Africa', *South African Journal of International Affairs*, 1(1): 82–99.

van der Pijl, Kees (1998), *Transnational Classes and International Relations* (London: Routledge).

Vattel, E. de. (1916), *The Law of Nations or the Principles of Natural Law Applied to the Conduct of Nations and of Sovereigns*, translated by C. Fenwick (Washington, DC: Carnegie Institute).

Vincent, R. J. (1974), *Nonintervention and International Order* (Princeton: Princeton University Press).

—— (1978), 'Western Conceptions of a Universal Moral Order', *British Journal of International Studies*, 4(1): 20–46.

—— (1980), 'The Factor of Culture in the Global International Order', *The Yearbook of World Affairs, 1980* (London: Stevens and Sons for the London Institute of International Affairs), pp. 235–47.

—— (1983), 'Change in International Relations', *Review of International Studies*, 9(1): 63–70.

—— (1984a), 'Racial Equality', in H. Bull and A. Watson (eds.), *The Expansion of International Society* (Oxford: Clarendon Press), pp. 239–54.

—— (1984b), 'Race in International Relations', in R. B. J. Walker (ed.), *Culture, Ideology and World Order* (Boulder, CO: Westview Press), pp. 173–85.

—— (1986a), *Human Rights and International Relations* (Cambridge: Cambridge University Press).

—— (1986b), 'Introduction' and 'Concluding Observations', in L. Freedman et al. (eds.), *Terrorism and World Order* (London: Routledge and Kegan Paul).

—— (1988), 'Hedley Bull and Order in International Politics', *Millennium: Journal of International Studies*, 17(2): 195–213.

—— (1990), 'Order in International Politics', in J. D. B. Miller and R. J. Vincent (eds.), *Order and Violence: Hedley Bull and International Relations* (Oxford: Clarendon Press), pp. 38–64.

—— (1992), 'The Idea of Rights in International Ethics', in T. Nardin and D. Mapel (eds.), *Traditions of International Ethics* (Cambridge: Cambridge University Press), pp. 250–69.

Vogler, J. (2000), *The Global Commons: A Regime Analysis*, 2nd edn. (London: Wiley).

—— (2003), 'Taking Institutions Seriously: How Regime Analysis can be Relevant to Multilevel Environmental Governance', *Global Environmental Politics*, 3(2): 25–40.

Von Moltke, K. (2001), 'The Organization of the Impossible', *Global Environmental Politics*, 1(1): 23–8.

Von Wright, G. H. (1971), *Explaining and Understanding* (London: Routledge and Kegan Paul).

—— (1997), 'Explanation and Understanding of Actions', in G. Holmstrom–Hintikka and R. Tuomela (eds.), *Contemporary Action Theory, Vol. 1: Individual Action* (Dordrecht: Kluwer), pp. 1–20.

Walker, R. B. J. (1988), *One World, Many Worlds: Struggles for a Just World Peace* (London: Zed Books).

—— (1990), 'The Concept of Culture in the Theory of International Relations', in J. Chay (ed.), *Culture and International Relations* (New York: Westport), pp. 3–17.

Waltz, K. N. (1979), *Theory of International Politics* (Reading, MA: Addison-Wesley).

—— (1986), 'A Response to my Critics', in R. O. Keohane (ed.), *Neorealism and its Critics* (New York: Columbia University Press), pp. 322–45.

Walzer, M. (1977), *Just and Unjust Wars: A Moral Argument with Historical Illustrations* (New York: Basic Books).

Watson, A. (1984a), *Diplomacy: The Dialogue Between States* (London: Routledge).

—— (1984b), 'European International Society and its Expansion', in H. Bull and A. Watson (eds.), *The Expansion of International Society* (Oxford: Clarendon Press), pp. 13–32.

—— (1987), 'Hedley Bull, States Systems and International Societies', *Review of International Studies*, 13(2): 147–53.

—— (1990), 'Systems of States', *Review of International Studies*, 16(2): 99–109.

—— (1992), *The Evolution of International Society: A Comparative Historical Analysis* (London: Routledge).

Wæver, O. (1995), 'Securitization and Desecuritization', in R. D. Lipschutz (ed.), *On Security* (New York: Columbia University Press), pp. 46–86.

—— (1998), 'Four Meanings of International Society: A Transatlantic Dialogue', in B. A. Robertson (ed.), *International Society and the Development of International Relations Theory* (London: Pinter), pp. 80–144.

Weaver, M. A. (2000), 'Ghandi's Daughters: India's Poorest Women Embark on an Epic Social Experiment', *The New Yorker*, 10 January, pp. 50–7.

Weber, C. (1995), 'Dissimulating Intervention: A Reading of the US-Led Intervention into Haiti', *Alternatives*, 20(2): 265–77.

Weiss, T. G. (2003), 'The Illusion of UN Security Council Reform', *Washington Quarterly*, 26(4): 147–61.

Weldes, J., M. Laffey, H. Gusterson, and R. Duvall (eds.) (1999), *Cultures of Insecurity: States, Communities and the Production of Danger* (Minneapolis: University of Minnesota Press).

Weller, C. (2000), 'Collective Identities in World Society', in M. Albert, L. Brock, and K. D. Wolf (eds.), *Civilizing World Politics: Society and Community Beyond the State* (Lanham, MD: Rowman and Littlefield), pp. 45–68.

Welsh, J. (1995), *Edmund Burke and International Relations* (London: Macmillan).

Wendt, A. (1987), 'The Agent-Structure Problem in International Relations', *International Organization*, 41(3): 335–70.

Wendt, A. (1992), 'Anarchy is What States Make of it: The Social Construction of Power Politics', *International Organisation*, 46(2): 391–425.

—— (1994), 'Collective Identity Formation and the International State', *American Political Science Review*, 88(2): 384–96.

—— (1999), *Social Theory of International Politics* (Cambridge: Cambridge University Press).

Whalley, J. and B. Zissimos (2001), 'What Could a World Environmental Organization Do?', *Global Environmental Politics*, 1(1): 29–34.

Wheeler, N. J. (1992), 'Pluralist or Solidarist Conceptions of International Society: Bull and Vincent on Humanitarian Intervention', *Millennium*, 21(3): 463–87.

—— (1996), 'Guardian Angel or Global Gangster: A Review of the Ethical Claims of International Society', *Political Studies*, 44(1): 123–35.

—— (2000), *Saving Strangers: Humanitarian Intervention in International Society* (Oxford: Oxford University Press).

—— (2003), 'The Bush Doctrine: The Dangers of American Exceptionalism in a Revolutionary Age', *Asian Perspective*, 27(4): 183–216.

—— and T. Dunne (1996), 'Hedley Bull's Pluralism of the Intellect and Solidarism of the Will', *International Affairs*, 72(1): 91–107.

—— and —— (1998*a*), 'Hedley Bull and the Idea of a Universal Moral Community: Fictional, Primordial or Imagined?', in B. A. Roberson (ed.), *International Society and the Development of International Relations Theory* (London: Pinter), pp. 43–59.

—— and —— (1998*b*), 'Good International Citizenship: A Third Way in British Foreign Policy', *International Affairs*, 74(4): 847–70.

White, N. J. (1999), *Decolonisation: The British Experience Since 1945* (London: Longman).

White, S. K. (1991), *Political Theory and Postmodernism* (Cambridge: Cambridge University Press).

—— (2000), *Sustaining Affirmation: The Strengths of Weak Ontology in Political Theory* (Princeton: Princeton University Press).

Wight, M. (1966*a*), 'Why is there no International Theory?', in H. Butterfield and M. Wight (eds.), *Diplomatic Investigations* (London: Allen and Unwin), pp. 17–34.

—— (1966*b*), 'Western Values in International Relations', in H. Butterfield and M. Wight (eds.), *Diplomatic investigations: Essays in the Theory of International Politics* (London: Allen and Unwin), pp. 89–131.

—— (1966*c*), 'The Balance of Power', in H. Butterfield and M. Wight (eds.), *Diplomatic Investigations* (London: Allen and Unwin), pp. 149–75.

—— (1977), *Systems of States*, edited and introduced by Hedley Bull (Leicester: Leicester University Press).

—— (1979), *Power Politics*, 2nd edn., edited by H. Bull and C. Holbraad (London: Penguin).

—— (1987 [1960]), 'An Anatomy of International Thought', *Review of International Studies*, 13(3): 221–7.

—— (1991), *International Theory: The Three Traditions*, edited by Gabriele Wight and Brian Porter (London: Leicester University Press).

Williams, B. (2002), *Truth and Truthfulness* (Princeton: Princeton University Press).

Williams, H. and K. Booth (1996), 'Kant: Theorist Beyond Limits', in I. Clark and I. B. Neumann (eds.), *Classical Theories of International Relations* (London: Macmillan), pp. 71–98.

Wilson, G. M. (1989), *The Intentionality of Human Action* (Stanford: Stanford University Press).

—— (1997), 'Reasons as Causes for Actions', in G. Holmstrom–Hintikka and R. Tuomela (eds.), *Contemporary Action Theory, Vol. 1: Individual Action* (Dordrecht: Kluwer), pp. 65–82.

—— (1989), 'The English School of International Relations: A Reply to Sheila Grader', *Review of International Studies*, 15(1): 49–58.

—— (1998), 'The Myth of the "First Great Debate"', in T. Dunne, M. Cox, and K. Booth (eds.), *The Eighty Years Crisis: International Relations 1919–1999* (Cambridge: Cambridge University Press), pp. 1–17.

Wohlforth, William (1994/95), 'Realism and the End of the Cold War', *International Security*, 19(3): 91–129.

Wolfers, A. (1962), *Discord and Collaboration: Essays on International Politics* (Baltimore: John Hopkins Press).

Woods, N. (ed.) (2000), *The Political Economy of Globalisation* (Basingstoke: Macmillan).

WSRG: World Society Research Group (1995), 'In Search of World Society', Darmstadt/ Frankfurt/M.: World Society Research Group Working paper no. 1. Updated version as 'Introduction: World Society', in M. Albert, L. Brock, and K. D. Wolf (eds.), (2000) *Civilizing World Politics. Society and Community Beyond the State* (Lanham, MD: Rowman and Littlefield), pp. 1–17.

Wyn Jones, R. (1995), '"Message in a Bottle?": Theory and Praxis in Critical Security Studies', *Contemporary Security Policy*, 16(3): 299–319.

—— (1999), *Security, Strategy, and Critical Theory* (Boulder, CO: Lynne Rienner).

Young, O. R. (1994), *International Governance: Protecting the Environment in a Stateless Society* (Ithaca: Cornell University Press).

—— (ed.) (1997), *Global Governance: Drawing Insights from the Environmental Experience* (Ithaca: Cornell University Press).

Zhang, Y. (2001), 'System, Empire and State in Chinese International Relations', in M. Cox, T. Dunne, and K. Booth (eds.), *How Might We Live? Global Ethics for a New Century* (Cambridge: Cambridge University Press), pp. 225–46.

Zehfuss, M. (2002), *Constructivism in International Relations: The Politics of Reality* (Cambridge: Cambridge University Press).

Index

Lightning Source UK Ltd.
Milton Keynes UK
13 November 2009

146195UK00002B/7/P